African Histories and Modernities

Series Editors
Toyin Falola
The University of Texas at Austin
Austin, TX, USA

Matthew M. Heaton
Virginia Tech
Blacksburg, VA, USA

This book series serves as a scholarly forum on African contributions to and negotiations of diverse modernities over time and space, with a particular emphasis on historical developments. Specifically, it aims to refute the hegemonic conception of a singular modernity, Western in origin, spreading out to encompass the globe over the last several decades. Indeed, rather than reinforcing conceptual boundaries or parameters, the series instead looks to receive and respond to changing perspectives on an important but inherently nebulous idea, deliberately creating a space in which multiple modernities can interact, overlap, and conflict. While privileging works that emphasize historical change over time, the series will also feature scholarship that blurs the lines between the historical and the contemporary, recognizing the ways in which our changing understandings of modernity in the present have the capacity to affect the way we think about African and global histories.

Editorial Board
Akintunde Akinyemi, Literature, University of Florida, Gainesville
Malami Buba, African Studies, Hankuk University of Foreign Studies, Yongin, South Korea
Emmanuel Mbah, History, CUNY, College of Staten Island
Insa Nolte, History, University of Birmingham
Shadrack Wanjala Nasong'o, International Studies, Rhodes College
Samuel Oloruntoba, Political Science, TMALI, University of South Africa
Bridget Teboh, History, University of Massachusetts Dartmouth

More information about this series at
http://www.palgrave.com/gp/series/14758

Hlengiwe Portia Dlamini

A Constitutional History of the Kingdom of Eswatini (Swaziland), 1960–1982

palgrave
macmillan

Hlengiwe Portia Dlamini
University of the Free State
Bloemfontein, South Africa

African Histories and Modernities
ISBN 978-3-030-24776-8   ISBN 978-3-030-24777-5   (eBook)
https://doi.org/10.1007/978-3-030-24777-5

© The Editor(s) (if applicable) and The Author(s), under exclusive license to Springer
Nature Switzerland AG, part of Springer Nature 2019
This work is subject to copyright. All rights are solely and exclusively licensed by the
Publisher, whether the whole or part of the material is concerned, specifically the rights
of translation, reprinting, reuse of illustrations, recitation, broadcasting, reproduction
on microfilms or in any other physical way, and transmission or information storage and
retrieval, electronic adaptation, computer software, or by similar or dissimilar methodology
now known or hereafter developed.
The use of general descriptive names, registered names, trademarks, service marks, etc. in this
publication does not imply, even in the absence of a specific statement, that such names are
exempt from the relevant protective laws and regulations and therefore free for general use.
The publisher, the authors and the editors are safe to assume that the advice and
information in this book are believed to be true and accurate at the date of publication.
Neither the publisher nor the authors or the editors give a warranty, expressed or implied,
with respect to the material contained herein or for any errors or omissions that may have
been made. The publisher remains neutral with regard to jurisdictional claims in published
maps and institutional affiliations.

Cover illustration: Fabian Plock/Alamy Stock Photo

This Palgrave Macmillan imprint is published by the registered company Springer Nature
Switzerland AG
The registered company address is: Gewerbestrasse 11, 6330 Cham, Switzerland

PREFACE

I took on the challenge of writing *A Constitutional History of the Kingdom of Eswatini (Swaziland), 1960–1982* to fill a gap in Swazi constitutional history that Swazi historians have avoided due to its sensitive nature. Thus, a particular era in the constitutional history of Swaziland has remained a neglected field of historical scholarship. This fact is compounded by the specificity of Swaziland's constitutional developments in Southern Africa where, during the colonial and post-colonial era, the Swazi political scene was dominated by traditionalists, in the person of King Sobhuza II, rather than leaders of modern political parties. This scenario is puzzling to those not initiated in Swazi studies and needs to be unpacked. Swaziland was a British dependency like other erstwhile British colonies in Africa, but there is a marked difference in its constitutional development. How do we explain the resilience and consolidation of Swazi monarchism in the context of the British colonial school of constitutionalism against a backlash of aggressive competing political party leaders? What were the substantive issues that dominated the constitutional debates in Swaziland and why were they so contentious? And what was the outcome of the heated constitutional engineering in the colonial and post-colonial periods up to 1982?

This book is concerned with the complexity and specificity of Swaziland's constitutional history from 1960, when the constitutional processes started in earnest, to 1982, when King Sobhuza, the ferocious nationalist leader that led Swaziland to independence, departed this life. As was typical with British decolonization politics in Africa, Britain laid down

v

the Westminster parliamentary constitutional framework and involved the various Swazi stakeholders—the monarchists, the white Swazis, and the leaders of modern political parties—for constitutional talks. The monarchists were disadvantaged from the beginning of the talks because of the British post-World War II decolonization policy, which envisaged the transfer of power to the Western-educated political leaders, rather than to the traditional rulers. Britain intended to establish what they deemed to be a new 'modernizing political order' under modern political leaders that emanated from ballot box democracy. Power was not to be transferred to King Sobhuza II, Swaziland's *Ngwenyama* [the lion], who was an offshoot of the Dlamini dynasty. Swazi political party leaders were in total agreement with the British that the Swazi king should be assigned a mere token role in Swazi politics, as with the Queen of England, and not perform an effective role. These political party leaders enjoyed the external support of Ghana's Kwame Nkrumah.

The monarchists smelled danger from both the British and the modern political leaders at the onset of the decolonization process. As a result, they campaigned hard for the Swazi traditional political status quo should be upheld, and for its integration within Britain's modernizing Westminster constitutional framework. Consequently, they stood against the implementation of full-scale liberal democracy in the shape of one-man-one-vote on the grounds that it was 'unAfrican' and very 'alien'. The beneficiary of the post-colonial state was not to be a 'commoner' but, rather, the 'natural ruler of the Swazi people', who was the Swazi *Ngwenyama*. They rejected the idea of the existence of political parties as unwarranted Westernization, and argued forcefully that political power in Swaziland was not up for grabs between contestants because there was no such practice in Swazi culture and tradition.

If King Sobhuza did not find the British a reliable ally, he could count on the White Swazis and apartheid South Africa. By rejecting the whole idea of one-man-one-vote and subscribing to the upholding of private property, the White Swazis and South Africa felt safe with the King. The White Swazis owned more than 70% of the land in Swaziland, which they had expropriated under the 1907 Land Act, and they controlled the entire colonial economy. They were therefore fearful of the political rhetoric and posturing of the political party leaders, who were branded 'Progressives'. Because of Swaziland's geographical location inside the belly of South Africa, with which it shares over 80% of its borders, there were concerns about the rise of radical nationalist ideas that could be harmful to that bastion of apartheid.

King Sobhuza took advantage of the fears of White Swazis and South Africa to establish a political alliance of convenience with them against the political party leaders and their British supporters. While rejecting the idea of universal adult suffrage and political parties, Sobhuza conceded that Whites could be allowed to vote according to the Western tradition of secret ballot, but that Africans would be restricted to the choice of candidates for the legislature by acclamation with royal sanction. In order to ensure White support, King Sobhuza II took the unpopular stance of advocating that Whites, who numbered a mere 10,000, should be accorded equal representation in the Legislature as Blacks, who numbered 270,000. The monarchists' justification for this was that the Whites were significant contributors to the colonial economy, and their economic weight should be compensated.

The political viewpoints of the Progressives, on the one hand, and the monarchists and their White allies, on the other, were so diametrically opposed and unbridgeable that constitutional talks could barely make any progress in Swaziland. The British finally convened the Swazi constitutional stakeholders to London in January 1963 for the London Constitutional Conference. The talks were to no avail, as each party feared giving in to the other because it was tantamount to political suicide. Britain imposed the 1963 Constitution on the Swazis and proceeded to schedule elections for June 1964. The elections were the determining factor in the political history of Swaziland, because they were expected to produce the Legislature from which the Constitutional Committee responsible for designing Swaziland's independence constitution would be drawn. The nature and direction of Swaziland's constitution was to be determined by the winners of the June 1964 elections.

But King Sobhuza had no political party, implying that he could not contest the June 1964 elections. The Whites and South Africa acted promptly by encouraging the King to found a political party, the *Imbokodvo* National Movement (INM), while the Whites on their part formed the United Swaziland Association (USA) to protect their interests and property rights (which had already been guaranteed by the King), while supporting INM on the land and mineral issues. The royal INM and White USA quickly constituted an alliance to fight the elections against the Progressive parties, of which the most prominent was Dr. Ambrose Zwane's Ngwane National Liberatory Congress (NNLC). The royal INM and the White USA won all the seats at the expense of

viii   PREFACE

the Progressives, and this allowed the monarchists to shape Swaziland's independence constitution.

No sooner had the INM and USA started constitutional talks, than the two allies fell out. King Sobhuza, a cunning political fox, realized he longer needed the White USA because he had the overwhelming majority in the Legislature. He was therefore in a strong position to call the shots, and he reneged on the unpopular agreement that Whites should have equal representation in Parliament with Blacks in favour of one-man-one-vote. He betrayed the Whites to follow the will of the Swazi people, who wanted a non-racial society. The Whites also disagreed with the Swazi Black majority in fierce debates in Swaziland's bicameral Legislature that King Sobhuza II should be allowed absolute power in the independence constitution. The Whites contended that there must be checks on the powers of the King in the spirit of modern governance, while the Swazis were adamant and maintained that all powers should go to the King. Britain was the final arbiter and bequeathed to Swaziland a constitutional monarchy with checks and balances on its attaining independence in 1968.

In the post-colonial era, the Swazi monarchy persevered with constitutional monarchism forced down their throats by the British until 1973, when the independence constitution was torpedoed in what I have labelled a royal auto-coup d'état. This was followed by a period of constitutional void that King Sobhuza never filled before his demise. The King literally substituted himself for the constitution. This development reflected not only the long-held desire of King Sobhuza to concentrate all powers in his hands, but also a common trend in the African continent, where there was a general move towards one-party rule and constitutionalized political monolithism. That constitutional developments in post-colonial Swaziland culminated in monarchical absolutism is beyond question. The three arms of government—the Executive, Legislature and Judiciary—belonged to the King. But this absolute political order has been qualified as Swaziland's brand of benevolent monarchical despotism. This is so because King Sobhuza II established an absolute monarchical order sprinkled with heavy doses of benevolence and paternalism. He was a true king of Swazis: he did not transform his kingdom into imprisonment camps and graveyards for his political opponents, unlike some of his contemporaries, such as Idi Amin of Uganda and Macias Nguema of Equatorial Guinea. At the time of Sobhuza II's death,

Swaziland was free of political prisoners, but not of absolutism, making his country a 'paradise of human rights' in an African continent that could be accurately labelled a stretch of human rights abuses.

Bloemfontein, South Africa   Hlengiwe Portia Dlamini
2019

ACKNOWLEDGEMENTS

This book is evidence-based and I needed the assistance of many people in assembling the sources used. The cooperation of the staff of the Eswatini National Archives at Lobamba, the libraries at the University of Eswatini (Swaziland) and the University of Pretoria, the National Archives in the United Kingdom, and the Bodleian Libraries at Oxford was greatly appreciated. I would therefore like to express my profound gratitude to these archivists and librarians. They exhibited professionalism, and kindly and generously assisted me in locating and ordering the material that I needed for this book.

Financial challenges were obviously posed by the exorbitant cost of travelling and researching abroad. My unreserved gratitude goes to the Oppenheimer Memorial Trust and the International Studies Group at the University of the Free State for making funding available for my research in Eswatini, South Africa, and the United Kingdom. Without their financial support, I would not have been able to travel to distant venues for data collection.

This book engaged me in a series of interviews with several Swazis by virtue of their direct involvement in the exercise of constitution-making, or their expertise in constitutional matters. My sincere thanks go to all these interviewees, and their families and relatives, who spared their time to sit with me. Their interviews were a very rewarding experience; they constituted the voice of Swazis in their constitutional history, and helped shape the direction of this book. I shall be forever indebted to all my interviewees for their time and frankness with me. Some of my invaluable

xii ACKNOWLEDGEMENTS

interviewees have passed on without seeing this book, but they remain in my memory and in my prayers.

I would like to thank Professor I. Phimister, the anchor Senior Professor of the International Studies Group of the University of the Free State, from the bottom of my heart. He persisted in encouraging me to write this book. He is most definitely very resourceful, and directly supported me in the most unimaginable and creative ways in realizing the writing of this book. Apart from sponsoring my academic trips to the USA, he also linked me up to a number of US and European universities at which I had to present chapters of this book to academics who subjected them to serious scrutiny, and I benefited immensely from their rich, critical perspectives. These academic interactions helped me in articulating and rethinking the course of this book and greatly improved its quality. Professor Phimister is, indeed, a superb mentor and motivator, and his invaluable support is what I really needed to accomplish the task of writing this book.

Professor A. S. Mlambo, my doctoral supervisor at the University of Pretoria, is somebody I can never forget, because he has been a permanent source of encouragement to me, and his inspiring supervisory methodology served as a beacon in the writing of this book. It was not just the methodology of historical writing that I acquired from him, but also what it meant to work under pressure. Because my manuscripts never remained on his table for long, I was compelled always to work exceedingly hard and to the best of my ability to keep pace with him. By working under someone as inspiring and erudite as Professor Mlambo, and reading his fresh publications at the same time, I definitely learned a great deal from him. He continued to support me and follow up on my academic activities after I obtained my Ph.D. It was an absolute joy to work with him.

Professor N. F. Awasom deserves a special mention in these acknowledgments for a singular reason: he made available his own publications and some thrilling, iconic works on constitutional history. His resources constituted a springboard for my intellectual journey along the path of constitutional history. To him, I owe a sincere debt of gratitude.

I am very obliged for the extensive feedback I received from the series editors and the anonymous reviewers on the draft of this book. Their contributions impacted significantly on its quality.

ACKNOWLEDGEMENTS   xiii

On a very personal note, I would like to thank the Lord Almighty for the gift of strength, good health, perseverance, and hope. To Him be given all the praise and glory. My parents were very supportive and meant everything to me. My father, Prince Majawonke Dlamini, literally became my driver, tirelessly taking me to Pretoria and to various places in Swaziland for interviews, most of which he arranged for me. To my mother, Inkhosikati Glory Ntombi Dlamini, I extend my loving gratitude. My brother, Mhlonishwa, and his wife, Inkhosikati Philile Dlamini, deserve special thanks for their care and availability each time I needed their assistance. My sister, Lenhle Dlamini, was magnetically and cheerfully attached to me through my research on this book and kept my spirits high. If she were not physically present, she kept in close contact with me in the follow-up of my research, and always had warm, cheerful, and generous words encouraging to me not to falter.

Although several experts have gone through this the book and made useful comments, I would like to emphasize that any shortcomings are my exclusive responsibility. A pioneering book of this nature simply sets the pace for further debate and improvements, to which I am willing to commit myself. One thing is certain: a scholar is always a student willing to learn.

Bloemfontein, South Africa   Hlengiwe Portia Dlamini
2019

CONTENTS

Part I Introduction

1 Introduction   3

Part II Colonial Phase

2 The Major Players in the Making of the Independence
   Constitution of Swaziland (Eswatini)   33

3 The Beginning of the Great Constitutional Debate:
   Agreeing to Disagree   65

4 The Imposed 1963 Constitution, the Maiden
   Legislative and Executive Councils,
   and the Select Constitutional Committee   129

5 The 1967 Constitution, Internal Self-Government,
   and the 1968 Independence Constitution   183

xvi CONTENTS

Part III Post-Colonial Phase

6 The 1968 Westminster Constitution, the 1972 General Election, and Serious Challenges Confronting Constitutional Monarchism — 237

7 From King Sobhuza II's Auto-Coup D'état to the Era of Constitutional Void and Royal Benevolent Despotism — 279

8 Conclusion — 339

Appendix A: King Sobhuza II's Speech of April 1960 — 349

Appendix B: Members of Parliament Under the *Tinkhundla* System — 361

Index — 363

LIST OF FIGURES

Fig. 1.1   Map of Swaziland (Eswatini) and its neighbours (*Source* The US Central Intelligence Agency, courtesy of the Perry-Castañeda Library Map Collection)   10

Fig. 3.1   Swazi Delegates at the London Constitutional Conference, 28 January–12 February 1963. Names of delegates from left to right: J. M. B. Sukati, M. P. Nhlabasti; S. T. M. Sukati; P. L. Dlamini, A. K. Hlophe (*Source* ZUMA Press, Inc./Alamy Stock Photo)   105

Fig. 5.1   Leading opposition leader Dr A. Zwane and K. T. Samketi demonstrating at the entrance of Marlborough House, UK (*Source* Keystone Press/Alamy Stock photo)   226

Fig. 7.1   King Sobhuza II, dressed in traditional attire and barefoot to empathize with Swazi masses, September 6, 1968 (*Source* Eswatini National Archives)   306

LIST OF TABLES

Table 3.1	Members of the Maiden Swazi Constitutional Committee	85
Table 3.2	Results of the EAC's referendum on the Constitutional Committee's proposals for a Constitution for Swaziland	110
Table 3.3	Delegates to Church House, London, Constitutional Conference on Swaziland in January 1963	118
Table 4.1	The January 1964 Referendum Results	143
Table 4.2	Members of the 1964 Legislative Council	172
Table 4.3	Members of the Executive Council	174
Table 4.4	The 1965 Constitutional Review Committee	177
Table 5.1	Constitutional Review Committee	185
Table 5.2	Results of general elections held in Swaziland on 19–20 April 1967	208
Table 5.3	Members of the Swazi National Assembly after the April 1967 general elections	210
Table 5.4	Senators elected by the House and appointed by King Sobhuza	212
Table 5.5	1967 ministers and assistant ministers	213
Table 5.6	Senate vote on amendment of government White Paper to give the *Ngwenyama* absolute power over minerals and mineral oils	224
Table 5.7	Members of the Swazi delegation to the UK to negotiate the Independence Constitution in February 1968	225
Table 6.1	The results of the May 1972 elections	254
Table 6.2	The members of the Special Tribunal to examine the Ngwenya citizenship affair	266

xx LIST OF TABLES

Table 7.1	Swaziland Royal Constitutional Committee	317
Table 7.2	Members of the Electoral Committee	322
Table 7.3	Members of Cabinet emanating from the tinkhundla system	327
Table 7.4	Deputy ministers and assistant ministers	327

PART I

Introduction

CHAPTER 1

Introduction

WHY A BOOK ON THE CONSTITUTIONAL HISTORY OF SWAZILAND?

Swaziland is the smallest country in continental Southern Africa and has a fascinating history of constitutional development under a traditional monarchy. This work is historical in the sense that, almost everywhere, African traditional leaders vanished from the political scene as they made way for the new political elite,[1] none of whom had royal blood flowing in their veins. This is not the case in Swaziland, where the monarch played a preponderant role in its constitutional developments and effectively succeeded the departing British colonial administration. The constitutional history of Swaziland (renamed Eswatini in 2018 by King Mswati III) is

---

[1] Even where chiefs were recognised in the constitution, they were banned from getting involved in modern politics as is the case in Ghana. (For more on the eclipsing of African traditional rulers in modern politics at the end of colonial rule, see D. I. Ray, 'Divided Sovereignty: Traditional Authority and the State in Ghana', *The Journal of Legal Pluralism and Unofficial Law* 28, 37–38 [1996], 181–202; A. Keese, 'Understanding Colonial Chieftaincy from Its Final Phase: Responses to the Crisis of an Institution in French-Ruled West Africa and Beyond, 1944–1960', *Africana Studia*, 15 [2010], 11–28; R. Rathbone, 'Kwame Nkruma and the Chiefs: The Fate of "Natural Rulers" Under Nationalist Governments', *Transactions of the Royal Historical Society*, 10 [2000], 45–63; R. C. Crook, 'Decolonization, the Colonial State, and Chieftaincy in the Gold Coast', *African Affairs*, 85, 338 [1986], 75–106; and A. S. Anamzoya, 'Chieftaincy Is Dead: Long Live Chieftaincy: Renewed Relevance of Chieftaincy in Postcolonial Ghana', *The African Review*, 40, 2 [2017], 115–139).

© The Author(s) 2019
H. P. Dlamini, *A Constitutional History of the Kingdom of Eswatini (Swaziland), 1960–1982*, African Histories and Modernities,
https://doi.org/10.1007/978-3-030-24777-5_1

4   H. P. DLAMINI

largely unexplored, and yet it is a rich area for scholarly investigation by historians. This book responds to this hiatus in Swazi historiography. It focuses on the history of the constitution of Swaziland during the era of King Sobhuza II, and deals with colonial and post-colonial Swaziland from 1960 to 1982.

The encouragement and motivation I received from academics to write a book on the constitutional history of Swaziland can be contrasted with the sceptical attitude of many in Swaziland who felt it was not achievable: it was considered that such a work was too political and that embarking on such an endeavour was treading on dangerous ground. People are hyper-sensitive about political issues, which are rightly or wrongly associated with political activists labelled in Swaziland as 'Progressives', and who have been clamouring for multipartyism and a new constitutional dispensation since the ban on political activities in the 1970s.

I took up this challenge to write on a such a sensitive topic to demonstrate that academics have a privileged role to play in their societies in deconstructing myths and removing fear. African scholars have legitimate fears of indulging in political discussions due to victimization, but they cannot afford to distance themselves from the situation. The challenge of this book is to give a critical account of the history of Swaziland's constitutional development, and to evaluate the label imposed on Swaziland as 'the last absolute monarchy'[2] in Africa in constitutional terms. If Swaziland is the last absolute monarchy in Africa, where is the line-up of the other absolute regimes? Does the problem lay in absolutism or regime type? Generally, the African presidentialism displayed by most 'life presidents' is actually disguised absolutism.

---

[2] See, for instance, D. Woods, 'Monarchical Rule in Swaziland: Power Is Absolute but Patronage Is (for) Relative(s)', *Journal of Asian and African Studies*, 52, 4 (2017), 497–513; D. Woods, 'Patrimonialism (Neo) and the Kingdom of Swaziland: Employing a Case Study to Rescale a Concept', *Commonwealth & Comparative Politics*, 50, 3 (2012), 344–366; C. M. Fombad, 'The Swaziland Constitution of 2005: Can Absolutism Be Reconciled with Modern Constitutionalism?', *South African Journal on Human Rights*, 23, 1 (2007), 93–115; L. N. Mnisi, 'From Absolutism to Constitutional Monarchy: Has the New Constitution Transformed Prospects for Human Rights in the Kingdom of Swaziland' (PhD diss., University of Essex, 2010); A. K. Domson-Lindsay, 'Neopatrimonialism and the Swazi State', *Politeia (02568845)*, 32, 3 (2013); and D. Motsamai, 'Swaziland's Non-Party Political System and the 2013 Tinkhundla Elections Breaking the SADC Impasse?', *Africa Portal* (2012).

The mainstream media[3] also styles the Swazi monarchy as the 'last absolute monarchy' in Africa, which is clearly negative and alarmist, and generates generalized fear and uneasiness. Swazis have fallen easy prey to the Western notion of 'political absolutism' without fully appreciating and giving value to Swazi absolutism. The critiques of the Swazi constitutional order seem to ignore the fact that Swaziland is a traditional African kingdom that has endeavoured to design an original African political system that may not fit squarely within the Western framework.[4] Furthermore, there is an exaggeration in the labelling of Swazi monarchical absolutism because, on a comparative basis, it is no more absolute than any other African political regime. The spotlight is on Swaziland due to its original African political system, and because it does not conform to the prescriptions of Western liberal democratic dictates. China would definitely not be treated in the same way as Swaziland.

Surprisingly, Swazi monarchists inadvertently subscribe to the thesis of an absolute monarchy when they clamour that the king's powers should not be reduced but should, in fact, be expanded. They proclaim in public that the king of Swaziland should be given more powers because all powers belong to the king. This urgent desire for the king's powers to be increased is captured in *siSwati* as *Emandla eNkhosi*. By publicly calling for the king to be given more powers, pro-monarchists are negotiating for an ultra-absolute monarchy. This stance should be contrasted with that of Swazi civil society and opposition groupings classified as Progressives, who are diehard opponents of absolute monarchism that have consistently and vehemently called for a return to constitutionalism and liberal democracy in Swaziland.[5]

---

[3] Reuters, 'Africa's Last Absolute Monarch Renames Swaziland as "eSwatini"', Mbabane, April 19, 2018; News24, 'eSwatini, Africa's Last Absolute Monarchy', September 9, 2018; BBC News, 1. eSwatini Country Profile—BBC News—BBC.com, 'The Kingdom of eSwatini Is One of the World's Last Remaining Absolute Monarchies', www.bbc.com/news/world-africa-14095303, September 3, 2018; CNN, 'Absolute Monarch Changes Swaziland Name to "eSwatini"', www.cnn.com/2018/04/20/africa/swaziland-eswatini-africa-monarchy-intl/index.html; and CNN, April 21, 2018 … The king of Swaziland, Africa's last absolute monarch, has changed the name of his country to the "Kingdom of eSwatini" to mark the 50th (Alain Vicky, 'Africa's Last Absolute Monarchy', *Le Monde diplomatique*, mondediplo.com/2018/10/10swaziland).

[4] See H. P. Dlamini, 'The Tinkhundla Monarchical Democracy: An African System of Good Governance?', In O. Bialostocka (ed.), *New African Thinkers Agenda 2063: Culture at the Heart of Sustainable Development* (Cape Town: HSRC Press, 2018).

[5] See J. B. Mzizi, 'Leadership, Civil Society and Democratisation in Swaziland', Development Policy Management Forum (DPMF), 2002; M. V. Mthembu, 'Participation of

6   H. P. DLAMINI

It should be noted that royal absolutism as expressed in *siSwati* is seen as positive and, even, desirable. If monarchical absolutism is translated into English to describe the Swazi constitutional order, it becomes pejorative. So, the positive or negative attribute of monarchical absolutism is also a function of the language in which it is expressed. One could ask: What is wrong with having an absolute monarchy that ensures a fairly comparative distribution of state resources in an African continent inflicted with the force of inertia?[6] I make a clear case for the historical processes of the making of an absolute monarchy in Swaziland: however, I qualify Swazi monarchical absolutism as the end product of this evolution as 'benevolent' and 'functional' absolutism. Following independence in 1968, King Sobhuza II instituted a benevolent despotic regime in Swaziland, the hallmark of which was the bringing together of all Swazis of different shades of political opinion under the firm control of a paternal monarch without necessarily resorting to persecution. Before King Sobhuza II's demise in 1982, Swaziland recorded zero political prisoners in its cells and was described as 'a paradise of human rights in the African continent'.[7] In contrast, the notorious Idi Amin, Macías Nguema, and others made headlines as the greatest human butchers in contemporary Africa.[8] I have not shied away from describing the constitutional system that King Sobhuza instituted as

---

Swazi Women in the Traditional Public Sphere, Sibaya, in the Kingdom of Swaziland', *Communicare: Journal for Communication Sciences in Southern Africa*, 37, 1 (2018), 74–93; K. A. Acheampong and A. K. Domson-Lindsay, 'Unlocking the Security Puzzle in Swaziland: The Centrality of Human Rights and Democracy', *African Security Review*, 20, 3 (2011), 3–14; B. Masuku and P. Limb, 'Swaziland: The Struggle for Political Freedom and Democracy', *Review of African Political Economy*, 43, 149 (2016), 518–527; and H. P. Sereo, 'The Contribution of the People's United Democratic Movement (PUDEMO) to Democratic Change in Swaziland, 1983–2013' (PhD diss., University of Zululand, 2018).

[6] The Democratic Republic of Congo is not comparable to Swaziland in terms of natural resources and stands as one of the most endowed countries in Africa. Yet generalised poverty, civil war and total chaos is the trade mark of the DRC (see C. W. Mullins and D. L. Rothe, 'Gold, Diamonds and Blood: International State-Corporate Crime in the Democratic Republic of the Congo', *Contemporary Justice Review*, 11, 2 [2008], 81–99; E. Dearaujo, 'Chaotic Congo', *Harvard International Review*, 23, 3 [2001], 10).

[7] J. Daniel, 'The Political Economy of Colonial and Post-colonial Swaziland', *South African Labour Bulletin*, 7, 6 (1982), 106.

[8] For more on African tyrants, see R. H. Jackson, R. H. Jackson, and C. G. Rosberg, *Personal Rule in Black Africa: Prince, Autocrat, Prophet, Tyrant* (London: University of California Press, 1982); S. Decalo, *Psychoses of Power: African Personal Dictatorships*. Vol. 3 (Boulder: Florida Academic Press, 1998); and Ali A. Mazrui, 'Between Development and Decay: Anarchy, Tyranny and Progress Under Idi Amin', *Third World Quarterly*, 2, 1 (1980), 44–58.

1 INTRODUCTION   7

'absolute' because it was. However, I have qualified and illustrated in this book the nature of Swaziland's exceptional benevolent despotism, which stands out as a classic case in the African continent from an objective perspective. The problem and perception of royal absolutism lays in the way it is presented and in the agenda of the presenter.[9]

WHAT IS A CONSTITUTION, AND WHAT DOES CONSTITUTIONAL HISTORY REPRESENT?

The term 'constitution' has been defined by a variety of scholars in various ways. On the one hand, Lane defines a constitution as a compact document that encompasses a number of articles about a state, laying down the rules that state activities are supposed to follow.[10] According to this definition, a constitution is simply a list of instructions written in a document for a country. Lane further asserts that a constitution can be regarded as a single document that makes up the bulk of constitutional law.[11] On the other hand, Nwabueze defines a constitution as a document that has a force of law by which a society organizes government for itself, and defines and limits its powers, and prescribes the relations of its different organs.[12] Grimm describes the function of the constitution as follows:

> By submitting all government to rules, a constitution makes the use of public power predictable and enables the governed to anticipate government

[9]The way the question of monarchical absolutism in Swaziland is presented in popular media as the "last absolute monarchy" in Africa carries some grain of exaggeration and prejudice. Absolutism, otherwise referred to as neopatrimonialism, is a political regime based on the personalisation of power, the use of public resources, and the preferential (instead of meritocratic) appointment of civil servants Neopatrimonialism affects almost all sub-Saharan states to differing degrees (see A. Pitcher, M. H. Moran, and M. Johnston, 'Rethinking Patrimonialism and Neopatrimonialism in Africa', *African Studies Review*, 52, 1 [2009], 125–156; D. C. Bach and M. Gazibo [eds.], *Neopatrimonialism in Africa and Beyond* [Routledge, 2013]; M. Bratton and N. Van de Walle, 'Neopatrimonial Regimes and Political Transitions in Africa', *World Politics*, 46, 4 [1994], 453–489; and G. Erdmann and U. Engel, *Neopatrimonialism Revisited: Beyond a Catch-All Concept*, 2006). The pervasive nature of absolutism or neopatrimonialism in Africa seems not to have been fully appreciated by the propagandists of the "last absolute monarchy theory in Africa with reference to the Swazi political regime.

[10]J. E. Lane, *Constitutions and Political Theory* (Manchester: Manchester University Press, 1996), 5.

[11]Ibid., 7.

[12]B. O. Nwabueze, *Constitutionalism in the Emergent States* (New York: C. Hugh and Company, 1973), 2.

8   H. P. DLAMINI

behaviour vis-à-vis themselves and allows them to face government agents without fear. A constitution provides a consensual basis for persons or groups with different opinions and interest to resolve their disputes in civilised manner and enables peaceful transitions of power.[13]

Akpan defines a constitution as a political contract between the government and the governed.[14] Ndulo and Kent asserted that a constitution represents the basic structure of any organized society.[15] These authors argued that a constitution can be written or unwritten; however, concepts of formality appeared in post-colonial Africa. As a result, a constitution is now described as a single document, a charter for the exercise of political power.[16] In essence, a constitution is that formal governance document that provides checks and balances on the powers of the state, and defines the distribution and operation of power amongst the various components of the country.

Maseko[17] emphasizes that the constitution of a nation should not simply be a statute that mechanically defines the structures of government: it should be a 'mirror reflecting the national soul', the identification of ideals and aspirations of a nation, and the articulation of the values bonding its people and disciplining its government. A constitution should not be the act of a government but, rather, of a people constituting a government; a government without a constitution is power without right. A constitution is an account of the ways in which a people establish and limit the power by which they govern themselves, in accordance with the ends and purposes that define their existence as a political community. This elaborate definition is a pointer to the process of making a constitution that should be as important as the document and its observance.[18]

Constitutional history deals with the processes of the lawful formulation, adoption, and amendment of constitutions over time, as a constitution is

---

[13]D. Grimm, 'Types of Constitutions', In M. Rosenfeld and A. Sajo (eds.), *The Oxford Handbook of Comparative Constitutional Law* (Oxford: Oxford University Press, 2012), 104.

[14]M. E. Akpan, *Constitution and Constitutionalism* (Calabar: Paico Ltd., 1984), 1.

[15]M. B. Ndulo and R. B. Kent, 'Constitutionalism in Zambia: Past Present and Future', *Journal of African Law*, 40, 2 (1996), 256.

[16]Ibid., 256.

[17]T. Maseko, 'The Drafting of the Constitution of Swaziland, 2005', *African Human Rights Law Journal* (2005), 317.

[18]Ibid., 317–318.

not a static document. In typical British fashion, political actors of society—the legislature, executive officers, judiciary, political parties, and the general public—were continually engaged in the constitutional debates to design a constitution that represented the aspirations of the people. The study of constitutional history must, therefore, consider the full range of political and social institutions in a given country, and their involvement in shaping constitutional developments. The constitution that the British bequeathed to the Swazis was a product of several meetings involving several stakeholders. Constitutional history thus represents the processes involved in providing Swaziland with a constitution over time.

THE GEO-POLITICAL LOCATION, ETHNIC COMPOSITION, AND OUTLINE OF THE HISTORY OF SWAZILAND

Swaziland is the smallest country in continental Southern Africa and is devoid of any coastline. Sandwiched between Mozambique and South Africa, it encompasses an area of 17,363 square kilometres. It measures 135 kilometres from east to west, and 176 kilometres from north to south. It lies between the 26th and 27th latitudes south, and 31st and 32nd meridians east (Fig. 1.1).[19]

Swaziland has four distinctly different topographical and climatological zones that run from north to south, and exist in parallel belts along the entire length of the country. Despite its diminutive size, Swaziland is divided from east to west into four well-defined regions: the High-Veld, Middle-Veld, Low-Veld, and the Lubombo plain and escarpment. Their height ranges from 1850 metres in the High-Veld in the west, to just 300 meters above sea level in the Low-Veld. Swaziland is traversed by rivers and streams, providing the country with one of the most plentiful water supplies in southern Africa.

During the decolonization era of the 1950s and 1960s, Swaziland's neighbours—apartheid South Africa and colonial Mozambique—'provided an enclosed, insulated environment for Swaziland',[20] and kept it 'out of the full force of the winds of change for over a decade, so that even when political and ideological intrusions occurred, their impact was muted'.[21]

---

[19] S. S. Vilakati, *Geography for Swaziland* (Manzini: Macmillan Boleswa Publishers, 1997); Andrew Goudie, *The Atlas of Swaziland*, No. 4, Swaziland National Trust Commission, 1983.

[20] Ibid.

[21] Ibid.

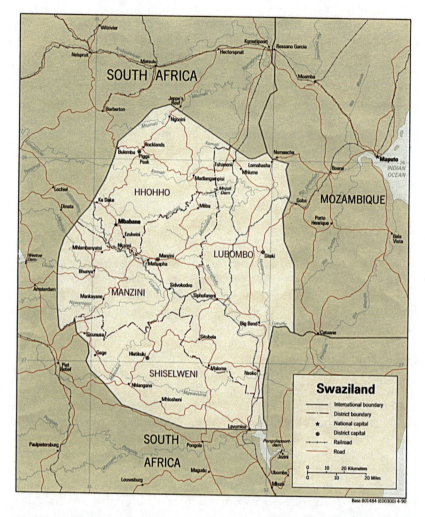

Fig. 1.1 Map of Swaziland (Eswatini) and its neighbours (*Source* The US Central Intelligence Agency, courtesy of the Perry-Castañeda Library Map Collection)

The Swazi traditional authorities capitalized on their geo-political insularity to contest their modern African rivals far more easily than they would have been able if they had been struggling in a more open, less controlled context. If Swaziland's neighbours were under Black majority rule who

1 INTRODUCTION   11

favoured universal adult suffrage, events could have turned out differently. The Swazi king supported European presence and business interests in Swaziland, and successfully used this group and South Africa for the country's survival during the colonial period against the British colonial authorities and the leaders of political parties considered Progressives, as I shall demonstrate.

If the international environment aided the Swazi traditional authorities by affording them a wide scope for political manoeuvre to play one group off the other successfully, they were also assisted by the fact that Swaziland is ethnically homogeneous despite the fact that the population contains a handful of Europeans and non-Swazi Africans, primarily Zulu and Shangane. The ethnic cohesion of Swaziland made it difficult for one group to be manipulated against another, as was the case with other African nation-states with multiple ethnic groups, such as Cameroon, Nigeria, Kenya, and South Africa.[22] In Swaziland, ethnicity becomes an important factor in facilitating political integration by reducing centrifugal strains; this had a profound repercussion on the quest for political hegemony that the monarch sought to establish.[23]

The Swazi monarch, and not political party leaders, successfully manoeuvred to position itself at the forefront of constitution-making in Swaziland. This was unlike the case elsewhere in Africa and, perhaps, in South Africa, during the making of the post-apartheid constitution.[24] An overview of the political history of Swaziland illuminates this phenomenon of monarchical preponderance to a large extent.

Historically, the Dlamini dynasty played a significant role in the founding and expansion of the Swazi Kingdom. After settling in the area of Delagoa Bay in Mozambique after migratory movements, the Dlamini clan later moved west, across the Lubombo escarpment in the late eighteenth century into southern Swaziland. Owing to mounting pressure from the Zulu

---

[22]See, for instance, R. H. Jackson and C. G. Rosberg, 'Popular Legitimacy in African Multi-Ethnic States', *The Journal of Modern African Studies*, 22, 2 (1984), 177–198.

[23]This in no way implies that a homogeneous ethnic nation-state is a guarantee for peace and harmony as the Somali case has demonstrated (see K. Menkhaus, *Somalia: State Collapse and the Threat of Terrorism* [Routledge, 2013]).

[24]For constitution making in British Africa and South Africa in the 1990s, see R. M. Maxon, *Kenya's Independence Constitution: Constitution-Making and End of Empire* (Fairleigh Dickinson, 2011); G. S. K. Ibingira, *The Forging of an African Nation: The Political and Constitutional Evolution of Uganda from Colonial Rule to Independence, 1894–1962* (Viking Adult, 1973).

12   H. P. DLAMINI

and the Ndwandwe incursions from the south, in the 1820s king Sobhuza I, an offshoot of the Dlamini dynasty, led his people further north into central Swaziland and brought this group into contact with others who were assimilated into the fold. When king Sohbuza I died in 1821, he was succeeded by his son, King Mswati II, who turned out to be the greatest of the Swazi warrior-kings to expand his kingdom. At the height of his career, his domain extended from the Pongola River in South Africa to the southern reaches of Rhodesia.

King Mswati II's successors had to deal with a succession of European powers in connection with land concessions for grazing and mineral exploitation, and the signing of international conventions. European manoeuvres culminated in the Anglo-Boer war (1899–1903), which resulted in the British establishment of a protectorate over Swaziland.[25] The Dlamini dynasty represented a strong political imprint in the minds of the ethnically homogeneous Swazi people. This explains why Swaziland's constitutional developments are *sui generis*, because it is the only African country where the traditional royal class, and not the Western-educated elite, dominated the constitutional processes. In British colonial Africa and South Africa in the 1990s, for instance, constitutional debates were the monopoly of political parties, to the exclusion of African chiefs and kings who represented the traditional ruling elite. This Swazi exceptionality gives the reading of this story of constitution-making a different flavour.

Antecedents of Scholarly Works on the History of Swaziland's Constitution

The history of constitutional developments in Swaziland has not yet been subjected to scholarly enquiry by historians, and the isolated historical writings on them are far from thorough. This study, therefore, sets out to fill this yawning gap in the historiography of Swaziland's constitution. This book is informed by literature on constitutional developments in British Africa in general, and in Swaziland in particular. The importance of this approach is explained by the fact that the process of Britain's imperial disengagement from Africa was generally similar, and was accompanied by the introduction

---

[25] P. Bonner, *Kings, Commoners and Concessionaires: The Evolution and Dissolution of the Nineteenth-Century Swazi State*. Vol. 31 (New York: Cambridge University Press, 2002).

of, and experimentation with, a succession of constitutions accompanied by power devolution to Africans culminating in independence.

Britain held several constitutional talks with the African political elite in the territory and the United Kingdom before finalizing the constitutional document leading to the granting of independence. Therefore, it goes without saying that the constitutional history of any erstwhile British dependency cannot be complete without reference to the constitutional talks held in London. A study of Swaziland's constitutional developments in the colonial period requires an examination of the constitutional talks that took place in Swaziland and the United Kingdom, and experimentations with the constitution designed to test its feasibility.

Several authors have demonstrated the preponderance of the metropolitan factor in constitution-making in colonial Africa, and how the British experimented with a succession of constitutions in their dependencies in the run-up to independence[26] Nigeria is a classic example of British constitutional engineering in Africa and therefore worth examining, and this study has devoted some attention to this case as it provides a framework for further analysis of the Swaziland case. The process of constitution-making in Nigeria started in earnest in the context of the World War II as a response to demands and agitation by some sections of the Western-educated elite for self-government and greater participation in governance. Consequently, in December 1944, Governor Richards published a proposal for a new constitution. The most distinguished feature of the constitution was the introduction of regionalism, and the establishment of a central legislature that was empowered to lay down the law for the whole of Nigeria. Three regions—the North, East and West—were established, each endowed with a Regional Council.

The Richards constitution took effect in 1946, but the constitution soon ran into problems when the nationalists complained that they were not properly consulted to give their viewpoint and, thus, the constitution was a *diktat*.[27] The British registered this grievance and consented to consult the African people in revising the constitution. This practice of consulting

---

[26] See K. Ezera, *Constitutional Developments in Nigeria* (London: Cambridge University Press, 1964); B. O. Nwabueze, *A Constitutional History of Nigeria* (London: C. Hurst and Company, 1982).

[27] That is to say, the British imposed the Richards Constitution on Nigerians instead of involving them in the formulation of the constitution (see Ezera, *Constitutional Development in Nigeria*, 107–111).

14   H. P. DLAMINI

indigenous peoples in designing a constitution for them became typical of the British process of the devolution of power. Thus, the agitation against the Richards constitution forced the colonial administration to review it. Governor Macpherson set up a Select Committee of the Legislative Council to review the constitution. This was done through wide consultations by holding conferences in each of Nigeria's three regions, starting with rural communities and district meetings through Provincial and Regional Conferences and culminating with the General Conference in Ibadan. Thus, constitution-making was a thorough and a consultative process, which will also be observed in the case of Swaziland.

The next constitution, the Macpherson constitution, was introduced in 1951. In the course of its implementation, certain shortcomings were revealed that led to its collapse. Protracted deliberations were held in 1953 and 1954 between Lagos and London, where the Macpherson constitution was reviewed. A new constitution, the Lyttelton constitution, was introduced that enshrined the federal system of government in Nigeria. More autonomy was granted to the three regions of the Nigerian Federation. In 1957 and 1958, further constitutional conferences were held, with the full participation of all Nigerian political parties, at Lancaster House in London, where the federal constitution for an independent Nigeria was prepared. In 1960, the independence constitution came into effect, modelled on the British Westminster parliamentary model.[28]

In the making of Cameroon's independence constitution, Awasom drew attention to two important issues: the role of the metropolitan or colonial powers—Britain and France—in setting the stage for constitution-making in Africa after 1945, and the participation of African nationalists.[29] He critically analysed the nature of the constitutional debates among the Western-educated elite and the controversies surrounding the constitution-making exercise, which were also present in the Swazi case.

Although the British constitution-making methodology may have been similar in Africa, Swaziland departed significantly from the British West African model, in that it was a settler colony and was surrounded by White

---

[28] A. E. Afigbo, 'Background to Nigerian Federalism: Federal Features in the Colonial State', *Publius: The Journal of Federalism*, 21, 4 (1991), 13–29; B. O. Nwabueze, *A Constitutional History of Nigeria* (Addison-Wesley Longman Ltd., 1982).

[29] N. F. Awasom, 'Politics and Constitution-Making in Francophone Cameroon, 1959–1960', *Africa Today* (2002), 3–30.

1 INTRODUCTION 15

minority regimes. The fact that a significant White population had permanently settled in Swaziland made them important actors in the constitutional processes in colonial Swaziland.

In a paper presented at a conference in Swaziland in 2003, the historian B. A. B. Sikhondze examined constitutional developments in Swaziland over a specific period, from the 1970s to 2003, and highlighted the challenges of not having a written constitution after the 1973 repeal.[30] Political scientists and scholars in the legal field have dominated scholarship on Swaziland's constitutional developments from their disciplinary perspectives.[31] Their writings are generally epochal, covering short time spans or specific topics. This approach has some drawbacks for the historian. First, the short time frames do not allow for a comprehensive and a longitudinal view of Swaziland's constitutional developments. Second, the studies do not provide detailed and critical analyses of the social groupings or stakeholders engaged in the making of Swaziland's constitutions to enable the evaluation of what was at stake in the whole process.

The common denominator of the writings of political scientists, anthropologists, and scholars in the legal field is their emphasis on power shifts in favour of the Swazi monarchy. Macmillan and Kuper's characterization of the emergence and consolidation of the Swazi monarchy from colonialism as an exceptional victory of the Dlamini dynasty, in contrast to its counterparts elsewhere in Africa, is quite instructive in understanding

---

[30] B. A. B. Sikhondze, 'Factors That Have Stalled Efforts Towards a Constitution in Swaziland, 1970s to 2003: A Constitutional History', Paper presented for a Workshop of the Swaziland OSSREA Chapter, November 27, 2003.

[31] J. Baloro, 'The Development of Swaziland's Constitution: Monarchical Response to Modern Challenges', *Journal of African Law*, 38, 1 (1994), 19–34; C. P. Potholm, *Swaziland: The Dynamics of Political Modernization* (London: University of California Press, 1972.); C. Potholm, 'Swaziland Under Sobhuza II: The Future of an African Monarchy', *The Round Table: The Commonwealth Journal of International Affairs*, 64, 254 (1974), 219–227; B. P. Wanda, 'The Shaping of Modern Constitution in Swaziland: A Review of Some Social and Historical Factors', *Lesotho Law Journal*, 6, 1 (1990), 137–178; T. Maseko, 'Constitution Making in Swaziland: The Cattle-Byre Constitution Act 001 of 2005', Paper presented at African Network of Constitutional Law Conference on Fostering Constitutionalism in Africa, Nairobi, 2007; T. Maseko, 'The Drafting of the Constitution of Swaziland, 2005', *African Human Rights Law Journal*, 8, 2 (2005), 312–336; and I. G. Dlamini, 'Socio-economic and Political Constraint on Constitutional Reform in Swaziland' (MA thesis, University of West Cape, 2005).

16   H. P. DLAMINI

the foundations of the Swazi monarchical constitutional system.[32] Stevens examines the constitutional developments in Swaziland in the 1960s from the perspective of the British model and Swazi tradition.[33] Baloro examines the increasing power of the Swazi monarchy under Swaziland's constitutions at the expense of the legislative and the judicial arms of government under the independence constitution.[34] These studies are useful, but are not sufficiently historicized.

Matlosa, Baloro, Dlamini, Maseko, and Mzizi examine the repeal of the independence constitution in 1973 without clearly demonstrating the significant of this act.[35] This author has adopted a more critical approach in studying the repeal of the independence constitution, and argues that constitutional repeal was a royal auto-coup d'état that can be defined as a civilian overthrow of the institutions of the state, which act is similar in

---

[32] H. Macmillan, 'Swaziland: Decolonization and the Triumph of "Tradition"', *Journal of Modern African Studies*, 23, 4 (1985), 643–666; H. Kuper, *Sobhuza II Ngwenyama and King of Swaziland: The Story of an Hereditary Ruler and His Country* (London: Gerald Duckworth and Co. Ltd., 1978).

[33] R. P. Stevens, 'Swaziland Political Development', *The Journal of Modern African Studies*, 1, 3 (1963), 327–350.

[34] J. Baloro, 'The Development of Swaziland's Constitution: Monarchical Responses to Modern Challenges', *Journal of African Law*, 38 (1994), 19–34.

[35] K. Matlosa, 'Democracy and Conflict in Post-apartheid Southern Africa: Dilemmas of Social Change in Small States', *International Affairs*, 74, 2 (1998), 319–337; Baloro, 'The Development of Swaziland's Constitution: Monarchical Responses to Modern Challenges'; T. Maseko, 'Constitution Making in Swaziland: The Cattle-Byre Constitution Act 001 of 2005', Paper presented at African Network of Constitutional Law Conference on Fostering Constitutionalism in Africa, Nairobi, 2007; T. Maseko, 'The Drafting of the Constitution of Swaziland, 2005', *African Human Rights Law Journal*, 8, 2 (2005), 312–336; I. G. Dlamini, 'Socio-economic and Political Constraint on Constitutional Reform in Swaziland' (MA thesis, University of West Cape, 2005); and J. B. Mzizi, 'The Dominance of the Swazi Monarchy and the Moral Dynamics of Democratisation of the Swazi State', *Journal of African Elections*, 3, 1 (2004), 94–119.

1 INTRODUCTION 17

several respects to typical military coups in Africa and elsewhere.[36] Governance by Orders-in-Council and Decrees are the hallmark of coup regimes. In light of the above, it is clear that, while literature on constitution-making in British West Africa is well-developed and informative, it is not so with Swaziland. The studies on Swaziland's constitutions neither address Swaziland's constitutional history over time, nor provide comprehensive analyses of the circumstances, factors, and actors that shaped the development of that history. This study seeks to fill this gap in the existing scholarship.

The Purpose of This Book

The main purpose of this book is to trace and analyse how Swaziland's constitutional history unfolded from 1960 to 1982, and the factors that helped shape its development. In attempting to address this problem, the book provides a comprehensive account that traces the development of Swaziland's constitutions over time. This study of Swaziland's constitutional developments takes into consideration the historical context, actors, and processes involved in each delineated historical epoch: the pre-independence years; the period of constitutional monarchy, 1968–1973; and the period of constitutional void that followed the 1973 royal auto-coup d'état.

The constitution-making process in Swaziland started in earnest in 1960, when the British invited various Swazi groupings to submit ideas on the type of constitution they would want for an independent Swaziland. Swaziland's independence constitution was, thus, designed under the guidance of the British colonial authorities. Those involved in constitution-making in Swaziland included King Sobhuza II and the Swazi National Council, the

---

[36] Recent scholarship informed this conceptualization of this category of civilian coup d'états which have taken place elsewhere (see, for instance, C. Sampford, 'Making Coups History', *World Politics Review*, 22 [2010], 1–10; J. Protzel, 'Changing Political Cultures and Media Under Globalism in Latin America', *Democratising Global Media: One World, Many Struggles* [2005], 101–120; M. Hutt, 'King Gyanendra's Coup and Its Implications for Nepal's future', *Brown Journal of World Affairs*, 12 [2005], 111; K. Hachhethu, 'Legitimacy Crisis of Nepali Monarchy', *Economic and Political Weekly* [2007], 1828–1833; K. M. Dixit, 'Absolute Monarchy to Absolute Democracy', *Economic and Political Weekly* [2005], 1506–1510; M. Hutt, 'Nepal and Bhutan in 2005: Monarchy and Democracy, Can They Co-exist?' [2006], 120–124; and D. Kumar, 'Proximate Causes of Conflict in Nepal', *Contributions to Nepalese Studies*, 32, 1 [2005], 51–92).

18   H. P. DLAMINI

Western-educated elite referred to as Progressives, and the White settlers who had gained the status of Swazi citizens. These processes culminated in the making of the 1968 Independence Constitution, which proved to be unsatisfactory to the monarch and was overthrown in 1973, thereby creating a period during which Swaziland was ruled without a constitution. Although I concede that royal absolutism characterized the period of constitutional void, I argue that a benevolent despotic political model prevailed in Sobhuza's Swaziland. This model was characterized by the concentration of powers in the hands of King Sobhuza II, which made him a despot *par excellence*. Nonetheless, it was monarchical despotism with a human face, as the Swazi King exhibited a high propensity towards the rehabilitation of his political opponents, and did not engage in the massive and protracted imprisonment and extermination of his political opponents, unlike some of his contemporaries.[37] The benevolent despotism component is not to be found in extant literature on Swaziland.

Significance of the Study

There is no historical study on the development of Swaziland's constitution from 1960 to 1982, even though Swaziland stands out in Africa as a traditional kingdom with a peculiar African constitutional order. The constitutional question in Swaziland is a topical and hotly contested issue, particularly by civil society. In order to arrive at an informed decision about the trajectory of Swaziland's constitutional development, there is need for a historical study of this nature.

Methodology

The study used a qualitative and historical research design to trace the development of Swaziland's constitution-making process, and to investigate the forces that helped shape the country's constitutional history. The

---

[37] See, for instance, G. Glentworth and I. Hancock, 'Obote and Amin: Change and Continuity in Modern Uganda Politics', *African Affairs*, 72, 288 (1973), 237–255; J. S. Saul, 'The Unsteady State: Uganda, Obote and General Amin', *Review of African Political Economy*, 3, 5 (1976), 12–38; A. A. Mazrui, 'Between Development and Decay: Anarchy, Tyranny and Progress Under Idi Amin', *Third World Quarterly*, 2, 1 (1980), 44–58; S. Cronjé, *Equatorial Guinea, the Forgotten Dictatorship: Forced Labour and Political Murder in Central Africa* (No. 2) (Anti-Slavery Society, 1976); and S. Baynham, 'Equatorial Guinea: The Terror and the Coup', *The World Today*, 36, 2 (1980), 65–71.

1 INTRODUCTION   19

design enabled the researcher to collect, verify, and synthesize evidence to establish historical facts. A qualitative research method was used, where the researcher sought to understand Swaziland's constitutional history by comparing, contrasting, cataloguing, classifying, and analysing information collected from a wide variety of sources. The study was based mainly on archival sources, official government documents, newspapers, and interviews.

Archival materials from the National Archives in Lobomba in Swaziland, the National Archives in London, and the Ghana National Archives in Accra were indispensable in the writing of this book. The core documents on constitutional developments included official reports, such as the Swaziland Legislative Council Reports, Swaziland National Assembly Reports, the Swaziland Senate Reports, and the Swaziland Government Gazettes. These reports covered the important debates on constitutional issues among the stakeholders. When Swaziland was endowed with self-governance in 1967, the bicameral legislature became a site of hotly contested debates on the race question, voting rights, and the powers of the Swazi monarch—the *Ngwenyama* of Swaziland—in an independent Swaziland. Government decisions having important consequences—such as the withdrawal of the citizenship of an opposition candidate, B. Ngwenya of the NNLC; and King Sobhuza II's 1973 repeal of the Independence Constitution and Proclamations by Decree and Orders-in-Council—are all captured in the Swaziland Government Gazettes. The official reports of the Swaziland government were, therefore, invaluable sources for this book.

The White Swazis, operating under the canopy of the European Advisory Council (EAC), were important players in the constitutional history of Swaziland, particularly during the colonial period. This book benefited from the minutes of the EAC, which cover issues on White voters' rights, and arguments for and against a common electoral roll in Swaziland. Of equal importance were minutes of the traditional Swazi National Council, which reflect the position of the Swazi traditionalists on the constitutional question in Swaziland. King Sobhuza's speeches and the minutes of the meetings of the Swazi National Council were useful to this study, as they clearly reflect the evolving relationship between King Sobhuza II and the EAC from one of hostile partners to real friends in need. Before 1960, King Sobhuza II and the White community had strained relationships over the issue of land appropriation and the reluctance of the White community to address the issue. But when decolonization fever gripped Swaziland, King Sobhuza and the White community realized that they had to cooperate to

20   H. P. DLAMINI

check the rising tide of radical nationalism in Swaziland before it was too late. The documents reveal this thawing of the relationship between the Swazi monarch and the EAC.

Newspaper reports were also of great importance to this study. Mac-Dowell notes that newspaper reports offer a day-to-day record of events and are therefore a vital source of historical reconstruction,[38] their shortcomings notwithstanding. This author depended heavily on *The Times of Swaziland*, obtained from the Swaziland National Archives, the Library of the University of Swaziland, and the University of Pretoria. *The Times of Swaziland*, which was the principal newspaper in Swaziland, provided this author with a broader picture and understanding of Swaziland's constitutional developments. It published communiqués on the outcome of Swaziland's constitutional talks in London and in Swaziland. The pictures of the constitutional meetings appeared in *The Times of Swaziland*, and one could sometimes assess the mood of the meeting by the pictures captured in the media with accompanying headlines. Given that this newspaper was central to this study, it is instructive to offer some insights into its origins and development.

The Times of Swaziland was founded in 1897 by Allister Miller, who became the mouthpiece of White settler interests. Between 1897 and 1909, it was used as a platform for settlers to criticize the colonial government for not doing enough to prioritize settler interests. It stopped publication in 1909, due to a financial crisis, and resumed publication again in 1931, once again as the White settlers' mouthpiece. In the 1960s, *The Times of Swaziland* became the platform used by White settlers to express their constitutional views on the establishment of the Legislative Council, and the rights and privileges of White voters. Carl Todd, the Leader of the White community, used *The Times of Swaziland* to campaign for the conservative constitutional stance of King Sobhuza and the Swazi National Council. He also used it to mobilize settler support for King Sobhuza II as Swaziland headed towards independence. The editorial policy of *The Times of Swaziland* changed in 1973 when King Sobhuza abrogated the Independence Constitution of 1968 and declared a state of emergency. *The Times of Swaziland* started writing critical reports of the monarch.[39] As with other

---

[38]W. H. MacDowell, *Historical Research: A Guide* (London: Longman, 2002), 57; J. Tosh, *The Pursuit of History* (London: Longman, 1991), 37–38.

[39]V. S. Hlatshwayo, 'The Reality of Media Freedom in Swaziland Under the New Constitutional Dispensation' (MA thesis, University of Cape Town, 2011), 31.

sources for historical reconstruction, *The Times of Swaziland* had its short-comings. Details of the actual constitutional discussions and debates were not usually published in the *Times of Swaziland*; they were published in the official reports of the government of Swaziland. By scrutinizing written sources and complementing them with interviews, the margin of bias was minimized.

Oral data was also useful in this study, and was collected through face-to-face, in-depth, and open-ended interviews. The advantage of this method of interview was to allow the interviewees some freedom and flexibility in responding to questions raised about the study. The interviews were recorded on a tablet with the permission of the interviewees.

The selection of interviewees was based on their knowledgeability of the history of Swaziland's constitution. Most of the interviewees were comfortable and conversant with constitutional developments in Swaziland. Over 20 people were interviewed between December 2014 and December 2016. Of the 20 interviews, 13 were with people in the legal field, while the rest were politicians. Interviews were later transcribed and analysed for use in the study.

Most of the interviewees chose not to be identified as they consider this book to be based on a politically hot issue and that they may be perceived negatively for having contributed to this book on a topic with which they are not very comfortable. Since 2015, the government of Swaziland has been under intense pressure from civil society and international stakeholders to review its political system along liberal democratic lines, which the monarch has been reluctant to entertain. Nonetheless, talks have been going on between the European Union and the underground Swazi opposition movement, otherwise referred to as the Progressives. On 8 November 2015, *The Times of Swaziland* carried a story about a select group of Swazis including government and progressive officials on tour to the Kingdom of Morocco and elsewhere to familiarize themselves with the working of multipartyism.[40] Nonetheless, government functionaries do not want to be overtly associated with the ideas of the Progressives. Swazis do not know who to trust and any type of discussion that touches on the constitution, which is continuously contested by the Swazi civil society as not sufficiently democratic, is treated with caution. People are therefore uncomfortable to express their opinions about the constitution publicly. Where so requested

---

[40]'Jan, Majahenkhaba, Mario's Trip', *Times of Swaziland*, November 8, 2015.

22   H. P. DLAMINI

by the interviewees, their names are not published in this study, as required by the ethics of scholarly writing.

STRUCTURE OF THE BOOK

This book is comprises four parts and contains eight chapters, each of which focuses on different phases of Swaziland's constitutional history. Part I presents the introductory chapter. Part II, comprising Chapters 2–5, covers constitutional developments during the colonial phase, which started in earnest in 1960 and culminated in the 1968 Independence Constitution. Part III, comprising Chapters 6 and 7, covers the post-colonial phase of the King Sobhuza era from 1968 until King Sobhuza's demise in 1982, and, Part IV, Chapter 8, concludes.

Part I, this chapter, introduces the book. In Part II, Chapter 2 focuses on the major players who were engaged in discussing the appropriate constitutional framework for independence for Swaziland during the colonial period. Such discussions took place under the supervision of the British colonial authorities, who provided the directives to the stakeholders within which to navigate. The stakeholders included King Sobhuza II and his traditional Swazi National Council; Carl Todd, the leader of the White community operating under the European Advisory Council in Swaziland; and the leaders of Swaziland's nascent political parties: John June Nquku and Dr Ambrose Zwane. Apartheid South Africa was an outsider but, nonetheless, an important stakeholder in Swaziland's political evolution by virtue of its geo-political location and the prospects of the spillover of developments of Swaziland into South Africa. Whereas Swaziland's political elite had different ideas on the type of political system that the future constitution should reflect, South Africa was also interested in the direction of political change in Swaziland due to the potential political implications for the life of the apartheid regime.

Chapter 3 explores the period from the commencement of the constitutional talks in 1960 up to the deadlock in the talks in 1963. Swaziland was comparatively tardy in commencing constitutional talks in preparation for independence owing to historical circumstances related to its relationship with South Africa and its settler colony status. Nonetheless, it took its cue from constitutional developments in the continent and started its own constitutional talks in 1960 under the British. Although the stakeholders did not contest the Westminster constitutional frame provided by the British, they engaged in a ferocious battle of conflicting ideologies that divided them into two camps. The first camp comprised the conservative Swazi monarchy and their White allies; the second was made of up leaders of Swaziland's nascent political parties who espoused an unbridled liberal democratic dispensation and a radical nationalist platform. Both the Swazi monarchy and the political leaders were jockeying and struggling to succeed the departing British colonial administration, and this made it difficult for them to arrive at a consensus. The protagonists agreed to disagree in Swaziland and in London on the issue of race, voting rights, the powers of the legislature, and the future role of the Swazi monarchy: this resulted in a stalemate that compromised the prospects of Swaziland's early independence. This chapter also highlights South Africa's behind-the-scenes interference in the constitutional processes in Swaziland as a major stakeholder through its Swazi proxies—the Swazi monarchy and the White community.

The constitutional stalemate that was created by the discord between Swaziland's political elite had to be unlocked. Chapter 4 examines how Britain unlocked the stalemate by imposing the 1963 Constitution on all the Swazi stakeholders, and by calling for elections to pave the way for the emergence of a clear party that would be charged with drawing up a constitution for Swaziland and leading the territory to independence. The 1963 Constitution that Britain imposed on Swaziland provided for limited internal self-government, with Her Majesty's Commissioner having veto rights over every subject.

The chapter highlights the clash between British constitutional values, on the one hand, and those of the Swazi monarchy, on the other, before and after the June 1964 elections. Whereas the British struggled to convince the traditional monarch to maintain absolute neutrality in modern politics in the same way as the English monarchy, King Sobhuza II refused to do so and opted to join modern politics. He was backed by the White Swazis and the South African government, who advised him to form a political party and enter modern politics so as to avoid being eclipsed by the modern political party leaders. King Sobhuza's *Imbokodvo* party and the White Swazi party, the United Swaziland Association, swept all the seats in the June 1964 elections at the expense of Swaziland's progressive political parties. The political implication of the defeat of the Progressives was that they were excluded from the Constitutional Committee for the formulation of Swaziland's independence constitution. Constitution-making in colonial Swaziland was, therefore, largely monopolized by King Sobhuza's party, while the Progressives were left out in the cold.

24   H. P. DLAMINI

Chapter 5 examines the processes involved in making Swaziland's independence constitution. It started with the making of the 1967 Constitution, which led to internal self-government and the completion of 1968 Independence Constitution. The making of the independence constitution was the sole business of the royal *Imbokodvo* and the United Swaziland Association Party, who won the June 1964 elections and constituted members of the Legislative Council from which the Constitutional Review Committee was selected. The relationship between the two allies quickly fell apart after the 1964 elections. They bitterly disagreed over the issue of race and the privileges of the Europeans in parliament. There were also disagreements between the indigenous Swazis and Whites, in both the House of Assembly and Senate, over the *Ngwenyama*'s control of minerals and mineral oils—disagreements that were carried over to London. Britain was reluctant to endorse what it perceived as a constitutional order in which the *Ngwenyama* was elevated to the position of a total autocrat who was above the cabinet in the management of mineral resources. The question that the two sides could not easily resolve was whether a traditional monarch should be above the constitution in a modern state, or whether it should be subjected to constitutional checks and balances. Britain had the last word in these matters before the independence of Swaziland in 1968 and bequeathed a constitutional monarch to independence Swaziland.

In Part III, Chapter 6 deals with the period of the Westminster-modelled 1968 constitution up to its overthrow in 1973. The constitution, which provided for a Swazi-type constitutional monarch, was overthrown in 1973, following which there was a constitutional void. Constitutional monarchism, which had a very short life span, was compromised by the African political environment, which favoured executive absolutism in the shape of a one-party dictatorship. King Sobhuza had been expressing his discontentment with multipartyism and the checks and balances of liberal democracy, which contested his authority. The courts' ruling against the government in the Ngwenya affair was considered intolerable by the monarch. The stand-off that ensued between the government and the courts resulted in a constitutional crisis culminating in Sobhuza's 1973 auto-coup d'état in the repeal of the independence constitution. This extraordinary development in the history of Swaziland's post-colonial development is a reflection of the difficulties of a nascent African state in engaging in constitutional engineering where the three arms of government were to serve as checks or counter-balance to each other.

Chapter 7 amplifies the political implications of King Sobhuza's 1973 auto-coup d'état. It demonstrates how, in the absence of parliament, king Sobhuza instituted a governance system by Orders-in-Council and Decrees that evolved into a fully fledged absolute monarchy with an arsenal of draconian laws to contain any opposition to his rule. This chapter clearly brings out the point that, although King Sobhuza decreed a succession of draconian legislations, they were more or less akin to paper tigers. This was so because his reign was not tyrannical and he did not make political martyrs, unlike some of his contemporaries who killed hundreds of thousands of people and threw others in jail. King Sobhuza struggled to reconcile with and rehabilitate his political opponents, and was the quintessence of a paternal king for all Swazis. He was therefore a benevolent despot *par excellence*. The *tinkhundla* system of governance he instituted in 1978 reflected his desire to have total control of the entire political system in the kingdom of Swaziland. King Sobhuza II was definitely an absolute monarch, but the benevolent element of his despotism cannot be dismissed. He succeeded in endowing Swaziland with a bicameral legislature in 1978 under the *tinkhundla* system of democracy.

Part IV, Chapter 8, concludes the book. Britain engaged the various Swazi stakeholders in designing the constitution of the territory during the colonial phase within a framework laid down by the colonial office. Britain bequeathed to Swaziland a constitutional monarch that the ruling monarchical class reluctantly accepted. After independence, the Swazi monarch discarded the constitution that provided for checks and balances in an auto-coup d'état in 1973, and made himself the constitutional reference point of the kingdom. He ruled by Orders-in-Council and Decrees; nonetheless, he governed Swaziland with a human face despite the draconian legislation at his disposal, quitting the political scene in 1982 without having endowed his country with another constitution.

References

Newspaper Articles

'Jan, Majahenkhaba, Mario's Trip', *Times of Swaziland*, November 8, 2015.

Books, Journal Articles and Theses

Acheampong, K. A., and Domson-Lindsay, A. K. 'Unlocking the Security Puzzle in Swaziland: The Centrality of Human Rights and Democracy', *African Security Review*, 20, 3 (2011), 3–14.

Afigbo, A. E. 'Background to Nigerian Federalism: Federal Features in the Colonial State', *Publius: The Journal of Federalism*, 21, 4 (1991), 13–29.

Akpan, M. E. *Constitution and Constitutionalism* (Calabar: Paico Ltd., 1984).

Anamzoya, A. S. 'Chieftaincy Is Dead: Long Live Chieftaincy: Renewed Relevance of Chieftaincy in Postcolonial Ghana', *The African Review*, 40, 2 (2017), 115–139.

Awasom, N. F. 'Politics and Constitution-Making in Francophone Cameroon, 1959–1960', *Africa Today* (2002), 3–30.

Baloro, J. 'The Development of Swaziland's Constitution: Monarchical Response to Modern Challenges', *Journal of African Law*, 38, 1 (1994), 19–34.

Bonner, P. *Kings, Commoners and Concessionaires: The Evolution and Dissolution of the Nineteenth-Century Swazi State*. Vol. 31 (New York: Cambridge University Press, 2002).

Crook, R. C. 'Decolonization, the Colonial State, and Chieftaincy in the Gold Coast', *African Affairs*, 85, 338 (1986), 75–106.

Daniel, J. 'The Political Economy of Colonial and Post-colonial Swaziland', *South African Labour Bulletin*, 7, 6 (1982), 90–113.

Dearaujo, E. 'Chaotic Congo', *Harvard International Review*, 23, 3 (2001), 10.

Decalo, S. *Psychoses of Power: African Personal Dictatorships*. Vol. 3 (Boulder: Florida Academic Press, 1998).

Dlamini, H. P. 'Constitutional Developments in the Kingdom of Swaziland 1960–2005' (PhD thesis, University of Pretoria, 2016).

Dlamini, H. P. 'The Tinkhundla Monarchical Democracy: An African System of Good Governance?', In O. Bialostocka (ed.), *New African Thinkers Agenda 2063: Culture at the Heart of Sustainable Development* (Cape Town: HSRC Press, 2018).

Dlamini, I. G. 'Socio-economic and Political Constraint on Constitutional Reform in Swaziland' (MA thesis, University of West Cape, 2005).

Dixit, K. M. 'Absolute Monarchy to Absolute Democracy', *Economic and Political Weekly* (2005), 1506–1510.

Domson-Lindsay, A. K. 'Neopatrimonialism and the Swazi State', *Politeia (02568845)*, 32, 3 (2013).

Ezera, K. *Constitutional Developments in Nigeria* (London: Cambridge University Press, 1964).

Fombad, C. M. 'The Swaziland Constitution of 2005: Can Absolutism Be Reconciled with Modern Constitutionalism?', *South African Journal on Human Rights*, 23, 1 (2007), 93–115.

Goudie, A. *The Atlas of Swaziland*. No. 4. Swaziland National Trust Commission, 1983.

Grimm, D. 'Types of Constitutions', In M. Rosenfeld and A. Sajo (eds.), *The Oxford Handbook of Comparative Constitutional Law* (Oxford: Oxford University Press, 2012).

Hachhethu, K. 'Legitimacy Crisis of Nepali Monarchy', *Economic and Political Weekly* (2007), 1828–1833.

Hlatshwayo, V. S. 'The Reality of Media Freedom in Swaziland Under the New Constitutional Dispensation' (MA thesis, University of Cape Town, 2011), 31.

Hutt, M. 'King Gyanendra's Coup and Its Implications for Nepal's Future', *Brown Journal of World Affairs*, 12 (2005), 111.

Hutt, M. 'Nepal and Bhutan in 2005: Monarchy and Democracy, Can They Co-exist?' (2006), 120–124.

Ibingira, G. S. K. *The Forging of an African Nation: The Political and Constitutional Evolution of Uganda from Colonial Rule to Independence, 1894–1962* (Viking Adult, 1973).

Jackson, R. H., Jackson, R. H., and Rosberg, C. G. *Personal Rule in Black Africa: Prince, Autocrat, Prophet, Tyrant* (London: University of California Press, 1982).

Keese, A. 'Understanding Colonial Chieftaincy from Its Final Phase: Responses to the Crisis of an Institution in French-Ruled West Africa and Beyond, 1944–1960', *Africana Studia* 15 (2010), 11–28.

Kumar, D. 'Proximate Causes of Conflict in Nepal', *Contributions to Nepalese Studies*, 32, 1 (2005), 51–92.

Kuper, H. *Sobhuza II Ngwenyama and King of Swaziland: The Story of an Hereditary Ruler and His Country* (London: Gerald Duckworth and Co. Ltd., 1978).

Lane, J. E. *Constitutions and Political Theory* (Manchester: Manchester University Press, 1996).

MacDowell, W. H. *Historical Research: A Guide* (London: Longman, 2002), 57.

Macmillan, H. 'Swaziland: Decolonization and Triumph of "Tradition"', *Journal of Modern African Studies*, 23, 4 (1985), 643–666.

Maseko, T. 'The Drafting of the Constitution of Swaziland, 2005', *African Human Rights Law Journal* (2005), 312–363.

Masuku, B., and Limb, P. 'Swaziland: The Struggle for Political Freedom and Democracy', *Review of African Political Economy*, 43, 149 (2016), 518–527.

Matlosa, K. 'Democracy and Conflict in Post-apartheid Southern Africa: Dilemmas of Social Change in Small States', *International Affairs*, 74, 2 (1998), 319–337.

28   H. P. DLAMINI

Maxon, R. M. *Kenya's Independence Constitution: Constitution-Making and End of Empire* (Fairleigh Dickinson, 2011).

Mazrui, Ali A. 'Between Development and Decay: Anarchy, Tyranny and Progress Under Idi Amin', *Third World Quarterly*, 2, 1 (1980), 44–58.

Menkhaus, K. *Somalia: State Collapse and the Threat of Terrorism* (Routledge, 2013).

Mnisi, L. N. 'From Absolutism to Constitutional Monarchy: Has the New Constitution Transformed Prospects for Human Rights in the Kingdom of Swaziland' (PhD diss., University of Essex, 2010).

Motsamai, D. 'Swaziland's Non-Party Political System and the 2013 Tinkhundla Elections Breaking the SADC Impasse?', *Africa Portal* (2012).

Mthembu, M. V. 'Participation of Swazi Women in the Traditional Public Sphere, Sibaya, in the Kingdom of Swaziland', *Communicare: Journal for Communication Sciences in Southern Africa*, 37, 1 (2018), 74–93.

Mullins, C. W., and Rothe, D. L. 'Gold, Diamonds and Blood: International State-Corporate Crime in the Democratic Republic of the Congo', *Contemporary Justice Review*, 11, 2 (2008), 81–99.

Mzizi, J. B. 'Leadership, Civil Society and Democratisation in Swaziland', Development Policy Management Forum (DPMF), 2002.

Ndulo, M. B., and Kent, R. B. 'Constitutionalism in Zambia: Past Present and Future', *Journal of African Law*, 40, 2 (1996), 256–278.

Nwabueze, B. O. *Constitutionalism in the Emergent States* (New York: C. Hugh and Company, 1973).

Potholm, C. P. *Swaziland: The Dynamics of Political Modernization* (London: University of California Press, 1972).

Potholm, C. P. 'Swaziland Under Sobhuza II: The Future of an African Monarchy', *The Round Table: The Commonwealth Journal of International Affairs*, 64, 254 (1974), 219–227.

Protzel, J. 'Changing Political Cultures and Media Under Globalism in Latin America', *Democratising Global Media: One World, Many Struggles* (2005), 101–120.

Rathbone, R. 'Kwame Nkruma and the Chiefs: The Fate of "Natural Rulers" Under Nationalist Governments', *Transactions of the Royal Historical Society*, 10 (2000), 45–63.

Ray, D. I. 'Divided Sovereignty: Traditional Authority and the State in Ghana', *The Journal of Legal Pluralism and Unofficial Law*, 28, 37–38 (1996), 181–202.

Sampford, C. 'Making Coups History', *World Politics Review*, 22 (2010), 1–10.

Sereo, H. P. 'The Contribution of the People's United Democratic Movement (PUDEMO) to Democratic Change in Swaziland, 1983–2013' (PhD diss., University of Zululand, 2018).

Stevens, R. P. 'Swaziland Political Development', *The Journal of Modern African Studies*, 1, 3 (1963), 327–350.

Tosh, J. *The Pursuit of History* (London: Longman, 1991), 37–38.

Vilakati, S. S. *Geography for Swaziland* (Manzini: Macmillan Boleswa Publishers, 1997).

Wanda, B. P. 'The Shaping of Modern Constitution in Swaziland: A Review of Some Social and Historical Factors', *Lesotho Law Journal*, 6, 1 (1990), 137–178.

Woods, D. 'Monarchical Rule in Swaziland: Power Is Absolute but Patronage Is (for) Relative(s)', *Journal of Asian and African Studies*, 52, 4 (2017), 497–513.

Woods, D. 'Patrimonialism (Neo) and the Kingdom of Swaziland: Employing a Case Study to Rescale a Concept', *Commonwealth & Comparative Politics*, 50, 3 (2012), 344–366.

NEWS CHANNELS

News24, 'eSwatini, Africa's Last Absolute Monarchy', September 19, 2018.

Reuters, 'Africa's Last Absolute Monarch Renames Swaziland as "eSwatini"', Mbabane, April 19, 2018.

SEMINAR PAPERS

Maseko, T. 'Constitution Making in Swaziland: The Cattle-Byre Constitution Act 001 of 2005', Paper presented at African Network of Constitutional Law Conference on Fostering Constitutionalism in Africa, Nairobi, 2007.

Sikhondze, B. A. B. 'Factors That Have Stalled Efforts Towards a Constitution in Swaziland, 1970s to 2003: A Constitutional History', Paper presented for a Workshop of the Swaziland OSSREA Chapter, November 27, 2003.

INTERNET SOURCES

BBC News, 1. eSwatini Country Profile—BBC News—BBC.com, 'The Kingdom of eSwatini Is One of the World's Last Remaining Absolute Monarchies' (*Source* www.bbc.com/news/world-africa-14095303, September 3, 2018).

CNN, 'Absolute Monarch Changes Swaziland Name to "eSwatini"', www.cnn.com/2018/04/20/africa/swaziland-eswatini-africa-monarchy-intl/index.html.

CNN, April 21, 2018 ... The king of Swaziland, Africa's last absolute monarch, has changed the name of his country to the "Kingdom of eSwatini" to mark the 50th (*Source* Alain Vicky, 'Africa's Last Absolute Monarchy', *Le Monde diplomatique*, mondediplo.com/2018/10/10swaziland, September 3, 2018).

PART II

Colonial Phase

CHAPTER 2

The Major Players in the Making of the Independence Constitution of Swaziland (Eswatini)

INTRODUCTION

The transfer of power to the Swazis during the decolonization era required the preparation of constitutional instruments for that purpose. It was typical of Britain, as the colonial administering authority, to engage the various stakeholders in the territory as a mentoring exercise before the transfer of power took place. This chapter focuses on Britain's involvement of the key players in the independence constitution-making processes in colonial Swaziland. The issue of stakeholders in constitution-making in colonial Swaziland is important due to the Swazi exceptionality.

In other British colonial dependencies such as Nigeria, Ghana, Kenya, Tanzania, Zambia, South Africa, and Malawi, constitution-making was the business of Western-educated nationalists under British tutelage, not traditional rulers.[1] In colonial Swaziland, it was a totally different scenario, as the Swazi monarch (or *Ngwenyama*, meaning lion in *siSwati*) was at the

---

[1] In Africa some of the prominent nationalists including N. Azikiwe, O. Awolowo, K. Nkrumah, J. Kenyatta, J. Nyerere, K. Kaunda, and A. Luthuli were educated elites without any royal connections (see C. Fyfe, 'Africanus Horton as a Constitution-Maker', *Journal of Commonwealth & Comparative Politics*, 26, 2 [1988], 173–184; G. Arrighi and J. S. Saul, 'Nationalism and Revolution in Sub-Saharan Africa', *The Socialist Register*, 6 [1969]; and C. Allen, 'Understanding African Politics', *Review of African Political Economy*, 22, 65 [1995], 301–320).

© The Author(s) 2019
H. P. Dlamini, *A Constitutional History of the Kingdom of Eswatini (Swaziland), 1960–1982*, African Histories and Modernities,
https://doi.org/10.1007/978-3-030-24777-5_2

34   H. P. DLAMINI

forefront of the exercise in total deviation from standard British practices. The other stakeholders included the White community, and the 'Progressives' (the radical Swazi nationalists operating under the banner of political parties). Another exceptionality in the constitution-making process was the interference of an outsider-apartheid South Africa, which positioned itself as a big player in Swazi colonial politics due to the strategic location of Swaziland within South Africa. These stakeholders were actively involved in Swaziland's constitution-making exercise under the British.

BRITAIN AND THE MAKING OF SWAZILAND'S INDEPENDENCE CONSTITUTION

Scholars are unanimous on the fact that metropolitan powers often assumed full responsibility in providing constitutions for their erstwhile dependencies before independence.[2] Independence constitutions were, therefore, identical, or similar, to metropolitan constitutions.[3] Of course, this similarity is explained by the fact that these constitutions were largely metropolitan impositions on newly constituted nation-states. The colonial powers had an interest in ensuring that the constitutions they bequeathed to their colonial dependencies followed their own constitutional model, satisfying their

[2] T. Lumumba-Kasongo, 'The Origin of African Constitutions, Elusive Constitutionalism, and the Crisis of Liberal Democracy', In *Democratic Renewal in Africa* (New York: Palgrave Macmillan, 2015), 63–96; B. Bujo, 'Springboards for Modern African Constitutions and Development in African Cultural Traditions', *African Ethics: An Anthology of Comparative and Applied Ethics* (2009), 391–411; and Y. Ghai, 'Constitutions and Governance in Africa: A Prolegomenon', In *Law and Crisis in the Third World* (London, Melbourne, Munich, and New Jersey: Hans Zell Publishers, 1993).

[3] See for instance, G. O. Julian, 'Modeling the State: Postcolonial Constitutions in Asia and Africa', *Southeast Asian Studies*, 39, 4 (2002), 558–583; M. Duverger, 'A New Political Model: Semi-Presidential Government', *European Journal of Political Research*, 8, 2 (1980), 165–187; A. Liijphart (ed.), *Parliamentary Versus Presidential Government* (London: Oxford University Press, 1992); T. O. Elias, *Nigeria: The Development of Its Laws and Constitutions* (London: Stevenson & Sons Ltd., 1967); B. Nwabueze, *Constitutionalism in the Emergent States* (London: C. Hurst & Company, 1973); K. Robinson, 'Autochthony and the Transfer of Power', In K. Robinson and F. Madden (eds.), *Essays in Imperial Government: Presented to Margery Perham* (Oxford: Basil Blackwell, 1963); M. G. De Winston, 'Decolonisation and the Westminster Model', In A. H. M. Kirk-Greene (ed.), *Africa in the Colonial Period III: The Transfer of Power: The Colonial Administrators in the Age of Decolonisation* (Oxford: Oxford University Inter-Faculty Committee for African Studies, 1979).

2 THE MAJOR PLAYERS IN THE MAKING ... 35

ego by realizing their modernization project[4] modelled on democratic values as the product of Western civilization. Metropolitan authorities and the local colonial administration wanted to have an honourable exit from Africa by leaving behind institutions that were structured along the same lines as theirs. This should not be interpreted as meaning that independence constitutions were enacted in the United Kingdom and imposed on African countries. These constitutions were always the outcome of full consultations and discussions, which are what this study sets out to examine. Colonial powers employed various methods to ensure constitutional isomorphism and this was clearly reflected in the processes that constitution-making underwent. Consequently, it was the colonial administration that appointed the committee that drafted the constitution following the British constitutional model. Critical decisions on the final outcome of the constitution had to be taken by policy-makers in the colonial office in Britain to emphasize the weight of metropolitan factors in constitution-making.[5] There was, therefore, a level of imperial imposition or *diktat* on the independent constitutions of African states.

Beyond colonial imposition was the fact that the Swazi political elite were engaged in the drafting of the independence constitutions under the supervision of Britain. The British colonial administration arrogated to itself the right to guide the Swazis through the intricacies of Western-style politics. The Swazis followed the British model as their reference point as far as they understood it and were, therefore, largely 'converts to Western Constitutionalism', as Nwabueze puts it.[6] Constitutional isomorphism with that of Britain was, therefore, a given because the British stood as a model in the eyes of the Swazis, who tried to copy British constitutional tradition insofar

---

[4]Yahia Mahmoud notes that concepts such as modernism, modernity, and modernisation are central to the concept of development studies. He argued that this often led to reductive representations of social realities 'through dichotomized and hierarchised categories: modern vs. traditional, rational vs. irrational,...developed vs. underdeveloped....' In the late 1960s modernisation revisionists criticised the modernisation approach on several key points. Amongst other things they argued that traditional institutions and attitudes were not necessarily hindrances to modernisation. British political modernisation in colonial Swaziland should be understood as the process of British introduction of new institutions, norms, and procedures of governance in contrast to the pre-colonial indigenous governance system (Y. Mahmoud, 'Modernism in Africa', *Routledge Encyclopedia of Modernism* [2016]).

[5]Constitutions of British colonial dependencies always needed to have final endorsement in a series of Lancaster House Conferences in the UK.

[6]Nwabueze, *Constitutionalism in the Emergent States*, 27.

as convenient. Colonial imitation or imposition, consequently, explains why the constitutional framework was usually a near-carbon copy of metropolitan frameworks, with some modifications to local circumstances. The differences in colonial constitutions may be seen in the structure of the government in terms of the distribution of power between the executive and the legislative arms of government, and the extent to which the parliamentary system, or any other inherited system, conforms to metropolitan systems.[7]

The constitutional development of Swaziland during the colonial period was comparatively tardy, owing to initial British uncertainty about the future of Swaziland.[8] Britain was counting on South Africa to incorporate the petty territory into its fold and did not intend to oversee its development into a sovereign entity. From the 1909 South African Act of Union to the birth of apartheid under the Nationalist Party, Swaziland, like the other High Commission Territories, was administered with a view to integrating

---

[7] The common tendency among Africans was to negotiate for a strong executive at the expense of the other arms of the government (see Y. Ghai, 'Constitutions and Governance in Africa: A Prolegomenon', *Law and Crisis in the Third World* [London, Melbourne, Munich, and New Jersey: Hans Zell Publishers, 1993]; B. Ibhawoh, 'Between Culture and Constitution: Evaluating the Cultural Legitimacy of Human Rights in the African State', *Human Rights Quarterly*, 22, 3 [2000], 838–860; M. Crowder, 'Whose Dream Was It Anyway? Twenty-Five Years of African Independence', *African Affairs*, 86, 342 [1987], 7–24; M. Meredith, *The Fate of Africa: A History of the Continent Since Independence* [Hachette UK, 2011]; and V. T. Le Vine, 'The Fall and Rise of Constitutionalism in West Africa', *The Journal of Modern African Studies*, 35, 2 [1997], 181–206).

[8] Constitutional developments in Ghana and Nigeria give us a clue to how comparatively fast these took place in the post Second World War era. In Ghana, the 1946 Burns constitution contained provisions for a Legislative and Executive Council and doubled African representations in these councils. A new constitution in 1951 gave the Executive Council a large majority of African Ministers and an Assembly dominated by Africans. But this was short of full self-government because executive powers still remained in British hands. In February 1951, the first elections were held for the Legislative Assembly under the new constitution and Nkrumah's Convention People's Party won two-thirds of the majority of 104 seats and was invited to form a government as leader of Government Business, which was a quasi-Prime Minister. In 1952 self-government was introduced and the position of Prime Minister was created and the Executive Council became a cabinet. Nkrumah was duly elected Prime Minister in 1952 and in 1957 Ghana became independent. Nigeria also experimented with a succession of Constitutions starting comprising the Richards constitution in 1946, the MacPherson constitution (1951), the Lyteltton constitution (1954) under which power was progressively transferred to Africans leading to independence in 1960 (see F. M. Bourret [ed.], *Ghana, the Road to Independence, 1919–1957*, Vol. 23 [Stanford: Stanford University Press, 1960]; B. O. Nwabueze, *A Constitutional History of Nigeria* [London: C. Hurst & Company, 1981]).

it with South Africa.[9] This explains why Swaziland was administered by British Resident Commissioners for the Protectorate, who were responsible to the British High Commissioner in South Africa, stationed in Pretoria. The South African adoption of apartheid in 1948 reduced the prospects of the integration of Swaziland into South Africa.[10] The withdrawal of South Africa from the Commonwealth and her change to a republic in 1960 invalidated the 1909 Act. The implication of this was that all South Africa's legal rights to lay claims to the High Commission Territories were rendered null and void, since the Republic was no longer a member of the Commonwealth and had severed all ties with the UK.[11] South Africa's withdrawal from the Commonwealth was, therefore, the last straw, and Britain had no choice but to prepare Swaziland for independence.

The United Kingdom had to play the role of political midwife in the birth of a sovereign Swaziland with the necessary constitution befitting a modern state. Consequently, Britain presented a draft constitutional document to a constitutional committee composed of the various interest groups for their information, appreciation, and necessary input. What Britain proposed as a draft constitution for Swaziland, as was the case with other British colonial dependencies,[12] was the prototypical British parliamentary form of government known as the Westminster system. This is characterized by the fact that the head of government's authority is dependent on the confidence of the legislature. The Prime Minister, usually the leader of the majority party, is chosen by the legislature and is dependent on parliament for his survival. The executive is bicephalic and includes the head of government (usually the Prime Minster), and a ceremonial head of state (who is usually a monarch). Britain intended to replicate a bicephalic executive in Swaziland. The draft proposed a bicameral legislature of an upper and lower house.[13]

[9] R. Hyam, *The Failure of South African Expansion, 1908–1948* (Africana Publication, 1972); W. M. H. B. Hailey, *The Republic of South Africa and the High Commission Territories* (London: Oxford University Press, 1963); and R. P. Stevens, *Lesotho, Botswana and Swaziland: The Former High Commission Territories in Southern Africa* (London: Pall Mall, 1967).

[10] R. P. Stevens, 'Swaziland Political Development', *The Journal of Modern African Studies*, 1, 3 (1963), 327–350.

[11] Zwane, 'The Struggle for Power in Swaziland', 4.

[12] In British Africa, the British bequeathed the Westminster parliamentary system of government with a bicameral legislature.

[13] G. O. Julian, 'Modelling the State: Postcolonial Constitutions in Asia and Africa', *Southern African Studies*, 39, 4 (2002), 558–560.

38   H. P. DLAMINI

In essence, the British proposed a parliamentary model of government that was a reflection of Britain's political history.

As the political midwife of the birth of new nation states in Africa, Britain bequeathed the Westminster model of government though a piecemeal process. The first thing the British intended to do was to establish a constitutional committee composed of the various interest groups in Swaziland to discuss voting procedures for the organization of general elections on a multiparty basis. From the elections would emanate the Legislative Council and an Executive Council. The Legislative Council would serve as the territory's Constituent Assembly, which would then oversee the drawing up of Swaziland's independence constitution. It was incumbent on Britain to achieve this political agenda by engaging all the interest groups in colonial Swaziland, including the White community, the Swazi monarch and his traditional Swazi National Council, and the progressives operating under the banner of political parties. South Africa did not intend to be indifferent to developments in Swaziland due to their possible impact on its apartheid system.

THE WHITE COMMUNITY AND MULTINATIONAL INVESTORS

The White community in colonial Swaziland numbered over 10,000 in 1960, sometimes being referred to in historical documents as 'South African immigrants' because most of them were of South African origin; they constituted a conspicuous exclusive ethnic minority. Kuper describes the exclusiveness of Whites as follows:

> The Whites … justify their exclusiveness on the grounds that that they have built up, and maintain, 'Western civilisation'. In fact, this Western civilisation … is a somewhat vague cultural complex, or syndrome, acquired over many centuries from many lands. It exists in the minds of Whites, for whom it includes monogamy, a monotheistic religion of Judaeo-Christian origin, a 'European language', a capitalist or mixed economy, and a wide assortment of material accessories (dress, building, food, liquors, furnishings and technical equipment …[14]

[14] H. Kuper, 'The Colonial Situation in Southern Africa', *The Journal of Modern African Studies*, 2, 2 (1964), 152.

The importance of the White community in Swaziland lies in the political economy of the territory represented in White and multinational capital.[15] The colonial economy was essentially in White hands, and they were therefore deeply involved in the politics of the territory in order to protect their economic interests. There is need here to trace the history of their economic domination of colonial Swaziland in order to demonstrate why and how the White community had high stakes in the constitutional developments of the territory.

The implantation of European settlements in Swaziland commenced in the mid-nineteenth century. During the peak period of the European scramble for African territories in the 1880s, there were over 750 White settlers in Swaziland, of whom 450 were of British origin, the remainder being Boers. The indigenous Swazis then numbered around 63,000.[16] By 1960, there were over 10,000 Whites and 270,000 Swazis.

Since the beginning of their settlement in Swaziland, Whites often organized themselves to pursue their common interests. For instance, in 1887 Whites established a White Committee of 25 men, with James Forbes as the chairman, to promote White interests.[17] The main responsibility of the White Committee was to resolve civil and criminal disputes among the Whites, subject, in principle, to the final authority of the Swazi king. The committee persuaded King Mbandzeni to grant them a charter, and he conceded on 1 August 1888.[18] The charter authorized Whites to form a committee that addressed all White matters. King Mbandzeni had a special adviser, Shepstone, to assist him in tackling the concession issues. Shepstone prevailed on the King to dismiss the White Committee for failing to manage intra-White conflicts and the King obliged.[19]

The White Committee was replaced by the Triumvirate Government, which existed from 1890 to 1894. It was composed of British, Boer, and Swazi representatives, and it established a concession court that operated on the basis of Roman Dutch law, which was used in South Africa.

---

[15] For details on this situation see J. Daniel, 'The Political Economy of Colonial and Post-colonial Swaziland', *South African Labour Bulletin*, 7, 6 (1982), 90–113.

[16] H. Kuper, *King Sobhuza II, Ngwenyama and King of Swaziland*, 26.

[17] A. N. Boyce, 'The Swaziland Concessions and Their Political Consequences 1876–1908', PhD thesis, University of South Africa (1946), 17; J. S. M. Matsebula, *A History of Swaziland* (Johannesburg: Longman Southern Africa Ltd., 1972), 99–100.

[18] Ibid.

[19] Ibid.

40   H. P. DLAMINI

The concession court was set up to pass judgement on the validity of European concessions owing to numerous conflicts over land claims arising between Whites.[20] The Triumvirate Government was disbanded in February 1895 following the implementation of the Third Swaziland Convention, under which the British agreed to allow the Boers to administer Swaziland and the Transvaal took over its administration.

The South African Boer Republic appointed Johannes Krogh as its special commissioner for Swaziland. With Swaziland under the Boers, a prominent White settler, Allister Miller, called for the transformation of Swaziland into a White man's country by convincing the Boers to set aside more land for Europeans. Miller founded many bodies to cater for White interests, such as the Mbandzeni Concession Syndicate in 1891, the Swaziland Corporation of 1898, and the Swaziland Mining, Industrial and Commercial Chamber in 1899.[21]

The relationship between the British and the Boers was strained, eventually degenerating into the Anglo-Boer War (1899–1902), which resulted in the ouster of the Boers and the establishment of a British Protectorate over Swaziland in 1903. Allister Miller, a prominent member of the Swaziland Concessions Commission, established in 1905, wanted the British to transform Swaziland into a White man's country like South Africa. He did this in two ways. First, he organized a media campaign to attract more Whites from South Africa and overseas to come and settle in Swaziland. Second, he wrote a report to the British colonial administration in which he called for the transferral of up to 90% of Swazi territory to White settlers. His argument was that the White community in Swaziland, like their counterparts in Kenya, South Africa, and elsewhere, were the economic backbone of the territory and therefore needed more land for that purpose.[22] There is no doubt that the White settlers were ruthless and had no conscience in land matters by asking for so much land without thinking of the consequences for the indigenous Swazis.

Miller's report appears to have influenced the British colonial administration because it became the basis for the ruthless British Land Partition Proclamation of 1907. The Proclamation allocated 43% of the land to

---

[20] Ibid.

[21] J. Crush, 'Landlords, Tenants and Colonial Social Engineers: The Farm Labour Question in Early Colonial Swaziland', *Journal of Southern African Studies*, 11, 2 (April 1985), 236.

[22] Ibid.

2 THE MAJOR PLAYERS IN THE MAKING … 41

White settlers and corporations, 24% to the British Crown, and the remaining 33% to the Swazi people.[23] The 1907 Proclamation was clearly engineered by the White settlers, who emerged as the biggest land owners in colonial Swaziland. The White settlers had to go beyond the 1907 Proclamation Act to protect their acquisitions by forming a lobby organization, the European Advisory Council (EAC), to protect their interests.

The need for the EAC was also underscored by the decision of the colonial government to increase taxes after World War I owing to increasing economic difficulties the government was facing. The Resident Commissioner, Sir De Symons Montagu George Honey, and the District Commissioners resolved in May 1921 that all male European residents in the territory should be levied with a poll tax and income tax in order to raise revenue to run the country. European residents in the territory would be levied personal taxes: a poll tax and surtax on incomes over £1000, along with a tax on undeveloped mineral concessions. Poll tax was applicable to all adult European males above 21 years and was set at £2 per annum.[24]

Whites were not happy with the increased tax rates and insisted that they would not submit to taxation without representation in the colonial administration. Consequently, they proposed the formation of the EAC, which would advise the colonial administration on issues affecting them in the territory, and the British administration consented.[25]

The EAC came into existence in October 1921. At its first meeting with the Resident Commissioner, the EAC proposed that it be transformed into a Legislative Council instead of being a mere advisory council. Whites argued that there were White Legislative Councils in British colonies, such as Kenya and Southern Rhodesia, with powers to implement policies without sometimes getting the approval of the colonial state. In response, Honey maintained that the EAC would be purely advisory, and that the colonial administration would not be obliged to implement recommendations made by the EAC. The colonial administration refused to give the

---

[23] Crush, 'Settler-Estate Production', 187; Matsebula, *A History of Swaziland*, 184.

[24] Ibid.

[25] J. Crush, 'The Culture of Failure: Racism, Violence and White Farming in Colonial Swaziland', *Journal of Historical Geography*, 22, 2 (1996), 177–197; M. Z. Booth, 'Settler, Missionary, and the State: Contradictions in the Formulation of Educational Policy in Colonial Swaziland', *History of Education*, 32, 1 (2003), 35–56.

EAC legislative powers because the number of White settlers in Swaziland was very low, just 2200 Whites against 110,295 Swazis.[26] Second, Swaziland was a British protectorate that was not entitled to a Legislative Council.[27] The EAC decided to appeal to the High Commissioner concerning its status but made no headway. The EAC therefore remained an advisory body responsible for White interests.

The mandate of the EAC was to advise the Resident Commissioner on matters directly affecting European residents, and on any matter specifically referred to the Council by the colonial government. Although not a Legislative Council, the EAC still managed to exercise considerable influence on government policy by virtue of the economic weight of the White residents.[28] The most influential leader of the EAC in the 1960s was Carl Todd. He was a director of more than 30 large companies in South Africa and had extensive land holdings in Swaziland.[29] Under Todd's leadership, the Whites jockeyed for political positioning by virtue of their economic relevance to the territory. Although Whites were a minority in statistical terms, they were an economic force to be reckoned with.

Whites were the biggest land owners in Swaziland under the land apportionment provisions of the 1907 Proclamations that allowed them to retain land with title deeds. They owned nearly 50% of the agricultural land and virtually 100% of the mines, industries, businesses, and trading enterprises. Their skills and capital, and their exploitation of Black labour, set the territory on the path to economic development.[30] Whites, therefore, legitimately claimed to belong to the country in which they had high economic stakes. As a result, they were determined to have a strong say in the political arena to protect their interests in the new political dispensation being negotiated during the decolonization era.

[26]SNA, RCS 613/21, Report of the First Meeting of the European Advisory Council, October 18–20, 1921; SNA, RCS 359/22, Suggested Deputation of the European Advisory Council to High Commissioner at Government House Cape Town, July, 21, 1922; and SNA, Colonial Annual Reports, 1923.

[27]Ibid.

[28]Daniel, 'The Political Economy of Colonial and Post-colonial Swaziland', 90–113; Stevens, 'Swaziland Political Development', 333.

[29]Ibid.

[30]Stevens, 'Swaziland Political Development', 333; J. Daniels, 'The Political Economy of Colonial and Post-colonial Swaziland', *South African Labour Bulletin*, 7, 6–7 (1981), 113; and J. S. Crush, 'The Parameters of Dependence in Southern Africa: A Case Study of Swaziland', *Journal of Southern African Affairs*, 4, 1 (1979), 56.

2 THE MAJOR PLAYERS IN THE MAKING ... 43

White and multinational interests in Swaziland were also dictated by the assumed mineral potentials of the territory. Swaziland was said to have rich iron ore, coal, and asbestos deposits of commercial value, which made it an enviable territory. Of the three High Commission territories, Swaziland was classified in the early 1960s as the only one that had any real prospect of becoming self-governing, due to its mineral wealth.[31] Swaziland was believed to be endowed with mineral wealth, unlike the other High Commission territories, in which the multinationals were interested.[32] Colonial investors, mainly the Commonwealth Development Corporation (CDC),[33] were the major investor in Swaziland's forestry and sugar industries, which employed thousands of Swazi workers, and had an interest in the maintenance of political stability, which was conducive for capital accumulation. The political economy of Swaziland dictated the type of support the Swazi traditional monarch was given by White economic interest groups, who were convinced it was easier to deal with the conservative Swazi monarch than the radical nationalists, who could not be trusted. Against a background of the wind of radical nationalism blowing over Africa, which threatened private investments and the Swazi traditional authorities, it is easy to understand the establishment of an alliance between the economic investors in Swaziland and the conservative Swazi monarch. Whites saw Swaziland as a potentially rich territory in which they had to invest but they needed a reliable ally to protect their investments, and they found this ally in the Swazi monarch and not the Progressives.

The economic prosperity of Whites was also dependent on exploiting Black labour. There was therefore a necessary White–Black economic partnership. The number of Swazi workers was ever-increasing and Swazis easily assimilated European standards, values, and ways of doing things, although they suffered discrimination in the hands of Whites and endured poor working conditions. The relationship between the Whites and indigenous Swazis during the colonial period was, essentially, one of masters and servants. White investors in Swaziland were worried about nationalist propaganda that pointed to the exploitation of Black labour.

[31] Zwane, 'The Struggle for Power in Swaziland', 4.

[32] J. Daniel, 'The Political Economy of Colonial and Post-colonial Swaziland', *South African Labour Bulletin*, 7, 6 (1982), 90–113.

[33] Macmillan, 'Swaziland: Decolonisation and the Triumph of "Tradition"', 661.

44   H. P. DLAMINI

King Sobhuza II was against the emergent labour unions in Swaziland, which was part of the expansion of the rights of association in the territory. He preferred that labour conflicts should be handled through traditional structures and that it was 'únSwazi' for workers to engage in industrial action because of wage disputes. This was the type of support the multinational consortium needed.

Whites and multinational business interests favoured King Sobhuza II at the expense of the Progressives due to their radical views and to their relationship with nascent labour movements, which they encouraged to strike for higher wages. Progressives were labelled communists, demagogues, and power-hungry individuals,[34] while King Sobhuza II was treated as a reliable ally.

THE SWAZI MONARCH AND HIS SWAZI NATIONAL COUNCIL

Important actors with whom the British had to collaborate in kick-starting the constitution-making process were King Sobhuza II and his traditional council, the Swazi National Council (SNC). The British avoided traditional leaders—kings and chiefs—in constitution-making in Africa, particularly in West and East Africa. The British dealt almost exclusively with Western-educated political leaders who formed political parties and pressure groups in their colonial dependencies.[35] Swaziland proved to be an exception to this standard practice because the British involved King Sobhuza II in the constitution-making exercise.

King Sobhuza II was a towering hereditary traditional figure of the Dlamini lineage in the kingdom of Swaziland. It was primarily through the leadership of a series of strong kings of the Dlamini dynasty that the Swazi nation not only came into existence, but also maintained its identity. King Sobhuza II was, therefore, a hereditary monarch, and he owed

---

[34]These labellings were common in the *Times of Swaziland* particularly from 1960 to 1963 when the constitutional debates were unfolding.

[35]The western educated elite like Julius Nyerere, Hastang Banda, Kenneth Kaunda, Kwame Nkrumah among others, were at the forefront of nationalist movements and constitutional talk and not traditional rulers (J. S. Coleman, *Nationalism and Development in Africa: Selected Essays* [University of California Press, 1994]; E. Schmidt, 'Anticolonial Nationalism in French West Africa: What Made Guinea Unique?' *African Studies Review*, 52, 2 [2009], 1–34; T. Falla, *Nationalism and African Intellectuals* [University Rochester Press, 2001]; and R. Onkwo, *Heroes of West African Nationalism* [Enugu: Delta, 1985], 35).

2 THE MAJOR PLAYERS IN THE MAKING ...   45

his position to the culture and tradition of a dynastic succession of the Dlaminis.[36] As with the historical European monarchs, Sobhuza's rights were considered divine, and were periodically reinforced by a succession of elaborate rituals in dance and song during the *incwala* and reed dance ceremonies.[37] King Sobhuza's legitimacy was, therefore, ancestral and not derived from universal adult suffrage, which he refused to have anything to do with on the grounds that it was un-African. The common folk viewed the Swazi king as a mystical figure who had direct association with the health of his subjects and the fertility of the soil.[38]

King Sobhuza II reigned over Swaziland, which is a largely ethnically homogeneous entity with a common language, custom, tradition, and history.[39] This uniform ethnic picture of Swaziland can be contrasted with that of other African countries, including Ghana, Nigeria, Kenya, Zimbabwe, and South Africa, where there was the absence of a single traditional authority to which the whole territory paid allegiance.[40] The heterogeneity of ethnic groups and traditional rulers in British colonial Africa, cleared the way for the Western-educated elite in these territories to emerge as the uncontested unifying forces to champion the anti-colonial struggle and,

[36] For more on the hereditary status of King Sobhuza II see H. Kuper, *King Sobhuza II, Ngwenyama and King of Swaziland: The Story of an Hereditary Ruler and His Country* (London: Africana Publication, 1978).

[37] For more on the traditional rituals of the Swazi monarchy as an instrument of legitimacy see P. Cocks, 'The King and I: Bronislaw Malinowski, King Sobhuza II of Swaziland and the Vision of Culture and Change in Africa', *History of the Human Sciences*, 13, 4 (2000), 25–47; R. Levin, 'Swaziland's Tinkhundla and the Myth of Swazi Tradition', *Journal of Contemporary African Studies*, 10, 2 (1991), 1–23; H. Kuper, *King Sobhuza II, Ngwenyama and King of Swaziland*; and H. Kuper, *An African Aristocracy: Rank Among Swazi* (London: Oxford University Press, 1980).

[38] This is a typical quality among African traditional rulers. See J. Middleton and D. Tait, *Tribes Without Rulers: Studies in African Segmentary Systems* (London: Routledge, 2013); P. Skalník, 'Authority Versus Power: Democracy in Africa, Must Include Original African Institutions', *The Journal of Legal Pluralism and Unofficial Law*, 28, 37–38 (1996), 109–121.

[39] H. Kuper, *King Sobhuza II, Ngwenyama and King of Swaziland: The Story of an Hereditary Ruler and His Country* (Africana Publication, 1978); W. J. Breytenbach, 'Sobhuza's Government: Old or New?' *Africa Insight*, 9, 2 (1979), 72–75.

[40] In a country like Nigeria and Cameroon, for instance, there are over 200 and 250 ethnic groups respectively (F. Gbenga, 'Ethnicity in Nigeria', *Philosophia Africana*, 11, 2 [2008], 141–156; F. A. Salamone, 'Ethnicity and Nigeria Since the End of the Civil War', *Dialectical Anthropology*, 22, 3–4 [1997], 303–333; and C. C. Fonchingong, 'Exploring the Politics of Identity and Ethnicity in State Reconstruction in Cameroon', *Social Identities*, 11, 4 [2005], 363–380).

46   H. P. DLAMINI

ultimately, to capture power from the departing colonial authorities. Furthermore, traditional leaders were perceived as retrogressive and divisive forces, while the educated elite were seen as the uniting and progressive forces that were most suitable to succeed the colonialists.

Swaziland was an exception and represented in Southern Africa what is referred to as a centralized polity[41] with twin monarchs, the *Ngwenyama* (the king), otherwise referred to as the 'lion', and the *Ndlovukati* (queen mother), otherwise referred to as 'the She-Elephant.'[42] This political system was generally considered and admired by Europeans as the peak of human historical achievement in governance.[43] The Swazi king worked closely with his traditional council, the *liqoqo*, which was composed of about 60 hereditary chiefs and nobles, together with a few commoners. Swaziland had a national body that was the rough equivalence of a parliament called *Libandla*, which met once a year and was attended by any adult male. Taken together, these traditional councils formed the SNC, which used to meet periodically with the representatives of the British government when the need arose.[44]

Swazis generally retained an emotional attachment to their King. King Sobhuza II championed the cause of retrieving Swazi land expropriated by Europeans, which had begun in the nineteenth century, and this made him

[41] Ethnologists eulogised centralized polities in contrast to segmentary or acephalous societies (see, for instance, P. Cocks, 'The King and I: Bronislaw Malinowski, King Sobhuza II of Swaziland and the Vision of Culture and Change in Africa', *History of the Human Sciences*, 13, 4 [2000], 25–47; S. N. Eisenstadt, 'Primitive Political Systems: A Preliminary Comparative Analysis', *American Anthropologist*, 61, 2 [1959], 200–220; and M. Fortes and E. E. Evans-Pritchard [eds.], *African Political Systems* [London: Oxford University Press, 1950]).

[42] H. Kuper, *King Sobhuza II, Ngwenyama and King of Swaziland: The Story of an Hereditary Ruler and His Country* (Africana Publication, 1978); H. Kuper, *The Swazi: A South African Kingdom* (Holt Rinehart & Winston, 1986); and P. Cocks, 'The King and I: Bronislaw Malinowski, King Sobhuza II of Swaziland and the Vision of Culture and Change in Africa', *History of the Human Sciences*, 13, 4 (2000), 25–47.

[43] Ethnologists eulogised centralised polities in contrast to segmentary or acephalous societies (see, for instance, P. Cocks, 'The King and I: Bronislaw Malinowski, King Sobhuza II of Swaziland and the Vision of Culture and Change in Africa', *History of the Human Sciences*, 13, 4 [2000], 25–47; S. N. Eisenstadt, 'Primitive Political Systems: A Preliminary Comparative Analysis', *American Anthropologist*, 61, 2 [1959], 200–220; and M. Fortes and E. E. Evans-Pritchard [eds.], *African Political Systems* [London: Oxford University Press, 1950]).

[44] H. Kuper, *King Sobhuza II, Ngwenyama and King of Swaziland: The Story of an Hereditary Ruler and His Country* (Africana Publication, 1978); W. J. Breytenbach, 'Sobhuza's Government: Old or New?' *Africa Insight*, 9, 2 (1979), 72–75.

2 THE MAJOR PLAYERS IN THE MAKING ...   47

popular among Swazis. A succession of European settlers that had started arriving in Swaziland from the 1840s resulted in the expropriation of large tracts of land. The Swazi people were generally displaced and were forced to relocate into a patchwork of 32 reserves that came to be known as Swazi Nation land held in communal tenure.[45] On ascending the throne, King Sobhuza II took up the issue of land expropriation with the British by sending deputations to London, but had little success. After World War II, he managed to organize the repurchase from Europeans of over 2,251,000 acres of land out of 4,280,000: this land became Swazi owned and was referred to as the Swazi Nation land. The struggle of the monarch to recover Swazi land from Whites, coupled with the fact that the King and his chiefs controlled one-third of the country's land space—the Swazi Nation Land, placed him in a strong position and made him an important central figure in colonial Swaziland.

The Swazi socio-political order fitted well with the British pattern of indirect rule because it was a centralized polity.[46] Typically, British policy in Africa was to administer colonial subjects through their indigenous political institutions. In 1950, the *Ngwenyama* and the SNC were recognized as the Native Authority, and the source of all delegated powers for matters related to Africans and this indirect rule system of government was given statutory recognition.[47] The *Ngwenyama* and the SNC were given such recognition, and they remained key political figures during the decolonization process.

[45] See K. Matthews, 'Squatters on Private Tenure Farms in Swaziland: A Preliminary Investigation', In M. Neocosmos (ed.), *Social Relations in Rural Swaziland: Critical Analyses* (Social Science Research Unit, University of Swaziland, 1987); H. S. Simelane, 'The State, Landlords, and the Squatter Problem in Post-colonial Swaziland', *Canadian Journal of African Studies/La Revue canadienne des études africaines*, 36, 2 (2002), 329–354. It should be noted that the other high Commission territories, Basutoland and Bechuanaland, did not suffer a similar fate like Swaziland. The British restricted the European ownership of land and recognized and protected the vital interests of Africans (see H. Kuper, 'The Colonial Situation in Southern Africa', *The Journal of Modern African Studies*, 2, 2 [1964], 149–150).

[46] J. R. Ayee, 'A Note on the Machinery of Government During the King Sobhuza II Era in Swaziland', *Institute of African Studies Research Review*, 5, 1 (1989), 54–68; H. Kuper, *King Sobhuza II, Ngwenyama and King of Swaziland: The Story of an Hereditary Ruler and His Country* (Africana Publication, 1978); H. Kuper, *The Swazi: A South African Kingdom* (Holt Rinehart & Winston, 1986); and P. Cocks, 'The King and I: Bronislaw Malinowski, King Sobhuza II of Swaziland and the Vision of Culture and Change in Africa', *History of the Human Sciences*, 13, 4 (2000), 25–47.

[47] Macmillan, 'Swaziland: Decolonisation and the Triumph of "Tradition"', 643–666; J. Gerring, D. Ziblatt, J. Van Gorp, and J. Arevalo, 'An Institutional Theory of Direct and Indirect Rule', *World Politics*, 63, 3 (2011), 377–433.

48   H. P. DLAMINI

Apart from his credentials as a traditional ruler, King Sobhuza II was Western-educated and had had good exposure to the rudiments of modern governance through the services of a coterie of White South African advisers. Born in 1880 of the ruling Dlamini clan, King Sobhuza II ascended the throne on 22 December 1921. He acquired primary and post-primary education in the Swazi National School and the Lovedale Institute in Cape Province in South Africa, which were the best available educational institutions for non-Whites.[48] King Sobhuza II was, therefore, fairly well-educated when compared to traditional rulers elsewhere in Africa, who were largely uneducated. King Sobhuza II was described as an 'intelligent and relatively well-educated ... [individual] ... who was fluent in English in speech and writing.'[49] Sobuza's education endeared him to the British, and they requested him to write and present a treatise on traditional political governance in Swaziland so that it could assist in the introduction of the indirect system of administration. Together with his legal adviser, Pixley Seme,[50] and A. G. Marwick, a long-serving British administrator who became Resident Commissioner in 1935, Sobhuza II prepared a lengthy document titled: 'The Original Swazi Political Organization'. The document illuminated the relative functions of the king, the queen mother, the *liqoqo*, the *libandla* and the chiefs.[51]

King Sobhuza II acquainted himself with Western politics by spending many hours reading parliamentary papers, with the assistance of his legal adviser, Pixley Seme.[52] He also had access to Johannesburg lawyers who clarified political and legal issues to him. Sobhuza's Western education did not endow him with progressive credentials because he remained a staunch believer of the Swazi traditional system of governance,[53] which

[48] P. Cocks, 'The King and I: Bronislaw Malinowski, King Sobhuza II of Swaziland and the Vision of Culture and Change in Africa', 25–47; J. B. Mzizi, 'The Dominance of the Swazi Monarchy and the Moral Dynamics of Democratisation of the Swazi State', *Journal of African Elections*, 3, 1 (2004), 94.

[49] M. Macmillan, 'Swaziland: Decolonisation and the Triumph of "Tradition"', *Journal of Modern African Studies*, 23, 4 (1985), 648.

[50] C. Saunders, 'Pixley Seme: Towards a Biography', *South African Historical Journal*, 25, 1 (1991), 196–217.

[51] Macmillan, 'Swaziland: Decolonisation and the Triumph of "Tradition"', 648.

[52] Saunders, 'Pixley Seme: Towards a Biography', 196–217.

[53] P. H. Bischoff, 'Why Swaziland Is Different: An Explanation of the Kingdom's Political Position in Southern Africa', *The Journal of Modern African Studies*, 26, 3 (1988), 457–471.

2 THE MAJOR PLAYERS IN THE MAKING ... 49

was the antithesis of liberal democracy and its corollary, periodic elections. He felt British political institution being transferred to Swaziland should be traditionalized to be meaningful to the Swazi people and to save the monarchy. He did not conceal his disdain for the progressive nationalists, whom he labelled a bunch of unSwazis that were bent on unseating him and seizing people's private property.[54]

THE PROGRESSIVE NATIONALISTS

The Progressives, otherwise referred to as radical nationalists, were the Western-educated Swazi elite who operated outside the traditional monarchical structures and who had imbibed Western modernist ideas of liberal democracy and the Nkrumah brand of nationalism. They wanted to see the wholesale implementation of the Westminster constitutional framework and the ideologies of modern African nationalism in Swaziland. They subscribed to the idea of popular sovereignty and Black majority rule, and the immediate independence of Swaziland. Beginning in 1960, they formed political parties with the aim of wresting power from the colonial authorities and shaping the independence constitution.[55]

Popular sovereignty in its modern sense dates from the social contract school represented by Thomas Hobbes (1588–1679), John Locke (1632–1704) and Jean-Jacques Rousseau (1712–1778). The central tenet of popular sovereignty is that legitimacy of governance or the law is derived from the consent of the people through elections. Republics and popular monarchies were theoretically based on popular sovereignty exercised in elections through the party system.[56] The Swazi Progressives were inspired

---

[54] Ibid. These invectives were commonly used by the SNC during the 2961 elections.

[55] J. Daniel and J. Vilane, 'Swaziland: Political Crisis, Regional Dilemma', *Review of African Political Economy*, 13, 35 (1986), 54–67; C. P. Potholm, *Swaziland: The Dynamics of Political Modernization*, Vol. 8 (University of California Press, 1972), 2, 72–73.

[56] For more on the idea of popular sovereignty see S. Chambers, 'Democracy, Popular Sovereignty, and Constitutional Legitimacy', *Constellations*, 11, 2 (2004), 153–173; R. Falk and A. Strauss, 'On the Creation of a Global Peoples Assembly: Legitimacy and the Power of Popular Sovereignty', *Stanford Journal of International Law*, 36 (2000), 191; F. M. Deng (ed.), *Sovereignty as Responsibility: Conflict Management in Africa* (Washington, DC: Brookings Institution Press, 1996); M. Mamdani, 'The Social Basis of Constitutionalism in Africa', *The Journal of Modern African Studies*, 28, 3 (1990), 359–374; and D. Strang, 'From Dependency to Sovereignty: An Event History Analysis of Decolonization 1870–1987', *American Sociological Review* (1990), 846–860.

50   H. P. DLAMINI

by Nkrumah's example: his Ghana Convention People's Party (CPP) stood in a series of elections in Ghana in the 1950s and won against other competing parties, and was invited to lead Ghana to independence in 1957. The Progressives intended to use modern political parties as instruments with which to obtain popular support from the people.

Nkrumah was the chief ideologue of the dominant brand of African nationalism that pervaded the modern African political class. His example to African nationalists across the continent was his use of his political party, the CPP, to mobilize the masses to protest against British colonial injustices, and to demand self-government and independence, which Ghana obtained in 1957.

Nkrumah argued that African workers and peasants needed to reclaim their dignity and independence, and advocated the use of force if necessary. On attaining independence, Nkrumah proclaimed that the independence of Ghana was meaningless until the entire continent was free from European imperialism and was united as a single country. In 1958, he organized the All Party African Congress, which attracted African nationalists from all over Africa, including Progressives from Swaziland, and during which he underscored the need for the unification the African continent and its liberation from European rule. 'Africa for the Africans' became the slogan for the Africanization or nationalization of all natural resources.[57] In essence, Nkrumah's intense abhorrence of colonial rule, his zealous enthusiasm for independence, and his ideal of a United States of Africa made him popular among Africans throughout the continent. Africans were, consequently, determined to take full control of their destinies in the political and economic domains as soon as possible.

At the United Nations, Nkrumah's Ghana was very active in the Afro-Asian bloc that called for the end of colonialism and was instrumental in the

---

[57]The brainchild of the Africa for Africans slogan was Marcus Garvey and his United Negro Improvement Association (UNIA) in the 1920s. For more on Nkrumah's political ideology see G. Shepperson, 'Notes on Negro American Influences on the Emergence of African Nationalism', *The Journal of African History*, 1, 2 (1960), 299–312; K. Nkrumah, *Handbook of Revolutionary Warfare: A Guide to the Armed Phase of the African Revolution*, Vol. 17 (New York: International Publishers, 1969); K. Nkrumah, *Towards Colonial Freedom* (London: Heinemann, 1962); K. Nkrumah, *Neo-Colonialism: The Last Stage of Imperialism* (London: Thomas Nelson & Sons, 1965); K. Nkrumah, R. Arrigoni, and G. Napolitano, *Africa Must Unite* (London: Heinemann, 1963); and K. Nkrumah, *Class Struggle in Africa* (New York: International Publishers, 1970).

2 THE MAJOR PLAYERS IN THE MAKING ... 51

1960 United Nations resolution to that effect. Ghana became the ideological training ground and pilgrimage centre for Africa's Western-educated political elite, who were still under colonial rule, and the Nkrumah government gave financial support to these political leaders.[58] The Nkrumah brand of the modern African nationalist ideology was clearly radical: it threatened White minority interests in Southern Africa, in general, and Swaziland, in particular, and Swaziland's Progressives were, consequently, treated with scorn by Whites and the conservative Swazi monarch.

The first Swazi political party to be formed was the Swaziland Progressive Party, in 1960, which represented the general aspirations of contemporary African nationalism. John J. Nquku was its founding President, Dr A. P. Zwane was its General Secretary, and M. O. Mabuza was an executive committee member. Although the party came into existence only in 1960, its roots can be traced to the Progressive Association, which was established by the colonial government in 1929 as a forum to bring together the British administrators and educated Swazis to discuss matters of common interest.[59] Swazi traditionalists viewed the organization with suspicion because it operated outside the tribal framework. King Sobhuza II intervened, and the colonial administration decreed that the organization should be affiliated to the traditional Swazi National Council. The organization made constructive recommendations on issues dealing with taxation and labour.[60]

Nquku transformed the Progressive Association, of which he had been the president since 1945, into a political party in 1960. Born in 1899 in Pietermaritzburg, South Africa, of Zulu parents, he had held various teaching and supervisory positions in Black schools in South Africa. He was appointed the first African inspector of schools in Swaziland in 1930, and he founded a vernacular newspaper, *Izwi Lama Swazi* (*The Voice of Swazi*), in 1934, serving as its editor until it was taken over by Bantu Press in 1954. He became an active member of the Swazi National Council and was responsible for educational affairs. In 1955, he founded a paper, *The Swazilander*, and became its first editor. His outlook was considerably widened by his travels to Europe and America in 1957, and by his contact with radical African nationalists, especially Nkrumah. Nquku transformed

[58] Stevens, 'Swaziland Political Development', 338.
[59] SNA, Swaziland's Report on the Constitution.
[60] Ibid.

52   H. P. DLAMINI

the Progressive Association into the Swaziland Progressive Party, following the decision of the British Resident Commissioner to initiate constitutional talks in Swaziland. He found the traditional tribal framework to be grossly inadequate to handle matters on Swaziland's proposed constitution.[61]

It was not easy to maintain the unity of Swaziland's nascent political party as it was soon faced with internal feuds, like its counterparts elsewhere in Africa.[62] By the end of 1961, a split occurred within the leadership of the SPP. Dr Zwane, the Secretary General of the party, and Clement D. Dlamini, the party's youth leader, accused Nquku of totalitarian tendencies and a lack of transparency in the management of party funds, and decided to remove him as president of the party in February 1961. This split should be seen as the result of personality clashes and not political ideology.

Nquku resisted dismissal and, in a bid to avoid any confusion, Dr Zwane announced in May 1963 that his own political party would, henceforth, be called the Ngwane National Liberatory Congress (NNLC). Macdonald Maseko, a former ANC leader in South Africa who had been banned by Dr Verwoerd, became Vice-President of the party. Dr Zwane became an outstanding political leader in Swaziland in the 1960s, and there is need to present his profile in some detail.

Dr Zwane was born on 30 April 1924 in Swaziland. His father, Amos Zwane, was a traditional physician. Dr Zwane attended Roman Catholic primary schools in Swaziland. For higher studies, he attended Inkanga High School in Natal in South Africa. He then studied medicine at the University of Witwatersrand. After graduating in 1951, he worked as a medical doctor in Mbabane. In April 1960, he resigned from practising medicine and took to politics full time by joining the newly formed Swaziland Progressive Party in July 1960, becoming the secretary general of the party. Owing to bitter disagreements with Nquku, he formed his own party, the NNLC.[63]

---

[61] Ibid.

[62] Nascent nationalist parties had the tendency of breaking up into factions under different names. In Zimbabwe, the Zimbabwe African People's Union split into two and the Zimbabwe African National Union was formed. See A. S. Mlambo, *A History of Zimbabwe* (New York: Cambridge University Press, 2014), 147; In Botswana, the Bechuanaland People's party broke into factions in 1964. The splinter party was called the Bechuanaland Independence Party. See R. Nengwekhulu, 'Some Findings on the Origins of Political Parties in Botswana', *Pula: Botswana Journal of African Studies*, 1, 2 (1979), 71–72.

[63] 'British Government Knows Our View-Nquku', *Izwi Lama Swazi*, January 19, 1963.

2 THE MAJOR PLAYERS IN THE MAKING … 53

Zwane's NNLC followed Nkrumah's footsteps by organizing strikes for better working conditions, and by protesting against colonial order. So, the strikes were not only for general economic change, but also for political reforms. On 20 January 1963, Prince Dumisa Dlamini, the Secretary of the NNLC, addressed a large number of workers at Big Bend. He advised the workers not to go back to work but, rather, to march to the company offices and stage a mass demonstration of their dissatisfaction with the conditions of work at the Ubombo Ranches. When the demands of the workers were not met, the leaders, Prince Dumisa Dlamini, Dr A. Zwane, Macdonald Maseko, and Stephen Twala called for a strike on 18 March 1963. The workers on the estate, including office staff and domestic servants, went on strike until 27 March 1963. The strike at Big Bend ignited other strikes at Peak Timbers in April, and the Havelock Asbestos Mine in May.[64] These strikes demonstrated the radical character of the Progressives and their relationship with the Swaziland nascent labour movement.

The Swaziland Progressive Party and the NNLC had close relations with revolutionary Ghana, and Nquku and Dr Zwane sent members of their political parties for training at the Nkrumah Ideological Institute. These nationalists demanded immediate independence and wanted 'Africa for the Africans', in line with Nkrumah's radical style of nationalism.

In March 1962, the Swazi Democratic Party (SDP) emerged under Simon Nxumalo. The party was nurtured, advised, and financed by a handful of White liberals. The SDP claimed to be the only non-racist party in Swaziland, and condemned the other political parties as racist and for subscribing to exclusivist pan-African ideals, as well as receiving outside financial assistance from Ghana.[65]

In July 1962, another political party was formed: the Mbandzeni National Convention (MNC). It was an amalgamation of the Mbandzeni Party led by Clifford Nkosi and Dr Msibi's Convention Movement. The MNC claimed that Swaziland had never lost its independence, and insisted that its sovereignty must be reasserted. Dr Msibi became the leader of the

---

[64] SNA, Swaziland Government Big Bend Strike Report 1963: A Report of the Commission Appointed to Inquire into the Causes and Circumstances of the Strike which took place in Big Bend area during March 1963, 10.

[65] J. B. Mzizi, Political Movements and the Challenges for Democracy in Swaziland, Research Report No. 18 (Johannesburg, EISA, 2005); D. Motsamai, Swaziland's Non-Party Political System and the 2013 Tinkhundla Elections Breaking the SADC Impasse? Institute for Security Studies Situation Report (Pretoria, August 15, 2012).

54 H. P. DLAMINI

MNC. He had received training in India for nine years and later furthered his education in Japan. He set out to establish a non-racial state.[66] Before the London constitutional talks in 1962, Dr Msibi joined Dr Zwane in demanding independence for Swaziland.

Swazi Progressives generally espoused ideals of modern African nationalism and pan-Africanism, as articulated by Nkrumah, and this did not find favour with the White community and the conservative Swazi traditional monarch. The call for independence and one-man-one-vote leading to Black majority rule was viewed with suspicion in Swaziland by both the Whites and the Swazi monarch, and this bifurcated the political class in Swaziland into Moderates and Progressives (or radicals).

THE BIFURCATION OF THE SWAZI POLITICAL PLATFORM: MODERATES VERSUS THE PROGRESSIVES

The Swazi political platform was clearly divided between the Moderates and the Progressives. The political debates were narrowed between these two camps, and they reflected their different orientations. Whites and the Swazi monarch claimed to be Moderate political leaders, as opposed to Progressive. The Whites' EAC and King Sobhuza II's SNC argued that the political economy of the colonial state should not be radically transformed through the adoption of nationalization of private property as it would discourage investors and negatively impact on the economic growth of Swaziland. They were opposed to universal adult suffrage and any political arrangement that would submerge the White minority.

The EAC and SNC defined themselves as Swazilanders who were concerned with the economic welfare of Swaziland, as opposed to the Progressives who were in a rush to destroy it. As Todd, the leader of the EAC, commented in a 1962 newspaper report:

> Swazilanders of all racial origins who love Swaziland, to whom Swaziland is home, who hope to see it prosper, to see rising standards of living and better opportunities in life for the Swazi; and who see only too clearly how those hopes can be imperilled by the reckless demands of extremists. This moderate element, conservative if you like, has never had any sympathy for reactionaries and diehards. It has never opposed political advance for the Swazis; it has stood for a programme of advance by stages, commensurate with the spread

[66]Ibid.

of education and growth of political maturity. It has pressed for the immediate deletion from the statute book of all kinds of racially discriminatory legislation, and for the abolition of all practices of this nature in our way of life. It has urged the government and industry to take steps to open up more avenues of skilled, more highly paid and more responsible employment for educated Swazis.[67]

The EAC, with the support of the SNC, advocated gradualism in the political transfer of power and not a rush because, they argued, Africans needed time to adjust to European political values. The EAC and SNC therefore posed as Moderates because they preferred the piecemeal introduction of political reforms, and argued that rushing matters was dangerous for Swaziland. The EAC differentiated themselves from Swaziland's nascent progressive leaders as follows:

Politically, the difference between us and the Progressives is the difference between moderation and extremism. But a more fundamental difference is that to us daily bread is as important as the vote, economic progress as important as political advance. To the Progressive, if the utterances of their more voluble members are any guide, industry, commerce, and finance are irrelevancies. The only worth considering [sic] is immediate universal suffrage and majority rule; and blow the consequences to industry, finance or anything else.[68]

Essentially the tension between the EAC and SNC, on the one hand, and the Progressives, on the other hand, was clear. The two camps were poised to struggle for political hegemony in colonial Swaziland in a bid to protect their interests.

APARTHEID SOUTH AFRICA

Apartheid South Africa was a key behind-the-scenes player in the decolonization politics of Swaziland for the simple reason that the territory was almost entirely surrounded by South Africa, and was a geographical and ethnic continuum of South Africa. There was no way South Africa could keep out of the politics of Swaziland given the brewing radical nationalism

[67]'Todd's Thoughts on Constitutional Proposals', *The Times of Swaziland*, March 23, 1962.

[68]Ibid.

56   H. P. DLAMINI

in the territory, and its possible rippling effects on the apartheid system. The South African establishment had often seen Swaziland as eventually becoming part of South Africa on the basis of the provision of the South African Act of Union (1909), which provided for the incorporation of the protectorates at some undefined future. South Africa, therefore, argued for incorporation in subsequent years, but this was complicated by South Africa's racial policies. South Africa's departure from the Commonwealth in 1960 further compounded the prospects of incorporation. However, that should not be taken to mean that South Africa had given up its designs on Swaziland.

South Africa had an eye on two groups in Swaziland as possible bridges to be used to achieve its incorporation dream: the Swazi monarchy and Whites that had taken up residence in Swaziland. Verwoerd's Bantustan project envisaged Swaziland as part of the unfolding South African political system because of its structured traditional political system with King Sobhuza II at the apex. The Tomlinson Report of 1954, which was actually the blueprint for Verwoerd's Bantustan project, was contained in the Promotion of Bantu Self-Government Act (1959), which limited African political rights to Black reserves.[69] The scheme planned for 10 such reserves, which were referred to as Black homelands or Bantustans, were to be established on ethnic basis.[70] The Bantustans were granted 'autonomy' partly in response to the wave of African decolonization that had begun with the independence of Ghana in 1957, and which had the effect of putting international pressure on Verwoerd to provide South Africa's African population with political rights.[71] Verwoerd enticed Swaziland to enter the Union by promising to increase the powers of the Swazi monarch as a fully sovereign leader. To the apartheid regime, Swaziland was essential to 'the scientific creation of a Swazi Bantustan.'[72] The extension and increase in the powers of the Swazi

---

[69] R. B. Beck, *The History of South Africa* (Santa Barbara, CA: ABC-CLIO, 2014), 144–146; D. H. Houghton, *The Tomlinson Report: A Summary of the Findings and Recommendations in the Tomlinson Commission Report* (South African Institute of Race Relations, 1956).

[70] Ibid. These Bantustans included Ciskei and Transkei for the Xhosa, and one for each of the other ethnic groups (The Venda, Shangana/Tonga, South Ndebele, North Ndebele, North Sotho, South Sotho, Tswana, Swazi and Zulu).

[71] Beck, *The History of South Africa*, 144–145.

[72] Stevens, 'Swaziland Political Development', 343–344.

2 THE MAJOR PLAYERS IN THE MAKING ...   57

king included a gift of land occupied by Swazis in the Republic as a positive benefit to be derived from cooperating with the apartheid regime.[73]

South Africa had become increasingly distressed by rising nationalism in Swaziland and elsewhere, which it labelled as subversion and which constituted a challenge to the principles of apartheid: universal adult suffrage and black majority rule, which was the platform of the Swazi Progressives, was anathema to the apartheid regime. South Africa was also opposed to pan-Africanism of the Nkrumah brand in Swaziland, owing to the numerical inferiority of the White population in Africa and the threat such an ideology posed to the apartheid system. Kuper maintained that 'whites constituted five per cent of the total population of Africa South of the Sahara, and over 80 per cent of them [were] located in South Africa and the Rhodesias.'[74] South Africa, therefore, had to contain nationalist developments in Swaziland through its allies—the Swazi monarch and Whites[75]—who were equally threatened by radical nationalism. The role of South Africa in political developments in Swaziland consisted of providing multiple forms of assistance to the Swazi monarch and Whites in order to contain the Progressives.

CONCLUSION

This chapter introduced the main actors in the deliberations leading to the crafting of Swaziland's independence constitution. There were four main stakeholders: (i) the British colonial authorities; (ii) Whites operating under the EAC led by Carl Todd, the Swazi monarch, and the SNC; (iii) the Progressives; and (iv) apartheid South Africa, which was a behind-the-scenes player. The chapter has demonstrated that the stakeholders had different and conflicting ideologies and agendas; which it is important to note as a way of understanding the direction that the constitutional talks would take. On the one hand were the 'conservative-traditionalist' Swazi monarch and his traditional council, who considered themselves the legitimate leaders of

---

[73] Stevens, 'Swaziland Political Development', 343–344.

[74] H. Kuper, 'The Colonial Situation in Southern Africa', *Journal of Modern African Studies*, 2, 2 (1964), 149–164.

[75] There is some popular discussion in Swaziland after the demise of apartheid that the Swazi monarchy did assist the ANC in the liberation of South Africa. Such reconstruction of history in the present does not give a full picture of Swaziland's real relationship with South Africa during the liberation years which is captured in Chapter 4, footnote 58.

the Swazi people and who derived their powers from inheritance according to Swazi culture and tradition. They felt legitimacy was conferred on them by custom and tradition, and that this qualified them to occupy the expanding political space created by the decolonization processes. King Sobhuza II found support from Carl F. Todd, the leader of the EAC, who was a wealthy South African businessman who had settled in Swaziland. The Swazi monarch and the White community, therefore, constituted the conservative camp, who were disturbed and frightened by the African nationalist ideology of the nascent Swazi political parties.

On the other hand, there were the Progressives, dubbed as radicals, who formed political parties to champion their cause. They were the typical African nationalists of the radical Nkrumah school who clamoured for immediate independence and 'Africa for Africans'. They shunned traditionalism and felt that the traditional Swazi monarch was ill-fitted to assume the complicated task of modern governance. These radical nationalists frightened both the Swazi monarch and the White community in Swaziland, who were concerned about the future security of their investments in the event of a radical nationalist assumption of the reins of the state from the departing colonial authorities. The White community and the Swazi monarch therefore had an interest in collaborating against the radical nationalists.

An important actor in Swaziland's constitutional development that was also examined in this chapter was apartheid South Africa, which played its role behind the scenes. The geographical position of Swaziland, which is almost entirely enclosed by South Africa, was such that the Republic could not be indifferent to the decolonization processes in the territory. The discourses of the Progressives in Swaziland were anathema to the philosophy of the apartheid regime and had to be contained by every means. South Africa was, therefore, an important actor because the Republic felt duty-bound to lend support to the White community and to the conservative Swazi monarch, which represented an ideal Bantustan in the eyes of the Boers. The stage was therefore set for the various protagonists to present their constitutional viewpoints, to defend them, and to arrive at a consensus. But was this possible?

REFERENCES

NEWSPAPERS

'British Government Knows Our View-Nquku', *Izwi Lama Swazi*, January 19, 1963.
'Todd's Thoughts on Constitutional Proposals', *The Times of Swaziland*, March 23, 1962.

FILES FROM THE SWAZILAND NATIONAL ARCHIVES (SNA)

SNA, RCS 613/21, Report of the First Meeting of the European Advisory Council, October 18–20, 1921.
SNA, RCS 359/22, Suggested Deputation of the European Advisory Council to High Commissioner at Government House Cape Town, July 21, 1922.
SNA, Colonial Annual Reports, 1923.
SNA, Swaziland Government Big Bend Strike Report 1963: A Report of the Commission Appointed to Inquire into the Causes and Circumstances of the Strike which took place in Big Bend area during March 1963, 10.
SNA, Swaziland's Report on the Constitution.

BOOKS AND JOURNALS

Allen, C. 'Understanding African Politics', *Review of African Political Economy*, 22, 65 (1995), 301–320.
Ayee, J. R. 'A Note on the Machinery of Government During the King Sobhuza II Era in Swaziland', *Institute of African Studies Research Review*, 5, 1 (1989), 54–68.
Arrighi, G., and Saul, J. S. 'Nationalism and Revolution in Sub-Saharan Africa', *The Socialist Register*, 6 (1969).
Beck, R. B. *The History of South Africa* (Santa Barbara, CA: ABC-CLIO, 2014).
Bischoff, P. H. 'Why Swaziland Is Different: An Explanation of the Kingdom's Political Position in Southern Africa', *The Journal of Modern African Studies*, 26, 3 (1988), 457–471.
Booth, M. Z. 'Settler, Missionary, and the State: Contradictions in the Formulation of Educational Policy in Colonial Swaziland', *History of Education*, 32, 1 (2003), 35–56.
Bourret, F. M. (ed.). *Ghana, the Road to Independence, 1919–1957*, Vol. 23 (Stanford: Stanford University Press, 1960).
Boyce, A. N. 'The Swaziland Concessions and Their Political Consequences 1876–1908', PhD thesis, University of South Africa, 1946.

60   H. P. DLAMINI

Breytenbach, W. J. 'Sobhuza's Government: Old or New?' *Africa Insight*, 9, 2 (1979), 72–75.

Bujo, B. 'Springboards for Modern African Constitutions and Development in African Cultural Traditions', *African Ethics: An Anthology of Comparative and Applied Ethics* (2009), 391–411.

Chambers, S. 'Democracy, Popular Sovereignty, and Constitutional Legitimacy', *Constellations*, 11, 2 (2004), 153–173.

Cocks, P. 'The King and I: Bronislaw Malinowski, King Sobhuza II of Swaziland and the Vision of Culture and Change in Africa', *History of the Human Sciences*, 13, 4 (2000), 25–47.

Coleman, J. S. *Nationalism and Development in Africa: Selected Essays* (London: University of California Press, 1994).

Crowder, M. 'Whose Dream Was It Anyway? Twenty-Five Years of African Independence', *African Affairs*, 86, 342 (1987), 7–24.

Crush, J. 'The Culture of Failure: Racism, Violence and White Farming in Colonial Swaziland', *Journal of Historical Geography*, 22, 2 (1996), 177–197.

Crush, J. 'Landlords, Tenants and Colonial Social Engineers: The Farm Labour Question in Early Colonial Swaziland', *Journal of Southern African Studies*, 11, 2 (1985), 236.

Crush, J. S. 'Settler-Estate Production, Monopoly Control, and the Imperial Response: The Case of the Swaziland Corporation Ltd.', *African Economic History*, 8 (1979), 183–197.

Crush, J. S. 'The Parameters of Dependence in Southern Africa: A Case Study of Swaziland', *Journal of Southern African Affairs*, 4, 1 (1979), 55–66.

Daniel, J., and Vilane, J. 'Swaziland: Political Crisis, Regional Dilemma', *Review of African Political Economy*, 13, 35 (1986), 54–67.

Daniel, J. 'The Political Economy of Colonial and Post-colonial Swaziland', *South African Labour Bulletin*, 7, 6 (1982), 90–113.

Deng, F. M. (ed.). *Sovereignty as Responsibility: Conflict Management in Africa* (Washington, DC: Brookings Institution Press, 1996).

De Winston, M. G. 'Decolonisation and the Westminster Model', In A. H. M. Kirk-Greene (ed.), *Africa in the Colonial Period III: The Transfer of Power: The Colonial Administrators in the Age of Decolonisation* (Oxford: Oxford University Inter-Faculty Committee for African Studies, 1979).

Duverger, M. 'A New Political Model: Semi-Presidential Government', *European Journal of Political Research*, 8, 2 (1980), 165–187.

Elias, T. O. *Nigeria: The Development of Its Laws and Constitutions* (London: Stevenson & Sons Ltd., 1967).

Eisenstadt, S. N. 'Primitive Political Systems: A Preliminary Comparative Analysis', *American Anthropologist*, 61, 2 (1959), 200–220.

Falk, R., and Strauss, A. 'On the Creation of a Global Peoples Assembly: Legitimacy and the Power of Popular Sovereignty', *Stanford Journal of International Law*, 36 (2000), 191.

Falola, T. *Nationalism and African Intellectuals* (Woodbridge: University Rochester Press, 2001).

Fonchingong, C. C. 'Exploring the Politics of Identity and Ethnicity in State Reconstruction in Cameroon', *Social Identities*, 11, 4 (2005), 363–380.

Fortes, M., and Evans-Pritchard, E. E. (eds.). *African Political Systems* (London: Oxford University Press, 1950).

Fyfe, C. 'Africanus Horton as a Constitution-Maker', *Journal of Commonwealth & Comparative Politics*, 26, 2 (1988), 173–184.

Gbenga, F. 'Ethnicity in Nigeria', *Philosophia Africana*, 1, 2 (2008), 141–156.

Gerring, J., Ziblatt, D., Van Gorp, J., and Arevalo, J. 'An Institutional Theory of Direct and Indirect Rule', *World Politics*, 63, 3 (2011), 377–433.

Ghai, Y. 'Constitutions and Governance in Africa: A Prolegomenon', In *Law and Crisis in the Third World* (London, Melbourne, Munich, and New Jersey: Hans Zell Publishers, 1993).

Hailey, W. M. H. B. *The Republic of South Africa and the High Commission Territories* (London: Oxford University Press, 1963).

Houghton, D. H. *The Tomlinson Report: A Summary of the Findings and Recommendations in the Tomlinson Commission Report* (South African Institute of Race Relations, 1956).

Hyam, R. *The Failure of South African Expansion, 1908–1948* (Africana Publication, 1972).

Ibhawoh, B. 'Between Culture and Constitution: Evaluating the Cultural Legitimacy of Human Rights in the African State', *Human Rights Quarterly*, 22, 3 (2000), 838–860.

Julian G. O. 'Modeling the State: Postcolonial Constitutions in Asia and Africa', *Southeast Asian Studies*, 39, 4 (2002), 558–583.

Kuper, H. *An African Aristocracy: Rank Among Swazi* (London: Oxford University Press, 1980).

Kuper, H. 'The Colonial Situation in Southern Africa', *The Journal of Modern African Studies*, 2, 2 (1964), 149–150.

Kuper, H. *King Sobhuza II, Ngwenyama and King of Swaziland: The Story of an Hereditary Ruler and His Country* (London: Africana Publication, 1978).

Kuper, H. *The Swazi: A South African Kingdom* (New York: Holt Rinehart & Winston, 1986).

Levin, R. 'Swaziland's Tinkhundla and the Myth of Swazi Tradition', *Journal of Contemporary African Studies*, 10, 2 (1991), 1–23.

Le Vine, V. T. 'The Fall and Rise of Constitutionalism in West Africa', *The Journal of Modern African Studies*, 35, 2 (1997), 181–206.

62   H. P. DLAMINI

Liijphart, A. (ed.). *Parliamentary Versus Presidential Government* (London: Oxford University Press, 1992).

Lumumba-Kasongo, T. 'The Origin of African Constitutions, Elusive Constitutionalism, and the Crisis of Liberal Democracy', 63–96, In *Democratic Renewal in Africa* (New York: Palgrave Macmillan, 2015).

Macmillan, H. 'Swaziland: Decolonisation and the Triumph of "Tradition"', *The Journal of Modern African Studies*, 23, 4 (1985), 643–666.

Mamdani, M. 'The Social Basis of Constitutionalism in Africa', *The Journal of Modern African Studies*, 28, 3 (1990), 359–374.

Matsebula, J. S. M. *A History of Swaziland* (Johannesburg: Longman Southern Africa Ltd., 1972).

Matthews, K. 'Squatters on Private Tenure Farms in Swaziland: A Preliminary Investigation', In M. Neocosmos (ed.), *Social Relations in Rural Swaziland: Critical Analyses* (Social Science Research Unit, University of Swaziland, 1987).

Meredith, M. *The Fate of Africa: A History of the Continent Since Independence* (Hachette UK, 2011).

Middleton, J., and Tait, D. *Tribes Without Rulers: Studies in African Segmentary Systems* (London: Rutledge, 2013).

Mlambo, A. S. *A History of Zimbabwe* (New York: Cambridge University Press, 2014).

Motsamai, D. Swaziland's Non-Party Political System and the 2013 Tinkhundla Elections Breaking the SADC Impasse? Institute for Security Studies Situation Report (Pretoria, August 15, 2012).

Mzizi, J. B. 'The Dominance of the Swazi Monarchy and the Moral Dynamics of Democratisation of the Swazi State', *Journal of African Elections*, 3, 1 (2004), 94–119.

Mzizi, J. B. Political Movements and the Challenges for Democracy in Swaziland. Research Report No. 18 (Johannesburg, EISA, 2005).

Nengwekhulu, R. 'Some Findings on the Origins of Political Parties in Botswana', *Pula: Botswana Journal of African Studies*, 1, 2 (1979), 71–72.

Nkrumah, K. *Class Struggle in Africa* (New York: International Publishers, 1970).

Nkrumah, K. *Handbook of Revolutionary Warfare: A Guide to the Armed Phase of the African Revolution*, Vol. 17 (New York: International Publishers, 1969).

Nkrumah, K. *Neo-colonialism: The Last Stage of Imperialism* (London: Thomas Nelson & Sons, 1965).

Nkrumah, K. *Towards Colonial Freedom* (London: Heinemann, 1962).

Nkrumah, K., Arrigoni, R., and Napolitano, G. *Africa Must Unite* (London: Heinemann, 1963).

Nwabueze, B. O. *A Constitutional History of Nigeria* (London: C. Hurst & Company, 1981).

Nwabueze, B. O. *Constitutionalism in the Emergent States* (London: C. Hurst & Company, 1973).

2 THE MAJOR PLAYERS IN THE MAKING ... 63

Okonkwo, R. *Heroes of West African Nationalism* (Enugu: Delta, 1985).

Potholm, C. P. *Swaziland: The Dynamics of Political Modernization*, Vol. 8 (London: University of California Press, 1972).

Robinson, K. 'Autochthony and the Transfer of Power', In K. Robinson and F. Madden (eds.), *Essays in Imperial Government: Presented to Margery Perham* (Oxford: Basil Blackwell, 1963).

Salamone, F. A. 'Ethnicity and Nigeria Since the End of the Civil War', *Dialectical Anthropology*, 22, 3–4 (1997), 303–333.

Saunders, C. 'Pixley Seme: Towards a Biography', *South African Historical Journal*, 25, 1 (1991), 196–217.

Schmidt, E. 'Anticolonial Nationalism in French West Africa: What Made Guinea Unique?' *African Studies Review*, 52, 2 (2009), 1–34.

Shepperson, G. 'Notes on Negro American Influences on the Emergence of African Nationalism', *The Journal of African History*, 1, 2 (1960), 299–312.

Simelane, H. S. 'The State, Landlords, and the Squatter Problem in Post-colonial Swaziland', *Canadian Journal of African Studies*, 36, 2 (2002), 329–354.

Skalník, P. 'Authority Versus Power: Democracy in Africa, Must Include Original African Institutions', *The Journal of Legal Pluralism and Unofficial Law*, 28, 37–38 (1996), 109–121.

Stevens, R. P. *Lesotho, Botswana and Swaziland: The Former High Commission Territories in Southern Africa* (London: Pall Mall, 1967).

Stevens, R. P. 'Swaziland Political Development', *The Journal of Modern African Studies*, 1, 3 (1963), 327–350.

Strang, D. 'From Dependency to Sovereignty: An Event History Analysis of Decolonization 1870–1987', *American Sociological Review* (1990), 846–860.

Zwane, T. M. J. 'The Struggle for Power in Swaziland', *Africa Today* (1964), 4–6.

CHAPTER 3

The Beginning of the Great Constitutional Debate: Agreeing to Disagree

INTRODUCTION

This chapter deals with the beginning of the constitutional processes in colonial Swaziland sparked by the momentum of the anti-colonial wave in the post-World War II era that culminated in the independence of Ghana in 1957, followed by the independence of a score of other African countries. When it became evident that independence was inevitable, Britain took the first preparatory step by establishing a Legislative Council in which to infuse parliamentary democracy such as that obtained in Britain with inputs from the political class in Swaziland; this proved to be exceptionally complicated. Britain endeavoured to lay the foundations of the Legislative Council as a crucible for the acquisition of their presumed political modernity,[1] but the exercise became tumultuous owing to the configuration of conflicting interests of monarchical traditionalists, Progressive nationalists, Whites, and multinational business interests. The traditional monarchy was determined

---

[1] Scholars have tended to treat the British colonial modernity project in the shape of introducing Westminster institutions in British Africa from a totalising, triumphant and transformative perspective with little or no regard for African agency. For more on colonial modernity in the introduction of western political institutions in colonial states see, for instance, C. Geertz (ed.), *Old Societies and New States: The Quest for Modernity in Asia and Africa* (New York: Free Press of Glencoe 1963); E. Laclau, 'Politics and the Limits of Modernity', *Social Text* (1989), 63–82; R. Shilliam (ed.), *International Relations and Non-Western Thought: Imperialism, Colonialism and Investigations of Global Modernity* (Abingdon: Routledge, 2010).

© The Author(s) 2019
H. P. Dlamini, *A Constitutional History of the Kingdom of Eswatini (Swaziland), 1960–1982*, African Histories and Modernities,
https://doi.org/10.1007/978-3-030-24777-5_3

65

66 H. P. DLAMINI

to resist being swept away by the British modernization political agenda, while the Progressives subscribed to the implementation of a radical political programme that would enable them to capture power and obtain immediate independence. As for the Whites, they were determined to negotiate a comfortable place in the legislature to have the political clout to protect their economic interests. That the Swazi monarch could challenge the political modernization endeavours of the British colonial administration and go unpunished with destitution, as was typical of British, points to the exceptionality of Swaziland's political history that has escaped the vigilance of historians. The traditionalists found common grounds with the White capitalists, with whom they allied to oppose the Progressives, and the two opposing camps were engaged in a battle of conflicting ideologies, which impeded the establishment of a consensus. The traditionalists and their White allies were of the view that the powers of the Swazi king should be conserved integrally, and an African traditional method of selecting the peoples' representatives to the legislature should be incorporated in the new constitutional order. Their conservative credentials were therefore clear. The Progressives disagreed, and proposed universal adult suffrage and a constitutional system of checks and balances as the essential components in the constitution being formulated. They subscribed to Nkrumah's brand of nationalism. Their radical credentials were therefore clear.

The debates and reactions of the stakeholders were essentially about the degree of compliance to the British proposed constitutional framework, and the extent to which it would affect their fundamental interests. This meant a great deal was at stake when the constitution was being made. The various stakeholders each wanted to have the upper hand, instead of establishing a consensus on a solid, lasting governance instrument of which posterity would be proud.[2]

Circumstances Leading to the Commencement of Constitutional Debates in Colonial Swaziland

A combination of factors explain the comparatively tardy commencement of constitutional talks in colonial Swaziland in late 1960. These included

---

[2]This is in no way comparable to the making of constitution of the US and elsewhere where the concept of 'founding fathers' is used to describe those Americans who made a significant intellectual contribution to the writing of the Constitution captured and conjured visionaries who set out to prepare a near-impeachable document for the moment and for posterity.

3 THE BEGINNING OF THE GREAT CONSTITUTIONAL DEBATE ... 67

World War II, the independence of a score of African states, the United Nations (UN) support for total independence of African territories under colonial rule, and Macmillan's 'wind of change' speech in South Africa.

WORLD WAR II AND THE DECOLONIZATION WHIRLWIND OVER AFRICA

Once unleashed, the World War II decolonization movement, which was the clamour for the birth of nation-statehood in Africa as the alternative to imperialism, was unstoppable. It provided the necessary ammunition for African nationalists to make claims for self-government from metropolitan powers. In 1941, US President F. D. Roosevelt and British Prime Minister W. Churchill signed the widely acclaimed Atlantic Charter document, which recognized the rights of all people to self-determination. After the War, this principle 'fired the zeal and aspirations of [African] nationalists everywhere to be free'.[3] Nationalist elements interpreted this declaration 'to mean that after the war they would have the right to choose their own form of government, namely, self-government and the independence.'[4] They challenged the imperial presence in Africa and demanded to be compensated for their services to the British Empire with greater economic and political opportunities.[5]

THE INDEPENDENCE OF A SCORE OF AFRICAN COUNTRIES

Developments in West, East and Central Africa had a snowball effect on the entire continent. In 1950, Nkrumah's Convention People's Party (CPP) orchestrated a campaign of civil disobedience in support of self-government, which led to Nkrumah's imprisonment for a brief period.[6]

---

[3] K. Ezera, *Constitutional Developments in Nigeria* (London: Cambridge University Press, 1964), 39; R. Emerson, 'Self-Determination', *American Journal of International Law*, 65, 3 (1971), 459–475.

[4] Ibid.

[5] B. Ibhawoh, 'Second World War Propaganda, Imperial Idealism and Anti-Colonial Nationalism in British West Africa', *Nordic Journal of African Studies*, 16, 2 (2007), 221–243; M. Sherwood, '"Diplomatic platitudes": The Atlantic Charter, The United Nations And Colonial Independence', *Immigrants & Minorities*, 15, 2 (1996), 135–150.

[6] K. Firmin-Sellers, 'The Concentration of Authority: Constitutional Creation in the Gold Coast, 1950', *Journal of Theoretical Politics*, 7, 2 (1995), 201–222.

68   H. P. DLAMINI

Further nationalist agitation led to the independence of Ghana in 1957, with Nkrumah as prime minister. Ghana's independence galvanized the general anti-colonial campaign movement in Africa. Nkrumah immediately became the spokesman for anti-colonial movements in Africa aimed at delivering the whole of Africa from colonial bondage. He advocated pan-Africanism, the idea of the unification of the whole continent.[7] In 1958, Guinea Conakry gained independence from France and, in 1960, a string of French-speaking West African states, Nigeria, and Congo Kinshasa gained independence.[8] In Kenya, the Mau Mau rebellion[9] put pressure on Britain to accelerate the independence of that country in 1962. These waves of independence increased agitation in Central and Southern Africa for similar developments.

The problem with British colonies in Central and Southern Africa is that they had significant settler White populations who dominated local politics and the economy. These Whites feared that independence and Black majority rule would jeopardize their economic privileges, so they convinced the British government to consolidate colonial rule in these territories at the expense of independence.[10] The reluctance to grant Black majority rule and the domination of Africans by White settlers led to racial tensions

---

[7] See K. Botwe-Asamoah, *Kwame Nkrumah's Politico-Cultural Thought and Politics: An African-Centered Paradigm for the Second Phase of the African Revolution* (New York: Routledge, 2013); M. Grilli, 'Nkrumah, Nationalism, and Pan-Africanism: The Bureau of African Affairs Collection', *History in Africa*, 44 (2017), 295–307.

[8] P. D. Curtin, S. Feierman, L. Thompson, and J. Vansina, *African History: From Earliest Times to Independence* (London: Longman, 1995); O. Enwezor and C. Achebe, *The Short Century: Independence and Liberation Movements in Africa, 1945–1994* (Munich: Prestel, 2001); and P. Nugent, *Africa Since Independence: A Comparative History* (New York: Palgrave Macmillan, 2012).

[9] The Mau Mau rebellion was a bloody uprising against British colonial rule in Kenya, championed by the Kikuyu ethnic group, which lasted from 1952 through 1960 and helped to hasten Kenya's independence. The uprising was caused by the expulsion of Kikuyu tenants from White settler farms, the loss of land to White settlers, poverty, and lack of true political representation for Africans. The revolt caused the lives of 32 White settlers and about 200 British police and army soldiers. Over 1800 African civilians were killed. White settlers in Southern Africa were very concerned about the revolt (see W. O. Maloba, *Mau Mau and Kenya: An Analysis of a Peasant Revolt* [Oxford: James Currey, 1993]; F. Furedi, *Mau Mau War in Perspective* [London: James Currey 1989]).

[10] In the Central Federation established in 1953, for instance, the Whites entrenched themselves in power at the expense of the Black majority and struggled to contain surging African nationalism (see A. S. Mlambo, *A History of Zimbabwe* [New York: Cambridge University Press], 119–127).

3 THE BEGINNING OF THE GREAT CONSTITUTIONAL DEBATE ... 69

and nationalist agitation. In January 1959, there was widespread rioting in Nyasaland, which prompted the British to declare a state of emergency and the arrest of nationalist leaders, including Hasting Banda of the Malawi Congress Party (MCP).[11]

Although Britain was able to contain violent local opposition to its rule in certain cases in the 1950s, there was growing concern among policy-makers in the Colonial Office that similar confrontations could get out of hand in the future, as African nationalists were becoming more and more successful in mobilizing popular support. These fears were reinforced by the domestic and international instability that accompanied the French reversals in their colonial wars in Indochina and Algeria.[12] The local demonstrations against British colonial rule and the repressive response of the British colonial government gave justification to imperial critics on the international scene that colonialism was evil and must come to an end.

THE UN SUPPORT FOR THE TOTAL INDEPENDENCE OF AFRICAN TERRITORIES UNDER COLONIAL RULE

The UN, established on 24 October 1945 following the end of World War II, increasingly supported the oppressed colonial peoples as more and more African and Asian nations obtained independence and became members of the international body. In 1960, these countries, acting as the Afro-Asian bloc, secured the passage of General Assembly Resolution 1514 (XV)

[11]Dr. K. Banda's Nyasaland African Congress (NAC) organised widespread disturbances starting in early 1958 in Nyasaland. This radical African nationalism took the form opposition to the Federation of Rhodesia and Nyasaland, particularly its farming and rural conservation policies, and demands for speedy progress towards majority rule. The British colonial government declared a state of emergency in March 1959 which lasted until June 1960. Dr. Banda and 1300 people were detained without trial. Over 2000 were imprisoned for offences related to the emergency and the Congress itself was banned. A total of 51 people were killed by colonial troops. Dr. Banda was released from detention 1960 and the Federation was dissolved in 1963 (see P. C. Banda and G. W. Kayira, 'The 1959 State of Emergency in Nyasaland: Process and Political Implications', *The Society of Malawi Journal* [2012], 1–19; O. J. M. Kalinga, 'The 1959 Nyasaland State of Emergency in Old Karonga District', *Journal of Southern African Studies*, 36, 4 [2010], 743–763).

[12]France was defeated in Indochina at Dien Bien Phu in 1954 and the Algerian War of independence started in 1954 culminating in the independence of Algeria in 1962 (B. B. Fall, *Street Without Joy: The French Debacle in Indochina* [Mechanicsburg: Rowman & Littlefield, 2018]; B. Shaev, 'The Algerian War, European Integration, and the Decolonization of French Socialism', *French Historical Studies*, 41, 1 [2018], 63–94).

70 H. P. DLAMINI

on the Granting of Independence unconditionally to Colonial People.[13] For the first time, the UN demonstrated some muscle on colonial issues by establishing the Special Committee on Colonialism, and by asserting the right of all peoples to self-determination irrespective of any inadequacy of political, economic, social, or educational preparedness. The UN defined the principle of self-determination to include the transition of colonial dependencies to independent states. Imperial powers were, therefore, expected to grant independence to their colonies without further delay.[14] The stance of the UN on decolonization was a source of great pressure on Britain, which had to address the racial situation and the decolonization of its Southern African dependencies.

THE PRO-INDEPENDENCE STANCE OF THE BRITISH LABOUR GOVERNMENT AND MACMILLAN'S 'WIND OF CHANGE' SPEECH, FEBRUARY 1960

The British Labour government, which had won the 1945 elections, was favourably disposed to decolonization.[15] British Prime Minister Harold Macmillan's public statements in South Africa—the bastion of White minority rule—during his official visit to that country in 1960 stirred nationalist feelings among Black people and scared White settlers. Macmillan made the famous 'wind of change' speech on 3 February 1960 in Cape Town against a background of increasing political pressure for rapid decolonization. The speech 'represented a defining moment in the history of the British Empire in Africa'.[16]

---

[13] Mittelman, James H. 'Collective Decolonisation and the UN Committee of 24', *The Journal of Modern African Studies*, 14, 1 (1976), 41–64; D. Birmingham, *The Decolonization of Africa* (London: Routledge, 2008).

[14] H. W. Barber, 'The United States vs. the United Nations', *International Organisation*, 27, 2 (1973), 139–163.

[15] For more on the new shift in the British post-1945 colonial policy see R. Pearce, 'The Colonial Office and Planned Decolonisation in Africa', *African Affairs*, 83 (1984), 77–93.

[16] S. Ward, 'Run Before the Tempest: The "Wind of Change" and the British World', *Geschichte und Gesellschaft*, 37, 2 (2011), 198.

3 THE BEGINNING OF THE GREAT CONSTITUTIONAL DEBATE ... 71

In the words of Macmillan, 'the wind of change is blowing through this continent and whether you like it or not, this growth of national consciousness is a political fact'.[17] In a press conference, Macmillan emphasized that the time had come for the existing groups in the colonies to reach a mutual understanding on peaceful coexistence. In his words: 'We should understand the other chaps' point of view as well as our own. Each group should recognize the needs and rights of others.' He further warned that:

> Angry words, partisan feeling, trying to score political points, whether at home or overseas; won't help: extremists' people [sic] holding entrenched positions – that won't do. What we have to do is to go quietly along with people of good will, trying to solve these difficult problems.[18]

The challenge that Macmillan was referring to was recognizing the needs and rights of other Africans—something that the European settlers in Southern Africa resented mostly because, for much of the colonial period, they had been entrenched in the position of masters, while Africans were treated in a subordinate position as servants. Macmillan's speech particularly targeted White settler communities that were resisting power-sharing with Blacks, and the notion of independence under Black majority rule.

THE REACTION OF SWAZI STAKEHOLDERS TO THE DECOLONIZATION WIND OF CHANGE

The Collective Quest of a Legislative Council of All the Races and the Worrying Question of Its Membership

Although Swaziland was generally quiet throughout the 1950s against a background of African nationalist stirrings, there was a strong anxiety among Swazis and Europeans about the real prospects and nature of self-government and independence.[19] This propelled them to start taking a public stance on decolonization with an emphasis on the establishment

---

[17] Cited in S. Ward, 'Run Before the Tempest: The "Wind of Change" and the British World', *Geschichfe und Gesellschaft*, 37, 2 (2011), 198–219.

[18] 'Prime Minister Returns to United Kingdom: Press Conference', *Times of Swaziland*, February 20, 1960.

[19] T. M. J. Zwane, 'The Struggle for Power in Swaziland', *Africa Today* (1964), 5; E. White, 'Last Steps Towards Independence: The Three African Protectorates,' *African Affairs*, 64, 257 (1965), 261–270.

72   H. P. DLAMINI

of a modern nation-state, beginning with giving consideration to ending racial discrimination and establishing an inclusive Legislative Council as a framework for the commencement of tutoring in modern governance. Unlike other High Commission territories in Southern Africa, Swaziland had never had a representative legislative body.[20] An economic survey mission, headed by Professor Chandler Morse, that visited the three High Commission territories in 1959 had made a similar recommendation. The Chandler Morse Commission published 'A Report of the Economic Survey Mission of Swaziland', which advocated that the establishment of a joint advisory body with elected membership of all races was necessary for the sound economic advancement of the territory. Composed of both Africans and Whites, the body's main role would be to advise government on the best economic policies to adopt for the territory. The Report stated that the economic welfare of all the groups in the territory was interdependent, and should be the objective of a single integrated plan.[21] The SNC, EAC, and the Progressives favoured the idea of a Legislative Council for Swaziland. But the composition of the Council and the method of selecting its membership divided the stakeholders. It mattered whether elections were to be conducted on the basis of universal adult suffrage, and whether the membership of the legislature would be composed of Progressives or Conservatives.

The Progressives in Swaziland were inclined towards Nkrumah's brand of nationalism: in essence, this included a call for African solidarity and the liberation of Southern Africa from White settler rule, African independence and continental unity, universal adult suffrage, and the nationalization of

---

[20] Legislative Councils had been established in Bechuanaland and Basutoland in 1960 but none existed in Swaziland (see J. E. Spence, 'The New States of Southern Africa', *The Journal of Modern African Studies*, 5, 4 [1967], 541–555). In the absence of a legislative council the Resident Commissioner had, hitherto, relied on the Ngwenyama (the Swazi King) and the Swazi National Council matters affecting Swazi inhabitants, and on the European Advisory Council on matters affecting whites.

[21] SNA, Swaziland Progressive Party, 'Swaziland: Report on Constitutional Proposals', Swaziland Progressive Party, 1961.

3 THE BEGINNING OF THE GREAT CONSTITUTIONAL DEBATE ...   73

all private investments.[22] Swaziland's Progressives paid regular political pilgrimage to Ghana and visited eastern bloc countries; this articulated their leftist leanings. J. J. Nquku and Dr Zwane, for instance, made several overseas trips to England, the USA, and Ghana so as to reinforce their liberal democratic ideas and their quest for independence; this was given media coverage in Swaziland.[23] The nationalist posture of the Progressives was inimical to the apartheid regime, White settler interests, and the Swazi monarchy.

South Africa was an important stakeholder in the political developments in Swaziland because of the geo-political location of Swaziland. The consuming momentum of radical nationalism in the African continent made South Africa determined to checkmate similar developments in Swaziland that could potentially spill over into South Africa. For the apartheid regime to remain unscathed, and for stability to be maintained in its Bantustans, South Africa had to contain the wind of radical nationalism in Swaziland at all costs. South Africa did not want to see developments in Swaziland that would contradict the White supremacist philosophy of the apartheid regime—particularly the concept of universal suffrage allowing for one-man-one-vote, or Black majority rule when the Black majority in South Africa were politically neutralized by the apartheid system. Apartheid South Africa was therefore determined to use both the White Swazis and the monarchy as proxies in achieving its goals.[24]

[22] D. Birmingham, *Kwame Nkrumah: The Father of African Nationalism* (Athens, OH: Ohio University Press, 1998); M. Grilli, 'Nkrumah's Ghana and the Armed Struggle in Southern Africa (1961–1966)', *South African Historical Journal*, 70, 1 (2018), 56–81; M. Grilli, 'Nkrumah, Nationalism, and Pan-Africanism: The Bureau of African Affairs Collection', *History in Africa*, 44 (2017), 295–307; and M. Grilli, 'African Liberation and Unity in Nkrumah's Ghana: A Study of the Role of "Pan-African Institutions" in the Making of Ghana's Foreign Policy, 1957–1966' (PhD dissertation, Institute for History, Faculty of Humanities, Leiden University and Department of Political and Social Sciences, University of Pavia, 2015).

[23] 'Nquku Questioned by the United Nations', *Times of Swaziland*, January 25, 1963; FCO 141/17507: Conference of African Dependent States; Ghana's Contacts with the High Commission Territories 1961–64.

[24] Zwane, 'The Struggle for Power in Swaziland', 5; C. P. Potholm, 'Changing Political Configuration in Swaziland', *The Journal of African Studies*, 4, 3 (1966), 316. The hand of South African in manipulating political developments in Swaziland is corroborated by the Swaziland Progressive Party in which Nquku categorically stated that Sobhuza's constitutional proposal and that it was the handiwork of the EAC and South Africa. The document was, therefore, imposed on the SNC (also see SNA, Swaziland Progressive Party, 'Swaziland: Report on Constitutional Proposals', Swaziland Progressive Party, 1961).

74   H. P. DLAMINI

The Stance of the European Advisory Council on the Issue of a Legislative Council for Swaziland

The White community in Swaziland was worried about the surge of radical nationalism, particularly in the 1950s. In a bid to avert the emergence of radical nationalism such as that of Kenya's Mau Mau, in 1959 the White community petitioned the British High Commissioner in South Africa, P. Liesching, to transform the EAC into a Legislative Council and to open it to Africans. Their fears were further underscored by the public statements of the Progressives, echoed Nkrumah's radical ideas. The EAC indicated its willingness to collaborate with King Sobhuza II, the conservative traditional authority, who did not subscribe to the ideology of radical nationalism. Consequently, on 18 January 1960, the EAC requested a Joint Advisory Council between the EAC and the Swazis in which both European and Swazi interests would be represented.[25] In a memorandum presented to the Resident Commissioner for transmission to London, the EAC stated that 'the time has been reached ... for the examination of a multiracial council in which both European and Swazi interests should be represented'. It urged the SNC to nominate its Swazi representatives to be considered for inclusion.[26]

Macmillan's speech in February 1960 put more pressure on the White settlers. Macmillan invited Whites to recognize the rights of Africans. The Whites were not comfortable with Macmillan's speech as they considered it a direct incitement of the educated African elite to revolt against them and to engage in the processes of political change, culminating in Black majority rule with unforeseen consequences on their businesses. The speech also fired the enthusiasm of the educated elite but worried King Sobuza II, who feared Swazis would start agitating for political rights outside the realm of their culture and tradition.[27] Perhaps not surprisingly, the EAC—which

---

[25]SNA, Swazi Constitution Presented to Parliament by the Secretary of State for Colonies by command of Her Majesty, May 1963; FCO 141/17579–17582: Resolution Passed by the Swaziland European Advisory Council; Session Dealing with the Question of Responsible Government for the Territory 1953–59.

[26]SNA, Government of Swaziland, Proposals for the Swazi Constitution (March 1962), 12.

[27]In expressing his views on 23 April 1960 on the constitutional future of Swaziland, King Sobhuza stated that he was in agreement with Macmillan's speech to the Union Parliament in Cape Town and admonished that Africas should not abandon their culture and should stay clear of East-West ideological confrontations (see, 'The Ngwenyama, Sobhuza II C.B.E.,

3 THE BEGINNING OF THE GREAT CONSTITUTIONAL DEBATE ...   75

was worried about Britain's favourable disposition towards the educated political elite as the heirs of the post-colonial state at the expense of the Swazi monarchy—supported South Africa's incorporation of Swaziland in a manner that would allow the *Ngwenyama* to enjoy increased political powers. The EAC also communicated the proposal for a joint Advisory Council to the *Ngwenyama* for his consideration as an important project.

The Stance of the Ngwenyama on the Rise of African Nationalism and the Issue of a Legislative Council for Swaziland

The Swazi monarch was aware of nationalist stirrings in Africa from newspapers and radio reports, which caused him to develop a phobia for the Western liberal democratic framework that the British had introduced and the nascent political parties. He developed an anti-political party and anti-liberal democratic credentials as his response to the resurgence of African nationalism.

What worried him most was the rise of the Western-educated elite and their craving for power at the expense of traditional African rulers everywhere in Africa. Nationalist leaders often targeted traditional rulers for destruction as relics of a feudal past who had no place in modern nation-states. In Egypt, the Free Officers Movement forced King Farouk to abdicate in 1952, launching a period of successive military rule. President Habib Bourguiba deposed Bey Muhammad VIII al-Amin, declaring Tunisia a republic on 25 July 1957. In Rwanda, a referendum led to the deposing of King Kigeli V Ndahindurwa on 25 September 1961.On assuming power in Guinea Conakry in 1958, Seke Toure abolished the institution of chieftaincy. In Nkrumah's Ghana, traditional rulers were relegated to the background of modern politics. The admonition of Ghanaian Kwame Nkrumah, 'Seek ye first the political kingdom', had a particularly strong appeal to the African Western-educated elite, who formed political parties in order to capture political power from the departing colonial administrations. King Sobhuza's suspicion of radical nationalists and of the concept of political parties and universal adult suffrage was profound and shaped his thinking. He therefore developed a strong phobia of Western liberal democratic culture, because he saw it as a medium for the destruction

Gives Expression to His Views on the Constitutional Future of Swaziland', *Times of Swaziland*, July 1, 1960).

76   H. P. DLAMINI

of monarchical powers. The Western-educated elite were feared as demagogues who had the capacity to sway crowds and use their votes to capture power. Political modernity, seen in the formation of political parties and the use of universal adult suffrage, threatened the Swazi monarchy, which was not only constructed on a dynastic lineage, but also based on culture and tradition. King Sobhuza II did not see himself as a replaceable political figure because the Dlamini dynasty represented the continuity of the Swazi nation. He believed a king did not need a political party to be in power because, by virtue of the people's culture and tradition, he was the king of all Swazis. A king was not made or voted, but was born. The rise of nationalist leaders in Swaziland with a new political modernizing agenda challenged the notion and the place of the Swazi monarch in modern governance.

The nascent political parties in Swaziland manifested leftist leanings,[28] which qualified them as Progressives. They were bent on capturing power and implementing Nkrumah's radical nationalism, including the nationalization of private property and, through land reforms and pan-Africanism, a non-racial and anti-apartheid Swaziland. King Sobhuza's woes were compounded by the fact that the British Colonial Office envisaged the exclusive transfer of political power, on departing Swaziland, to political party leaders and not traditional rulers, whose role was limited to culture and tradition. The Swazi monarchists logically developed cold feet about political modernization in the shape of political parties and universal adult suffrage because they sounded the death knell of the monarchy, as had happened elsewhere on the African continent. The White settlers and multinational

---

[28] In this study the term left-wing refers to "the radical, reforming, or socialist oriented political party that included nationalisation of private property in its programme". The political terms "Left" and "Right" were coined during the French Revolution (1789–1799) and generally refers to those opposed to the monarchy and supported the revolution, including the creation of a republic and secularization while those on the right were supportive of the traditional institutions of the Old Regime. Left-wing politics supports social equality and egalitarianism, often in opposition to social hierarchy. It typically involves a concern for those in society whom its adherents perceive as disadvantaged relative to others as well as a belief that there are unjustified inequalities that need to be reduced or abolished (by advocating for social justice) (see L. Diamond and R. Gunther [eds.], *Political Parties and Democracy* [Baltimore: Johns Hopkins University Press, 2001]; J. Cupples and K. Glynn, 'Decolonial Social Movements, Leftist Governments and the Media', 11–16, In J. Cupples and K. Glynn [eds.], *Shifting Nicaraguan Mediascapes: Authoritarianism and the Struggle for Social Justice* [Newcastle: Springer, Cham, 2018]).

3 THE BEGINNING OF THE GREAT CONSTITUTIONAL DEBATE ...   77

corporations in Swaziland, concerned for the vulnerability of their investments and private property in the event of a leftist take over from the British, found a natural ally in King Sobhuza II, who was out to conserve the traditional status quo and protect private property.

Macmillan's February 1960 'wind of change' speech impacted on King Sobhuza and underscored the necessity of responding to these new political pressures as, inevitably, they had to impact directly on the survival of the traditional Swazi monarchy. The challenge facing the Swazi king was how traditional kingship had to appropriate the veritable forces of political modernity without fizzling out.

The *Ngwenyama* convened an important meeting in the Royal Residence on 23 April 1960 to which he invited the local British government officials, members of the SNC, and prominent White businessmen. The invitees included the Acting Resident Commissioner, the Secretary for Swazi Affairs, Dr D. Hynd, and W. G. Lewis. The members of the Swazi Traditional Council who were invited were Prince Magongo, Prince Madevu, Councillor S. Matsebula, Councillor B. Simelane, Councillor S. A. Sibiya, Councillor M. Sukati, Councillor J. M. S. Matsebula (otherwise referred to as the *Lisolenkosi*, meaning 'the King's eye'), Prince Matsafeni, Councillor A. K. Hlophe, and Councillor M. Nhlabatsi.[29]

The *Ngwenyama* made a historic speech in which he clearly stated his political views about the future of Swaziland in his dual capacity as a member of the educated elite and the traditional ruler of the Swazi people. Although a product of Western education and political culture, he was also meticulously groomed in the royal culture and tradition of the Swazi people. He understood that the exigencies of Western democracy were not compatible with traditional monarchism and therefore articulated his political views through the prism of Swazi culture and tradition, which he intended to conserve as much as possible.

King Sobhuza II's political views were captured in his April 1960 speech, which is of enormous importance in the constitutional annals of Swazi history.[30] While agreeing with Macmillan's 'winds of change' speech, he expressed the wish that Africans should be allowed to conserve and operate

---

[29] Excepts of this speech are published in: 'The Ngwenyama, Sobhuza II C.B.E. Gives Expression to His Views on the Constitutional Future of Swaziland', *The Times of Swaziland*, July 1, 1960; Also see Appendix A for the full reproduction of this speech given the fact it constituted an important milestone in the constitutional history of Swaziland.

[30] See Appendix A.

78 H. P. DLAMINI

their own traditional system of government. By so doing, King Sobhuza II was advocating a conservative political ideology in changing political times framed in Britain's modernizing political machinery that was unfolding towards independence. Sobhuza stated that Swaziland was not exempt from nationalist explosions that were occurring in Africa, and he called for vigilance. He attributed the ongoing unrest in Africa to nationalist agitation, and to the tense relations between Whites and Blacks.

The *Ngwenyama* stated that the upsurge of nationalist agitation in North and Central Africa, particularly in Nyasaland, was because of the fact that Africans had forgotten their culture and tradition, and were adopting European norms to which they were not used. He accused the African educated elite at the forefront of nationalist agitation of being 'power-greedy individuals' who were using Western political ideology to arrogate power. Such agitation was tied to modern political parties, which were foreign to Swazis and were undesirable. Sobhuza stated that the correct political procedure was the traditional one, which required all Swazis to be brought to the *Libandla* (a traditional gathering in the form of an informal parliament) for discussions about national issues, and for a proper decision to be taken by the assembly on the basis of a consensus.

According to Sobhuza, Swazis needed the White settlers for the economic development of the territory and, therefore, their properties must be protected and not nationalized. Without identifying the radical Swazi nationalists by name, Sobhuza stated that those who were advocating the nationalization of private property were 'victims of bad upbringing ... they had been brutally and badly brought up and were now acting to their early treatment [sic]'. He stated that Africans must co-exist with White immigrants, because Swaziland was also their country and it was wrong to target the confiscation of their property.[31]

Concerning the White community's invitation to the monarch to send representatives to the proposed EAC, which would be transformed into the Legislative Council, Sobhuza rejected the idea on the grounds that it would mean a derogation of Swazi power, because the SNC already had legislative and executive powers, whereas the EAC was only advisory. In his estimation, the SNC was superior to the EAC. He stated:

[31] Ibid.

3 THE BEGINNING OF THE GREAT CONSTITUTIONAL DEBATE ... 81

the legislature of the modern state. The King would, thus, have to handpick those he deemed fit to represent the Swazi people in the spirit of traditional democracy.

The Swazi monarch and the SNC, which represented the traditional elite, felt threatened by the spread of the more radical form of African nationalism into Swaziland, and by the emerging labour force that would emulate industrial action from other African countries and arrogate to themselves alternative centres of political influence other that the monarch. Consequently, Sobhuza was against the formation and operation of political parties. He preferred the African consensual system of consultation in which the last word lay with the traditional authorities. He was also against the idea of one-man-one-vote because it could potentially threaten the traditional monarch, as had already happened elsewhere in Africa in the last years of colonial rule[36] and would certainly submerge the White minority in the territory. In essence, Sobhuza was advocating political hybridity by selecting elements from Swazi culture and tradition that favoured him, and integrating them into a modern political frame while rejecting liberal democracy as presented by the British and advocated by the Progressives, which were a threat to him.

Sobhuza's political stance expectedly found sympathy with the White minorities and multinational business interests, who were anti-nationalization. The White community was more comfortable with the question of land and mineral rights being excluded from the jurisdiction of the Legislative Council and left in Sobhuza's hands, because they could more easily manipulate Sobhuza than a Legislative Council the composition of which they could not trust. Sobhuza's political ideology ran contrary to that of the British colonial administration, which intended to bequeath parliamentary democracy to Swaziland with the Progressives as its main beneficiaries.

---

[36] See M. Crowder and O. Ikime (eds.), *Their Changing Status Under Colonial Rule and Independence* (New York: Africana Publishing Corporation, 1970); R. Rathbone, 'Kwame Nkrumah and the Chiefs: The Fate of Natural Rulers Under Nationalists Governments', *Transactions of the Royal Historical Society*, 10 (2000), 45–53.

82   H. P. DLAMINI

The Stance of the Progressives on the Issue of a Legislative Council for Swaziland

The Progressives subscribed fully to the idea of the establishment of a Legislative Council in Swaziland as a preliminary step to self-government and independence. They espoused the radical nationalism and parliamentary democracy constructed on the platform of universal adult suffrage, which was a contrast to Sobhuza's position. In August 1960, under Nquku's leadership, the Swaziland Progressive Party (SPP) issued a manifesto that hinged on four cardinal points.

First, it advocated a non-racial society that would bring about democratic enfranchisement of all Swazi inhabitants irrespective of race, colour, or creed; second, it opposed the incorporation of Swaziland into South Africa; third, it adopted the UN Declaration of Human Rights; and, lastly, it advocated for complete integration of all Swazis in every walk of life and the ending of all forms of racial discrimination,[37] which was the hallmark of settler colonies. The position of the Progressives is understandable when one takes into consideration the fact that Swaziland was a settler colony, and White discriminatory practices and South African influences were all-pervasive.

By calling for universal suffrage when advocating the enfranchisement of all peoples, the Progressives showed that they felt that the traditional structures advocated by the Swazi monarch and the SNC were inappropriate for modern governance, and that they needed to be streamlined in the modern constitution in such a way that there would be an opening for modern political development. British political institutions and practices were their reference points. By alluding to the UN, the Progressives wanted to have international pressure brought to bear in order to bring about genuine political developments in Swaziland with respect to human rights and equality for all, irrespective of race. The United Nations had taken a position in favour of decolonization and it was logical for the Progressives to invoke this institution.

The Progressives were different from King Sobhuza and the SNC, but the British lumped them together as Swazis, considering the Whites as a distinct European group. The British had to consult the Swazis and the

---

[37] SNA, Swaziland Progressive Party, 'Swaziland: Report on Constitutional Proposals', Swaziland Progressive Party, 1961; FCO 141/17472, 17670: Constitutional Proposals; Land Issues; Africanisation of the Civil Service.

3 THE BEGINNING OF THE GREAT CONSTITUTIONAL DEBATE ...   83

Europeans as two distinct blocs in the making of the constitution. The responsibility of appointing Swazis fell under the purview of King Sobhuza II. This was so because, in 1944, the British High Commissioner issued a Native Authorities Proclamation that recognized King Sobhuza II as the Native Authority for the territory to issue legally enforceable orders to the Swazis subject to restrictions and directions from the Resident Commissioner. This proclamation was revised in 1952 to grant King Sobhuza II a degree of autonomy unprecedented in British colonial indirect rule in Africa.[38] The British therefore relied on King Sobhuza to appoint the Swazi delegates who would serve in the maiden Constitutional Committee to deliberate on the establishment of the modern political institutions of the colonial state. It was clear the Swazi political elite were divided along progressive and conservative lines and this division would magnify when the constitutional talks took off.

THE COMMENCEMENT OF THE SWAZI CONSTITUTIONAL TALKS

The independence of Swaziland was inevitable: the British were conscious of this fact and took appropriate measures in preparation for it. On 16 June 1960, the British Secretary of State for the Colonies, Alexander Douglas-Home, directed the British Resident Commissioner in Swaziland, Brian Marwick, through the High Commissioner in Pretoria, to initiate formal constitutional talks in the territory in a typically British style of preparing to exit their colonial dependencies.[39]

What Britain set out to bequeath to its dependencies as a constitutional legacy was the principle of separation of powers as enshrined in the Westminster system of government. Fombad notes that:

---

[38] A. M. Kanduza, 'Evolving Significance of Sobhuza's 1941 Petition', *Transafrican Journal of History* 25 (1996), 110; P. Cocks, 'The King and I: Bronislaw Malinowski, King Sobhuza II of Swaziland and the Vision of Culture Change in Africa', *History of the Human Sciences*, 13, 4 (2000), 25–47.

[39] Britain often introduces a succession of constitutional instruments in its colonies which are improved upon before independence is finally granted (For example from Nigeria, Ghana and Malawi see B. O. Nwabueze, *A Constitutional History of Nigeria* [London: C. Hurst and Company, 1982]; T. P. Biswal, *Ghana, Political and Constitutional Developments* [New Delhi: Northern Book Centre, 1992]; and Z. D. Kadzamira, 'Constitutional Changes in Malawi 1891–1965,' In *Malawi Past and Present: Selected Papers from the University of Malawi History Conference* [1967]).

84   H. P. DLAMINI

A major challenge faced by *constitutional engineers has been to design a system of governance that maximizes the protection of individual members of society while minimizing the opportunities for governments to harm them.* Of the theories of government that have attempted to provide a solution to this dilemma, the doctrine of separation of powers...has been the most significant both intellectually and in terms of its influence upon institutional structures....This is not surprising, for the French considered this doctrine so important that Article 16 of their Declaration of the Rights of Man and of the Citizen of 1789 stated that any society in which the separation of powers is not observed 'has no constitution'.[40]

British constitutionalism consisted of the separation of powers, a cabinet system of government with an executive prime minister, while the monarch was merely a ceremonial figure. The task before the British in Swaziland was to initiate, establish and drill a British political order as the independence governance package to the people of Swaziland. How could the socio-political reality of Swaziland be moulded to fit into British constitutional thought?

The British Resident Commissioner prepared the grounds for constitutionalism by holding separate meetings with representatives of Sobhuza's SNC and Todd's EAC, and it was agreed to set up a Constitutional Committee under the chairmanship of the Resident Commissioner. The Committee was composed of 28 members and included British officials of the Swazi colonial government and representatives of the SNC, the EAC, and the Swaziland Combined Executives Association.[41] The full Constitutional Committee appointed by the British is presented in Table 3.1.

Table 3.1 reveals that Europeans were in the majority on the committee, followed by the representatives of the SNC. However, the reality was that the colonial government was introducing the constitutional stakeholders into the rudiments of modern governance. When the constitutional discussions started in earnest, the Swazis and White settlers were seen at the forefront of the discussions.

The Swazi king appointed the SNC delegates to the Constitutional Committee, including the three Progressive Party leaders: J. J. Nquku,

---

[40]C. M. Fombad, 'The Separation of Powers and Constitutionalism in Africa: The Case of Botswana', *Boston College Third World Law Journal* (2005), 301.

[41]SNA, Swazi Constitution Presented to Parliament by the Secretary of State for Colonies by command of Her Majesty, May 1963; FCO 141/17472, 17670: Constitutional Proposals; Land Issues; Africanisation of the Civil Service;

3 THE BEGINNING OF THE GREAT CONSTITUTIONAL DEBATE ... 85

Table 3.1 Members of the Maiden Swazi Constitutional Committee

	Name	Rank	Affiliation
1.	Brian Marwick	Resident Commissioner in Swaziland	Government representative
2.	E. Long	Government Secretary	Government representative
3.	J. F. B. Furcell	Secretary of Swazi Affairs	Government representative
4.	W. E. C. Fitcher	Director of Education	Government representative
5.	H. D. G. Fitzpatrick	Ex-Government Official on Pension	European member
6.	C. F. Todd	Member of the European Advisory Council	European member
7.	S. Hubbard	Director of Colonial Development Corporation	European member
8.	R. P. Stephens	Director of Peak Timbers	European member
9.	S. W. J. Gaiger	Proprietor of Swazi Inn Hotel, Mbabane	Affiliated European member
10.	P. Steward	Treasury Department, Farmer and Member of the EAC	
11.	J. D. Weir	Farmer and Member of EAC	
12.	B. Bordihn	Farmer and Member of EAC	
13.	S. Bowman	Farmer and Member of EAC	
14.	Chief J. M. Dlamini	(Swazi) Chief of Enkungwini area	Member of the Swazi Royal House.
15.	L. Dlamini	(Swazi) Member of the Swazi Royal House	Secretary of the Swazi National Council
16.	K. Hlope	(Swazi)	Private Secretary of King Sobhuza
17.	D. Lukhele	(Swazi)	Lawyer with headquarters in South Africa
18.	J. S. M. Matsebula	Swazi (Iselenkosi or the eye of the King)	Senior African Protectorate Officer
19.	M. P. Mhlabatsi	Son-in-law of King Sobhuza	Member of the Swazi National Council
20.	J. M. B. Sukati	Commander of the Swazi Royal Regiment	Senior African Protectorate Officer

(continued)

86   H. P. DLAMINI

Table 3.1   (continued)

Name	Rank	Affiliation
21. S. T. M. Sukati	Brother of J. M. B. Sukati	Senior African Protectorate Officer
22. Chief L. Dlamini	Chief of Royal House. Chief of Embo area	Member of SNC
23. Chief S. Dlamini	Chief of Valozizwani area	President of the Swazi High Court of Appeal
24. Prince D. M. Somhlolo	Swazi	Member of SNC
25. Dr A. M. Nxumalo	Cousin of King Sobhuza	Medical officer
26. J. J. Nquku	President	Swaziland Progressive Party
27. Dr A. P. Zwane	General Secretary	Swaziland Progressive Party
28. O. M. Mabuza	Member of Executive Committee	Swaziland Progressive Party

Source Compiled from SNA: Constitutional Proposals: Written Comments of the Public Chapter XIV, Membership of the Swaziland Constitutional Committee, 1962

Dr A. P. Zwane, and O. M. Mabuza.[42] It should be understood that, at this point, all Swazi elites were co-opted onto the SNC. The Progressives had to belong by virtue of their social standing in Swazi society, and the monarch had to recognize this fact. They were, therefore, members of the committee 'in their capacity as members of the *Libhandla* [SNC] and not as members of the Swaziland Progressive Party.'[43] British expected the Swazi representation to be broad-based and would not have endorsed the exclusion of the educated elite, whom they considered an important element in the transfer of power to Africans. Nonetheless, the Coloured community, otherwise referred to as Euro-Africans, were not accorded any representation, notwithstanding the fact that they comprised a substantial minority and, under the laws of race-sensitive colonial Swaziland, were treated as

---

[42] SNA: Constitutional Proposals: Written Comments of the Public Chapter XIV, Membership of the Swaziland Constitutional Committee, 1962; FCO 141/17472, 17670: Constitutional Proposals; Land Issues; Africanisation of the Civil Service.

[43] Ibid.

3 THE BEGINNING OF THE GREAT CONSTITUTIONAL DEBATE ...   87

a separate group possessing a separate status.[44] A seasoned British colonial administrator, Sir Charles Arden-Clarke, who oversaw the independence processes of Nkrumah's Ghana,[45] was sent to Swaziland to serve as the constitutional adviser of the colonial administration. The British were therefore set to engage the Swazis in the important constitution-making exercise.

DISAGREEMENTS BETWEEN THE CONSTITUTIONAL DELEGATES LEADING TO THE EXCLUSION AND WITHDRAWAL OF THE PROGRESSIVES

Constitution-making was a prelude to the methodology of the acquisition of the art of modern governance and power transfer to the local elite under the British. In order to proceed with its business of constitution-making, the Constitutional Committee appointed a small Working Committee, drawn from Sobhuza's SNC and Todd's EAC, which invited submissions on the British constitutional framework from interested parties.

The first meeting of the Constitutional Committee started in earnest on 4 November 1960 in Mbabane. The Resident Commissioner held talks with Constitutional Committees representing the European community of the territory and the Swazi National Council to initiate formal discussion on the constitutional development of Swaziland. The Committee had to consider the agenda of the meeting established by the Secretary of State and the British proposal for a Legislature Council based on universal suffrage. He indicated that the administration intended to guide Swaziland to responsible self-government within the commonwealth in conditions that ensured the people enjoyed a fair standard of living and freedom from oppression. The Resident Commissioner said that, in accordance with this

---

[44] For more on the race question in colonial Swaziland see Larry W. Bowman, 'The Subordinate State System of Southern Africa', *International Studies Quarterly* 12, 3 (1968), 231–261; J. Crush, 'The Colonial Division of Space: The Significance of the Swaziland Land Partition', *The International Journal of African Historical Studies*, 13, 1 (1980), 71–86; and N. Dlamini, *The Legal Abolition of Racial Discrimination and Its Aftermath: The Case of Swaziland, 1945–1973* (Doctoral dissertation University of the Witwatersrand, 2007).

[45] Sir Charles Arden-Clarke was a seasoned colonial administrator with a wealth of experience from Ghana in particular where he served as the last governor from August 1949 until 1957. After Ghana's independence, he was named the first Governor-General of Ghana in 1957. The credit for Ghana's relatively smooth transition to independence goes to him (D. Rooney, *Sir Charles Arden-Clarke* (London: Rex Collings Limited, 1982)).

88   H. P. DLAMINI

policy, the Secretary of State had instructed him to initiate discussions with a view to examining the means by which the people of the territory could more effectively play a part in its government. The Resident Commissioner indicated his awareness of the desire of both Swazis and Europeans for the establishment of a joint Legislative Council in the territory. He cautioned both sides that they lacked experience of working together following parliamentary procedure of modern governance, and expressed the view that an essential preliminary to any examination of constitutional reform would be the attainment of a proper mutual understanding. He pointed to the fact that there would be a number of problems and conditions that would require close consideration and suggested that, because of the complexities of these issues and of the machines of constitution framing, it would seem desirable to appoint a small working committee representative of the interested parties: government, the Swazi, and the Europeans. Each of these committees would be answerable to its parent body and, eventually, to the Swazi general public. The Resident Commissioner suggested that the task of the working committee included:

a. examination of the circumstances that militated against common purpose and co-existence;
b. consideration which form of constitution was desirable for Swaziland, and the drafting of it accordingly; and
c. consideration of the need for subordinate or local forms of government in Swaziland: for example, at district level and for urban areas.[46]

The meeting endorsed the analysis of the exigencies of constitution-making presented by the Resident Commissioner. The representatives of the EAC expressed the view that no objection existed to the early establishment of a Legislative Council and agreed forthwith that three of their members should serve on a working committee. The representatives of the Swazi Council stated that they would report back to the King before any decision on the way forward could be made. The meeting accordingly adjourned to

---

[46] SNA, Government of Swaziland, Proposals for the Swazi Constitution (March 1962), 12; FCO 141/17380, 17385–17387: Constitutional Reforms 1959–63; 'Constitutional Advance in Swaziland', *Times of Swaziland*, November 11, 1960.

3 THE BEGINNING OF THE GREAT CONSTITUTIONAL DEBATE ... 89

enable the representatives to consult.[47] The constitution-making exercise had started in earnest.

The British political modernization agenda had to start with the involvement of the Swazis and Europeans in the establishment of a Legislative Council, which was an instrument *par excellence* for the political training of Africans in the art of modern governance in British dependencies. The Legislative Council was usually composed of British colonial officials and Africans, and it is within this institution that power was gradually transferred to Africans in the spirit of self-government leading to independence. The Legislative Council was therefore an important political institution for British political modernization project.

The members of the maiden Legislative Council were to be selected through elections. British preferred the implementation of the concept of universal adult suffrage, which consists of the right of all adult citizens to vote, regardless of property ownership, income, race, or ethnicity, subject only to minor exceptions.[48] The British idea of universal adult suffrage was based on the logic that the beneficiary of the transfer of power from the colonial government to the post-colonial government should emerge from the will of the sovereign people of Swaziland. In other words, the will of the Swazi people should dictate the post-colonial government of modern Swaziland according to democratic principles. Politics should be open to all, and the political playing field should be level for all interested political contestants of political parties seeking to solicit the mandate of the Swazi people. The logic of the British was that the attainment of political modernity, starting with the establishment of a Legislative Council, should be achieved through the instruments of electoral competition by modern political parties. This position was agreeable to Swaziland's nascent political leaders, who knew how effective popular suffrage could be and that it was the channel Nkrumah pursued to ascend to power in Ghana. But the SNC and the EAC did not share such sentiments.

The representatives of the SNC and EAC consulted with their principals, returning to the meeting with apprehensions of the British idea of universal adult suffrage and the ultimate transfer of power to elected political leaders. King Sobhuza II's SNC rejected the principle of elections on the grounds

---

[47]'Constitutional Advance in Swaziland', *Times of Swaziland*, November 11, 1960.

[48]L. Beckman, 'Who Should Vote? Conceptualizing Universal Suffrage in Studies of Democracy', *Democratisation*, 15, 1 (2008), 29–48.

90   H. P. DLAMINI

that Swaziland was a protectorate under a traditional monarch who had inherited his powers from the Dlamini dynasty and did not owe his authority to an election process. As far as the monarchy was concerned, political power in Swaziland was not open to contestation because it was not the Swazi way of doing things. It was anathema for Swazi political culture to be sacrificed on the altar of British modernity by contesting the powers of the king, who was seen as the continuity of the Swazi nation. There was, therefore, the feeling among the royal class that the British were out to invite every Tom, Dick and Harry to contest political power at the expense of the Dlamini dynasty. In the words of Prince Masitsela, a member of the Swazi National Council: *EmaNgisi ajika live etulu*, which can be loosely translated as 'the British are throwing up the country for anyone to 'catch' and 'lead it'. He stated that the British made it clear that they were not just going to hand over Swaziland directly to King Sobhuza after their departure. They were going to 'throw it up in the air' for anyone who had the support of the people to take it. This modern practice did not tally with Swazi culture and tradition, and King Sobhuza II was against being placed on the same footing with other Swazis to contest political power when he was already a king.[49] Prince Masitsela did not realize that the British did not even envisage the possibility of King Sobhuza II engaging in modern politics because the post-1945 Labour government policy programmed the Western-educated elite, who were not traditional rulers, to succeed to the role of post-colonial government.

The White minority supported King Sobhuza II, although they were not necessarily traditionalists or admirers of African political traditionalism. They were against popular elections for another reason. As a minority with heavy investments in the private sector, they were very concerned that they would be swamped in the legislature and their economic interests would be jeopardized by the Black majority under the sway of the Progressives, whom they could not trust. They preferred to support the Swazi monarch, to have King Sobhuza's powers intact and undiluted, because they trusted he would defend their economic interests against the rising radical nationalists who were threatening them with nationalization. It is, therefore, important to

---

[49]The Swazi king is a towering figure that wields a lot of power and the ordinary country folk could not conceive an alternative form of power (For more on the Swazi king's dominance in public space see P. T. Khoza, 'A Study of the Powers of the Swazi Monarch in Terms of Swazi Law and Custom Past, Present and the Future' [MA dissertation, Rhodes University, 2002]).

3 THE BEGINNING OF THE GREAT CONSTITUTIONAL DEBATE ... 91

appreciate the conflicting viewpoints of the protagonists as this divergence of interests complicated the constitutional talks in the early 1960s and soon led to a stalemate. The SNC and EAC were forced into an alliance by the British political modernization agenda and the political posture of the Progressives. This SNC–EAC alliance had the backing King Sobhuza enjoyed from White multinational investors and apartheid South Africa.[50] It is from this position of strength that King Sobhuza II had the temerity to oppose the British constitutional proposals, and to propose an alternative agenda that ran contrary to British constitutional tradition, which was being laid down in the territory.

A succession of constitutional meetings were held behind closed doors because they were expected to be stormy, since the political viewpoints of the various protagonists had been topics of elaborate discussion in the media and were, therefore, well-known.[51] As was expected, when the Constitutional Committee began serious discussions regarding the submission on the British constitutional framework for Swaziland, a conflict developed between the conservative camp, comprising King Sobhuza II's SNC and the Todd's EAC, on the one hand, and the three Progressive members of the Progressive party, on the other hand. The dispute was based on the following issues.

First, the three members of the Progressive wing of the Committee wanted to participate in the constitutional talks freely without any restraint, and to be guided by common logic and their conscience. As members of the SPP, they wished to express their party's views about the constitution without any restrictions. The Swazi traditionalists of the SNC retorted that a true Swazi should speak through the mouth of the *Ngwenyama* and not independently of him. The Progressives rejected this reactionary traditionalism on the grounds that it impeded free debates.

Second, the Progressives espoused the multiparty politics that was in vogue in Africa as the best way to gauge people's preferences. Freedom of association was the hallmark of modernity and development. Their opponents argued that there was no room for multiparty politics for Africans

---

[50] H. P. Dlamini, 'South African Interventionism in Swazi Colonial Politics' (Conference Paper).

[51] FCO 141/17380, 17385–17387: Constitutional Reforms 1959–63; FCO 141/17579–17582: Resolution Passed by the Swaziland European Advisory Council; Session Dealing with the Question of Responsible Government for the Territory 1953–59; FCO 141/17479: Reform Committee of the Swaziland National Administration 1959–61.

92   H. P. DLAMINI

in Swaziland on the grounds that the *Ngwenyama* had not endorsed such a political culture. The traditionalists stated that multiparty politics were against the strong wishes of the *Ngwenyama*.

Third, the Progressive Party resented the charge contained in the working paper presented by the Working Committee that the Progressive Party had not been approved by the *Ngwenyama*. The SNC stated that political organizations existing outside the SNC were inimical to the traditional ethnic structure of the Swazi state. The Progressives retorted that the last word on the authorization of the formation of political parties was the exclusive prerogative of the colonial state, and not that of a tribal chieftain.

Lastly, the Progressive Party were upset by the suggestion of the British administration that discussions for formulation of the constitution would take place on the basis of the submissions of King Sobhuza's SNC. As expected, C. F. Todd, the leader of the EAC, supported Sobhuza's submissions as a basis for discussion. He admonished members of the Committee that they were expected to make comments within the framework of the *Ngwenyama*'s constitutional proposals for Swaziland. Todd reminded the Progressive leaders that their views on adult universal suffrage were unacceptable to the *Ngwenyama*, who had argued that it was un-African and un-Swazi.[52]

The Progressives retorted that the SNC–EAC constitutional proposals were simply about protecting capitalist big business interests. Nquku stated:

> Those whom Mr Todd regard as Ngwenyama's 'people' constitute the clique from which privilege on the White side selects the 'loyal Swazis' to sit on Boards of Company Directors. This clique and White privilege ganged up and produced a fifty-fifty formula to muzzle public opinion and establish a government dominated by the financial corporations.[53]

The Progressives argued that power should emanate from the sovereign people, and therefore supported the British proposal for one-man-one-vote, which was rejected outright by the conservative SNC and their EAC ally. The Swazi monarch and the White minority were not happy with the

---

[52]FCO 141/17380, 17385–17387: Constitutional Reforms 1959–63; 'Ngwenyama Warns Swazi Nation Politics Can Lead Us to Hardship', *Times of Swaziland*, November 4, 1960; and 'Constitutional Advance in Swaziland', *Times of Swaziland*, November 11, 1960.

[53]'Swaziland Democratic Part 1961 Policy Speech' In S. N. Ndwandwe, Politics in Swaziland 1960–1968: A Selection of Reports in the Tmes of Swaziland. University of Witwatersrand, Johannesburg, 4, n.d.

British constitutional proposals for adult universal suffrage, which created room for nationalist agitation for political rights in Swaziland. The SNC and EAC were convinced that 'the British administration was bent on sacrificing their interests to the causes of modern African nationalism and majority rule'.[54] Under the British constitutional arrangement, the Whites would be wiped off the political scene and Sobhuza's reign would be compromised by the competing political parties, as had happened elsewhere in Africa, where traditional rulers were steadily relegated to the background in modern politics.[55] These four issues were compounded by a fifth, which was a proposal for a 50–50 representation in the envisaged legislature for Europeans, who numbered a mere 10,000, and the Swazis, who numbered 270,000. It was further proposed that the two groups were to be selected separately according to European and African political traditions. The Progressives described the 50–50 political representation of Swazis and Europeans as a pure 'political monstrosity'.[56] The equal representation submission for the White minority and the Swazi majority was so bitterly opposed by the political parties and the British colonial administration, and so strongly supported by Sobhuza's SNC and Todd's EAC, that the constitutional talks dragged on for almost two years with no end in sight.[57] This issue remained a bone of contention and could hardly be

[54] C. P. Potholm, 'Changing Political Configuration in Swaziland', *The Journal of African Studies*, 4, 9 (1966), 314.

[55] R. Rathbone, 'Kwame Nkrumah and the Chiefs: the Fate of Natural Rulers Under Nationalists Governments', *Transactions of the Royal Historical Society*, 10 (2000), 45–63; E. A. B. Van Rouveroy van Nieuwaal, 'Chiefs and African States: Some Introductory Notes and an Extensive Bibliography on African Chieftaincy', *The Journal of Legal Pluralism and Unofficial Law*, 19, 25–26 (1987), 1–46.

[56] Sishayi Simon Ndwandwe, Politics In Swaziland 1960–1968: A Selection of Reports in the *Times of Swaziland*, University of the Witwatersrand Institute for Advanced Social Research, African Studies Programme University of the Witwatersrand, Johannesburg, 1968, 8.

[57] This constitutional feet-dragging can be compared to developments in Botswana, another British High Commission Territory. In Botswana, a Joint Advisory Council comprising Africans and Europeans established a constitutional committee with the support of the colonial administration in 1959. The committee recommended the establishment of a legislative council in 1960. A National Assembly replaced the Legislative Council in 1963. During a conference held in Lobatse in 1963, a constitution for a self-governing Botswana was agreed upon. A period of self-government ended with full independence on 30 September 1966 (see P. Fawcus and A. Tilbury, *Botswana: The Road to Independence* [Gaborone: Pula Press and the Botswana Society, 2000]).

94   H. P. DLAMINI

resolved, even with the intervention of the British, because they were not only confronted with the Swazi monarch, but also with White settlers and multinational interests.

The British proposal on the method of voting members of the legislature raised a storm of protest from the SNC and EAC because it touched directly on the issue of empowerment and disempowerment, and political ideology. The Swazi monarchy saw itself as the natural leader of the Swazis but feared the ability of the Progressives to manipulate the electorate to their advantage, given the performance of the educated elite elsewhere in Africa at the polls—the radical Nkrumah who was swept to power in the February 1951 elections in Ghana being a classical example. The possibility of the Progressives ousting the Swazi king from power was a stark reality. The White minority, who were the economic backbone of the territory, feared they would be eclipsed in the event of the introduction of universal suffrage, and that they would have no space in parliament to defend their interests. Both the Swazi monarchy and the Whites were uncomfortable with the idea of elections organized on basis of one-man-one-vote.[58] The British introduction of universal adult suffrage was further compounded by the fact that British colonial policy in the post-war era clearly envisaged the transfer of power to the educated elite at the expense of traditional rulers. The battle line between the SNC–EAC alliance and the Progressives was drawn without any sign of surrender by one camp to the other.

The disagreements between the SNC–EAC and the Progressive camp were so intense that the Constitutional Committee initially concealed them from the public, and the media was mute about the deliberations. The silence on the constitutional talks caused Swaziland's Student Union to complain about the fact that all the deliberations, which concerned the entire Swazi nation, were conducted behind closed doors, and that the only information they could get was that there was an agreement to terminate racial discrimination.[59] The students were not happy being kept in the dark and began agitating to have information about the constitutional talks.

In February 1961, there were public discussions that Sobhuza's SNC and Todd's EAC had proposed to accord numerical equality to Whites and Swazis on the Legislative Council, and to endorse the traditional method of selecting indigenous Swazi legislators by royal appointment and not

[58]'Ngwenyama warns Swazi Nation Politics Can Lead Us to Hardship', *Times of Swaziland*, November 4, 1960.

[59]'All Quiet on Constitutional Front: A Widening Gulf?' *Times of Swaziland*, January 26, 1962.

3 THE BEGINNING OF THE GREAT CONSTITUTIONAL DEBATE ... 95

by election on the basis of universal suffrage. Todd supported the Swazi traditional system of voting, ostensibly on grounds that Swazi culture and tradition, and the monarchy, should not be destroyed by those he perceived to be 'radical' nationalists. The Progressives under Nquku protested vehemently against the proposal to accord equal representation to Whites and Blacks in the legislature, and to have different voting systems for the two races. They stood for universal suffrage and a non-racial electoral system as the best system for Swaziland. The SNC denounced the Progressives for disrespecting the Swazi king by contesting his constitutional proposal.[60]

Since the SNC had appointed Nquku, the leader of the Progressives, to the Constitutional Committee on its ticket, it quickly suspended him for being undisciplined by not adhering to the SNC constitutional standpoint. Other Progressive elements in the Constitutional Committee were unhappy with Nquku's suspension for having opposing views to those of the monarch. Consequently, in June 1961, Dr Zwane, the Secretary General of the SPP, and Mabuza decided to resign from the Constitutional Committee.[61] Dr Zwane explained that the position of the Progressive members on the Constitutional Committee was untenable. In his resignation and protest letter, addressed to the Resident Commissioner, Dr Zwane stated that the Progressive members in the Committee were expected to surrender their convictions on constitutional matters in deference to opinions put forward by the conservative traditionalists. He stated that, if they failed to speak out, they would have given the public the impression that the SPP had a hand in shaping the new constitution for Swaziland when, in fact, it was the handiwork of the monarch. Dr Zwane stated:

If we are to be discouraged from speaking out, as in Mr. Nquku's case, we will be false to our convictions while giving the public the misleading impression that the Swaziland Progressive Party is having a hand in the shaping of the new constitution when, in fact, the position is quite different.[62]

The Progressives resigned from the Committee, leaving behind the SNC and the EAC. Since the Progressives were on the Constitutional Committee as members of Sobhuza's SNC, they now formally made a request to the

[60] FCO 141/17380, 17385–17387: Constitutional Reforms 1959–63.

[61] Swaziland Progressive Party, 'Swaziland Report on Constitutional Reform', Cape Town, 1961.

[62] Cited in H. Kuper, *Sobhuza II: Ngwenyama and King of Swaziland*, 339.

96 H. P. DLAMINI

Resident Commissioner to be readmitted in their own right as the SPP members, but this was refused.[63] The Progressives were in the committee on the ticket of the SNC, and the Council was acting within the ambit of the law to expel a recalcitrant member. The exit of the Progressives from the Constitutional Committee did not mean they had abandoned their participation in the formulation of Swaziland's future constitution.

THE PROGRESSIVES GO ON THE OFFENSIVE

The Progressives decided to hire the services of Professor D. V. Cowen, an expert in Comparative Law at Cape Town University, to assist them in articulating their constitutional viewpoints, which they packaged for the attention of the British Colonial Office for consideration and necessary action. With the assistance of Professor Cowen, the Progressives articulated their constitutional positions in clear terms. They upheld the idea of a Swazi Legislative Council but argued that it should be established through universal adult suffrage, and that there should be a provision for a common voters roll, including African Swazis, White Swazis, and Coloureds. They advocated, among other things:

i. the establishment of a non-racial, as opposed to a multiracial, Swaziland in the political, economic, and social spheres, and the elimination of all legislation that enforced racial discrimination in Swaziland;
ii. the constitutional entrenchment of a court-enforced Bill of Human Rights, including full freedom of association, particularly with regard to political organizations;
iii. the peaceful integration of the traditional Swazi monarchical institution into the modern democratic structures of government;
iv. the recognition of Swaziland as a Protected State, and the establishment of the Swazi monarch's position as a Head of State, with a similar status to that of the Sultan of Zanzibar, which was merely ceremonial;
v. the establishment of a responsible government; and
vi. the establishment of a democratic form of government, especially in the main townships in Swaziland.[64]

[63] Ibid.
[64] Ibid.

3 THE BEGINNING OF THE GREAT CONSTITUTIONAL DEBATE … 97

In essence, the Progressives drafted a petition that called for the establishment of a Legislative Council on the basis of a common voters roll and universal adult suffrage. The SPP requested the abolition of racism in all spheres of life in Swaziland. There were a large number of racially discriminatory laws, some of which dated back to when Swaziland was subjected to the jurisdiction of the Transvaal Republic in the nineteenth century. The SPP asked for an entrenched clause in the constitution on the Bill of Rights, including full freedom of political association,[65] an issue to which the conservative Swazi monarch, with the support of the EAC, was reluctant to agree. It asked for the integration of the traditional monarchy into the modern democratic structures of government similar to that of the UK—a request Sobhuza was against, for he preferred the monarchy to be at the apex of the political system.

The SPP requested that the urban agglomerations in Swaziland should be run by democratically elected local governments. Furthermore, Swaziland was to be recognized as a Protected State and the position of the traditional monarch, referred to in the sources as Paramount Chief, was to be a Head of State in the form of a constitutional monarch. In essence, the Progressives drafted a petition based on the advice of Professor Cowen and forwarded it to the Colonial Office in London.[66]

The issue of Swaziland's status as a protectorate arose from the erroneous argument that Swaziland had long been independent and was recognized in the succession of European Conventions in the 1880s, later being taken over by Britain as a protected territory and not a colony.[67] Sobhuza then argued that the territory should be handed over to him and not to a political party, and was opposed to the attempt of the Progressives to neutralize his powers in any way. Since, historically, Swazi kings were effective rulers, and

---

[65] See SNA, File 3311/1 Newsletter: Swaziland Democratic Party, No. 5, Vol. 1, 5 October 1962, Mbabane.

[66] Ibid.

[67] There is this confusion over the terminology "Protectorate" in history because of its theoretical and practical dimension. In theory, a protectorate territory is one which the protecting power undertook to defend from external aggression without the responsibility for internal administration and was not supposed to be a colony. Professor C. Fombad points out that in Africa the term, protectorate was almost irrelevant because protectorates were treated exactly the same way as a colonies, if not worst (see C. Fombad, 'Botswana Introductory Notes: Origins and Historical Development of the Constitution', University of Pretoria. www.icla. up.ac.za/images/country_reports/botswana. Accessed August 5, 2018).

98   H. P. DLAMINI

not figureheads, Sobhuza found it difficult to accept the stance of the SPP to render him a ceremonial Head of State.

The Progressives also engaged in an international offensive as a way of keeping their agenda alive and courting international sympathy. J. J. Nquku and Dr Zwane travelled abroad to solicit support for their Progressive agenda and the condemnation of the Swazi monarch as a retrogressive colonial lackey.[68] In May 1961, Nquku testified before the Committee on Non-Self-Governing territories of the UN about the political situation in Swaziland being manipulated by imperial forces through traditional chiefs and White settlers. At the end of May 1962, both Nquku and Zwane left for the All African People's Conference in Accra, Ghana, which was chaired by Kwame Nkrumah, the radical pan-Africanist.[69] Thereafter, both leaders visited the Soviet Union, the anti-imperialist champion.[70]

In October 1962, Nquku flew to New York to petition the UN to intervene in the constitutional stalemate in Swaziland. Again, in January 1963, Nquku returned to the UN in New York to protest the composition of the Constitutional Committee, which had excluded Progressive forces in favour of the conservatives and South African White immigrants. At the meeting of the UN Fourth Committee, which dealt with the problems of non-self-governing territories, including Swaziland, Nquku made an urgent appeal to the UN to intervene in Swaziland and establish an effective UN presence there. He told the Committee that the future of Swaziland depended on the rapid implementation by the UN General Assembly of the declaration on the granting of independence to colonial countries and peoples, and of those UN resolutions aimed at eliminating aggression in all its forms. He explained that the gravity of the situation in Swaziland was due to the failure of the United Kingdom to live up to its obligation under the UN Charter. Nquku claimed to be speaking as a leader of the Progressive Party on behalf of the Swazi people, and drew a distinction between the Swazi people and

---

[68]C. A. Johnson, 'Conferences of Independent African States', *International Organization*, 16, 2 (1962), 426–429; R. P. Stevens, 'Swaziland Political Development', *The Journal of Modern African Studies*, 1, 3 (1963), 327–350; M. Grilli, 'Nkrumah, Nationalism, and Pan-Africanism: The Bureau of African Affairs Collection', *History in Africa*, 44 (2017), 295–307; and Matteo Grilli, 'Nkrumah's Ghana and the Armed Struggle in Southern Africa (1961–1966)', *South African Historical Journal*, 70, 1 (2018), 56–81.

[69]Johnson, 'Conferences of Independent African States', 426–429; Stevens, 'Swaziland Political Development', 338.

[70]Ibid.

3 THE BEGINNING OF THE GREAT CONSTITUTIONAL DEBATE ... 99

the Swazi nation. To him, the Swazi nation was ruled by chiefs and civil servants who were simply puppets at the beck and call of imperialists and White settlers.

The real leaders of Swaziland were the Progressives, who spoke freely on behalf of all the inhabitants of the territory, regardless of race, colour, or creed, and who pursued the interests and wellbeing of all its inhabitants. The political development of Swaziland was being stalled by the British and White settlers, who sought only to promote their interests. He accused the British government and White settlers of denigrating Swazis as inexperienced, immature, and unfit to take over the administration of their country. He stated that Sobhuza's SNC was led by the puppets of the White settlers, interested only in increasing their own rights and privileges, with the connivance of the British. Lastly, he complained about the eviction of Africans from their lands and the influx of White settlers from South Africa into Swaziland to further marginalize the Swazi people. Thus, outside the Constitutional Committee, the Progressives remained a powerful political force to be reckoned with. Their international credentials added weight to their relevance in Swazi politics.

THE DISCONTENTED COLOURED COMMUNITY JOIN THE PROTEST AGAINST THE CONSTITUTIONAL COMMITTEE

The Coloured community were also unhappy with the Constitutional Committee because of their total exclusion. The Euro-African Welfare Association, which represented the Coloured community in Swaziland, pointed out that they were Swazis and obligatorily had a say in the constitutional future of the territory. They also hired the services of Professor D. V. Cowen of the University of Cape Town, who had been consulted by the Progressives to make a case for them about their representation on and contribution to the Constitutional Committee. The Coloured community emphasized the fact that they were a substantial minority group who were in danger of being eclipsed and forgotten. They paid taxes like Swaziland's Whites, but they were not given any political representation on the Constitutional Committee. They were legally excluded from the SNC and were not regarded as part of the country's political structure. They did not have any financial support for their school-aged children. They regretted the fact that they were not given representation on the Constitutional Committee, despite the fact that they had a contribution to make and the laws of Swaziland recognized their special status as a separate group.

100   H. P. DLAMINI

In giving evidence to the Constitutional Committee on request, the Coloured people asked for special provision to be made for them. They feared they would be bundled together on a common roll with Whites, who largely outnumbered them. They felt they were a group only by rejection, exclusion, and legal definition. Because of this, they did not wish to perpetuate group or racial distinction of any type in Swaziland; they favoured the eradication of discriminatory laws that treated them as a separate group. The Coloureds therefore clamoured for the introduction of a common voters' roll on a wide suffrage, which would include Swazis as well as Whites and Coloureds.[71] What they were advocating for was exactly what Sobhuza was opposed to, for he did not want a common voters' roll. The Coloureds were craving recognition within a wider Swaziland nation in which there would be no discrimination on the basis of ethnicity or race. The protests of the Coloureds pointed to the fact that the British colonial administration had made a grievous omission in its composition of the Constitutional Committee. The inclusion of the Coloureds on the committee could possibly have strengthened the Progressives' opposition to the conservative royalists.

Constitutional Committee Delegation to London to Present Preliminary Report

A delegation of the Constitutional Committee of the SNC–EAC and members of the British colonial administration in Swaziland left for London in December 1961 to present the preliminary report of the Constitutional Committee's proposal to the Colonial Secretary of State. The SNC–EAC delegation comprised M. Dlamini, A. K. Hlophe, C. F. Todd, and D. Fitzpatrick. The Resident British High Commissioner in Swaziland, Brian Marwick, travelled separately, taking with him confidential reservations about the SNC–EAC constitutional proposals.[72]

The preliminary SNC–EAC report indicated that there was unanimity over its contents by its signatories. But the report of the Resident British High Commissioner, who was the Chairman and the Government official on the Committee, indicated that they had serious reservations on certain

[71] Ibid.

[72] FCO 141/17380, 17385–17387: Constitutional Reforms 1959–63; 'Points of View on Constitutional Reforms: Mr Todd Replies', *Times of Swaziland*, February 2, 1962.

3 THE BEGINNING OF THE GREAT CONSTITUTIONAL DEBATE ... 101

aspects of the SNC–EAC report, with particular reference to the composition and powers of the Legislative Council. The SNC–EAC report recommended an Executive and a Legislative Council for Swaziland. The Executive Council was to consist of the Governor, three ex-officio members, one official, and four nominated members, with an additional four unofficial members (two Swazis and two Europeans). The Legislative Council was to consist of equal numbers of Swazis (chosen by the traditional method of acclamation) and European members (elected by Western voting methods). This meant that Swazis and Whites were to be equally represented despite the disparity in the population of the two communities: 270,000 Swazis as opposed to only 10,000 Whites. The special place of the Swazi monarch in the constitution was to be recognized, giving him rights to withhold his consent to bills, which would be reserved for the Queen of England's pleasure. In matters affecting Swazi law and custom, Swazi land and minerals, and Swazi institutions, were to be excluded from the purview of the Legislative Council and left exclusively to the *Ngwenyama*'s discretion.

Finally, a Bill of Rights was included to protect personal liberties, such as freedom of expression and assembly, but also to prevent any major change in the socio-political framework, by pledging to maintain the position of the monarch and the property rights of racial groups, and specifically excluding constitutional reforms that would conflict with these principles.[73] The SNC–EAC took time to qualify the 'freedom of expression and assembly', with the clear intention of preventing the formation of political parties by Swazis outside the SNC and beyond the control of the Swazi monarch.

The British official members of the Constitutional Committee were not in total agreement with the SNC–EAC report. In a 'Note of Reservations', they pointed out to the Colonial Secretary that Sobhuza's idea of treating Blacks and Whites separately under the so-called racial federation was 'inimical to the achievement of the ultimate objective of a non-racial state' envisaged by the British. The preferred goal of the British was the achievement of a democratic, non-racial, stable form of government provided with checks and balances to safeguard all civil liberties. To achieve this, they considered it necessary to build one nation according to Western political procedures. Brian Marwick relied heavily on the advice of senior officials in the service who had worked on the British model of constitution-making in other African territories. Marwick pointed out that the British were anxious

[73] Ibid.

102   H. P. DLAMINI

to recast what has been described as the feudal Swazi society and transform its monarch into a modern constitutional king.

The Resident Commissioner and official members of the British colonial administration in Swaziland felt that the proposal in the report, that Europeans and Swazis should have equal representation in the legislature, was an arrangement that was difficult to justify and that it was time for the Europeans to give up such ridiculous claims of equality with Blacks, which did not tally with their tiny population in the territory. They warned that such a provision for a 50% representation for the White minority in the legislature would be wrested from Whites as soon as Swaziland became independent. The argument being advanced by King Sobhuza II and the Whites, that potential investment in the territory depended on a 50–50 arrangement, was described as 'illusionary and ridiculous', and was outweighed by the advantage of recognizing the true position of the European minority.[74] Marwick later wrote to Hilda Kuper, the British anthropologist in Swaziland, that the acceptance of the idea of a racial federation and a 50–50 principle would be tantamount to an unforgivable betrayal of Her Majesty's government responsibilities as the protecting power, and would compound the processes of attempting to satisfy Swazi grievances over the land issue caused by the expropriation of Swazi land by Whites and the erosion of Swazi institutions in the future. Marwick felt that the 50–50 principle would not favour indigenous Swazis and would, further, imperil the objective of ensuring that Swazi interests eventually predominated.[75] This important point may not have been evident to Sobhuza, who was according equal legislative weight to Whites who were responsible for the Swazis' land hunger. Sobhuza was giving Whites legislative instruments to obstruct the implementation of any land reforms in the long run, which would disfavour Whites to the benefit of the Swazis.

The British officials also had reservations about the exclusion of modern political organizations, which were an integral part of the modernization agenda in the SNC–EAC report. Sir Brian Marwick revealed that he was at pains to convince Sobhuza that, in the modern world, it was impossible to prevent people from forming political organizations according to their own persuasion. He had told Sobhuza that, if he wanted to participate in Swazi politics, he could use his supporters to form a political party, because

[74]SNA, DPMO 12, A.G. 100/316/56, July 26, 1979.

[75]Kuper, *Sobhuza II: Ngwenyama and King of Swaziland*, 216–217.

3 THE BEGINNING OF THE GREAT CONSTITUTIONAL DEBATE ... 103

it was the only instrument that could be used to enter modern politics and acquire political power.[76] The Secretary of State for the Colonies could, therefore, not agree with the constitutional proposals of the SNC–EAC alliance, which was, evidently, a bad document.

The official members conceded to the constitutional stand-off between the SNC–EAC alliance and Progressives by proposing a middle-of-the-road solution that would combine the nominations method and universal adult suffrage method. In accordance with this proposal, some would be nominated, while others would be elected through secret ballot. Under this British scheme, eight Swazi members were to be nominated by the *Ngwenyama*, eight Europeans were to stand for elections on a European roll, four officials (with voting powers) were to be nominated, and 12 members (eight Swazis and four Europeans) were to be elected on a common roll with qualified franchise. The British official members objected to the SNC–EAC proposal, that certain spheres such as Swazi traditional law and custom, Swazi traditional institutions, and Swazi land and minerals should be excluded from legislative control. The British were of the opinion that the legislature should have a complete say in these matters because it was made up of the people's elected representatives.[77]

The remarks of the British official members from Swaziland were taken seriously by the British Secretary of State for the Colonies. He commented elaborately on them in the form of a letter to the British High Commission in Swaziland, which was published together with the report of the Constitutional Committee in March 1962. The British Secretary of State rejected the recommendation of the SNC–EAC that the British official members of the Council in Swaziland should have no vote. While recognizing that certain matters should be reserved for the *Ngwenyama*-in-Council, he expressed serious concerns that too great a reservation had been made of interests vital to the whole country that should have come under the scrutiny of the legislature. He warned that a very powerful monarchical system that privileged the monarchy over other institutions of state was dangerous, and was a clear path to unbridled dictatorship.

The Secretary of State did not agree with the SNC–EAC's proposal that the legislature should be prevented from passing 'laws that might affect

---

[76] Ibid.

[77] SNA, Constitutional Proposals Comments of the Public 1962. This file is rich in the reactions of the public to the constitutional proposals.

104   H. P. DLAMINI

Swazi law and custom or from general legislation in respect of land and minerals.' He insisted that the legislature, and not the monarch, should have the final say in the resources of the country. The Secretary of State pointed out that it was dangerous for the monarch to have monopoly over such matters, including Swazi land and minerals. This would cause the ordinary Swazi to regard the Legislative Council as worthless and as something of very little interest to him. The Secretary of State was of the opinion that the Swazi people, through the legislature, should have the final say in a wide array of matters concerning them.

The issue of the franchise was also addressed. The Secretary of State felt that the educated class constituted an important element in Swazi society that could not be ignored. Consequently, he declared that a common roll, or something along those lines, would undoubtedly be required to cater for the educated non-tribal elements in Swazi society. The British officials were critical of the way the Progressives were treated, and considered it 'unrealistic and wrong' to force them to comply with the traditional monarchical system that hindered their right to participate in the modern democratic process in the legislature. They felt the Progressives should be the beneficiaries of the new political dispensation the British were trying to construct for Swazis, because they represented the modernizing forces of British colonial rule.[78]

The SNC–EAC report on the constitutional proposals, together with the reservations expressed by the British officials and the comments of the Colonial Office, were sent back to Swaziland with instructions that the general public should be invited to have input.[79] The Secretary of State indicated that he would await the reactions, both to the constitutional proposals and his comments, before taking a final decision. This was because the constitution being designed was for the Swazi people, and the British wanted them to take ownership of it.[80] By sending the report back to Swaziland and inviting the public to comment on it, the British were indirectly indicating that they were not satisfied with the SNC–EAC constitutional proposal. What this reflects is that the British colonial administration had

---

[78] SNA, Constitutional Proposals Comments of the Public 1962. This file is rich in the reactions of the public to the constitutional proposals; Kuper, *Sobhuza II: Ngwenyama and King of Swaziland*, 225.

[79] SNA, Constitutional Proposals Written Comments of the Public 1962. This file is rich in the reactions of the public to the constitutional proposals.

[80] Ibid.

found loopholes in the Constitutional report that needed to be addressed. The SNC and EAC were unhappy with the criticisms of the Colonial Office and local British administration in Swaziland. Inviting the public to comment on the report was another way of inviting the Progressives and their allies—especially the intelligentsia, liberals, and the churches—to start a virulent debate on the future constitution of Swaziland. The field was therefore open to the key players to sell and defend their constitutional standpoints to the populace (Fig 3.1).

Fig. 3.1 Swazi Delegates at the London Constitutional Conference, 28 January–12 February 1963. Names of delegates from left to right: J. M. B. Sukati, M. P. Nhlabasti; S. T. M. Sukati; P. L. Dlamini, A. K. Hlophe (*Source* ZUMA Press, Inc./Alamy Stock Photo)

The Involvement of the Swazi Public in the Constitutional Debates

The Colonial Office instructions, that the public should be given the opportunity to comment on the public involvement in the debate on the SNC–EAC constitutional proposals, took two forms. First, written comments were made that were sent to the British colonial administration for perusal and necessary action. Second, the media[81]—particularly, *The Times of Swaziland* newspaper—was used to air the viewpoints. When a meeting was convened two days after the release of the report on the proposed constitution, it broke up in chaos.[82] Civil society, acting as a united front for Christian Churches, political parties and academics, and trade unions, protested against the racial basis of the proposed constitution.

Public opinion gauged from newspaper reports[83] pointed to the fact that the 50–50 political formula that was intended to give the country's minority Whites an equal voice with the Black majority in the Legislative Council was ridiculous, and would be difficult for Britain to endorse because it was far off the mark of democratic principles. This 50–50 proposal was viewed by a growing number of politically conscious Swazis, Progressives, and White liberals as nothing more than a device to perpetuate the privileges of the White business class, who were essentially South African immigrants. This arrangement allowed Whites to exist as a separate community from Blacks, and this state of affairs hindered racial integration.[84]

A group of White Liberals under Vincent Rozwadowski, a Polish immigrant from Poland who had relocated from South Africa to Swaziland,[85] supported the programme of the Swazi Progressives, which considered radical by the monarch and the EAC. Rozwadowski argued that a more egalitarian society was more relevant to Swaziland than one constructed to

---

[81] Public opinion was gauged from letters and opinions expressed in the *Times of Swaziland* and in a file which contains written comments from various individuals from various works of life in society.

[82] FCO 141/17380, 17385–17387: Constitutional Reforms 1959–63; SNA, Constitutional Proposals Written Comments of the Public 1962.

[83] See *Times of Swaziland* in the first half of 1962 in particular and also SNA, Constitutional Proposals Written Comments of the Public 1962.

[84] SNA, Constitutional Proposals Written Comments of the Public 1962.

[85] Rozwadowski moved to Swaziland because of racism in South Africa.

3 THE BEGINNING OF THE GREAT CONSTITUTIONAL DEBATE ... 107

protect White privileges. They criticized the SNC–EAC constitutional proposal because of the racial division it contained, which strongly resembled apartheid. The proposal was far from being democratic and was backward-looking in every sense of the word. The Swazi intelligentsia were very critical of the constitutional proposals, and felt that the interests of the Swazi population were being sacrificed in favour of Whites and their royal allies. The Swaziland Student Union at St Christopher's High School attacked the Bill of Rights that the Constitutional Committee proposed should be incorporated in the constitution. They also attacked the 50–50 representation proposal for Swazis and Europeans, and the traditional way Swazis should be selected to the Legislative Council. They protested that the constitutional proposals did not fit in with the ideal of a non-racial Swazi state.[86]

The Catholic Church, through the voice of Father P. Burtwell, protested against the exclusion of the educated elite in these terms:

> I must resist any constitutional proposals that give representation to Europeans and to the tribal Swazis while ignoring the small [independent-minded] educated African class which has separated itself from tribal ways. To ignore these men is an offence against every man's God-given duty, to spend his life here on earth using God's gift fully to the Glory of God....[87]

Dr D. Hynd, a missionary and a medical doctor who represented special interest groups in Swaziland, disapproved the 50–50 representation in the SNC–EAC constitutional proposal. He argued that the both the SNC and the EAC represented an oligarchy. Whites representatives reflected only about 3% of the population in Swaziland, and it was unfair for them to claim a 50% representation in the legislature. On the other hand, the Swazi representatives were a royal oligarchy. With regard to the position of the *Ngwenyama*, Dr Hynd suggested that the monarch should assume the position of a constitutional ruler, and be much in the same relationship to the Legislative Council as the Queen of England was to the Parliament of the United Kingdom.

Swazi students under the canopy of the Swaziland's Student Union rejected 'unreservedly and unconditionally both the work of the Constitutional Committee and the Committee itself'. The students pointed out

---

[86]'The Nwenyama Denies Making 50–50 Offer', *Times of Swaziland*, June 22, 1962.

[87]'Priest Replies', *Times of Swaziland*, March 16, 1962.

108   H. P. DLAMINI

that the SNC–EAC alliance, in effect, produced a document that protected White and monarchical interests at the expense of those of the Swazi people. *The Guardian* commented on this as follows:

> A constitutional committee of local worthies, black and White, has put forward proposals for a timid advance towards communally elected legislative council which would entrench all the conservative characteristics of the [Swazi] Paramount Chief [*Ngwenyama*'s] regime.[88]

The criticisms were met with a vigorous riposte from the White settlers and multinational businesses though their spokesperson, Carl Todd. He came out publicly to defend the Swazi monarch by presenting the *Ngwenyama* as the only authority to make statements on behalf of Swazis. He derided public criticisms of the SNC–EAC constitutional proposal, and admonished British political theorists for trying to impose on Swazis what they did not desire, because they had no right to do so. He wrote:

> I am personally influenced by my thinking on the constitutional proposals to give great weight to the wishes of the Ingwenyama-in-council [sic], as it is the only truly established Swazi authority which has constitutional rights visa-a-vis the Europeans and the British government in the protectorate state of Swaziland. We have no right to force upon them our views but must carry them with us by argument and agreement. As a traditionalist I support orderly development in political affairs and would prefer the safe course of carrying the bulk of people with me than introducing innovations that may have support from a minority of theorists. We wish to have a constitution in Swaziland of our own choosing and not one forced upon us by political theorists ... Advanced political theorists applied to Africans and exploited by demagogues have proved disastrous elsewhere in Africa ... Europeans should cooperate with Ingwenyama-in-council to maintain a traditional system to which the Swazis are accustomed and to uphold their institutions as being a stabilizing force in the political and economic development of the territory and we should collaborate with them in perfecting the system in order to ensure that it is equal to the needs of a developing society rather than destroy it.[89]

---

[88] *The Guardian* (Manchester), March 7, 1962.

[89] 'Points of View on Constitutional Reform: Mr Todd's Reply', *Times of Swaziland*, February 2, 1962.

3 THE BEGINNING OF THE GREAT CONSTITUTIONAL DEBATE ... 109

Basically, Carl Todd challenged the British colonial administration as much as he struggled to defend the Swazi traditional political status quo and claimed to be a 'traditionalist'. To him, those propagating democracy in Swaziland were demagogues and theorists, and their propaganda was irrelevant to the Swazi situation. He underscored his unalloyed support to King Sobhuza and the SNC–EAC constitutional proposal. Todd accused the colonial state, White liberals, and Progressives of being 'anti-settler.'[90]

Carl Todd argued that the SNC–EAC constitutional proposals were not far-fetched and actually reflected the will of the Swazi people. In order to demonstrate European support for it, Todd decided unilaterally to organize a referendum among over half the European voting community (1368 persons were on the voters' roll), which was neither authorized by or binding on the British colonial government. Registered voters were asked to respond to the following question: 'Are you in favour or against the proposals for the constitution for Swaziland as recommended by the European Advisory Council?' A cross had to be placed in a square that recorded the decision of the voter and the paper had to be signed. Voters were urged to vote in favour of the committee's proposals. The results of the referendum were as documented in Table 3.2.

As anticipated, an overwhelming majority of Whites endorsed the proposals. This did not come as a surprise, given the fact that the proposals were designed to protect the dominance of Whites in the politics and economy of colonial Swaziland. It was only logical that Whites should support such a constitution, which upheld their interests and marginalized the overwhelming majority of the Swazi people whose survival was suffering from land scarcity. The referendum was, therefore, meaningless because the Swazi people who were the victims of the colonial order, and who suffered multiple deprivations because of that order, were not consulted. Carl Todd's referendum was, thus, a farce.

Todd stated that a Bill of Rights protected the Europeans who were committed to a duly established authority of the *Ngwenyama*, and that it was not binding on White liberals or any political party that was opposed to it. Todd indicated that the *Ngwenyama*-in-Council had offered Europeans equal partnership for the overall wellbeing of the territory and was opposed to the Westminster form of franchise, which he feared was going to destroy

[90] Ibid.

110   H. P. DLAMINI

Table 3.2   Results of the EAC's referendum on the Constitutional Committee's proposals for a Constitution for Swaziland.

Constituency	Number of registered voters	Number of votes cast	In favour of the Committee's recommendation	Against Committee's recommendation	Percentage poll
Pigg's Peak	134	66	66	Nil	49.10
Mbabane	316	156	145	11	49.36
Mankayane-Usutu	103	39	39	Nil	37.80
Manzini District	119	63	58	5	52.90
Manzini Urban	171	88	88	Nil	51.46
Stegi	116	66	63	3	56.90
Hlatikulu	60	39	39	Nil	65.00
Goedgegun-Dwaleni	194	121	121	Nil	62.23
Mhlotsheni-Mooihoek	52	14	14	Nil	26.90
Hluti-Gollel	103	64	64	Nil	62.20
Totals	1363	716	697	1952.23	

Source 'Constitution Referendum: 697 for and 19 Against 52.3 Per cent Roll', *Times of Swaziland*, May 18, 1962

the Swazi Traditional Council and its authority, as had happened elsewhere in Africa.

Todd warned that the future of the White minority would be in jeopardy if they endorsed the type of constitution the Progressives and White liberals were demanding. He stated that government officials were also supporting the stance of the Progressives blindly, without taking White interests into consideration. Todd declared that he would prefer to rely on agreements with the SNC and the provision for equal representation in the legislature, than rely on the British government and its officials who could not protect European interests against radical politicians who did not respect the rights of Whites and the true interests of Swaziland. Todd warned that the promising economic future of Swaziland would be jeopardized if Europeans were marginalized in the legislature. He referred to the importance of Whites in the economies of Kenya and Rhodesia, and argued that it

3 THE BEGINNING OF THE GREAT CONSTITUTIONAL DEBATE ... 111

would be vital for Swaziland to retain the confidence of foreign investors, especially Europeans.

Todd indicated that Whites needed to support and strengthen the position of the *Ngwenyama*, who saw the wisdom of rejecting the European franchise system, which was suitable for only Europe. For this reason, he was full of praises for the *Ngwenyama* when he stated:

> *Ngwenyama* is such a wise friend of the Europeans that we [the EAC] should support and strengthen his position and not undermine it, and it is politically wise to collaborate with the friends we know and trust than to try out experiments with politicians who are responsible to no one. We can move to a more advanced stage of political thinking after we have worked together in the new legislature, but it is unwise in the present stage of Swazi development to jump into a European franchise system from which you cannot withdraw once it is established.[91]

Todd concluded by calling on the public to support the SNC–EAC constitutional proposal and to resist being influenced by 'political agitators'—a term he used to describe the Progressives. He assured Europeans that the constitution would protect their stakes in the territory.[92]

Sobhuza also struggled to campaign for the acceptance of the 50–50 principle among Swazis to no avail. In February 1962, he convened a popular meeting of Swazi men at Lobamba and addressed them on the Committee's proposals: they overwhelmingly rejected the proposal. The Swazi youths were so rude that Sobhuza could hardly believe it, since they had the habit of being respectful towards royalty.[93] The Swazi National Council decided to hold another meeting in April but it broke up in confusion as the Progressives and the monarchists clashed on almost every point, particularly over the issue of equality between Whites and Swazis in the envisaged legislature.

The anti-50–50 sentiments were so pervasive that King Sobhuza started flip-flopping over the issue. When the King convened the *Sibaya* for June 1962 he denied that he had offered 50–50 Swazi–European representation on the Legislative Council in the Constitutional Committee Report

---

[91] 'Todd's Thoughts on Constitutional Proposals', *The Times of Swaziland*, March 23, 1962.

[92] Ibid.

[93] Zwane, 'The Struggle for Power in Swaziland', 2–5.

112   H. P. DLAMINI

and during a speech he made at Masundwini in April 1960. Rather, he emphasized equality between Blacks and Whites as imperative.[94]

Members of Sobhuza's SNC endeavoured to meet with the Swaziland Student Union at St Christopher's High School on 30 June 1962 to diffuse the tension arising from the SNC–EAC constitutional proposal. While addressing the student body, the delegation reiterated that the *Ngwenyama* did not say at his speech at Masundwini in April 1960 that the Swazis and the Europeans should have 50–50 representation on the proposed Legislative Council. They explained that what the *Ngwenyama* meant was that Europeans and Swazis should meet on an equal basis.[95]

Sobhuza convened another meeting at a local *inkhundla* (meeting place) at Mbabane at which the crowd was hostile to the 50–50 idea even before it had been raised. On 3 July 1962, he called another meeting of all adult Swazis at Lobamba to discuss the constitutional proposal. Swazis turned out in large numbers and this seems to have had an intimidating effect. The King and the SNC addressed the people on several issues, avoiding touching on the constitutional proposal because they were suspicious of the reaction of the crowd, who had come under the sway of the Progressives. The monarch preferred to interrogate the leaders of the Progressives privately, who were summoned to appear before the executive council of the SNC: the *liqoqo*. The Progressive leaders refused to budge from their objection to the 50–50 constitutional proposal. King Sobhuza resorted to threats and denounced all those who embraced the ideas of political parties, which he had denounced as 'unSwazi'. Several similar meetings continued in August without achieving anything, until people soon got tired and stopped attending the meetings.[96] The Swazi population was clearly not in favour of the constitutional proposal, which favoured the White minority outright by giving them representation equal to that of the Swazi majority. The 50–50 issue united the Swazis against their king.

[94]'The Ngwenyama Denies Making 50–50 Offer', *Times of Swaziland*, June 22, 1962.

[95]'The Ngwenyama Denies Making 50–50 Offer', *Times of Swaziland*, June 22, 1962.

[96]Kuper, *Sobhuza II: Ngernyama and King of Swaziland*; FCO 141/17472, 17670: Constitutional Proposals; Land Issues; Africanisation of the Civil Service; FCO 141/17380, 17385–17387: Constitutional Reforms 1959–63.

The Looming Prospects of an Imposed Constitution

Among the SNC–EAC alliance, there was the fear that the British colonial administration could end up imposing a constitution on Swaziland, if no negotiated solution could be found. In a letter published on 1 June 1962 in the influential *The Times of Swaziland*, a mouthpiece of the White community in Swaziland, the editor of the paper attempted to avert such a likelihood by suggesting that round table talks should be held with the various dissenting parties so as to arrive at a compromise before the British government stepped in, a *deus ex machina*, to impose a constitution on Swaziland.[97] The editor of *The Times of Swaziland* was directly targeting Todd, the influential chairman of the EAC, who was a hardliner and a close ally of the Swazi monarch. Todd was not in favour of the idea of a round table conference in Swaziland before the London conference with British officials because the outcome was a foregone conclusion, given the public outcry against the SNC–EAC constitutional proposal. He believed that all differences between the parties and with the British government would be resolved when the delegates went London. He explained that the Swazis were still to communicate their position on the SNC–EAC constitutional report to the *Ngwenyama* and that he did not see any use for a constitutional conference, which the Resident British High Commissioner would have to chair. Todd did not believe such a conference would produce any better results than the existing SNC–EAC constitutional proposals. He recognized the fact that the five British official members of the Constitutional Committee were totally at loggerheads with the EAC because they were against-White settlers, but he insisted that their dissenting views were not binding on the British government's position on the matter. While agreeing that delays at arriving at a consensus on a constitution were intolerable, Todd pointed out that they could not be avoided. Todd further pointed out that the delays in making progress with the constitutional talks were having a negative effect on the economy, and that one of the major contributions to economic stagnation was the threat contained in the dissenting views of the British officials that Europeans should be reduced to a minority in the legislature despite their economic weight in the territory. Todd pointed out that this factor would restrict European investment in the territory. The EAC was therefore not ready for any compromise on the issue of equal European representation in the envisaged Legislative Council, and

---

[97] 'Todd Replies to Times Leader', *The Times of Swaziland*, June 15, 1962.

114   H. P. DLAMINI

they had the full backing of the *Ngwenyama*-in-Council. Europeans had already expressed their opinion on the constitutional proposal that the committee drafted in a referendum.[98] The EAC was not ready to budge from its position, and neither was it ready for any round table conference.

Todd's argument that the dissenting views of the British official members may not necessarily be those of the British government appeared plausible at face value. However, a perusal of the despatch of the British Colonial Secretary containing his preliminary views on the proposed constitution shows that the Colonial Office was in total agreement with the position of the British official members in colonial Swaziland. The EAC deliberately ignored this fact. They were not ready to budge an inch on the 50–50 representation in the Legislative Council and negotiate with the Progressives, whom they consistently belittled and disregarded as senseless radicals.[99]

After the Swazi public had given their views on the SNC–EAC constitutional Project and the comments made on it by the British colonial administration, the British Secretary of State for the Colonies, B R. Maudling, proceeded to the next step. He appointed D. S. Stephens in July 1962 to undertake a thorough evaluation of public opinion about the constitutional project in Swaziland, taking into consideration their concerns and making concrete recommendations. Stephens was well-equipped for the job. He had been Crown Counsel in Nigeria from 1948, and was promoted to Senior Crown Counsel from 1952. In 1957, he was appointed Legal Secretary in Malta and served there until 1962.[100] Like the other officials of the British administration before him, Stephens advised that the proposed 50–50 White–Swazi representation in the Legislative Council, the whole idea of racial federation, and the exclusion of modern political organizations should not be considered. The 50–50 principle would not favour indigenous Swazis and would further imperil the objective of ensuring that Swazi interests eventually predominated. He supported the middle-of-the-road position that would embrace the views of all the political stakeholders by proposing that eight Swazi members should be nominated by the *Ngwenyama*, that there be eight Europeans on a European roll, four nominated officials (with voting powers), and 12 members (eight Swazis and

---

[98] Ibid.

[99] Ibid.

[100] 'Constitutional Adviser from UK Due in Swaziland This Week', *Times of Swaziland*, July 13, 1962.

3 THE BEGINNING OF THE GREAT CONSTITUTIONAL DEBATE ... 115

four Europeans) elected on a common roll with a qualified franchise. He also emphasized the supremacy of parliament in controlling the actions of the government. What Stephens recommended was a simply reiteration of Westminster parliamentary practices, with sovereignty belonging to the people and parliament being supreme in every facet of governance.[101]

The SNC–EAC alliance did not like the position of the British legal advisor and, in a funny twist of events, they issued a joint statement on 14 September 1962 stating that the 50–50 proposal was acceptable to an overwhelming majority of the people of Swaziland.[102] The joint statement also requested Her Majesty's government to promulgate the recommendations of the SNC–EAC constitutional proposals as the constitution of Swaziland as a matter of urgency, because it had been accepted by an overwhelming majority of the people of Swaziland.[103] Todd's referendum concerned Whites only and, as anticipated, the overwhelming majority voted in favour of the 50–50 constitutional proposal. Indigenous Swazis were overwhelmingly opposed to the draft constitution that favoured Whites, contrary to what Sobhuza was purporting—that was clear to the British colonial administration.

The British Colonial Secretary of State still nursed the hope of reaching an agreement among the various Swazi political protagonists by inviting them to London for a conference. On 8 December 1962, he issued an invitation to Whitehall in London to the various stakeholders for constitutional talks on the future of Swaziland. The announcement of the British Colonial Office that a constitutional conference for Swaziland would be held in London was welcomed by Progressives, in the belief that the constitutional deadlock created by the obstinacy of the SNC–EAC alliance would be unlocked. The Progressives saw the London conference as an opportunity to speak directly to the Colonial Office about their position on the constitution for Swaziland, which was close to that of the British.

The SNC–EAC alliance was sceptical of the London conference owing to the unpredictable attitude of British liberals and the prevailing anti-colonial mood in the UK. The British Liberal Party and liberals in general were in favour of a liberal democratic system tailored along Westminster

[101]FCO 141/17472, 17670: Constitutional Proposals; Land Issues; Africanisation of the Civil Service; FCO 141/17380, 17385–17387: Constitutional Reforms 1959–63.

[102]'50–50 Accepted by Swazis and Europeans: Joint Statement', *Times of Swaziland*, September 14, 1962.

[103]Ibid.

116   H. P. DLAMINI

lines, and that was precisely what the SNC–EAC alliance was against.[104] Nonetheless, they did not have much of a choice, because the directives came from the Colonial Office in Britain.

In preparation for the London conference, the Progressives decided to coordinate their tactics and approach. On the initiative of the Swazi Democratic Party leader, S. Nxumalo, the Progressives, including Dr Zwane and H. Y. Samketi, issued a four-point programme calling for the establishment of a non-racial democratic state, a sovereign and independent Swaziland, recognition of the *Ngwenyama* as a constitutional monarch, and universal adult suffrage. They protested vehemently against the inclusion of people holding dual citizenship in the EAC delegation and requested the government to give each party a minimum of four delegates.[105]

The persistent virulent criticism of the 50–50 position of the SNC–EAC alliance by the Progressives shook the unity of the royalist SNC camp, as some of them started wavering and withdrawing their support for it. Just barely a fortnight before the opening of the London constitutional talks on Swaziland, a trusted and leading figure of the Constitutional Committee, Dr Allen M. Nxumalo, withdrew his support for the 50–50 arrangement that placed Whites and Swazis at par in the legislature. Dr Nxumalo, who had come under the influence of the arguments of the Progressive political leaders, felt that such an arrangement was unfair to the Swazi population of 270,000 and favoured the Whites, who numbered barely 10,000. He charged that there was no sincere intention on the part of the Swazi monarch of allowing the Swazi people to have a frank and honest discussion on the constitutional document, and obtaining a real mandate from the people. He charged that the Swazi monarchical scheme of a federation of races was simply disguised apartheid in Swaziland.[106] Nxumalo's attacks on the SNC–EAC alliance were an embarrassment, and an indication that the propaganda of the Progressives was having an effect. Essentially, before the London constitutional talks on Swaziland, there were cracks within the ranks of the SNC group, as some members felt Sobhuza was not prepared

[104]Stevens, 'Swaziland Political Development', 348; FCO 141/17380, 17385–17387: Constitutional Reforms 1959–63.

[105]'Bid to get Dr. Zwane to London fails, Mr. Nquku to represent the Progressives', *Times of Swaziland*, January 18, 1963.

[106]'Political Alliance', *Times of Swaziland*, January 18, 1963.

3 THE BEGINNING OF THE GREAT CONSTITUTIONAL DEBATE ... 117

to listen to the voice of the Swazis. Nonetheless, the hope for a compromise of all Swazi nationalists was pinned on the London Constitutional Conference.

THE LONDON CONFERENCE ON SWAZILAND, 28 JANUARY–12 FEBRUARY 1963

The holding of a Constitutional Conference in London between the British Colonial Office and the Swazi nationalists was a typical aspect of the British decolonization process, as various African colonies participated in constitutional conferences in London as a prelude to independence.[107] The Government Secretary, A. Long, was responsible for selecting the delegates to the London Constitutional Conference. The British ensured that a wide spectrum of the stakeholders were invited, including the members of the SNC, EAC, the Progressives, the Euro-Africans, and special interest groups. After the delegates from colonial Swaziland were selected, the Secretary of State for the Colonies, Duncan Sandys, issued invitations to two delegates to represent the government, six representatives of the SNC, four representatives of the European Advisory Council, one representative of the SPP, one representative of the Swaziland Democratic Party, one representative of the Mbandzeni National Convention, and a representative of the Eurafrican community. Dr D. Hynd, a European missionary and long-term resident in Swaziland, was also invited. Table 3.3 gives a list of all the delegates present at the Church House Conference in London and their affiliation.

The choice of delegates to the London talks was more representative of Swazi society than the members of the Constitutional Consultative

---

[107]With reference to British Nigeria, for instance, the African political elite attended the Lancaster House Constitutional conference in 1949, 1951, 1954, 1958 and 1959. In British Kenya the African political elite attended the Lancaster House constitutional conference in 1960, 1962 and 1963 during which constitutional arrangements for Kenya's independence were made (see J. B. Ojwang, *Constitutional Development in Kenya: Institutional Adaptation and Social Change* [Nairobi: Acts Press, African Centre for Technology Studies, 1990]; J. Darwin, 'British Decolonization Since 1945: A Pattern or a Puzzle?' *The Journal of Imperial and Commonwealth History*, 12, 2 [1984], 187–209; R. L. Sklar, *Nigerian Political Parties: Power in an Emergent African Nation*, Vol. 2288 [Princeton: Princeton University Press, 2015]; and J. O. Adeyeri, 'Nationalism and Political Independence in Africa', In *The Palgrave Handbook of African Politics, Governance and Development* [New York: Palgrave Macmillan, 2018], 203–215).

118   H. P. DLAMINI

Table 3.3   Delegates to Church House, London, Constitutional Conference on Swaziland in January 1963

	Name	Affiliation
1.	B. Marwick	British Resident Commissioner in Swaziland
2.	M. Fairlie	Secretary for Social and Political Affairs in the Swaziland Government
3.	P. L. Dlamini	Swazi National Council
4.	B. A. Dlamini	Swazi National Council
5.	A. K. Hlope	Swazi National Council
6.	M. P. Nhlabatsi	Swazi National Council
7.	S. T. M. Sukati	Swazi National Council
8.	J. M. B. Sukati	Swazi National Council
9.	C. Todd	Leader of the European Advisory Council
10.	B. Habbard	European Advisory Council
11.	R. P. Stephens	European Advisory Council
12.	D. Fitzpatrick	European Advisory Council
13.	J. J. Nquku	Progressive Party of Swaziland
14.	Dr G. L. M. Msibi	Mbandzeni National Party of Swaziland
15.	S. Nxumalo	Swaziland Democratic Party
16.	A. Sellstroom	Euroafrican Welfare Association
17.	Dr D. Hynd	Missionary, freelance, not tied to government or political party

Source Compiled from the Times of Swaziland, 'Political Alliance', *The Times of Swaziland*, January 18, 1963

Committee. Apart from the SNC–EAC alliance, political parties and the Euro-African Welfare Association were included. The Coloureds, operating under the Euro-African Welfare Association, had protested to the colonial administration about their exclusion, and they were now represented in the London talks. Dr Hynd, who represented missionary interest, was also included. He was the head of a Christian mission station in Swaziland that ran schools, a teacher training college, a nursing training college, a large hospital, and several clinics.

The constitutional deliberations started in earnest on 28 January 1963 and there was an air of optimism, as the delegates were visibly excited at the prospects of independence and Britain's commitment towards that goal.[108] The opening session was presided over by the British Colonial Secretary

---

[108]The pictures in The *Times of Swaziland* showed the delegates all smiling and the caption read as follows: 'Talks Begin with Smiles But End in Deadlock', February 15, 1963.

3 THE BEGINNING OF THE GREAT CONSTITUTIONAL DEBATE ... 119

of State, Duncan Sandys, while the subsequent meetings were presided over by Lord Lansdowne, Minister of State for Commonwealth Affairs. After welcoming the delegates, Sandys announced that the British had no preconceived plan but would try to look into the views of all concerned parties and put forward a compromise formula on both the political and economic fronts.

The SNC delegates were fully aware of the determination of the British to replicate a political system in Swaziland that would undo the existing traditional African political system, and they therefore made an ardent plea in London that, before a constitution could be made, the following conditions must be met:

i. The status of Swaziland as a protectorate state should be restored;
ii. The position of the *Ngwenyama*, Sobhuza II and his successors, as King of Swaziland should be fully recognized and not tampered with; and
iii. All rights and minerals of the Swazi people should be returned to them.

The SNC deplored the haste with which the British were attempting to institute political change without being patient with the people of Swaziland. It asserted that SNC was the only established authority in Swaziland for the Swazi people, not political parties or any other organization. The SCN stated that it was 'a matter of life and death, and [they] would appeal to the Resident Commissioner and the Secretary of State to give to the people all the time necessary to make up their minds' and not to be rushed to have any type of constitution.[109]

When the contentious constitution proposal of the SCN/EAC was presented, the mood of the delegates became grim. The contentious 50–50 proposal split the delegates into two camps. On the one side of the situation were the political parties, the Euro-Africans, and Dr Hynd, who were ferociously against the proposal; on the other was the SNC–EAC alliance that were in favour. Neither camp was prepared to change its mind.

The EAC delegates expressed their wish to see the incorporation of Swaziland into or, at least, for it to be part of, a federal arrangement with

---

[109] 'Constitutional Talks: Swazi National Council Delegates Report Back to the Council', *Times of Swaziland*, March 15, 1963; FCO 141/17380, 17385–17387: Constitutional Reforms 1959–63.

120 H. P. DLAMINI

South Africa. They felt that this could be better achieved with the assistance of the Nationalist Party in power. The SNC supported their ally and calculated that they could successfully stem the rise of radical African nationalism by accepting a Bantustan status within the protective shield of South Africa.[110] This was conceived as a safe route for Sobhuza to escape the British neutralization of his powers under Britain's new post-World War II decolonization policy, which favoured the ascension of Progressives to power. The British ignored the request to hand over Swaziland to the apartheid regime.

Meanwhile, the British government and the Progressives wanted mineral rights to be vested in the Legislative Council and not in the monarch, while the SNC–EAC alliance wanted Sobhuza to be in control. The British government rejected the SNC–EAC constitutional proposal and tried to propose a formula that would allow for a degree of universal adult suffrage, the African traditional method of voting, and European universal adult suffrage, but this was rejected by all delegates. When discussions seemed to be getting nowhere, Sandys became increasingly impatient. In the words of Kuper:

> On Sunday 12 February, about 10.00 pm, [Sandys] came into the meeting and announced harshly that since agreement could not be reached; he would have to impose a constitution. There was a brief stunned silence.[111]

Sandys then adjourned the meeting and, when it resumed, Lord Lansdowne took the chair, but there was no progress. On 13 February, the London Conference ended in a deadlock and the delegates returned home.[112] The London Conference had failed to resolve the Swaziland constitutional deadlock.

---

[110]Stevens, 'Swaziland Political Development', 328. It should be noted that this author was resident in Basutoland. Consequently he was very close to the events he is describing and knew most of the actors.

[111]Kuper, *Sobhuza II: Ngwenyama and King of Swaziland*, 232–233. Kuper was in a position to give a graphic account of what transpired in Church House in London because of her close relationship with Sobhuza for decades and because she was the *Ngwenyama*'s official biographer. She therefore had privileged information about the day-to-day activities of the *Ngwenyama*. Her book, therefore, contains a lot of first hand reporting.

[112]'Talks begins with smiles but end in deadlock', *Times of Swaziland*, February 15, 1963; 'Constitutional Talks End', *Izwi Lama Swazi*, February 23, 1963. Also see Stevens, 'Swaziland Political Development', 22.

Conclusion

The constitution-making process in colonial Swaziland was triggered by the rise of nationalism in the post-World War II era. This culminated in the independence of Ghana and a score of African states, and Swaziland had to follow the trend. The British embarked on the constitution-making process in 1960 with the establishment of the Constitutional Committee, which comprised the officials of the British administration, Swazis, and European settlers. In a bid to bequeath a legacy of Westminster parliamentary democracy, Britain opted for the establishment of a Legislative Council, which was a popular demand in the territory. The constitutional debate hinged on two interconnected issues: first, who should be the successor of the departing British colonial authorities, the modern political leaders or the Swazi monarch? Second, should entry into the Legislative Council be achieved through popular sovereignty exercised by the nascent political parties, or through the traditional structures of the Swazi monarchy? The British were unequivocal that the Progressives operating under the banner of political parties were programmed to succeed the departing colonial authorities through the mechanism of universal adult suffrage. The Progressives were agreeable to this agenda, but King Sobhuza II's SNC and Todd's EAC joined forces to oppose it on grounds that political power was not up for grabs by anybody in the kingdom of Swaziland. The next issue was the method of gaining admission into the Legislative Council. The SNC and EAC allies advocated a dual electoral system of adult universal suffrage votes by secret ballot for Whites, and nomination by traditional methods for Swazis. The SNC–EAC alliance was against political parties and universal adult suffrage for Swazis on the grounds that they were 'unAfrican'. Furthermore, the SNC–EAC agreed that there should be equal representation for Swazis and Whites on the Legislative Council in recognition of the economic weight of the White community in the economy. The Whites trusted the traditional monarch as a reliable ally who could protect their economic interests, unlike the Progressives, whose radical ideology was a threat to their economic investments. Consequently, investing in the survival of an all-powerful traditional monarch was the best shield for their economic interests. For the South African regime to enjoy tranquillity, it had to replicate its ideology in Swaziland through its proxies—the traditional Swazi monarch and the White immigrant community, who were largely of South African origin.

Essentially, the SNC–EAC constitutional proposals were intended to stymie the rise of radical nationalism, which was anathema to Swazi political traditionalism, the economic interests of the White community in Swaziland, and the South African apartheid regime. Radical nationalism represented by the leaders of the nascent political parties echoed themes such as universal adult suffrage and a single electoral roll, equality of all races, nationalization, Africa for Africans, and pan-Africanism. The White economic interest groups trusted the conservative Swazi monarch as the guarantor and insurer of their economic interests, rather than the legislature. Todd's EAC therefore lobbied for overwhelming powers to be vested in the Swazi monarch.

The radical political leaders countered the constitutional stance of the SNC–EAC and were either fired or forced to resign from the Constitutional Committee. For over three years, no consensus could be reached on the way forward for the establishment of a Legislative Council for Swaziland owing to unbridgeable differences between the conservative stance of the SNC–EAC alliance and the progressive stance of the nascent political parties. In essence, Sobhuza, with the support of the Whites, wanted to enter modern politics with the traditional structures of the Swazi kingdom intact under Sobhuza II and with separate privileges for Whites. This political stance smacked of historical anachronism and disguised apartheid.

By the time the British government invited the various protagonists in Swaziland for the London Conference in early 1963, no agreement had been reached owing to the rift between the SNC–EAC alliance and the Progressives, and their public sympathisers. The Church Hall Conference expectedly ended in a puff smoke, despite the efforts of the colonial administration to strike a compromise. Chapter 4 deals with the return of the delegates to Swaziland and the response of the British colonial administration to the constitutional stalemate.

References

Archival Sources

Swaziland National Archives
SNA, Constitutional Proposals Comments of the Public 1962.
SNA, Constitutional Proposals: Written Comments of the Public Chapter XIV, Membership of the Swaziland Constitutional Committee, 1962.
SNA, DPMO 12, A.G. 100/316/56, July 26, 1979.

SNA, File 3311/1 Newsletter: Swaziland Democratic Party, No. 5, Vol. 1, October 5, 1962, Mbabane.

SNA, Government of Swaziland, Proposals for the Swazi Constitution, March 1962.

SNA, Swazi Constitution Presented to Parliament by the Secretary of State for Colonies by command of Her Majesty, May 1963.

SNA, Swaziland Progressive Party, 'Swaziland: Report on Constitutional Proposals', Swaziland Progressive Party, 1961.

The National Archives (UK) Archives

FCO 141/17380, 17385–17387: Constitutional Reforms 1959–63.

FCO 141/17472, 17670: Constitutional Proposals; Land Issues; Africanisation of the Civil Service.

FCO 141/17479: Reform Committee of the Swaziland National Administration 1959–61.

FCO 141/17507: Conference of African Dependent States; Ghana's Contacts with the High Commission Territories 1961–64.

FCO 141/17579–17582: Resolution Passed by the Swaziland European Advisory Council; Session Dealing with the Question of Responsible Government for the Territory 1953–59.

Newspaper Articles

'50–50 Accepted by Swazis and Europeans: Joint Statement', *Times of Swaziland*, September 14, 1962.

'All Quiet on Constitutional Front: A Widening Gulf?' *Times of Swaziland*, January 26, 1962.

'Constitution Referendum: 697 for and 19 Against 52.3 per cent roll', *Times of Swaziland*, May 18, 1962.

'Constitutional Advance in Swaziland', *Times of Swaziland*, November 11, 1960.

'Constitutional Adviser from UK Due in Swaziland this week', *Times of Swaziland*, July 13, 1962.

'Constitutional Talks End', *Izwi Lama Swazi*, February 23, 1963.

'Constitutional Talks: Swazi national Council Delegates Report Back to the Council', *Times of Swaziland*, March 15, 1963.

'Dr. Zwane to London Fails, Mr. Nquku to Represent the Progressives', *Times of Swaziland*, January 18, 1963.

'Ngwenyama Warns Swazi Nation Politics Can Lead Us to Hardship', *Times of Swaziland*, November 4, 1960.

'Nquku Questioned by the United Nations', *Times of Swaziland*, January 25, 1963.

124   H. P. DLAMINI

'Points of View on Constitutional Reforms: Mr Todd Replies', *Times of Swaziland*, February 2, 1962.
'Political Alliance', *Times of Swaziland*, January 18, 1963.
'Priest Replies', *Times of Swaziland*, March 16, 1962.
'Prime Minister Returns to United Kingdom: Press Conference', *Times of Swaziland*, February 20, 1960.
'Swaziland Democratic Part 1961 Policy Speech', In S.N. Ndwandwe, Politics in Swaziland 1960–1968: A Selection of Reports in the *Times of Swaziland*. University of Witwatersrand, Johannesburg, 4, n.d.
'Talks Begins with Smiles but End in Deadlock', *Times of Swaziland*, February 15, 1963.
'The Ngwenyama, Sobhuza II C.B.E., Gives Expression to His Views on the Constitutional Future of Swaziland', *Times of Swaziland*, July 1, 1960.
'The Nwenyama Denies Making 50–50 Offer', *Times of Swaziland*, June 22, 1962.
'Todd Replies to Times Leader', *Times of Swaziland*, June 15, 1962.
'Todd's Thoughts on Constitutional Proposals', *Times of Swaziland*, March 23, 1962.
Ndwandwe, S. S. Politics in Swaziland 1960–1968: A Selection of Reports in the *Times of Swaziland*, University of the Witwatersrand Institute for Advanced Social Research, African Studies Programme University of the Witwatersrand, Johannesburg, 1968.
The Guardian (Manchester), March 7, 1962.

BOOKS AND JOURNALS

Adeyeri, J. O. 'Nationalism and Political Independence in Africa', In *The Palgrave Handbook of African Politics, Governance and Development* (New York: Palgrave Macmillan, 2018), 203–215.
Banda, P. C., and Kayira, G. W. 'The 1959 State of Emergency in Nyasaland: Process and Political Implications', *The Society of Malawi Journal* (2012), 1–19.
Barber, H. W. 'The United States vs. the United Nations', *International Organisation*, 27, 2 (1973), 139–163.
Beckman, L. 'Who Should Vote? Conceptualizing Universal Suffrage in Studies of Democracy', *Democratisation* 15, 1 (2008), 29–48.
Birmingham, D. *Kwame Nkrumah: The Father of African Nationalism* (Athens, OH: Ohio University Press, 1998).
Birmingham, D. *The Decolonization of Africa* (London: Routledge, 2008).
Biswal, T. P. *Ghana, Political and Constitutional Developments* (New Delhi: Northern Book Centre, 1992).
Botwe-Asamoah, K. *Kwame Nkrumah's Politico-Cultural Thought and Politics: An African-Centered Paradigm for the Second Phase of the African Revolution* (New York: Routledge, 2013).

Bowman, L. W. 'The Subordinate State System of Southern Africa', *International Studies Quarterly* 12, 3(1968), 231–261.

Cocks, P. 'The King and I: Bronislaw Malinowski, King Sobhuza II of Swaziland and the Vision of Culture Change in Africa', *History of the Human Sciences*, 13, 4 (2000), 25–47.

Cupples J., and Glynn, K. 'Decolonial Social Movements, Leftist Governments and the Media', 11–16, In J. Cupples and K. Glynn (eds.), *Shifting Nicaraguan Mediascapes: Authoritarianism and the Struggle for Social Justice* (Newcastle: Springer, Cham, 2018).

Curtin, P. D., Feierman S., Thompson, L., and Vansina, J. *African History: From Earliest Times to Independence* (London: Longman, 1995).

Crowder M., and Ikime, O. (eds.), *Their Changing Status Under Colonial Rule and Independence* (New York: Africana Publishing Corporation, 1970).

Crush, J. 'The Colonial Division of Space: The Significance of the Swaziland Land Partition', *The International Journal of African Historical Studies*, 13, 1 (1980), 71–86.

Darwin, J. 'British Decolonization Since 1945: A Pattern or a Puzzle?' *The Journal of Imperial and Commonwealth History*, 12, 2 (1984), 187–209.

Dlamini, N. *The Legal Abolition of Racial Discrimination and Its Aftermath: the Case of Swaziland, 1945–1973* (Doctoral dissertation University of the Witwatersrand, 2007).

Diamond, L., and Gunther, R. (eds.). *Political Parties and Democracy* (Baltimore: Johns Hopkins University Press, 2001).

Emerson, R. 'Self-determination', *American Journal of International Law*, 65, 3 (1971), 459–475.

Enwezor O., and Achebe, C. *The Short Century: Independence and Liberation Movements in Africa, 1945–1994* (Munich: Prestel, 2001).

Ezera, K. *Constitutional Developments in Nigeria* (London: Cambridge University Press, 1964).

Fall, B. B. *Street Without Joy: The French Debacle in Indochina* (Mechanicsburg: Rowman & Littlefield, 2018).

Fawcus, P., and Tilbury, A. *Botswana: The Road to Independence* (Gaborone: Pula Press and the Botswana Society, 2000).

Firmin-Sellers, K. 'The Concentration of Authority: Constitutional Creation in the Gold Coast, 1950', *Journal of Theoretical Politics*, 7, 2 (1995), 201–222.

Fombad, C. M. 'The Separation of Powers and Constitutionalism in Africa: The Case of Botswana', *Boston College Third World Law Journal* (2005), 301.

Furedi, F. *Mau Mau War in Perspective* (London: James Currey 1989).

Geertz, C. (ed.). *Old Societies and New States: The Quest for Modernity in Asia and Africa* (New York: Free Press of Glencoe 1963).

Grilli, M. 'African Liberation and Unity in Nkrumah's Ghana: A Study of the Role of "Pan-African Institutions" in the Making of Ghana's Foreign Policy,

1957–1966' (PhD dissertation, Institute for History, Faculty of Humanities, Leiden University and Department of Political and Social Sciences, University of Pavia, 2015).

Grilli, M. 'Nkrumah, Nationalism, and Pan-Africanism: The Bureau of African Affairs Collection', *History in Africa*, 44 (2017), 295–307.

Grilli, M. 'Nkrumah's Ghana and the Armed Struggle in Southern Africa (1961–1966)', *South African Historical Journal*, 70, 1 (2018), 56–81.

Ibhawoh, B. 'Second World War Propaganda, Imperial Idealism and Anti-colonial Nationalism in British West Africa', *Nordic Journal of African Studies*, 16, 2 (2007), 221–243.

Johnson, C. A. 'Conferences of Independent African States', *International Organization*, 16, 2 (1962), 426–429.

Kalinga, O. J. M. 'The 1959 Nyasaland State of Emergency in Old Karonga District', *Journal of Southern African Studies*, 36, 4 (2010), 743–763.

Kadzamira, Z. D. 'Constitutional Changes in Malawi 1891–1965', In *Malawi Past and Present: Selected Papers from the University of Malawi History Conference* (1967).

Kanduza, A. M. 'Evolving Significance of Sobhuza's 1941 Petition." *Transafrican Journal of History*, 25 (1996), 110.

Khoza, P. T. 'A Study of the Powers of the Swazi Monarch in Terms of Swazi Law and Custom Past, Present and the Future' (MA dissertation, Rhodes University, 2002).

Laclau, E. 'Politics and the Limits of Modernity', *Social Text* (1989), 63–82.

Maloba, W. O. *Mau Mau and Kenya: An Analysis of a Peasant Revolt* (Oxford: James Currey, 1993).

Mittelman, J. H. 'Collective Decolonisation and the UN Committee of 24', *The Journal of Modern African Studies*, 14, 1 (1976), 41–64.

Mlambo, A. S. *A History of Zimbabwe* (New York: Cambridge University Press, 119–127).

Nugent, P. *Africa Since Independence: A Comparative History* (New York: Palgrave Macmillan, 2012).

Nwabueze, B. O. *A Constitutional History of Nigeria* (London: C. Hurst and Company, 1982).

Ojwang, J. B. *Constitutional Development in Kenya: Institutional Adaptation and Social Change* (Nairobi: Acts Press, African Centre for Technology Studies, 1990).

Pearce, R. 'The Colonial Office and Planned Decolonisation in Africa', *African Affairs*, 83 (1984), 77–93.

Potholm, C. P. 'Changing Political Configuration in Swaziland', *The Journal of African Studies*, 4, 9 (1966) 313–322.

Rathbone, R. 'Kwame Nkrumah and the Chiefs: The Fate of Natural Rulers Under Nationalists Governments', *Transactions of the Royal Historical Society*, 10 (2000), 45–53.

Rooney, D. *Sir Charles Arden-Clarke* (London: Rex Collings Limited, 1982).

Shaev, B. 'The Algerian War, European Integration, and the Decolonization of French Socialism', *French Historical Studies*, 41, 1 (2018), 63–94.

Sherwood, M. '"Diplomatic platitudes": The Atlantic Charter, The United Nations and Colonial Independence', *Immigrants & Minorities*, 15, 2 (1996), 135–150.

Shilliam, R. (ed.). *International Relations and Non-Western Thought: Imperialism, Colonialism and Investigations of Global Modernity* (Abingdon: Routledge, 2010).

Sklar, R. L. *Nigerian Political Parties: Power in An Emergent African Nation*, Vol. 2288 (Princeton: Princeton University Press, 2015).

Spence, J. E. 'The New States of Southern Africa', *The Journal of Modern African Studies*, 5, 4 (1967), 541–555.

Stevens, R. P. 'Swaziland Political Development', *The Journal of Modern African Studies*, 1, 3 (1963), 327–350.

Van Rouveroy van Nieuwaal, E. A. B. 'Chiefs and African States: Some Introductory Notes and an Extensive Bibliography on African Chieftaincy', *The Journal of Legal Pluralism and Unofficial Law*, 19, 25–26 (1987), 1–46.

Ward, S. 'Run Before the Tempest: The "Wind of Change" and the British World', *Geschichte und Gesellschaft*, 37, 2 (2011), 198.

White, E. 'Last Steps Towards Independence: The Three African Protectorates', *African Affairs*, 64, 257 (1965), 261–270.

Zwane, T. M. J. 'The Struggle for Power in Swaziland', *Africa Today* (1964), 4–6.

Internet Source

Fombad, C. 'Botswana Introductory Notes: Origins and Historical Development of the Constitution', University of Pretoria. www.icla.up.ac.za/images/country_reports/botswana. Accessed August 5, 2018.

Conference Paper

Dlamini, H. P. 'South African Interventionism in Swazi Colonial Politics', Paper presented at the University of Pretoria, Postgraduate Conference, 2015.

CHAPTER 4

The Imposed 1963 Constitution, the Maiden Legislative and Executive Councils, and the Select Constitutional Committee

INTRODUCTION

Britain was compelled to impose a somewhat compromise constitution on Swaziland in 1963, of which the highlight was the marginalization of King Sobhuza II in the governance machinery, and his relegation to the inconsequential role of guardian of culture and tradition. This constitution came on the heels of the fiasco of the London constitutional talks. This was too bad for the king. Neither the monarchists nor their White allies, who were banking on the King for the protection of their investments and private property against threats from the Progressives, could be pleased. Even the Progressives were also discontented, although for entirely different reasons. All the key political players created problems for the British by rejecting the constitution for reasons that are explored in this chapter. Britain could no longer tolerate the procrastination, manoeuvring, and jockeying of the political actors positioning themselves, and assumed its full responsibility by calling for elections for a Legislative Council in June 1964.

This chapter also discusses the clash, before and after the June 1964 elections, between British constitutional values, on the one hand, and those of the Swazi monarchy and its White allies, on the other hand. Whereas the British struggled to convince the traditional monarchy to maintain absolute neutrality in modern politics and to evolve into a mere ceremonial Head of State, as in the UK, the White Swazi community, investors, and multinational businesses wanted to see the emergence of a politically robust

© The Author(s) 2019
H. P. Dlamini, *A Constitutional History of the Kingdom of Eswatini (Swaziland), 1960–1982*, African Histories and Modernities,
https://doi.org/10.1007/978-3-030-24777-5_4

129

130   H. P. DLAMINI

Swazi king who would contain the radicalism of the Progressives, which was inimical to their interests. Together with apartheid South Africa, they advised Sobhuza to form a political party and enter modern politics so as to capture power, lest he found himself totally neutralized and irrelevant. The monarchists formed the *Imbokodvo* party, while King Sobhuza's White allies formed the USA party. The *Imbokodvo* and the USA party quickly formed an alliance to checkmate the leftist parties; they largely succeeded by winning all the 24 seats in the legislature. How King Sobhuza was convinced to join the bandwagon of modern politics and sailed to political victory in alliance with Whites at the expense of the Progressives is analysed. The implication of the overwhelming victory of *Imbokodvo*–USA alliance in the 1964 elections was that a Legislative and Executive Council were constituted and a constitutional committee was selected composed exclusively of monarchists and their White allies, who were entrusted with the responsibility of designing a new constitution for Swaziland. Sobhuza's victory emboldened him and endowed him with faith in modern politics, which he had so far dreaded.

THE BRITISH THREAT TO IMPOSE A CONSTITUTION ON SWAZILAND AND TO CALL FOR ELECTIONS

The Swazi constitutional delegates to the London Conference returned home frustrated by the stalemate just as the British colonial administration was fast running out of patience with the delegates. The Colonial Secretary, Duncan Sandys, threatened that the British were going to impose a constitution on the territory, since the delegates could not agree on a common platform.[1] This was not good news for the SNC–EAC alliance because it meant an unfavourable constitution that would provide a level political playing field that would be favourable to the Progressives. The SNC–EAC alliance was not popular with the people because of their 50–50 proposal, which was seen as favouring a handful of Whites, and the threat to impose a constitution with the prospects of universal adult suffrage by secret ballot was an ominous sign for them.

Todd naturally reacted angrily to the suggestion that a constitution would be imposed on Swaziland. With the full support of the SNC to

---

[1] 'Talks Begins with Smiles but End in Deadlock', *Times of Swaziland*, February 15, 1963; Izwi Lama Swazi, 'Constitutional Talks End', *Izwi Lama Swazi*, February 23, 1963. Also see Stevens, 'Swaziland Political Development', 22.

4 THE IMPOSED 1963 CONSTITUTION, THE MAIDEN LEGISLATIVE ... 131

speak on its behalf, Todd warned that an imposed constitution would not work and would simply be a dead letter. He stated that both the SNC and EAC had proposed that a monarchical form of government should be established in which the Swazi king would be the king of all the people of Swaziland, not only the indigenous Swazis.[2]

The Swazi constitutional delegates from the abortive London Conference equally expressed disappointment with the British. They briefed King Sobhuza II of the outcome of the Conference. On 9 March 1963, the delegates addressed a crowd of over 4000 people at Lobamba on what happened in London, making sure that the British and Progressives were castigated. They praised the SNC–EAC constitutional proposal as a good document for the consolidation of Swazi values and national unity, and one that needed to be supported by Swazis.[3]

Todd also reported to King Sobhuza his own version of the events that transpired in London and assured the *Ngwenyama* that all was not lost. He advised him that he had to demonstrate to the British that the Swazi nation was behind him and supported the SNC–EAC constitutional proposal, which the British had rejected. He suggested that King Sobhuza should write a letter to the Resident Commissioner asking the government to conduct a referendum to test the constitutional proposal that the British had rejected. A letter was therefore drafted to the Resident Commissioner on the question of the referendum, which the *Ngwenyama* then discussed with the SNC.[4] The British administration could not grant King Sobhuza's request. The British Resident Commissioner could not permit such a referendum because the issue of the constitution had already been examined in London and the Colonial Office had already taken a decision that a constitution was going to be imposed on Swaziland.

Even then, a free and fair referendum on the SNC–EAC constitutional proposal did not stand a chance of being adopted. The Swazi public had generally been very critical of King Sobhuza's 50–50 proposal and his idea

[2]'Todd on the Talk in United Kingdom: An Imposed Constitution Would Not Work', *Times of Swaziland*, March 1, 1963.

[3]Ibid.

[4]H. Kuper, *Sobhuza II, Ngwenyama and King of Swaziland: The Story of an Hereditary Ruler and His Country* (New York: Africana Publishing, 1978), 233. Kuper was in a position to give a graphic account of what transpired in London because of her close relationship with King Sobhuza II for decades and because she was the *Ngwenyama*'s official biographer. She therefore had privileged information about the day-to-day activities of the *Ngwenyama*.

of a racial federation, because it did not favour Swazis. Given the hostility of the Swazi public to the proposal, King Sobhuza II resorted to manipulating public opinion about the political stance of the SNC–EAC alliance. King Sobhuza proceeded to mobilize Swazi opinion in favour of a referendum on the rejected constitutional proposal, even though he had no authorization from the British colonial administration. King Sobhuza's SNC decided to send 12 men on a tour of the country to campaign for the King's referendum, placing emphasis on the importance of national unity under the *Ngwenyama* and the need for stability in a world endangered by strife from radical nationalism. In order to make the constitutional proposal document attractive, the SNC backtracked from the unpopular 50–50 equality clause regarding equal Black and White representation in the legislature by denying that such a proposal was ever made. The explanation given for the 50–50 proposal was that it meant Blacks and Whites should treat each other as equals. Furthermore, the SNC stated that it could not accept the full implementation of the Westminster European system of governance anchored on universal adult suffrage, because it would erode essential Swazi values.[5] They made sure that, on the campaign trail, they presented the Progressives as people who wanted to remove the *Ngwenyama* from power—a statement that ordinary folk did not like to hear. On their return from their sensitization campaign, the SNC delegation reported to the *Ngwenyama* that the people were solidly behind him and that they had rejected Western ideas of democracy. A committee of seven men were then selected to draft a national resolution to be submitted to the British on the people's wishes that the SNC–EAC constitutional proposal should be upheld.[6] The committee had hardly sat down to draft the resolution when a bombshell came from the Resident Commissioner on 13 March 1963: the Secretary of State for the Colonies had definitively rejected the SNC–EAC constitutional proposal and the British government was set to provide Swaziland with a constitution. The Swazi monarch had to prepare a quick response for the British in an effort to avert the situation, because they had not yet agreed on the terms of the constitution. Prince Masitsela responded to the Resident Commissioner on behalf of the SNC on 14 March 1963 as follows:

[5] Ibid., 233–237.
[6] Ibid.

We, the members of the SNC herein assembled in the Council Chambers, Lobamba, this 14 March 1963 resolve that:

1. We are very grateful for the Report on the Constitutional Talks in London, notably, the provisional conclusions of the Secretary of State for colonies.
2. As they are a complete departure from our proposals of a Legislative Council (LEGCO) based on racial federation or communal representation, these provisional conclusions of the Secretary of State must be referred to the people for whom we speak who will give us a fresh mandate.
3. Another meeting will be called for the 15th of April 1963 to crystallise these ideas.
4. Government will be furnished with the views of the Swazi Nation by the 23 April 1963. [7]

Meanwhile, Todd also tried communicating to the colonial administration, requesting that a constitution should not be imposed without taking local opinion into consideration. He stated that the White community was solidly united behind the SNC–EAC constitutional proposal. He polled the opinion of the White community on the committee's constitutional proposals in May 1963 and they proved to be overwhelmingly behind Todd's constitutional proposal. The Sobhuza–Todd political manoeuvrings were an indication of how nervous the two leaders were about the impending imposed constitution. Their worry was that space could be opened up for the Progressives to compete for power and succeed. Sobhuza and Todd therefore fought hard to stop the British from imposing a constitution. They were bent on protecting their interests, but the British were unstoppable in their resolve to endow Swaziland with its maiden governance instrument: a constitution.

SWAZILAND'S FIRST CONSTITUTION AND THE RELEGATION OF THE *NGWENYAMA* TO MANAGER OF CULTURE AND TRADITION

On 20 May 1963, the British government announced that a maiden constitution would be promulgated for Swaziland. Although the constitution was British-tailored, the views of the Swazi stakeholders were taken into consideration. William Dale notes that:

[7] Ibid., 233–234.

134   H. P. DLAMINI

The constitutions drafted in Whitehall were [usually] drawn up with meticulous care, in a style owing much to the style of an Act of Parliament, with the object—at least at first—*of reproducing the features, in detail, of parliamentary democracy as it obtains in Britain.* A Governor-General was to be responsible to the House, and there were safeguards for an independent judiciary. *But it would be wrong to regard these constitutions as forced on the countries...* They are always *the outcome of full consultation and discussion and in the majority of cases independence constitutions have been preceded by one or more full-scale conferences. It can justly be claimed that the constitution gives the people what they ask for...*[8] (Emphasis added)

The British, in essence, had consulted thoroughly with the Swazis in Swaziland and continued consultations in London. Although the delegates could not arrive at a consensus during the London Conference, the British still managed to design and implement a constitution that took into consideration their different viewpoints, because time was not on their side. The British had become impatient with Swaziland, because it was it was the least politically advanced of the three British High Commission territories[9] owing to wrangling over constitutional issues. Whereas Basutoland (Lesotho), in 1960, and Bechuanaland (Botswana), in 1961, has been endowed with Legislative Councils,[10] the Swazi political class was still engaged in feverish negotiations to ensure their political survival and economic interests. The British were therefore under pressure to move on with the decolonization process instead of marching on the spot. They endeavoured to strike a compromise between the conflicting viewpoints of the SNC–EAC alliance and the Progressive political leaders. The 1963 constitution was therefore not a totally a *diktat*.

The British compromise envisaged a constitution in which the membership of the Legislative Council would be elected by three distinctly separate methods to please the Swazi traditionalists, the White minority, and the Progressives. One-third of the members of the Council would be chosen by indigenous Swazis using the traditional way of acclamation that King Sobhuza wanted, one-third would be chosen by the White minority on a

[8] Dale William. 'The Making and Remaking of Commonwealth Constitutions', *International & Comparative Law Quarterly*, 42, 1 (1993), 67–68 (Emphasis mine).

[9] M. Laschinger, 'Roads to Independence: The Case of Swaziland', *The World Today*, 21, 11 (1965), 487.

[10] R. P. Stevens, *Lesotho, Botswana and Swaziland: The Former High Commission Territories in Southern Africa* (London: Pall Mall P, 1967).

4 THE IMPOSED 1963 CONSTITUTION, THE MAIDEN LEGISLATIVE ... 135

single territory-wide European roll, and the remaining one-third would be chosen by all qualified voters on a national roll.[11] The Secretary of State presented the proposed voting methods in the constitution for Swaziland to the British Parliament. Both the Lower and Upper House endorsed it and released a White paper on the constitution for Swaziland on 31 May 1963. The White Paper began with a statement that the Swazi constitutional document was in line with the Swaziland Order-in-Council of 1903, which established the British protectorate over Swaziland. The new constitution was finally enacted on 20 December 1963. It was published in the Swaziland Government Extraordinary Gazette on 2 January 1964 and came into operation the following day.[12]

The 1963 Swazi constitution was tardy when compared to that of other High Commissioner territories or other British territories in Africa, such as Ghana and Nigeria. Nonetheless, it was better late than never. The 1963 constitution had the merit of being the first constitution in colonial Swaziland and was the first clear step towards the introduction of full self-government leading to independence.

The constitution followed the typical pattern of British Commonwealth constitutions: it provided for an Executive and Legislative Council. Although Swaziland remained a protectorate state in which Her Majesty the Queen of England possessed full jurisdiction, some degree of power devolution was effected under the constitution in favour of the inhabitants of Swaziland. Executive powers were to be exercised by Her Majesty's Commissioner (formerly the Resident Commissioner), who was to be assisted by an Executive Council of three ex-officio members plus five others appointed by Her Majesty's Commissioner. The three ex-officio members were to be the Chief-Secretary, the Attorney General, and the Secretary for Finance and Development. One appointed member would be an official and the other four would be appointed from among the members of the Legislative Council. It was stated in the White Paper that Her Majesty's Commissioner had a right to veto any decision of the Council if he deemed it necessary to do so. In such a case, he would have to report the matter to the Secretary

---

[11] SNA: Swaziland Government Gazette Extraordinary, Vol. III, Mbabane, Thursday January 2, 1964; No. 15; 'New Swaziland Constitution Comes into Force Today: Order in Council Published', *Times of Swaziland*, January 3, 1964.

[12] SNA: Swaziland Government Gazette Extraordinary, Vol. III, Mbabane, Thursday January 2, 1964; No. 15; 'New Swaziland Constitution Comes into Force Today: Order in Council Published', *Times of Swaziland*, January 3, 1964.

of State and give reasons for his actions. This meant that Her Majesty's Commissioner had the last word in matters of the overall governance of the territory. The status of the Her Majesty's Commissioner was equivalent to that of a governor in other British dependencies. Her Majesty's Commissioner was to legislate by proclamation until the Legislative Council was formed under the new constitution after the holding of elections in the territory. Since executive power was vested in Her Majesty's Commissioner, power was still in the hands of the British.[13]

The Legislative Council was to consist of the Queen's Commissioner, the Speaker, 24 elected members, and four officials and nominated members. Her Majesty's Commissioner was entitled to use his discretion when appointing the Speaker, who was from without the Legislative Council. A triple electoral system was introduced in a bid to accommodate the viewpoints of those in favour of a special electoral roll for Whites, the traditional Swazi system of voting, and universal adult suffrage. In the light of this, the 24 members were to be elected as follows:

   i. Eight Swazis certified by the *Ngwenyama*-in-Council as elected by traditional methods;
   ii. Eight Europeans, four of whom would be elected by voters on a European roll and four of whom would be elected on national roll;
   iii. Eight persons of any race elected by voters on a national roll.[14]

In addition, the government would appoint up to three more persons to represent minority interests. Adult tax payers and their wives who were British subjects or British protected persons and had lived in Swaziland for at least three of the preceding five years could register on the national roll. A bill passed by the Legislative Council could not become a law until Her Majesty's Commissioner had assented to it. The Commissioner had a right to assent, refuse to assent, or reserve the Bill for the signification of Her Majesty's pleasure.[15]

---

[13] SNA: Swaziland Government Gazette Extraordinary, Vol. III, Mbabane, Thursday January 2, 1964; No. 15 'New Swaziland Constitution Comes into Force Today: Order in Council Published', *Times of Swaziland*, January 3, 1964.

[14] 'Swaziland Constitution Announced', *Izwi Lama Swazi*, June 8, 1963, 3; 'Swaziland Constitution Announced, 8 Seats Reserved for Whites Out of 24 Elected Members', *Times of Swaziland*, May 31, 1963.

[15] Ibid.

4 THE IMPOSED 1963 CONSTITUTION, THE MAIDEN LEGISLATIVE ... 137

Traditional matters were to be regulated by Swazi law and custom. These included the following:

i. The office of the *Ngwenyama*;
ii. The office of the *Ndlovukati* (the queen mother);
iii. The appointment, revocation of appointment, and suspension of chiefs;
iv. The composition of the Swazi National Council, the appointment and revocation of appointment of members of the Council, and the procedure of the Council;
v. The *Incwala* ceremony;
vi. The *Libufto* (regiments).[16]

All the 1963 constitution reserved for the *Ngwenyama* was his administration of culture and tradition. The Constitution did not treat the *Ngwenyama* fairly. The *Ngwenyama* was clearly an ambitious man who did not want to be subsumed and stripped of his powers by the politics of constitution-making in colonial Swaziland. In this struggle, he had the support of the White community and multinational capital in Swaziland, and the South African government, but not that of the British colonial administration, who wanted him to stay out of modern politics. The *Ngwenyama* was more trustworthy in the eyes of investors because of his conservatism, unlike the radical politicians who espoused the principles of the Africanization and nationalization of private property, and supported labour unions striking for improved wages. Although the *Ngwenyama* was relevant to the White and business community, he was not a consideration in the British political modernization project and had to be sacrificed in the 1963 constitution by relegating him to the background of modern politics. This act of keeping King Sobhuza out of active politics can only be understood in the context of British constitutional history.

---

[16]SNA: Swaziland Government Extraordinary Gazette, January 2, 1964; 'Constitution Now in Operation', *Times of Swaziland*, January 3, 1964.

138 H. P. DLAMINI

TOWARDS UNDERSTANDING THE BRITISH RELEGATION OF THE *NGWENYAMA* FROM THE REALM OF MODERN POLITICS

The British approach to constitutionalism was dictated by two factors: British monarchical parliamentary tradition, where the role of the monarch was merely ceremonial, and their post-1945 policy to relinquish power to the modernizing Western-educated elite. The British insisted that the Swazi traditional monarch should be restricted to a ceremonial role, as in the United Kingdom, while the Prime Minister would be the real executive head of the Cabinet. Lord Cohen of the British Colonial Office had clearly stated in 1951 that the beneficiaries of the transfer of power in British dependencies to the post-colonial modern states should be to the Western-educated elite through the instrument of multiparty political contestation, not to African traditional rulers.[17] African traditional rulers (African chiefs and kings) were to be restricted to the domain of culture and tradition—no more, no less. The supremacy of an elected parliament was underscored. Because of British insistence on the election of a Legislature and the supremacy of Cabinet as a cardinal point of its political modernization project in Swaziland, there is need to present a précis of British constitutional history with reference to the relationship between the British monarchy and the House of Commons (Parliament).

During the reign of Queen Elizabeth I of England (1533–1603), conflict arose between the monarch and the House of Commons. The monarch believed in the Divine Rights of Kings and opted for absolutism, while the elected members of the House of Commons claimed they had the right to deal freely with all matters of grievance and policy as the people's representative. When King James I ascended the throne in 1603, he challenged the claim of parliamentary supremacy and asserted royal supremacy over parliament, but it was under his successor that the conflict degenerated into a civil war. In January 1642, his son, Charles I, attempted to arrest and impeach five members of Parliament for challenging royal authority and was resisted by the House. This conflict deteriorated into a civil war between the King and Parliament, and resulted in the triumph of the parliamentary army over the royalists. The English King was tried and executed in 1649, and a period of chaos followed. The conflict was finally resolved in 1689 when

---

[17] R. E. Robison, *Andrew Cohen and the Transfer of Power in Tropical Africa 1940–1951* (Fondation nationale des sciences politiques, 1976).

4 THE IMPOSED 1963 CONSTITUTION, THE MAIDEN LEGISLATIVE ... 139

the British monarch accepted the Declaration of Rights, which upheld the supremacy of parliament over the monarch, meaning that only the Commons could make laws.[18] Essentially, the English revolution resulted in sovereignty devolving on the people, who became the sovereigns of the country in place of the monarch.[19] This background explains British political thinking about the supremacy of parliament in governance and the ceremonial role of the monarch. The British colonial administration also wanted the Swazi monarch to play a merely ceremonial role, as does the British monarch, and stay clear of partisan politics.

The Reactions of the SNC, EAC, and Progressives to the 1963 Constitution

The British struggled to present a compromise document by trying to please all the stakeholders by means of the 30–30–30 formula, which was intended to incorporate the viewpoints of the Conservative monarchists, the Whites, and the Progressives, but they ended up pleasing no one. The 1963 constitution was not a document that united, as all the protagonists took a shot at it. The SNC–EAC alliance was against the constitution, so were radical political parties.

[18] For more on the conflict between the British monarchy and parliament in the seventeenth century see D. C. North and B. R. Weingast, 'Constitutions and Commitment: The Evolution of Institutions Governing Public Choice in Seventeenth-Century England', *The Journal of Economic History*, 49, 4 (1989), 803–832; C. J. Davis, 'Blair Worden, Roundhead Reputations: The English Civil War and the Passions of Posterity', *Parliamentary History*, 21, 3 (2002), 397–398; and C. Hill, 'Parliament and People in Seventeenth-Century England', *Past and Present*, 92, (1981), 100–124.

[19] The sovereignty of the people or popular sovereignty is the principle that the authority of the state and its government is created and sustained by the consent of the people through their elected representatives who are the source of all political power. Power should therefore emanate from the people through their elective representatives. The idea of popular sovereignty is also closely associated with the political philosophies of Thomas Hobbes, John Locke and Jean-Jacque Rousseau (see S. Lee, 'A Puzzle of Sovereignty', 29–51, In N. Walker (ed.), *Relocating Sovereignty* [London: Routledge, 2018]; H. Lindahl, 'Sovereignty and Symbolization', *Rechtstheorie*, 28, 3 [1997], 347–371; and E. A. 'Or to the People: Popular Sovereignty and the Power to Choose a Government', *Cardozo Law Review*, 39, 6 [2018]).

140   H. P. DLAMINI

King Sobhuza and the SNC

The *Ngwenyama* appeared to be the greatest loser under the new constitutional dispensation, because he was given no significant role in modern governance beyond being allowed to manage cultural and traditional matters. The *Ngwenyama* called the SNC to a meeting to discuss the White Paper on Swaziland's constitution that treated him so shabbily. The meeting discussed certain clauses in the proposed constitution that clashed with the wishes of the SNC, which wanted to see the Swazi monarch given a more prominent role in the constitution. The *Ngwenyama* decided to send a petition to the British government to protest his marginalization. King Sobhuza sent a three-member delegation to London to submit the petition to the House of Commons. Prince Makhosini led the delegation, which included Polycarp Dlamini, the Secretary to the Swazi Nation, and A. K. Hlophe, the Private Secretary to the *Ngwenyama*. The delegation left Jan Smuts Airport on 14 July 1963.[20] The *Ngwenyama* objected to the following matters, none of which was new; namely, that the 1963 constitution:

i. sought to impose a system of electing members of the Legislative Council that was wholly unsuitable to and unacceptable by the people of Swaziland;
ii. ignored the protectorate status of Swaziland;
iii. ignored the petitioner's rightful position as king of Swaziland;
iv. took rights to land and minerals away from the Swazi nation; and also
v. took away from the Swazi nation, the Swazi National Council, and the *Ngwenyama*-in-Council powers in regard to its own institutions.[21]

The *Ngwenyama* also pointed out that the method of conducting elections was confusing, in the sense that it seemed that a person on the electoral roll could vote three times. The *Ngwenyama* suggested that there should be a Swazi traditional system, a European voters' roll, and a national roll. He pointed out that 'any qualified European should have a right to choose

---

[20] Historical Paper Research Archives, Collection Number AD 1715, News from Swaziland, July 15, 1963. http://www.historicalpapers.wits.ac.za/inventories/inv_pdfo/AD1715/AD1715-29-3-4-001-jpeg.pdf. Accessed January 22, 2015.

[21] 'Ngwenyama's Petition to the Commons: Wants Changes Made in the Constitution', *Izwi Lama Swazi*, November 30, 1963.

4 THE IMPOSED 1963 CONSTITUTION, THE MAIDEN LEGISLATIVE ... 141

to be registered either on the European roll or on the national roll, but not on both.'[22] Any qualified Swazi should participate in the traditional way of conducting elections but would also have a right at any time to claim to be registered on the national roll and cease to take part in the traditional roll. Coloured people would have a choice of either participating in the traditional roll, or the European roll. In essence, the *Ngwenyama* was unhappy because he was given little recognition in the constitution and was reduced to the role of manager of culture and tradition. The *Ngwenyama* was virtually neutralized in the 1963 constitution and reduced to a figurehead, like a British monarch.

The Minister of State for Colonial Affairs, Lord Landsdowne, received the Swazi delegation. The SNC delegation requested Conservative British Member of Parliament, Major Sir Patrick, to present a petition on their behalf to the House of Commons. Following the presentation of the Swazi petition, Sir W. Teeling asked Duncan Sandys, the Secretary of State for Colonial Affairs, whether he would:

- recognize the *Ngwenyama* as king of Swaziland;
- grant an interview to the Swazi delegation representing the *Ngwenyama* in the next 10 days to discuss the proposed constitutional changes in Swaziland;
- modify the constitutional proposals for Swaziland contained in the White Paper by providing that the ultimate decision as to mineral concessions should be with the Swazi nation; and
- modify the constitutional proposals for Swaziland contained in the White Paper by providing that the High Commissioner should not have power of unlimited nomination of members of the elected Legislative Council, but that his powers should be restricted to the constitution.[23]

In response, Duncan Sandys made it clear that he was no longer prepared to reopen constitutional negotiations with the Swazis. He stated

---

[22] Historical Paper Research Archives, Collection Number AD 1715, News from Swaziland. http://www.historicalpapers.wits.ac.za/inventories/inv_pdfo/AD1715/AD1715-29-3-4-001-jpeg.pdf. Accessed January 25, 2015.

[23] Historical Paper Research Archives, Collection Number AD 1715, News from Swaziland. http://www.historicalpapers.wits.ac.za/inventories/inv_pdfo/AD1715/AD1715-29-3-4-001-jpeg.pdf. Accessed January 25, 2015.

142   H. P. DLAMINI

that the White Paper on the 1963 constitution was a result of three years of exhaustive consultation with different parties in Swaziland. The delegates were told that the constitution was devised as the first step towards self-government. They were advised to go home and to make sure that the constitution worked.[24]

The stance of the British Colonial Secretary was not good news for King Sobhuza and his EAC allies. Todd advised King Sobhuza not to give up the fight and to organize a referendum similar to the one he had organized earlier to test European opinion on the constitutional proposal of the SNC–EAC, but with a specific agenda to repeal the 1963 British imposed constitution. King Sobhuza II agreed to organize a historic referendum to repeal the imposed constitution, which he opposed due to its democratic aspects and the weakening of his position. It was believed that the people's endorsement of the *Ngwenyama*'s petition in a referendum could influence British opinion to change in favour of the *Ngwenyama* and drop the constitution that rendered him irrelevant.

The SNC decided to organize a referendum in order to show the support of the Swazi people for the King's petition against the 1963 constitution. As anticipated, the EAC endorsed the referendum, while the political parties rejected it and tried to persuade people from participating in it. The British colonial administration made it clear that it would not recognize the referendum because it was of no value. That did not stop King Sobhuza from proceeding with his referendum.

During the campaign for the referendum, the SNC and Swazi chiefs accused political parties of being disloyal to the Swazi king, and of attempting to cause a civil war and divide the Swazi nation. They alleged that the colonial administration also wanted a civil war because it supported the political parties. Among the Swazi traditionalist and rural population, it became anathema to be associated with political parties, referred to in *siSwati* as *Uyiphathi*, a label for a traitor.[25]

Since the level of literacy was low in the 1960s, with less than 70%[26] of the people having received an education, the electorate were asked to

---

[24] Ibid.

[25] Ibid.

[26] The 70% statistics for the illiteracy rate in Swaziland was just an estimate and was probably higher. This estimate is contained in the petition written by the President of the Swaziland student Union (SSU) to the British Secretary of State in 1967 of the illiteracy rate in Swaziland (see, 'Student Leader Attacks Constitution', *Times of Swaziland*, May 12, 1967).

4 THE IMPOSED 1963 CONSTITUTION, THE MAIDEN LEGISLATIVE ... 143

choose between two symbols: a reindeer and a lion. The reindeer stood for the rejection of the King's petition, while the lion stood for the support of the *Ngwenyama*'s petition against the 1963 imposed constitution. The political parties were depicted in the symbol of the reindeer—a strange animal with horns lacking a straight direction. The Swazis, of course, could easily relate to the lion, since the King, in Swazi culture, is also referred to as the lion and his children are referred to as cubs.

The referendum on repealing the constitution was held in Swaziland on 19 January 1964 and was boycotted by political parties. The result was an overwhelming majority vote for the lion, meaning the people supported their King's petition against the 1963 imposed constitution (Table 4.1).

Those who voted for the *Ngwenyama*'s petition against the 1963 constitution numbered 124,218, while 162 voted for the imposed constitution.[27] The result was 99.87% in favour of repealing the British 1963 Constitution and in support of King Sobhuza II. The *Ngwenyama* was pleased with the results, which he interpreted as a vote of confidence in him by the Swazi people.[28] King Sobhuza used the outcome of the referendum to petition the British government to repeal the Constitution. *The Times of Swaziland* commented:

> Following Todd's recommendation [for the holding of a referendum] there has been a dramatic change of things in which the Swazi National Council says that practically the whole population was unanimous in rejecting the White Paper.[29]

Table 4.1 The January 1964 Referendum Results

	Lion	Reindeer
Swazis	122,505	154
Europeans	1400	8
Eurafricans	313	0

Source 'Sandys Answers Questions on the Referendum', *The Times of Swaziland*, February 28, 1964

[27] Matsebula, *A History of Swaziland*, 240.

[28] Interview with Prince Masitsela, Emafini, January 25, 2015.

[29] 'SNC Petitions the Queen: Cable Sent to Sandy', *Times of Swaziland*, September 6, 1963.

144   H. P. DLAMINI

Unfortunately, the referendum did not change anything, as the British government distanced itself from it, rejecting both the petition and the referendum.[30] The British government tenaciously stuck to the 30–30–30 voting arrangement and decided to press ahead with the election, which was scheduled for 23–25 June 1964.[31]

Todd and the EAC

Similarly, Todd was opposed to an imposed constitution when they had not yet agreed on its details on the grounds that it favoured the leftist politicians and it 'gave opportunities for the growing Swazi elite and professional class to exert [unnecessary] influence', which was not always favourable to the business class and investors.[32] He called on all Whites to support King Sobhuza's constitutional proposals, which had been endorsed by the EAC. In June 1963, Todd went to the United Kingdom to lobby for modifications to the franchise plan. He suggested the inclusion of South Africans on the national roll, because they were heavy investors in the Swazi economy, but the British refused. One commentator, referring to his efforts, described him as 'Roy Welensky',[33] because of his uncompromising position and his insistence on the rights of the Whites and the protection of the Swazi monarch.[34] Again, in August 1963, Todd revived the referendum plan for Swaziland under the auspices of King Sobhuza, which the British government treated as irrelevant.[35] This last-ditch attempt to torpedo the British-imposed constitution by standing together with King Sobhuza II was disappointing. Addressing the Swazilanders, Todd claimed that a great deal of effort had been made to prepare a constitutional document that

[30]'Make the Constitution Work: Urges Fletcher', *Times of Swaziland*, September 13, 1963.

[31]Levin 1997, 72; Macmillan 1985, 659.

[32]'Todd on the Talk in United Kingdom: An Imposed Constitution Would Not Work', *Times of Swaziland*, March 1, 1963.

[33]Roy Welensky was the Prime Minister of the federation of Rhodesia and Nyasaland from 1956–1963. He distinguished himself as a hard-fighting and stubborn politician who stood for White supremacy and resisted attempts by the black majority to achieve an inclusive democratic system of government (see A. S. Mlambo, *A History of Zimbabwe* [New York: Cambridge University Press, 2014, xxxii]).

[34]'Todd Doomed to Same Eclipse as Welensky', *Times of Swaziland*, July 12, 1963.

[35]'Todd: White Paper Turned Down by SNC: A New approach Suggested', *Times of Swaziland*, August 30, 1963.

4 THE IMPOSED 1963 CONSTITUTION, THE MAIDEN LEGISLATIVE ... 145

was acceptable to the majority of the people but that Britain preferred to act alone and set itself against the Swazi people. Todd stated:

> [We] spent a great deal of time of the past year negotiating with the British Government in London and with the Swazi National Council and Swazi leaders in trying to find a compromise that would be acceptable to the people of Swaziland and ensure a constitution that would give confidence to the bulk of their people in their future wellbeing. Unfortunately the British Government [had] pursued an uncompromising policy of imposing their will without reference to the vast majority of the people and this policy [had] brought the government into conflict with the Swazi nation led by the *Ngwenyama*.[36]

Todd maintained that he was sceptical of British Westminster democracy being applied to Swaziland, because events in other parts of Africa had shown how impossible it was for minority interests to be protected under such a political system.[37] Westminster democracy was bad for minority interests, while the traditional Swazi monarchical system was ideal. Todd therefore proved to be the King's man in the very sense of the word, because he saw in that relationship the protection of White interests. A pro-royalist, Prince Mfanasibili described Todd as somebody who was open-minded and was a staunch supporter of King Sobhuza II. He was always close to the *Ngwenyama* and preferred to be incorporated into Sobhuza's fief than lose his investment in Swaziland.[38] He always nursed the fear that a leftist-dominated legislature could amend the law in Swaziland in such a way that White businesses would be jeopardized and Sobhuza was seen as their own protective shield that they had to support.

Other Non-EAC White Interest Groups

There were some splinter White interest groups operating independently that pronounced on the 1963 constitution. Michael Fletcher, the President of the Swaziland Chamber of Industries in Swaziland, urged the nation to accept the constitution and give it a trial.[39] Fletcher pointed out that the

---

[36] SNA: 'Letter from Carl Todd to Swazilander', Minutes of the Forth Reconstituted European Advisory Council Held October 15 and 16, 1963.

[37] Ibid.

[38] Interview with Prince MfanasibiliDlamini, at Coates Valley, Manzini, March 7, 2014.

[39] 'Make Constitution Work Urges Fletcher', *Times of Swaziland*, September 13, 1963.

146   H. P. DLAMINI

main concern was the uncertainty about the political future, which was harmful to industrial progress. He, therefore, urged the nation to make the constitution work in order to achieve the political stability that was essential to industrial development in Swaziland.

S. Gaiger, a member of the Swaziland Chamber of Commerce and Industries, asserted that the constitution had recognized the contribution that the White community had made to the economic wellbeing of Swaziland. He pointed out that political differences should be put aside with the object of building a prosperous nation.[40] He argued that the constitution should be given a trial. Essentially, certain quarters in the White community demonstrated moderation by not rejecting the constitution outright and by calling for it to be given a trial.

The Progressives and the Swazi Educated Class

The Progressives and the Swazi educated class were not happy with the constitution, mainly because of a separate electoral roll for one set of Blacks and Whites, and another electoral roll for another set of the electorate. Furthermore, the reservation of one-third of the Legislative Council seats for the minority European community and the inclusion of the traditional methods of electing Swazis were unacceptable.

Ambrose Zwane's NNLC called an urgent National Executive Committee meeting on 1 June 1963 at Msunduza Hall in Mbabane to discuss the Constitution. At that meeting, the party resolved to boycott the Constitution, rejecting it on the grounds that:

i. it was discriminatory and 'racialistic', in that it allowed White South Africans to vote, while it denied the vote to the thousands of Swazis who worked in the Republic of South Africa;
ii. it blatantly and openly allowed separate voting of the 'White settler minority' from that of the indigenous African majority in order to give the former more political power in addition to their present economic control of the territory; and

---

[40]'Reactions to the Constitution: Whites Say Let's Do Our Best to Make it Work', *Times of Swaziland*, June 7, 1963.

4 THE IMPOSED 1963 CONSTITUTION, THE MAIDEN LEGISLATIVE ... 147

iii. it gave the Resident Commissioner or Her Majesty Commissioner enormous and uncontrolled power, while the position of the *Ngwenyama* as king of Swaziland was unsatisfactory.[41]

The NNLC maintained that they wanted a democratic system of governance based on universal adult suffrage with the *Ngwenyama* as king of Swaziland. They pointed out that the *Ngwenyama* should be the king of not only the Swazis, but also of Swaziland, and that all citizens, irrespective of colour, race or creed owe, allegiance to him. J. J. Nquku's faction of the SDP disapproved of the constitution, but indicated his intentions to cooperate to make it work.[42]

In reaction to the constitution, the SPP's President, J. Dlamini, and Secretary General, O. M. Mabuza, sent a letter to the Resident Commissioner, Brian Marwick, stating that the executive powers should not be vested in Her Majesty's Commissioner alone but should be shared with the Executive Council.[43] The party appealed for a change in the Legislative Council, suggesting that, of the 24 members, 16 should be elected on a national roll under the direct control of the *Ngwenyama*.

Apartheid South Africa

When it seemed obvious that the Sobhuza–EAC alliance was far from getting what they wanted, South Africa was worried about the prospects of a leftist regime emerging in Swaziland. Dr Verwoerd, the South African prime minister, moved swiftly and offered to incorporate the High Commission territories, including Swaziland, into the Republic of South Africa. In September 1963, Verwoerd offered South African guardianship of Swaziland and the other High Commission territories, which would be led to independence under the system of 'natural native democracy', which meant a system of the rule by African chiefs through Bantu authorities.[44] This was seen as a better alternative to the emergence and transfer of power to the Progressives at the expense of the Swazi traditional monarch. Instead

---

[41]'The Ngwane National Congress Rejects the Constitution', *Izwi Lama Swazi*, October 5, 1963.

[42]'The Constitution: A Fresh Start Even Now', *Times of Swaziland*, September 6, 1963.

[43]'Reactions to the Constitution', *Times of Swaziland*, June 7, 1963.

[44]Macmillan, 'Swaziland: Decolonisation and the Triumph of Tradition', 661.

148   H. P. DLAMINI

of neutralizing the monarch, as the British planned to do, it was better for Swaziland to be incorporated into South Africa where the traditional political institutions of the Swazi people would be allowed to survive and even be reinforced. Furthermore, the EAC viewed the incorporation of Swaziland into South Africa as a necessity for the White farmers, who would hopefully benefit from the open market and other advantages given to South African farmers.[45] At the opening of the Transvaal Congress of the National Party in Pretoria on 3 September 1963, Verwoerd suggested that the territories should be allowed to develop to independence under the guardianship of South Africa, instead of that of Britain. Verwoerd said he was 'making [the]…offer-almost a challenge', and that 'if South Africa were to become a guardian of these territories [the government] could lead them to independence and economic prosperity far more quickly and more efficiently than can Britain'. Verwoerd was particularly more interested in Swaziland than the other High Commission territories because of its 'White settler and Afrikaner farming populations'.[46] Verwoerd therefore wanted to annex Swaziland, if he had his way. If he could not do so, he was determined to insulate South Africa from simmering radical African nationalism in Swaziland. He viewed the rise of Black Nationalism in the High Commission territories under Britain as a threat to the apartheid state.

Verwoerd's government had a master plan in which Swaziland would become a state in the style of Bantustan pattern.[47] It was planned that this Swazi-stan would be linked with the *projischoff* (or the other Bantustan projects).[48] Verwoerd's aim was, no doubt, meant to exploit the problems Britain was having with the major political actors in establishing a constitution, and the disenchantment of the Swazi King with the British. Verwoerd's offer seemed to have been designed to undermine Britain's position in Swaziland, given its poor relationship with the Swazi monarch.[49] Britain's response to past South African demands for the incorporation of the High Commission territories was always that pledges had been made

---

[45] Stevens, 'Swaziland Political Development', 334.

[46] P. H. Bischoff, 'Why Swaziland Is Different: An Explanation of the Kingdom's Position in Southern Africa', *The Journal of Modern African Studies*, 26, 3 (1988), 459.

[47] Zwane, 'The Struggle for Power in Swaziland', 4–6.

[48] Ibid.

[49] Ibid.

to the inhabitants that they would have to be consulted on whether they wished to become part of apartheid South Africa or not. Verwoerd claimed that the path to multiracialism that Britain was pursuing was doomed to fail in Swaziland as it had failed elsewhere in Africa. South Africa was suspicious of Britain's policy of allowing the growth of Black nationalism in the High Commission territories and was determined to maintain stability in the Bantustans, which would be insulated from African nationalism. More than ever, South Africa was determined to influence developments in Swaziland, even if legal incorporation was impossible. Todd and a prominent White businessman, R. P. Stevens, supported Verwoerd's offer of partnering with Swaziland, because of the economic advantages to be derived. Todd maintained that Swaziland was already economically dependent on South Africa. According to him, it was possible for Swaziland to be linked to South Africa in a mutually beneficial way and still avoid being subjected to its apartheid policies:

> [Swaziland] may very well be able to find a basis of co-existence with Dr Verwoerd by establishing a form of government that is not in line with his Bantustan policy but which has objections of universal pattern on a Universal Suffrage on the Westminster…[model]…And particularly to defend [Swaziland's] economic wellbeing and avoid South African discrimination in Swaziland. Advantages [would] be that [Swaziland would] be a substantial winner of foreign exchange, all of which accrues to the Republic and a right to demand should be shared with [Swazis]. [Swaziland would] take advantage of Pongola dam which is flooding which can be used as a bargain over our water resources which is threatened.[50]

It seems most likely that this was a way the EAC could hit back at the British government for the imposed constitution by lobbying for some form of partnership between South Africa and Swaziland. Todd argued that a good neighbour policy was called for and that this would free Swaziland from economic threats, such as export duties, which inhibited free passage of persons and goods, and all the other prejudices of an independent antagonistic state.[51] Todd also proposed a possible partnership between South

---

[50]'People Impressed by Verwoerd's Offer Says Todd', *Times of Swaziland*, October 25, 1963.

[51]Ibid.

150 H. P. DLAMINI

Africa and Britain in exercising a common control over Swaziland as a protected state. Great Britain and South Africa would act in collaboration as protectors of the state under a defined treaty for their mutual interests.[52] It is clear that Todd had a sense of insecurity and that is why he felt South Africa was a partner to be considered seriously for a form of association. The problem with Todd's proposal was that Britain could not endorse it owing to the possible hostility of independent African states, given South Africa's racial policies.

Dr Zwane's NNLC reacted to Verwoerd's offer and Todd's stance negatively. Zwane suspected South Africa was concerned about a democratic Swaziland, because it would pose a serious threat to the apartheid system of government and its belief in the master race theory. He stated that 'nothing would be [more] undermining to Dr Verwoerd than to have a Swaziland on his boundaries in which Whites [were] equal to blacks.'[53] Zwane was not surprised that Todd was eager for incorporation into South Africa through trickery, because Todd was a strong supporter of Verwoerd and he had one foot in Swaziland and the other in South Africa. He was a South African-based businessman who spent most of his time in South Africa, and so he was bound to have interest in developing the South African connection because of his business interests. The British government ignored the criticisms of the 1963 Constitution and Verwoerd's and Todd's overtures, and proceeded to call for the June 1964 elections to be organized under the 1963 Constitution.

The June 1964 Elections and the Establishment of Swaziland's First Legislative and Executive Council

In June 1964, the British colonial administration decided to call for elections to be held under the 1963 constitution in order to establish governance structures that would constitute Swaziland's first steps into modern governance. The June 1964 elections were crucial for all the stakeholders, because the outcome was to determine the direction of constitutional change. As far as the British colonial administration was concerned, the *Ngwenyama* was not a consideration, because he was a traditional ruler who

[52] Ibid.

[53] 'NNLC's Reaction to Dr V's Offer', *Times of Swaziland*, December 13, 1963.

4 THE IMPOSED 1963 CONSTITUTION, THE MAIDEN LEGISLATIVE ... 151

was expected to remain neutral in modern politics. Britain banked on the nationalist political parties to participate in the 1964 elections. This upcoming election constituted a dangerous development for the *Ngwenyama*, the White community and the multinational investors, and apartheid South Africa, given that it represented the first step for the implementation of British decolonization policy involving the exclusion of traditional rulers. Apart from the British anti-traditional ruler policy, the *Ngwenyama* did not have a political party other than his White allies of the EAC.

King Sobhuza II had consistently kicked against the idea of political parties as being foreign and 'unSwazi', and he had dispatched the SNC delegation in the aftermath of the London Conference to tour the territory and speak against political parties. Sobhuza found himself in a quagmire over the issue of a political party because forming one meant he had to contest for power with commoners he was supposed to rule. Like his counterparts in other parts of Africa, the Swazi monarch initially found it difficult to contemplate forming a political party to contest elections with commoners when the origin of his power was hereditary and not the ballot box. The *Ngwenyama*'s conception of political power was true to the traditional realm of politics, not the modern. In the new political order created by the British, it was the Westminster institutions that dictated the nature and direction of governance, not Swazi traditionalism. The 1964 election was intended to endow Swaziland with its first modern governance institutions—institutions that would dominate the political space in Swaziland. It was expected to produce the Legislative Council, from which a constitutional committee would be selected to formulate a new constitution that would be acceptable to all. The stakes of the June 1964 elections were high, because of the far-reaching implications they had on the politics and economy of the territory.[54]

The elections were open to political parties that were generally of leftist leanings. But King Sobhuza had no political party. Yet, the power equation in the colonial order was being renegotiated between political parties and the British colonial authorities. The Progressive politicians demonstrated beyond reasonable doubt that they were a formidable alternative source of power by their ability to control the emergent labour movements to

---

[54]The political manifesto of the radical opposition parties published in the *Times of Swaziland* before the June 1964 elections was clear on a single electoral roll for all, and rapid Africanisation among other issues (see 'N.N.L.C. Chooses Candidates; Manifesto', *Times of Swaziland*, May 15, 1964).

152   H. P. DLAMINI

great effect. They sponsored a wave of strikes that began in 1962 and led to a general strike in June 1963 that culminated in the imposition of a state of emergency, the shipping in of a battalion of British troops from Kenya, and the curtailment of trade union activity.[55] The strikes reflected their influence, heightened the fears of White investors, and frightened the Swazi monarch. The SPP and NNLC were clearly behind the strikes, which exposed their radical agenda. Because of the Progressives, Swazi workers became more conscious of their rights and were determined to make their voices heard through industrial action.[56]

Workers had been operating under the traditional *indvuna* system[57] cleverly instituted by King Sobhuza's conservative SNC in which the *tindvuna* (senior advisors) were appointed to handle workers' interests by the Council, instead of being elected. This traditional system that King Sobhuza had instituted to regulate labour was intended to be a substitute for trade unions, which were viewed with scepticism, because of their propensity to organize strikes. The traditional *tindvuna* established by the Swazi monarch had to look into workers problems and sometimes even into their domestic affairs. The nascent trade unions that emerged with the birth of political parties in the logic of the right of association became an alternative counterforce to the authority of the Swazi monarch and a threat to White investors, particularly the investments of the Commonwealth Development Corporation (CDC) in the forestry and sugar industries.[58] Swazi workers felt the *indvuna* system was too traditional and did not represent their interests, so they started forming trade unions in the early 1960s with the encouragement of the radical political parties.[59]

---

[55] I. Raitt, 'Operation "Green Belt" in Swaziland', *Royal United Services Institution. Journal*, 109, 633 (1964), 40–44; A. R. Booth, *Swaziland: Tradition and Change in a Southern African Kingdom* (Boulder, CO: Westview Press, 1983); R. Levin, *When the Sleeping Grass Awakens: Land and Power in Swaziland* (Johannesburg: Witwatersrand University Press, 1997); and Hlandze, 'The Evolution of Worker's Consciousness in Swaziland'.

[56] R. Levin, *When the Sleeping Grass Awakens: Land and Power in Swaziland* (Johannesburg: Witwatersrand University Press, 2001), 65.

[57] A traditional method of using senior advisors to monitor the performance of group workers in a work place.

[58] Macmillan, 'Swaziland: Decolonisation and Triumph of Tradition', 661.

[59] For details on labour consciousness in Swaziland and the 1963 strike see S. Hlandze, 'The Evolution of Workers' Consciousness in Swaziland: The Case of Usuthu Pulp Company, 1948–1963', MA thesis, University of Swaziland, 2013. Also see Levin, *When the Sleeping Grass Awakens: Land and Power in Swaziland*, 66.

4 THE IMPOSED 1963 CONSTITUTION, THE MAIDEN LEGISLATIVE ... 153

On 18 March 1963, over 2500 sugar cane workers in Big Bend went on strike, demanding a monthly wage of R30 instead of the R7 they were receiving. In early April 1963, the newly formed Pulp and Timber Workers Union called a strike at Usuthu Pulp Mill after demands for a minimum wage were not met and two union members had been dismissed.[60] In response, the company's 800 workers supported the strike and only returned to work after they were promised higher wages.[61] The Usuthu Pulp Mill strike was successful and paved the way for further strikes in 1963. Workers of the railway station responsible for the transportation of iron ore to the port in Mozambique held a one-day strike over low wages and challenged the relevance of the SNC's *indvuna*, who were supposed to protect their interests.[62] In August 1962, the Swaziland Mining Workers Union was formed at the Havelock asbestos mine.

The Progressives engineered the pre-election 1963 strikes as a way of portraying themselves as champions of the workers' cause. In June 1963, the radical parties were able to use local grievances to instigate a general strike in Mbabane, the capital, in which over 8000 Swazis were involved. This led to the arrest and temporary incarceration of its ring leaders, Dr Zwane and Prince Dumisa Dlamini.[63] The fears that the Swazi monarch and the White community had often nursed about the radical nationalists were confirmed by these strikes. Of great significance was the fact that the strikes served notice to the White employers that politics and labour could find a common cause.[64] The strikes alarmed King Sobhuza, who saw them as driven by a Progressives' agenda to destabilize Swaziland and complicate its movement to independence. King Sobhuza II had no doubt in his mind that the Progressives were behind the strike.

> [He] wondered whether [there was] no more to the strikes in Mbabane and Havelock than a demand for higher wages. Strikes were usually engineered by people in industry but the document before him giving the resolution passed at the meeting in Msunduza Township last Sunday came from people in political parties. What puzzles me is what to call this thing that is happening.

---

[60] Ibid.

[61] Ibid.

[62] Macmillan 'Swaziland: Decolonisation and Triumph of Tradition', 661; Hlandze, 'The Evolution of Worker's Consciousness in Swaziland'.

[63] Potholm, 'Changing Political Configuration in Swaziland', 317.

[64] Ibid.

154　H. P. DLAMINI

Shall we call it a demonstration for a certain purpose? Or shall we call it a strike? What is it? We should make it perfectly clear in this council what the aim of all this is. [The *Ngwenyama*] ... said that when people gathered together in such large crowds a small spark could cause a big conflagration, and such damage could be done for no cause whatever ... Are we going to have strikes or are we going to talk amicably? What [do] they want [me] to do? ... Is this the way you will get your independence? ... I think this a setback for our people.[65]

The strike exposed the dangerous balance Sohhuza attempted to hold between the colonial state and the White investors he was expected to protect, on the one hand, and the Swazi workers he was supposed to defend against exploitation by White and multinational interests, on the other. His sympathy tilted towards the White investors and not the Swazi people, who were striking because of poor working conditions and who the *Ngyemyama* was supposed to protect against exploitation.

Sobhuza and the White community feared that the strikes, which the Progressives were sponsoring, had the potential of reducing the inflow of White capital so essential for the development of Swaziland, and of undermining traditional leadership. Workers defied Sobhuza II, who was against the strike and listened to the Progressives, who were for the strike and effectively went on strike. To allow the Progressives to dominate the public space through their control of labour unions and political organizations was dangerous.

The White community, multinational investors, and South Africa advised the Swazi monarch to form a political party to contest the June 1964 elections as a way of surviving politically, so that he could serve their interest as their ally. When King Sobhuza was set to form a political party, the British and the Progressives were opposed to it, because he could not be a king of the Swazis and indulge in competitive politics with his citizens, instead of being neutral. The British Commissioner, Brian Marwick, warned King Sobhuza in clear terms to stay out of party politics, because he was already the king of all the Swazi people. Following on the heels of Cohen's policy of the neutrality of traditional rulers in politics,[66] Brian Marwick told the *Ngwenyama* to steer clear of modern politics. Marwick

---

[65] Ibid., 69.

[66] See Robinson, 'Andrew Cohen and the Transfer of Power in Tropical Africa 1940–1951'.

advised King Sobhuza to prepare himself for the position of a constitutional monarch in the new political dispensation, similar to that of the United Kingdom.[67]

Marwick did not hesitate to underscore the official British position on the role of African traditional rulers in modern politics, which was neutrality and not direct engagement in party politics. He welcomed the proliferation of political parties in Swaziland as an inevitable part of political modernization and political apprenticeship, and called for a clear and unequivocal statement from the *Ngwenyama*-in-Council that 'no barriers [would] be placed in the way of political groups or electoral candidates who wished to make themselves and their policies known to the Swazis'. Marwick stressed his long-held conviction that the *Ngwenyama* should remain above party politics and that the SNC, which was in receipt of public funds, should not use its position to organize a political party in competition with others that did not have the advantage of such backing. He emphasized that the SNC should be a body representing Swazi law and custom, not a political party in disguise. Marwick stated that:

> if the traditional and conservative elements in Swaziland wished to form a political party to contest the June 1964 elections, they were free to do so by all means but they must not involve the King in that party and they must not use the Swazi National Council as a political instrument. They should stand and operate on equal basis with the other political parties and they should allow all contesting politicians to express their policies publicly.[68]

In a clear reference to White investors and South Africa, Marwick stated that he was aware of the fact that King Sobhuza and the SNC were in close collaboration with some powerful economic and political interest groups, and may be getting different advice from the advice he was giving. He warned that what was paramount was that the interests of the Swazi people should be protected and that, if the King were identified with a political party, this would promote intra-Swazi conflicts, which would bring Sobhuza's kingship into disrepute.

Similarly, Dr Zwane's NNLC argued against the King entering politics, because Sobhuza should stand as a symbol of unity and not become a divisive force. South Africa and the White minority in Swaziland did not

---

[67] 'Marwick, A Farewell Message', *Times of Swaziland*, April 24, 1964.

[68] Ibid.

156   H. P. DLAMINI

see things the same way as the British. The 1963 turbulence in Swaziland, sponsored by the radical political parties, convinced White investors, multinational business interests, and apartheid South Africa that King Sobhuza needed to form a political party to contest the June 1964 elections, in order to contain the radical nationalists, who represented a real danger to their interests. They were not comfortable with Marwick's political stance against the *Ngwenyama*, which appeared to create space for the cause of radical African nationalism.

Macmillan pointed to the CDC,[69] a major investor in Swaziland's forestry and sugar industries, as a strong lobby group behind the conservative Swazi monarch in colonial Swaziland. A British member of parliament, Geoffrey Lloyd, revealed that, after 1945, the CDC transformed the Big Bend area of the Great Usutu River into a pioneering region that was responsible for the production and export of half of Swaziland's sugar. In the 1960s, over 10,000 people lived there, dependent on the production of the sugar industry. The CDC made a loan of £100,000 to private enterprise development in the south of Swaziland, which was crucial in enabling the construction of a canal on the Great Usutu River and for the area to develop as a large, irrigated farming area. In collaboration with Courtaulds, the CDC was engaged in exploiting the great pine forests to produce sulphide pulp. The CDC was therefore the economic mover of Swaziland, and its investment was the largest the corporation had in any country.[70] The CDC and White investors abhorred industrial unrest, which was inimical to their investments, and 'had a direct interest in the maintenance of stability and the establishment of a conservative regime which would be unlikely to interfere with either capital accumulation or relations with South Africa'.[71]

---

[69] The CDC, a private liability company, was a Development Financial Corporation owned by the UK government. The Department for International Development was responsible for the CDC and the shareholders duties were managed by the Shareholder Executive Committee (see M. Cowen, 'Early Years of the Colonial Development Corporation: British State Enterprise Overseas During Late Colonialism', *African Affairs* [1984], 63–75).

[70] http://hansard.millbanksystems.com/commons/1968/jul/05/swaziland-independence-bill. HANSARD 1803–2005 → 1960s → 1968 → July 1968 →5 July 1968 → Commons Sitting → ORDERS OF THE DAY,SWAZILAND INDEPENDENCE BILL, HC Deb July 5, 1968, Vol. 767 cc1875-9031875. Accessed June 27, 2015.

[71] Macmillan, 'Swaziland: Decolonisation and Triumph of Tradition', 661.

White interest groups and apartheid South Africa[72] persuaded King Sobhuza to form a political party because they preferred him to the Progressive political leaders, and because staying out of modern politics would result in the monarch being eclipsed. As Potholm puts it, 'The White leadership [in Swaziland], feeling that they could deal most effectively with the traditional authorities, pressed the King to form his own political party, which could contest the national roll seats'.[73] Furthermore, prominent South African Afrikaner politicians such as the Broderbond member Van Wyk de Vries and MP, and later Prime Minister, B. J. Vorster also advised King Sobhuza to form a political party to contest the June 1964 elections, in order to remain relevant in Swazi politics. South Africa provided King Sobhuza with financial and organizational resources for the formation of his own political party to challenge the radical nationalists.[74]

King Sobhuza also relied on the technical advice of Douglas Lukhele, a junior partner in the Nelson Mandela and Oliver Tambo law firm.[75] In early April 1964, against the advice of the British, King Sobhuza liaised with the SNC and formed the *Imbokodvo* National Movement (INM) under the

---

[72] There is this apparent contradiction between South Africa's pro-Sobhuza policy and the Swazi monarchy's apparent toleration of the activities of South African liberation movements on its territory during the apartheid period. The Swazi monarchy was never a member of the front line states in Southern Africa and went as far as signing a secret non-aggression pact with South Africa in 1982 under which Swazi officials harassed African National Congress representatives in the capital, Mbabane, and eventually expelled them from Swaziland. South African security forces, operating undercover, also carried out operations against the ANC on Swazi territory (see B. Nyeko, 'Swaziland and South Africa Since 1994: Reflections on Aspects of Post-Liberation Swazi Historiography', *From National Liberation to Democratic Renaissance in Southern Africa* [2005]; P. H. Bischoff, 'Why Swaziland Is Different: An Explanation of the Kingdom's Political Position in Southern Africa', 457–471). Swaziland allowed the ANC to operate on its territory because it did not have an army of its own to stop them. In order to quell a labour unrest in 1962, the British had to import troops from Kenya. When one takes into consideration the fact that the Swazi ethnic group stretches into South Africa and there was no hardened line of demarcation between the two territories, it would be easy to understand why the control of the movement of South African guerrilla fighters was largely intractable. After Swazi independence, the building of a professional army was a slow and sluggish process meaning that the Swazi monarchy lacked the capacity to control the activities of the ANC and other rebel movements on its territories without direct South African involvement. The free operation of South African liberation forces on Swazi territory does not mean that Swaziland was officially pro-ANC.

[73] Potholm, 'Changing Political Configurations in Swaziland', 17.

[74] J. Daniel and J. Vilane, 'Swaziland: Political Crisis, Regional Dilemma', *Review of African Political Economy*, 13, 35 (1986), 56.

[75] Macmillan, 'Swaziland: Decolonisation and the Triumph of Tradition', 662.

158   H. P. DLAMINI

nominal leadership of Prince Makhosini but, in fact, under the King's complete control.[76] Potholm observes that the *Imbokodvo* was never a political party in the organizational sense of the word. It was, rather:

> an extension of the *Ngwenyama* and the Swazi National Council, which depended upon the prestige of the King, the concept of a unified Swazi nation, and the local authority of the chiefs, who owed their position to traditional Swazi law and custom and the largesse of the *Ngwenyama* at the centre.[77]

King Sobhuza was easily impressed by the arguments of his White allies that the Swazi political parties were a distinct threat to the traditional monarch and Swazi society. The programme of the radical political parties concerned the *Ngwenyama*, because it called for an overhaul of the traditional status quo, nationalization, and the end to racialism and tribalism. King Sobhuza was further perterbed by opposition party rallies of thousands of Swazis, and the opposition's ability to marshal mammoth strikes.[78]

Potholm makes a class argument about the reason why Sobhuza agreed to form a political party. He opines that *Imbokodvo* was actually established as a way of meeting the requirements of the Westminster electoral process to give political expression to the class interests of Swaziland's traditional nobility, made up of the royal family and chiefs, for whom Sobhuza was the principal spokesperson.[79] The establishment of the *Imbokodvo* goes beyond class interests. It was a response to the fear of the prospects of the rise of the Progressives, and the attendant implications regarding the future of the Swazi monarchy as a traditional institution and the investments of private investors. *Imbokodvo* was expected to defend the economic interests of White investors and check the rise of inimical ideas that were prejudicial to apartheid South Africa, an important economic backbone of the territory. *Imbokodvo* was therefore an offshoot of a wider and a formidable coalition of interests and economic investors that were fearful of radical nationalism and disruptive strikes.[80]

---

[76] C. P. Potholm, 'Changing Political Configuration in Swaziland', *The Journal of African Studies*, 4, 3 (1966), 314–315.

[77] Ibid., 315.

[78] Ibid.

[79] J. Daniel and J. Vilane, 'Swaziland: Political Crisis, Regional Dilemma', 56.

[80] Ibid.

4 THE IMPOSED 1963 CONSTITUTION, THE MAIDEN LEGISLATIVE … 159

The British Commissioner, Brian Marwick, came to be seen as a thorn in the flesh of King Sobhuza II and the business community, because of his attacks on Sobhuza and the embargo he placed on him not to indulge directly in party politics, which was reserved for the non-royal Western-educated political elite. The CDC and White investors abhorred the industrial unrest being sponsored by the Progressives, as it was inimical to their investments. They 'had a direct interest in the maintenance of stability and the establishment of a conservative traditional regime which would be unlikely to interfere with either capital accumulation or relations with South Africa', which they cherished for business.[81] Macmillan states that the multinational investors successfully lobbied the Colonial Office to orchestrate Marwick's retirement in April 1964, because of his steadfastness in ensuring the transfer of power to leaders of political parties in the territories who were overwhelmingly leftist in inclination.[82] This was clear evidence of the sacrifice of post-World War II British decolonization policy in Swaziland on the altar of economic pragmatism.

The *Ngwenyama*'s formation of a political party, *Imbokodvo*, was a welcome relief to White investors and apartheid South Africa. Once the *Ngwenyama* formed a political party, the White community in Swaziland had to follow suit in order to contest the seats on the White roll and national roll provided in the 1963 constitution. The Whites formed a political party, the United Swaziland Association (USA), led by three ranchers: Willie Meyer, R. P. Stevens, and J. D. Davies. The USA was out to preserve the primal position of Europeans in Swaziland, particularly their economic investments and property rights (which had already been guaranteed by the *Ngwenyama*), while supporting the *Imbokodvo* on land and mineral issues would be under the control of the Swazi monarch. The USA, like the *Imbokodvo*, was fearful of the rise of radical Black nationalism in Swaziland espoused by the leftist parties. Another party of liberal Whites was formed: the Swaziland Independent Front (SIF), which was also to contest elections for the seats on the European roll. This party was different from the USA by virtue of its composition and ideology. It was non-racial, because it opened its doors to Blacks, and it stood for a political order that respected the wishes of the people and not those of a particular race.

[81] Macmillan, 'Swaziland: Decolonisation and Triumph of Tradition', 661.
[82] Ibid.

160   H. P. DLAMINI

With the formation of the *Imbokodo*, the SNC formally asked King Sobhuza to contest the June Legislative Council elections at a meeting of 2500 Swazis at Royal Cattle Kraal, Lobamba, on 16 April 1964. King Sobhuza accepted the invitation. At the meeting, King Sobhuza said that Swazis of all colours had demonstrated their solid support for him in the January 1964 referendum. He therefore, called them *Imbokodvo Emabalabala* (the grinding stone of many colours), reflecting the image of something compact and hard to break to stand behind him.[83] This was a clear political statement indicating the toughness of his political organization with regard to other political formations in the territory, and calling on all Swazis to stand behind him. The *Imbokodo* articulated its campaign platform on protecting peasant lands from nationalization and assisting the peasants, while labelling the other parties as 'foreign', 'unSwazi', divisive, and hostile to Swazi tradition and the King. They promised to keep traditional land tenure unchanged, and distanced themselves from any form of nationalization, while vesting mineral and land rights in the hands of the *Ngwenyama*.

King Sobhuza II appointed Prince Makhosini Dlamini to tour Swaziland and explain to the Swazi people what the elections were all about. Both before and after Sobhuza's referendum, the SNC travelled the length and breadth of Swaziland speaking against political parties and elections. After the formation of the *Imbokodvo* in April 1964, the pro-monarchists were on the road again, explaining to Swazis why they had to vote for the King in the forthcoming legislative elections.

The outgoing British High Commissioner in Swaziland, Brian Marwick, was furious at King Sobhuza's formation of a political party and at his entry into modern politics, contrary to British constitutional tradition. Marwick condemned the King in very harsh terms for bringing Swazi traditional institutions into disrepute, and for enjoying unfair competition with other political formations in the territory by virtue of being the king of all Swazis. Marwick pointed out that modern politics was not meant for traditional rulers, who were the product of a totally different civilization and system of governance, and that King Sobhuza's entry into modern politics was not healthy for the political future of Swaziland. He insisted that King Sobhuza should restrict himself to traditional matters and leave politics to modern politicians.

---

[83]'Ngwenyama and Swazi Council Enter Politics', *Times of Swaziland,* April 24, 1964.

4 THE IMPOSED 1963 CONSTITUTION, THE MAIDEN LEGISLATIVE … 161

Marwick had no kind words for King Sobhuza and the SNC in his farewell speech as the outgoing High Commissioner for Swaziland. He described Sobhuza as being 'obstructive' to the electoral process, as reports reaching him indicated that opposition candidates were oppressed and disallowed from freely campaigning, and that this was a bad omen for Swaziland's first experiment with modern elections. He questioned the impartiality of the *Ngwenyama*. Marwick stated:

> I have been told the *Ngwenyama* himself addressed the Lobamba meeting and identified himself beyond doubt with the political group 'Imbokodo'. I was also told another meeting called for May 15th at which the names of the 'Imbokodo' candidates for elections would be announced and instructions issued presumably through the Swazi National Council and tribal channels to voters to choose these men.[84]

What this meant, in essence, was that the *Ngwenyama*-in-Council, who was supposed to be answerable to the whole Swazi nation, was entering the political arena backed by the prestige of the King and the machinery of the SNC which was, incidentally, paid for by all Swaziland's tax payers. Marwick accused the King of misusing public funds:

> I put it to you gentlemen that by identifying the *Ngwenyama* with the Swazi National Council or 'Imbokodo' political thinking and by misusing your staff and machinery for electioneering purposes as I have no doubt you intend to do, you will do more to put Swazi against Swazi and to bring kingship into disrepute than by any other acts.[85]

Marwick warned that Sobhuza would lose his throne, if he continued to indulge in modern politics.[86] He stated that, by listening to advice from interest groups and lobbyists who did not care about the Swazi people, King Sobhuza was not being of service to his country. He enjoined Sobhuza to 'think well on this' as his advice was genuine and not motivated by any personal interests. He stated that his 'advice [came] to [Sobhuza] a few days before [he] finally [left] Swaziland' and that '[he had] nothing to gain by misleading [the King], and [that] after over 30 years of service to

---

[84] 'Strong Criticism of Country's Political Direction: Sir Brian Hits Out Sharply in Last Big Speech', *Times of Swaziland*, April 24, 1964.

[85] Ibid.

[86] 'Strong Criticism of Country's Political Direction: Sir Brian Hits Out Sharply in Last Big Speech', *Times of Swaziland*, April 24, 1964.

162   H. P. DLAMINI

Swaziland, [he thought he had] a right to ask that [the King] give [his advice] due weight.'[87]

The Swazi traditionalists in the *Imbokodvo* royal party responded promptly to Marwick's criticisms. They stated that Sir Brian Marwick had ignored the will of Swazis by imposing the 1963 Constitution on them – a constitution that completely marginalized King Sobhuza. They pointed out that, under the Constitution, the *Ngwenyama* had 'become a mere useless little tail, a relic which [was] to be done away with as soon as expedient', and that the will of the Swazi people had been ignored and the *Ngwenyama* 'was reduced to a caricature'. They urged the British colonial administration 'to respect and acknowledge the position of *Ngwenyama* as King of Swaziland' in the governmental machinery.[88] The traditionalists stated that the *Ngwenyama* was just doing his job and that the people of Swaziland looked to him for leadership. They further argued that, in Africa, 'kings are leaders as well as kings', and Sobhuza should be recognized and respected as such. In response to Sir Brian Marwick's plea for political parties to develop freely and operate without harassment, the *Imbokodvo* stated that political parties had, so far, 'used despicable methods of bribery, intimidation, calumny and defamation', and that they had demonstrated little or nothing of an honest attempt to propagate policy. Yet, the British were silent about their excesses and were focusing their criticism solely on the *Imbokodvo*.[89]

Dr Zwane of the NNLC said that the decision of the *Imbokodvo* to fight the legislative elections in June would do the monarch the greatest harm. The monarch should be a symbol of national unity and an independent part of the constitution.[90] He pointed out that the *Imbokodvo* was making the people vote on royalty rather than on policy, and warned that the King would end up in trouble in the same way that King John of England, at the time of the Magna Carta, was forced to come to terms with his people.[91]

[87] 'Sir Brian to the King: This Is the Advice I give to You. Preserve Your Office', *Times of Swaziland*, April 24, 1964.

[88] 'Imbokodo Reply to Sir Brian', *Times of Swaziland*, May 8, 1964.

[89] 'National Council to Reply to Sir Brian Next Week. The King's Speech to Sir Brian Marwick', *Times of Swaziland*, May 1, 1964; 'In Africa Kings Are Leaders as Well as Kings: Imbokodo Reveals Itself, Attacks Sir Brian Marwick', *Times of Swaziland*, May 8, 1964.

[90] 'Zwane Objects to Council in Politics', *Times of Swaziland*, April 24, 1964.

[91] Ibid.

4 THE IMPOSED 1963 CONSTITUTION, THE MAIDEN LEGISLATIVE ...   163

The NNLC concluded that the King should stay clear of politics if he expected to conserve his throne. The agitations of the monarchical traditionalists was a pointer to the fact that, if they had their way in the June 1964 elections, they would overhaul the British-tailored 1963 Constitution to place King Sobhuza at the centre of the governmental machinery. Swaziland's radical political parties were also determined to pursue their agenda of one-man-one-vote and a constitutional monarch. The outcome of the June 1964 elections was, therefore, crucial in determining the constitutional future of Swaziland with reference to the role of the monarch, which the British and the radical nationalists were determined to neutralize. The June 1964 election was a struggle for the survival of the Swazi monarch and the stakes were therefore very high for all the stakeholders of Swazi politics.

THE JUNE 1964 ELECTIONS AND THE STRATEGY OF THE *IMBOKODVO*–USA COALITION

For the first election, there was general euphoria that the colonial government was organizing in the territory to initiate the process of internal self-government as a prelude to the departure of the British. Candidates seeking election were required to meet certain criteria. For instance, a Swazi had to be a British subject or British protected person who had resided in the country for at least three years, and who had paid direct tax or, in the case of women, be the wife of a man who had paid tax. Only one wife of a polygamous man could vote. However, the inclusion of the clause restricting voting to one wife for polygamous men was criticized by the Swazis, as it violated Swazi culture.[92] There were two main camps involved in the June 1964 elections: the monarchists and the Progressives. Each camp came up with a strategy, with or without a support base. Various White business interests stood or lobbied for King Sobhuza to win the elections as insurance for their interests, just as they abhorred the Progressives and conspired to sink them.

For the purposes of the June 1964 elections, the British colonial administration redrew Swaziland's districts or constituencies, reducing them from six to four: Hhohho, Lubombo, Manzini, and Shiselweni. The previous six districts into which Swaziland had earlier been divided were Mbabane,

---

[92]Matsebula, *A History of Swaziland,* 241.

164 H. P. DLAMINI

Mankayane, Piggs Peak, Siteki, Manzini, and Hlatikulu.[93] The reconstitution of electoral constituencies is usually politically motivated, intended to favour a particular political party and disfavour another by playing on the concentration of the adherents of a political party. It was not an innocent act by the British colonial administration, which had come under the sway of White business interest groups and multinationals and their wish to contain the Progressives. It was clear to them that supporters of the Progressives were professionals, workers, and the educated elite, who were concentrated in the urban centres of Manzini and Mbabane. By reducing the number of electoral constituencies to four, and by integrating urban constituencies with the rural ones, the support base of the Progressives was inundated by the additional rural population, who were faithful supporters of the Swazi monarch. The rural votes were bound to swamp the urban votes. This was a clear case of flagrant gerrymandering by the colonial administration, which had come under the influence of White capitalist classes and was bent on suffocating the radical political parties.

At the level of political parties in Swaziland, the leaders of the White USA Party convinced King Sobhuza that they should form a coalition and plan a common strategy. The strategy devised was that the USA Party should take all the White reserved seats, while the *Ngwenyama* would appoint members to fill the Swazi reserved seats. The rest of the seats would be shared between the USA and the *Imbokodvo*. According to this logic, the *Imbokodvo*–USA coalition would realize their dream of dividing the national roll seats in the legislature between themselves at the expense of the radical nationalist parties, who would have zero seats and would be excluded from Swazi politics. The *Imbokodvo*–USA coalition was a good marriage of convenience and 'would not have arisen had not both groups feared the power of the other [radical] political parties'[94] Essentially, the USA Party and the *Imbokodvo* went into the elections as a coalition with the aim of eclipsing the radical political parties.

The *Imbokodvo*–USA coalition had the full backing of apartheid South Africa, which contributed financially to their election funds. The South African government gave King Sobhuza £25,000 for electoral expenses, leading to a widespread rumour that he was planning to sell his kingdom

---

[93] Macmillan 1989, 306; Potholm 1966, 316.

[94] Potholm, 'Changing Political Configuration in Swaziland', 316.

4 THE IMPOSED 1963 CONSTITUTION, THE MAIDEN LEGISLATIVE ... 165

to South Africa.[95] King Sobhuza campaign was well-funded from diverse sources from White interest groups and multinational business organizations, and supported by the South African radio station, which was used to carry campaign messages.[96] In this way, South Africa intended to promote the emergence of a pro-South African regime and, thus, avert the prospects of hostile Black majority rule in Swaziland. The *Imbokodvo* unfairly enjoyed extra facilities and support from the SNC derived from Swazi tax payers.

The Progressives were disadvantaged by the fact that they had failed to close ranks and form a united front in the same way as the *Imbokodvo* and USA had done. As if it were not enough, the hostile attitude of the traditional chiefs in the rural areas, who were subservient to King Sobhuza, targeted Progressive supporters. The chiefs threatened to expel anybody who voted for the Progressives. They prevented Progressive candidates from campaigning in some areas. Furthermore, over 7500 Black South Africans who had escaped the horrors of apartheid and were living in Swaziland were disenfranchised, unlike White South African residents who were likely to be favourable to the *Ngwenyama*.[97] The Progressives accused the *Imbokodvo* of negative campaigning, as it disparaged the Progressives and charged them with being disrespectful to the *Ngwenyama* and attempting to cause a civil war.

During the campaign, the Progressives presented a platform that was almost meaningless to the rural masses, and was far from comparable to that of the *Imbokodvo*. Progressive rhetoric on pan-Africanism, nationalization of private property in favour of Swazis, and the improvement of workers' overall working conditions had little meaning to the rural population. The issues that bothered the largely illiterate and rural electorate were the land confiscated by White settlers and loyalty to the *Ngwenyama*. The traditional monarch was seen by the royal population as the champion of the recovery of their land from Whites. The *Imbokodvo* platform was simple for the rural population to understand, as it promised to maintain the traditional land tenure system controlled by the chiefs, protect the interests of peasants, and protect the culture and tradition of the Swazi people and

---

[95] Macmillan, 'Swaziland: Decolonisation and the Triumph of Tradition', 662.

[96] Ibid.

[97] Macmillan, 'Swaziland: Decolonisation and the Triumph of "Tradition"', 661.

166   H. P. DLAMINI

the *Ngwenyama*.[98] Sobhuza's astute dealing with the British, with whom he had been engaged in a war of words, and the persuasive and coercionary power of the hierarchy of chiefs all played in his favour.[99] Sobhusa was able to tap into an 'immense reservoir of rural political conservatism on the nation-wide common roll to inundate the urban centres, so that even where the radical political parties did well [as in the urban areas of Mbabane and Manzini] they were unable to compensate for the huge rural votes of the *Imbokodvo*'. The fact that there was a referendum in January 1964, and calls for Swazis to stand behind the *Ngwenyama* and be watchful of political parties that were out to divide and destroy the Swazi nation, caused many to focus the minds on voting for the King. The assumption of many Swazis was that the election was simply a plebiscite for the *Ngwenyama*, and the rural population had no problem with that.[100] In essence, the election was not so much about competing platforms per se but, rather, about a vote for the King and the Swazi nation. Voters were persuaded to believe the interests of the King and the survival of the nation were one and the same thing.[101]

It should be noted that Todd was not a member of the USA Party. By agreement with King Sobhuza, and much to the surprise of the Whites in the territory, Todd joined the *Imbokodvo* and, in the June 1964 elections, stood as an *Imbokodvo* candidate.[102] He was the first White member of the *Imbokodvo*, a symbol of racial integration, according to the Swazi monarch. For Sobhuza, this was the best way to keep Todd within the system, knowing how resourceful the man could be to him.[103]

[98] M. Dlamini, *The Philosophy, Policies and Objectives of the Imbokodvo National Movement* (Swaziland Printing and Publishing Company, 1972).

[99] Ibid.

[100] C. P. Potholm, 'Swaziland in Transition to Independence', *Africa Report*, 12, 6 (1967), 49; C. P. Potholm, 'Changing Political Configurations in Swaziland', *The Journal of Modern African Studies*, 4, 3 (1966), 313–322.

[101] R. Levin, *When the Sleeping Grass Awakens: Land and Power in Swaziland* (Johannesburg: Witwatersrand University Press, 1997), 72, 73.

[102] Ibid. Also see Kuper, *Sobhuza II: Ngwenyama and King of Swaziland*, 253; L. Rubin and R. P. Stevens. 'Swaziland: A Constitution Imposed', Africa *Report*, 9, 4 (1964), 9.

[103] Ibid.

4 THE IMPOSED 1963 CONSTITUTION, THE MAIDEN LEGISLATIVE ... 167

Nomination of Candidates

The nominations of candidates for the first Legislative Council elections took place on 19 May, while the first elections for the Legislative Council were held on different dates in June 1964.

Election Proper and Distribution of Seats

Imbokodvo's victory was overwhelming for it won all eight elective seats with 85.47% of the vote, the SNC supplied them to the eight *tinkhundla* seats and they won one of the White seats; their allies, the USA, took a further six seats. Carl Todd won his White seat as an *Imbokodvo* member. Commentators such as Christian Potholm[104] who assert that the USA took all the White seats are almost surely wrong.

The 1963 constitution provided for a Legislative Council of 28 members. The Queen's Commissioner had the right to appoint four of the 28 members. There was a provision for two electoral rolls-one exclusively for Europeans and the other one national. Four Whites would be elected on a White roll and four others would be elected on a national roll. Eight legislative seats would be 'elected' through the traditional *tinkhundla* system (chiefdoms grouped for age regiment mobilization) which was essentially by appointment while eight Swazis would be elected on a national roll bringing the total to 16.

The nominations of candidates for the first Legislative Council elections took place on 19 May, while the first elections for the Legislative Council were held on different dates in June 1964. For the European roll, the following parties and individuals contested the elections: The (USA), the SIF and two independent candidates. The elections under this European roll took place on 16 June and all four seats were won by the USA. The elected candidates were B. P. Stewart (1129 votes), J. D. Weir (992 votes), E.G. Winn (983 votes), and W. P. Meyer (983 votes).[105]

Fifty-eight candidates representing four political parties were nominated under the national roll to run for 12 seats, eight for Swazis and four for Europeans. The parties were: the SPP, the SDP, the INM (*Imbokodvo*), and the USA. The voters on the national roll went to the polls on 24–25 June 1964 to choose 12 candidates. The results were announced on 27

---

[104]C. P. Potholm, *The Journal of Modern African Studies* 4, 3 (1966), 316.

[105]'USA Takes All Four Seats on European Roll', *Times of Swaziland*, June 19, 1964.

168 H. P. DLAMINI

June 1964, and showed that all nine *Imbokodvo* and three USA candidates were elected. By agreement with King Sobhuza, and much to the surprise of the Whites in the territory, Todd joined the *Imbokodvo* and, in the June 1964 elections, stood as an *Imbokodvo* candidate.[106] For Sobhuza, retaining Todd within the system was a boon.[107]

On 26 June 1964, in accordance with the requirements of the Constitution, the SNC presented to the chief electoral officer the eight members who had been selected by the Council by following the traditional Swazi way of acclamation. Thus, the SNC supplied them with eight *tinkhundla* seats.

Imbokodvo's victory was crushing: it won all eight elective seats with 85.47% of the vote, the SNC afforded them eight *tinkhundla* seats, bringing the total to 16, and they won one of the White seats, giving an overall total of 17 seats. The *Imbokodvo* allies, the USA, won a further seven seats.[108] The *Imbokodvo*–USA coalition, which had been formed to fight the 1964 elections, turned out to be very effective, because it successfully stifled the other political parties that had been operating in Swaziland since 1960. In the share-out strategy of the *Imbokodvo*–USA coalition, the *Imbokodvo* nominated candidates were acclaimed on the traditional roll, while USA candidates won every European seat. As for the remaining seats on the national roll as provided in the Constitution, the *Imbokodvo*–USA candidates won all the seats.[109] Thus, once the *Imbokodvo* and USA decided to close ranks and cooperate, victory was a foregone conclusion. It should be pointed out that the *Imbokodvo* candidates were virtually appointees of King Sobhuza II. The implication was that they had to be totally loyal and answerable to him. A legislature with an overwhelming representation of pro-monarchical traditional and conservative elements would be expected to formulate a constitution that had the King at the centre of all affairs.

The odds mounted against the Progressives, as the outcome of the June 1964 elections was virtually insurmountable. The parties were largely disfavoured by lack of funds and by inexperience in political campaigns.

---

[106]Ibid. Also see Kuper, *Sobhuza II: Ngwenyama and King of Swaziland*, 253; L. Rubin and R. P. Stevens. 'Swaziland: A Constitution Imposed', *Africa Report*, 9, 4 (1964), 9.

[107]Ibid.

[108]Ibid.

[109]'Clean Sweep for Sobhuza: All Elected Seats Go to Traditionalists', *Times of Swaziland*, July 3, 1964.

They were blackmailed and completely misrepresented to the rural population, who came to see them as a bunch of misguided educated people who had forgotten their culture and tradition, and who wanted to destroy the monarch. The Progressives went into the elections in divided ranks, instead of endeavouring to establish a coalition. The Progressives were therefore badly defeated in the elections. While the *Imbokodvo*–USA candidates received 8000–14,000 votes in each of the four national constituencies, Dr Zwane's NNLC was able to muster a mere 2438 votes. Dr A. Nxumalo's SDP received 237 votes; J. J. Nquku's faction of the SDP, 56 votes; while O. B. Mabuza, of the other splinter Swazi Progressives, received 26 votes. Likewise, the liberal White parties, including the hastily contrived SIF represented by F. Corbett and R. J. Lockart, were defeated by large majorities.[110]

The Progressive political parties protested in vain about election malpractices in which the King and the SNC were engaged in including intimidation, political blackmail, and the disenfranchisement of Black South African residents. The Queen's Commissioner, Sir Francis Lloyd, referred the petitions to the Colonial Office, advising that the courts should handle the matter. The British Colonial Secretary, Duncan Sandys, responded to the joint memorandum regarding the protest from political parties over election malpractices by pointing out that 'the test for alleged malpractices during the elections lies with the courts, and that the parties should seek legal counsel from their legal advisers'.[111] Although the British government responded to the petitioners by suggesting that the matter should be referred to the courts, there was more to the matter than that. The British colonial government in Swaziland was disinclined to pay heed to any petitions about the unfairness of the elections owing to the influence of multinational capital that was behind the *Imbokodvo*. The fate that befell Brian Marwick was still hovering over the head of his successor, Sir Francis Lloyd, and he merely forwarded the complaints to the Colonial Office with a commentary that it was the responsibility of the courts to look into such matters.

The June 1964 election did not turn out to be the dangerous game of which King Sobhuza II had been fearful. The idea of forming political

---

[110] Ibid.

[111] 'Sandys Replies to Political Parties: Test for Alleged Electoral Offences Lies in Courts', *Times of Swaziland*, July 10, 1964.

170   H. P. DLAMINI

parties and engaging in multiparty elections had been a real nightmare for King Sobhuza, because of the electoral successes of the Western-educated elite in other parts of Africa, and because of the propaganda and mobilizing crowd-pulling capacity of the Progressives in Swaziland. The 1964 election favoured the Swazi monarch in a significant way, and brought him back to the centre of Swazi politics to start calling the shots. C. P. Potholm explains that 'the June 1964 election enabled the *Imbokodvo* leaders to take a more relaxed view of Western-style elections and removed some of their doubts concerning majority rule'.[112] The election brought King Sobhuza II into the modern politics of he had often been suspicious of joining as a player.

The political implications of the crushing defeat of the radical political parties at the polls and the victory of the *Imbokodvo*–USA need to be analysed in order to establish their significance to Swaziland's colonial politics. The dismal performance of the Progressives in the June 1964 elections was demoralizing, and some started vacillating between whether to continue in their parties, or to cross the carpet and join the royal *Imbokodvo* party. Dr G. Msibi, leader of the MNC, left his party to join the royal *Imbokodvo*, and was rewarded with an appointment as its Secretary General. Two months later, S. Nxumalo resigned from the executive of the SDP to join the *Imbokodvo*. In March 1965, Dr A. M. Nxumalo, President of the SDP, abandoned his party and joined the *Imbokodvo*, calling on his followers to do same.[113] These defections were sufficiently serious to cause the SDP and MNC to dissolve. The SPP and NNLC continued to exist as the main extra-parliamentary opposition, despite continuous defections from their ranks. For instance, Arthur Khoza, the Secretary General of the NNLC, resigned and joined the *Imbokodvo*, and was rewarded with an appointment as the Private Secretary to Prince Makhosini.[114] These defections and carpet-crossings in favour of the *Imbokodvo* royalists emboldened Sobhuza, but they also compromised the political significance of his White USA allies, who were the brainchild of the destruction of the radical opposition.

[112]C. P. Potholm, 'Changing Political Configurations in Swaziland', *The Journal of Modern African Studies*, 4, 3 (1966), 313–322.

[113]'Democratic Party Joins the Imbokodvo', *Times of Swaziland*, April 23, 1965.

[114]Potholm, 'Changing Political Configurations in Swaziland'; H. Macmillan, 'Swaziland: Decolonisation and the Triumph of "Tradition"', *The Journal of Modern African Studies*, 23, 4 (1985).

4 THE IMPOSED 1963 CONSTITUTION, THE MAIDEN LEGISLATIVE ... 171

SWAZILAND'S FIRST LEGISLATIVE AND EXECUTIVE COUNCILS AND THE SELECTION OF THE CONSTITUTIONAL COMMITTEE FOR CONSTITUTIONAL REVIEW

The June 1964 elections produced members of Swaziland's first Legislative and Executive Councils. The Legislative Council was made up of three Europeans, elected on the national roll; four Europeans elected on the European roll; eight Africans and one European elected on the national roll; and eight others elected in accordance with Swazi traditional methods; four officials; and one nominated member. The Africans elected by Swazi traditional methods were J. M. Dlamini, M. K. Mamba, P. K. Dlamini, J. B. M. Sukati, D. A. Hlophe, G. L. M. Msibi, G. M. E. Mabuza, and J. Rose (who was Coloured). Thus, the membership of the first Legislative Council included six White USA members, one independent member, and 17 *Imbokodvo* members, including Carl Todd.[115] Sir Francis Lloyd used his discretion to appoint more members from the ranks of the *Imbokodvo* and the USA, bringing the total to 34.

The inauguration of Swaziland's maiden Legislative Council took place on 9 September 1964. It was a historic occasion and was given all the ceremonial importance it deserved. Her Majesty's Commissioner, Sir Francis Lloyd, appointed I. B. Aers, the Speaker of the House, while the members of the Legislative Council, as documented in Table 4.2, were sworn in as prescribed by section 27 of the Swaziland Order-in-Council.

Thereafter, Her Majesty's Commissioner delivered a message of good wishes from the Queen of England and the Secretary of State for the Colonies. The Commissioner noted that the inauguration of the Legislative Council was 'an important step in the constitutional advance of [the territory]', and wished the Swazis success in their work. He further stated:

> First, I want to congratulate you on your membership of Swaziland's first Legislative Council, which marks a very significant step in the constitutional advance [of the territory], and to express the hope that the deliberations will be attended by goodwill and understanding for the benefit of the people of this country. This is a great and important occasion in the history of Swaziland, and its significance lies in many things. But first and most important of all is that you met here, together today for the opening of a Council which

---

[115]Compiled from SNA: Swaziland Legislative Council Official Report (Hansard), First Session, Sittings from November 9 and 14, 1964.

172   H. P. DLAMINI

Table 4.2   Members of the 1964 Legislative Council

	Member	Political affiliation	Remarks
1	A. C. E. Long, C.B. E.	Chief Secretary	
2.	Prince M. N. Dlamini	Imbokodvo	Member
3.	Chief M. K. Magongo	Imbokodvo	Member
4	F. M. Mbelu	Imbokodvo	Member
5.	Prince J. M. Dlamini, B.E.M.	Imbokodvo	Member
6.	Dr G. L. M. Msibi	Imbokodvo	Member
7.	D. A. Hlophe	Imbokodvo	Member
8.	M. N. Gamede	Imbokodvo	Member
9.	B. A. Dlamini	Imbokodvo	Member
10.	M. G. Dlamini	Imbokodvo	Member
12.	N. M. Hlatshwako	Imbokodvo	Member
13.	W. M. M. Magongo	Imbokodvo	Member
14.	J. M. B. Sukati	Imbokodvo	Member
15.	Dr G. L. Msibi	Imbokodvo	Member
16.	J. Rose	Imbokodvo	Member
17.	W. P. Meyer	United Swaziland Association	Member
18.	E.G. Winn	United Swaziland Association	Member
19	J. D. Weir	United Swaziland Association	Member
20.	R. P. Stephens	United Swaziland Association	Member
21.	B. P. Steward, M.C.	United Swaziland Association	Member
22.	P. K. Dlamini	Imbokodvo	Member
23.	J. J. Dickie	Attorney-General	
24.	C. F. Todd	Imbokodvo	Member
25.	J. R. Masson	United Swaziland Association	Member
26.	H. D. G. Fitzpatrick	United Swaziland Association	Member
27.	M. J. Fairlie	United Swaziland Association	Member
28.	G. M. E. Mabuza	Imbokodvo	Member
29.	S. M. K. Mamba	Imbokodvo	Member
30.	A. K. Hlope	Imbokodvo	Member
31.	A.Z. Khumalo	Imbokodvo	Member
32.	M. N. Dlamini	Imbokodvo	Member
33.	C. A. B. Mandy	United Swaziland Association	Member
34.	Prince M. Dlamini	Imbokodvo	Member

Source Compiled from SNA: Swaziland Legislative Council Official Report (Hansard), First Session, Sittings from November 9 and 14, 1964

had been elected by people of all races throughout the country. This is the first time that such a joint Council has existed in Swaziland, and while I should like to take this opportunity to pay tribute to the work done in the past by such bodies as the European Advisory Council and the Swazi National

4 THE IMPOSED 1963 CONSTITUTION, THE MAIDEN LEGISLATIVE ... 173

Council, no group which is not composed of all the races in the territory can be truly representative of its people.[116]

He warned that no racial discrimination would be tolerated, and that there should be mutual respect for each other among the Swazi people, Black and White.

The *Ngwenyama* could not attend the inauguration, because he was very ill. He was represented by the *Ndlovukati* (queen mother) and S. T. M. Sukati, who read the King's speech on his behalf. The *Ngwenyama*'s speech hailed the historic opening of the first Legislative Council for Swaziland, and recounted that 'it was after many years of government by Proclamation...that the constitutional talks were initiated on 23 April 1960...'. He recognized the fact that Swaziland had arrived at this point only after many 'disappointments and tribulations' with particular reference of the refusal of the British to recognize the February 1964 referendum in which the imposed 1963 Constitution was rejected. The *Ngwenyama* expressed the intention of Swaziland to be independent within the Commonwealth of Nations and that the Constitution should serve as a vehicle to attain such a goal.[117] He expected the Legislative Council to make laws in the land in which all were treated equally, irrespective of race or colour.

Lloyd also appointed members of the Executive Council as prescribed by section 27 of the Swaziland Order-in-Council. The Council's membership is documented in Table 4.3.

Lloyd appointed A. K. Hlophe Member for Local Administration and Social Development, and Polycarp Dlamini Member for Education and Health. D. Fitzpatrick was appointed Member for Public Works and Communications, and C. F. Todd was appointed for Natural Resources. The royalist *Imbokodvo* and the White USA political parties made up the Legislative and Executive Councils in addition to the Commissioner's appointees.

Radical opposition parties were not represented in parliament owing to their poor performance at the polls. Dr A. Zwane's NNLC barely managed to garner 12% of the vote, which did not translate into any seat in the legislature, while the other Progressive parties simply fizzled out. In an editorial, *The Times of Swaziland* regretted the losses of dynamic parties in the elections, and emphasized that a vigorous opposition was a good thing

---

[116]SNA: Swaziland Legislative Council Official Report (Hansard), First Session, Sittings from November 9 and 14, 1964.

[117]Ibid.

174   H. P. DLAMINI

Table 4.3   Members of the Executive Council

Ex-officio members	Appointed members	Party affiliation
1. A. C. E. Long, Chief Secretary	Polycarp Dlamini	Imbokodvo
2. J. J. Dickie, Attorney General	A. K. Hlophe	Imbokodvo
3. J. C. Martin, Secretary for Finance and Development	C. F. Todd	Imbokodvo
4.	H. D. G. Fitzpatrick	United Swaziland Association
5.	M. J. Fairlie	United Swaziland Association

Source Compiled from SNA: Swaziland Legislative Council Official Report (Hansard), First Session, Sittings from November 9 and 14, 1964; News From Swaziland, http://www.historicalpapers.wits.ac.za/inventories/inv_pdfo/AD1715/AD1715-29-3-4-001-jpeg.pdf. Accessed January 25, 2015

for a healthy political atmosphere.[118] The newspaper observed that, in the absence of an opposition, no lively debates could be expected to come out of the Legislative Council, and there could be no checks and balances on the activities of the government.[119]

At the inaugural session of the Legislative Council, Prince Makhosini, *indunankhulu*,[120] (leader) of the *Imbokodvo* royalist group, which held majority seats in the House, indicated that the *Imbokodvo* would work for the advancement of Swaziland, and for the preservation of its kingship, customs, culture, and language, which must be recognized by the law. With reference to the election campaign and newspaper write-ups by Progressives, Prince Makhosini complained that some of his kinsmen and local newspapers considered the *Imbokodvo* royalist group as 'being retrogressive' and as 'tribalist'. This hurt the *Imbokodvo*, because the Swazi nation was represented by the king as its head, the traditional Council as the trunk, and the nation as the limbs. Alluding to the radical opposition parties, Prince Makhosini said the Progressive political leaders had gone

[118]'Comments', *Times of Swaziland*, July 19, 1964.

[119]Ibid.

[120]In siSwati *ndvunankhulu* means Prime Minister. King Sobhuza referred to Prince Makhosini as *Ndvunankhulu*. But Prince Makhosini was the leader of the majority party in parliament and not Prime Minister because there was no provision for that position in the 1963 constitution.

4 THE IMPOSED 1963 CONSTITUTION, THE MAIDEN LEGISLATIVE ... 175

to overseas organizations to lobby against the independence of Swaziland because, they claimed, the *Imbokodvo* is 'tribalistic and retrogressive'. He argued that the Swazis were a nation and not a tribe, and complained that the King of Swaziland was degraded and had not been accorded the place he deserved in the 1963 Order-in-Council. He declared that the *Imbokodvo* wanted to correct the situation. Prince Makhosini rejected the view that the Swazi king should be neutral in politics, and vowed that his party would fight for the recognition of the *Ngwenyama* of Swaziland. He pointed out that his party had won the elections under a constitution that it did not like and would, therefore, want to review it. Consequently, Prince Makhosini called for a committee to be set up from among the members of the Council to review the 1963 Order-in-Council to recommend amendments. The *Imbokodvo* had sent the signals for constitutional debates in the legislature's select committee.

THE 1965 CONSTITUTIONAL REVIEW COMMITTEE FROM THE LEGISLATIVE COUNCIL

Developments in Britain and the other High Commission territories put pressure on Swaziland to quicken its pace of constitutional development.[121] A change in government in Britain, with the coming of the Labour Party to power in October 1964 after 13 years of conservative rule, was dramatic: the new government set 1966 as the year for the independence of Basutoland and Bechuanaland. The *Imbokodvo*, which had initially preferred to move slowly on the issue of independence,[122] had to reconsider its position. Furthermore, when Prince Makhosini attended an ordinary session of the Organisation of African Unity (OAU) in March 1965, the clamour for independence was high on the agenda of African statesmen. These developments put pressure on Swaziland to speed up its campaign to effect constitutional amendments that would help it attain independence.

Prince Makhosini wrote to the British colonial administration requesting the Secretary of State to reconsider the revision of the imposed 1963

---

[121]Sobhuza's attitude towards independence is captured properly by his biographer, Kuper, who remarks that he was not opposed to independence but he was reluctant to push too hard on that because everything had its appropriate moment (see Kuper, *Sobhuza II: The Ngwenyama and King of Swaziland*).

[122]Attitude of Sobhuza captured by Kuper, *Sobhuza II: The Ngwenyama and King of Swaziland*.

176 H. P. DLAMINI

Constitution. The *Imbokodvo* received the support of their USA allies on the assumption that their own interests would also be served. Meanwhile, Carl Todd had written a confidential letter to King Sobhuza seeking reassurance that the existing privileges of Whites that had been negotiated with the monarch in the early 1960s would be safeguarded.[123]

On 18 August 1965, Commissioner Lloyd announced that the Colonial Secretary had agreed to review the 1963 Constitution, and had authorized the appointment of a constitutional committee to submit proposals for the establishment of internal self-government leading to independence.[124] Commissioner Lloyd proceeded to appoint the constitutional committee under his chairmanship, comprising two official members,[125] eight *Imbokodvo* members, four USA members, and two secretaries (see Table 4.4).

The 1965 Constitutional Review Committee was drawn almost exclusively from the Legislature, because its elected members had the people's mandate to act on their behalf. The SPP under Nquku, the NNLC under Dr Zwane, and a joint Council of Swaziland Political Parties under O. M. Mabuza made separate submissions to the Constitutional Review Committee, and sent memorandums of protest to the OAU and to sympathizers in different countries regarding their admission into the Constitutional Review Committee, but to no avail. As in previous constitutional conferences, King Sobhuza did not directly participate in the talks; instead he teleguided its proceedings through the *Imbokodvo*, the members of which were totally faithful to him. The Constitutional Review Committee was

---

[123] This confidential letter in which Sobhuza was expected to safeguard White interests in Swaziland was stolen by the opposition NNLC from national files and published in the times of Swaziland of November 1966 to discredit Sobhuza as a puppet of the White minority. Kuper states that King Sobhuza did not reply Todd's letter and did not therefore commit himself (see Kuper, *Sobhuza II: The Ngwenyama and King of Swaziland*, 265).

[124] 'Proposals for Constitution Sent to London', *Times of Swaziland*, March 11, 1966.

[125] In British Colonial Africa the British members of the colonial administration were technically referred to as "officials'. African members who were progressively incorporated in the executive and legislative structures of colonial Africa were technically referred to as unofficial members (see K. Ezera, *Constitutional Developments in Nigeria* [London: Cambridge University Press, 1964]; B. O. Nwabueze, *A Constitutional History of Nigeria* [London: C. Hurst and Company, 1982]). The files from Swaziland National Archives have also consistently referred to British officials in the colonial administration as "official" members and the non-British officials as unofficial members.

4 THE IMPOSED 1963 CONSTITUTION, THE MAIDEN LEGISLATIVE ... 177

Table 4.4 The 1965 Constitutional Review Committee

	Member	Affiliation	Comment
1.	Sir Francis Lloyd	British Commissioner and Chair	Official member
2.	A. C. E. Long	Chief Secretary	Official member
3.	J. J. Dickie	Attorney-General	Official member
4.	Prince Makhosini	Imbokodvo	Unofficial member
5.	Prince Masitsela	Imbokodvo	Unofficial member
6.	Prince Mfanasibili	Imbokodvo	Unofficial member
7.	A. K. Hlope	Imbokodvo	Unofficial member
8.	P. Dlamini	Imbokodvo	Unofficial member
9.	M. Sukati	Imbokodvo	Unofficial member
10.	Dr G. Msibi	Imbokodvo	Unofficial member
11.	C. Todd	Imbokodvo	Unofficial member
12.	A. H. Fitzpatrick	United Swaziland Association	Unofficial member
13.	R. P. Stephens	United Swaziland Association	Unofficial member
14.	W. Meyer	United Swaziland Association	Unofficial member
15.	A. G. Winn	United Swaziland Association	Unofficial member
16.	H. M. Roemmele	Assistant Chief Secretary	Served as secretary
17.	Rev. A. B. Gamedze	Senior Liaison Officer	Served as secretary

Source Compiled from SNA: Legislative Council Official Report, Hansard, 1965–1966

tasked with the work of reviewing the constitution and making recommendations to the Secretary of State for Colonies on the form of a new constitution. Chapter 5 focuses on the debates of the Constitutional Review Committee.

Conclusion

The British imposed the 1963 Constitution on Swaziland, because the delegates failed to arrive at an agreement at the 1963 London Conference. The Constitution provided limited internal self-government for the inhabitants of the territory, with the British Commissioner having veto powers. The Constitution was intended to be a compromise document, but it did not produce the desired effect. The SNC–EAC alliance was fearful of the document, and struggled to have their version of the constitution proposal, which protected them, adopted by the British, but to no avail. The Progressives felt the Constitution did not go far enough to institute adult universal suffrage by secret ballot.

178   H. P. DLAMINI

The traditional monarchists cried foul, because King Sobhuza was provided a token ceremonial role in the constitution. He sent a delegation to London to protest against the Constitution, but the delegation was turned back. He then organized an fruitless plebiscite on the Constitution to demonstrate that Swazis were against it in the hope that the British would repeal it, but they ignored the referendum. Todd's White community rejected the Constitution, because equal European representation was not included in it and the traditional monarchy, which they preferred to the radical political parties, was excluded. Radical political leaders rejected the Constitution on the grounds that it did not provide for one-man-one-vote under universal adult suffrage, and also because it introduced the 'federation of races', which favoured the White minority due to their disproportionate representation in the Legislature. Against a background of this wrangling, Britain announced elections for June 1964, and the various key players quickly readjusted and indicated their willingness to participate in the elections.

Events leading to the elections revealed tensions between Britain's project to modernize the constitutional and the conservative project of the *Ngwenyama* and his White allies. Whereas Britain insisted that African traditional rulers should maintain neutrality in modern politics, involving themselves exclusively with cultural and traditional matters, the *Ngwenyama* and his SNC disagreed. They felt the *Ngwenyama* should be the central figure in traditional and modern governance.

The labour unrest from 1962 to 1963 sponsored by the radical political party leaders threatened King Sobhuza's leadership, caused White investors concern, alarmed apartheid South Africa, and underscored the necessity of the *Ngwenyama* to enter modern politics. Against the wishes of the British, the *Ngwenyama* was persuaded to form a political party, the *Imbokodvo*, and to contest the 1964 elections. Clearly, British colonial policy favoured the transfer of power to the Western-educated elite operating under the banner of political parties. The White minority also formed the USA party to contest the elections and, possibly, minimize the influence of the radical nationalist parties. Thus, Sobhuza and the White community, who had long been opposed to the notion of political parties as 'unAfrican', made a U-turn and quickly formed political parties to join the existing ones, in order to contest the June 1964 elections, against the advice of the British Commissioner.

The stakes in the 1964 elections were high, because their outcome would shape the direction of the future constitutional development of Swaziland.

The royal *Imbokodvo* and the White USA party formed a coalition to contest the elections, and received logistical and financial support from White investors and apartheid South Africa, while opposition parties contested the elections in dispersed ranks. Not surprisingly, the *Imbokodvo*–USA alliance won all the seats. Swaziland's maiden Legislative Council was, therefore, monopolized by the conservative political elements. The Constitutional Review Committee, which was an offshoot of the Legislative Council, was composed exclusively of the *Imbokodvo* and the USA party. The initiative for the revision of the 1963 imposed constitution, therefore, fell on the *Imbokodvo* and USA parties, from which the Constitutional Review Committee was established. King Sobhuza II's throne was therefore safe; the Progressives had been completely eclipsed and were out of the Legislative and Executive Council.

REFERENCES

ORAL INTERVIEWS

Interview with Prince Masitsela, Emafini, January 25, 2015.
Interview with Prince Mfanasibili Dlamini, at Coates Valley, Manzini, March 7, 2014.

ARCHIVAL SOURCES

Swaziland National Archives
SNA: Swaziland Government Gazette Extraordinary, Vol. III, Mbabane, Thursday January 2, 1964; No. 15.
SNA: 'Letter from Carl Todd to Swazilander', Minutes of the Forth Reconstituted European Advisory Council Held October 15 and 16, 1963.
SNA: Swaziland Legislative Council Official Report (Hansard), First Session, Sittings from November 9 and 14, 1964.

NEWSPAPER ARTICLES

'Talks Begins with Smiles but End in Deadlock', *Times of Swaziland*, February 15, 1963.
'Constitutional Talks End', *Izwi Lama Swazi*, February 23, 1963.
'Todd on the Talk in United Kingdom: An Imposed Constitution Would Not Work', *Times of Swaziland*, March 1, 1963.
'Swaziland Constitution Announced, 8 Seats Reserved for Whites Out of 24 Elected Members', *Times of Swaziland*, May 31, 1963.

180   H. P. DLAMINI

'Reactions to the Constitution: Whites Say Let's Do Our Best to Make it Work', *Times of Swaziland*, June 7, 1963.

'Swaziland Constitution Announced', *Izwi Lama Swazi*, June 8, 1963.

'Todd Doomed to Same Eclipse as Welensky', *Times of Swaziland*, July 12, 1963.

'Todd: White Paper Turned Down by SNC: A New approach Suggested', *Times of Swaziland*, August 30, 1963.

'The Constitution: A Fresh Start Even Now', *Times of Swaziland*, September 6, 1963.

'SNC Petitions the Queen: Cable Sent to Sandy', *Times of Swaziland*, September 6, 1963.

'Make the Constitution Work: Urges Fletcher', *Times of Swaziland*, September 13, 1963.

'The Ngwane National Congress Rejects the Constitution', *Izwi Lama Swazi*, October 5, 1963.

'People Impressed by Verwoerd's Offer Says Todd', *Times of Swaziland*, October 25, 1963.

'Ngwenyama's Petition to the Commons: Wants Changes Made in the constitution', *Izwi Lama Swazi*, November 30, 1963.

'NNLC's Reaction to Dr V's Offer', *Times of Swaziland*, December 13, 1963.

'Constitution Now in Operation', *Times of Swaziland*, January 3, 1964.

'New Swaziland Constitution Comes into Force Today: Order in Council Published', *Times of Swaziland*, January 3, 1964.

'National Council to Reply to Sir Brian Next Week. The King's Speech to Sir Brian Marwick', *Times of Swaziland*, May 1, 1964.

'Imbokodo Reply to Sir Brian', *Times of Swaziland*, May 8, 1964.

'In Africa Kings Are Leaders as Well as Kings: Imbokodo Reveals Itself, Attacks Sir Brian Marwick', *Times of Swaziland*, May 8, 1964.

'N.N.L.C. Chooses Candidates; Manifesto', *Times of Swaziland*, May 15, 1964.

'Marwick, A Farewell Message', *Times of Swaziland*, April 24, 1964.

'Strong Criticism of Country's Political Direction: Sir Brian Hits Out Sharply in Last Big Speech', *Times of Swaziland*, April 24, 1964.

'Ngwenyama and Swazi Council Enter Politics', *Times of Swaziland*, April 24, 1964.

'Sir Brian to the King: This Is the Advice I Give to You. Preserve Your Office', *Times of Swaziland*, April 24, 1964.

'Zwane Objects to Council in Politics', *Times of Swaziland*, April 24, 1964.

'USA Takes All Four Seats on European Roll', *Times of Swaziland*, June 19, 1964.

'Clean Sweep for Sobhuza: All Elected Seats Go to Traditionalists', *Times of Swaziland*, July 3, 1964.

'Comments', *Times of Swaziland*, July 19, 1964.

'Sandys Replies to Political Parties: Test for Alleged Electoral Offences Lies in Courts', *Times of Swaziland*, July 10, 1964.

'Democratic Party Joins the Imbokodvo', *Times of Swaziland*, April 23, 1965.

'Proposals for Constitution Sent to London', *Times of Swaziland*, March 11, 1966.
'Student Leader Attacks Constitution', *Times of Swaziland*, May 12, 1967.

BOOKS AND JOURNALS

Bischoff, P. H. 'Why Swaziland Is Different: An Explanation of the Kingdom's Position in Southern Africa', *The Journal of Modern African Studies*, 26, 3 (1988), 457–471.

Booth, A. R. *Swaziland: Tradition and Change in a Southern African Kingdom* (Boulder, CO: Westview Press, 1983).

Cowen, M. 'Early Years of the Colonial Development Corporation: British State Enterprise Overseas During Late Colonialism', *African Affairs* (1984), 63–75.

Daniel, J. 'The Political Economy of Colonial and Post-Colonial Swaziland', *South African Labour Bulletin* 7, 6 (1982), 90–113.

Daniel, J., and Vilane, J. 'Swaziland: Political Crisis, Regional Dilemma', *Review of African Political Economy*, 13, 35 (1986), 54–67.

Davis, C. J. 'Blair Worden, Roundhead Reputations: The English Civil War and the Passions of Posterity', *Parliamentary History*, 21, 3 (2002), 397–398.

Dlamini, M. *The Philosophy, Policies and Objectives of the Imbokodvo National Movement* (Swaziland Printing and Publishing Company, 1972).

Ezera, K. *Constitutional Developments in Nigeria* (London: Cambridge University Press, 1964).

Hill, C. 'Parliament and People in Seventeenth-Century England', *Past and Present*, 92, (1981), 100–124.

Hlandze, S. 'The Evolution of Workers' Consciousness in Swaziland: The Case of Usuthu Pulp Company, 1948–1963', MA thesis, University of Swaziland, 2013.

Kuper, H. *Sobhuza II, Ngwenyama and King of Swaziland: The Story of an Hereditary Ruler and His Country* (New York: Africana Publishing, 1978).

Laschinger, M. 'Roads to Independence: The Case of Swaziland.' *The World Today*, 21, 11 (1965), 486–494.

Lee, S. 'A puzzle of sovereignty', 29–51, In N. Walker (ed.), *Relocating Sovereignty* (London: Routledge, 2018).

Levin, R. *When the Sleeping Grass Awakens: Land and Power in Swaziland* (Johannesburg: Witwatersrand University Press, 1997).

Lindahl, H. 'Sovereignty and Symbolization', *Rechtstheorie*, 28, 3 (1997), 347–371.

MacMillan, H. 'Swaziland: Decolonisation and the Triumph of "Tradition"', *The Journal of Modern African Studies*, 23, 4 (1985), 643–666.

Matsebula, J. S. M. *A History of Swaziland* (Johannesburg: Longman Southern Africa Ltd., 1972).

Mlambo, A. S. *A History of Zimbabwe* (New York: Cambridge University Press, 2014).

North, D. C., and Weingast, B. R. 'Constitutions and Commitment: The Evolution of Institutions Governing Public Choice in Seventeenth-Century England', *The Journal of Economic History*, 49, 4 (1989), 803–832.

Nwabueze, B. O. *A Constitutional History of Nigeria* (London: C. Hurst and Company, 1982).

Nyeko, B. 'Swaziland and South Africa Since 1994: Reflections on Aspects of Post-Liberation Swazi Historiography', *From National Liberation to Democratic Renaissance in Southern Africa* (2005).

Potholm, C. P. 'Changing Political Configuration in Swaziland', *The Journal of African Studies*, 4, 3 (1966), 313–322.

Raitt, I. 'Operation "Green Belt" in Swaziland', *Royal United Services Institution. Journal*, 109, 633 (1964), 40–44.

Reese, E. A. 'Or to the People: Popular Sovereignty and the Power to Choose a Government', *Cardozo Law Review*, 39, 6 (2018).

Robison, R. E. *Andrew Cohen and the Transfer of Power in Tropical Africa 1940–1951* (Fondation nationale des sciences politiques, 1976).

Rubin, L., and Stevens, R. P. 'Swaziland: A Constitution Imposed', Africa *Report*, 9, 4 (1964), 9.

Stevens, R. P. 'Swaziland Political Development', *The Journal of Modern African Studies*, 1, 3 (1963), 327–350.

Stevens, R. P. *Lesotho, Botswana and Swaziland: The Former High Commission Territories in Southern Africa* (London: Pall Mall P, 1967).

William, D. 'The Making and Remaking of Commonwealth Constitutions', *International & Comparative Law Quarterly*, 42, 1 (1993), 67–68.

Zwane, T. M. J. 'The Struggle for Power in Swaziland', *Africa Today* (1964), 4–6.

Internet Sources

Historical Paper Research Archives, Collection Number AD 1715, News from Swaziland, July 15, 1963. http://www.historicalpapers.wits.ac.za/inventories/inv_pdfo/AD1715/AD1715-29-3-4-001-jpeg.pdf. Accessed January 22, 2015.

http://hansard.millbanksystems.com/commons/1968/jul/05/swaziland-independence-bill. HANSARD 1803–2005 → 1960s → 1968 → July 1968 → 5 July 1968 → Commons Sitting → ORDERS OF THE DAY, SWAZILAND INDEPENDENCE BILL, HC Deb July 5, 1968, Vol. 767 cc1875-9031875. Accessed June 27, 2015.

CHAPTER 5

The 1967 Constitution, Internal Self-Government, and the 1968 Independence Constitution

INTRODUCTION

This chapter examines the making of the 1967 Constitution that led to the introduction of internal self-government characterized by the Cabinet system that ushered in independence. Whereas the 1963 Constitution was the result of consultations with selected delegates with no any elective mandate from Swazis, the post-1964 Constitutional Review Committee was composed of elected delegates from the *Imbokodvo* and the White USA party, and representatives and appointees of the Legislative Council. The *Imbokodvo* and the USA allies were expected to cooperate in the Constitutional Review Committee, but this was not the case. The conservative monarchists operating under the *Imbokodvo* party became political chameleons in the aftermath of the 1964 elections when they abandoned their former political platform of conceding special political privileges for their White allies and the postponement of Swaziland's independence, and adopted the stance of the Progressives, to the utter chagrin and discomfort of the White allies. The *Imbokodvo* was able to flex their muscles owing to the newfound political weight of King Sobhuza II following the elections. The overwhelming numerical strength of *Imbokodvo* placed them in a position to undermine their White USA allies, and renege on promises made earlier to guarantee equal representation of Whites and Blacks, and special political rights for Whites. The *Imbokodvo* betrayed the Whites on the

© The Author(s) 2019
H. P. Dlamini, *A Constitutional History of the Kingdom of Eswatini (Swaziland), 1960–1982*, African Histories and Modernities, https://doi.org/10.1007/978-3-030-24777-5_5

184   H. P. DLAMINI

altar of populist nationalist symbols of the equality of all races, and independence for political survival. Although the two allies were unanimous in recommending the *Ngwenyama* as a central figure and executive Head of State in the new constitution, they bitterly disagreed over the issue of race and the privileges of the Europeans earlier agreed on in the early 1960s. This resulted in hotly contested and acrimonious debates in the Legislative Council between the *Imbokodvo* and USA party. This chapter affords voices to the protagonists of the two camps to reveal the substantive contentious issues in order, which enables the appreciation of the difficulties of designing a constitution in a racially polarized society.

This chapter also examines disagreements between the indigenous Swazis and White Swazis in both the House of Assembly and Senate regarding the *Ngwenyama*'s absolute powers to control minerals and mineral oils. These disagreements were carried over to the London Constitutional Conference on the Independence Constitution, at which Britain was reluctant to endorse a constitutional order in which the *Ngwenyama* was elevated to a total autocrat. The question that the two sides could not easily resolve was whether a traditional monarch should be above the constitution in a modern state, or whether it should be subjected to constitutional checks and balances. Britain had the last word in these matters before the independence of Swaziland in 1968.

Further, this chapter looks at the promulgation of the 1967 Constitution and the holding of elections that led to the inauguration of internal self-government in colonial Swaziland under Prince Makhosini Dlamini, as Prime Minister. The new government debated the White Paper on the 1968 Independence Constitution in preparation for the Constitutional Conference in London, following which the independence constitution was passed by the Act of the British parliament.

THE CONSTITUTIONAL REVIEW COMMITTEE AND THE MAKING OF THE 1967 CONSTITUTION

The British government established the Constitutional Review Committee in 1965 to revise the 1963 Constitution, which was not entirely satisfactory, and to make recommendations for a new constitution. The membership of this Constitutional Review Committee is given in Table 5.1.

The Committee was made up of British officials and members of the *Imbokodvo* and USA party. When the second session of the Legislative

5 THE 1967 CONSTITUTION, INTERNAL SELF-GOVERNMENT ... 185

Table 5.1 Constitutional Review Committee

	Official members	Non-official members	Affiliation
1.	Sir Francis Loyd, Chairman	Prince Makhosini Dlamini	Imbokodvo
2.	A. E. C. Long, Chief Secretary	Prince Masitsela Dlamini	Imbokodvo
3.	J. J. Dickie, Attorney General	Prince Mfanasibili Dlamini	Imbokodvo
4.		J. M. B. Sukati	Imbokodvo
5.		C. F. Todd	Imbokodvo
6.		P. Dlamini	Imbokodvo
7.		Dr. G. L. Msibi	Imbokodvo
8.		A. K. Hlophe	Imbokodvo
9.		W. Meyer	United Swaziland Association
10.		R. P. Stephens	United Swaziland Association
11.		H. D. G. Fitzpatrick	United Swaziland Association
12.		E. Winn	United Swaziland Association

Source Compiled from *The Times of Swaziland*, '12 Appointed to constitutional Committee: 8 Imbokodvo, 4 USA', 27 August 1965

Council opened on 12 October 1965, the British Commissioner, Sir Francis Lloyd, attended this session, during which he underscored in his speech to the House the intentions of the government to pursue its constitutional review exercise. He expressed the hope that the recommendations of the Committee would be ready by early 1966, and concluded on a personal optimistic note that 'there was enough wisdom in [Swaziland] ... for the right decision to be taken.[1]

The Constitutional Review Committee started its work on 26 August 1965. The Committee held a total of 18 sessions from August 1965 to March 1966, and was informed in its deliberations by constitutional practices in other British dependencies, and memoranda and suggestions received from interested bodies, organizations, and members of the general public.[2] On 3 March 1966, the government published the Committee's

---

[1] SNA: Legislative Council Official Report, Hansard, 1965–1966.

[2] SNA: Swaziland Government. Report of Swaziland Constitutional Committee, 1966.

186 H. P. DLAMINI

report in both English and *siSwati* as a White Paper for debate in the Legislative Council in April 1966. The non-official members affirmed 'their desire and intension for complete independence as soon as possible' in the report. The Secretary of State for the Colonies accepted the recommendation of the Committee in principle, and expressed the wish to see independence granted before the end of 1969.[3]

It was anticipated that the members of the *Imbokodvo* and USA on the Constitutional Review Committee would work in harmony due to their common ideological stance vis-a-vis that of the Progressives. Unfortunately, the political position of the *Imbokodvo* had changed in the aftermath of the June 1964 elections, when they discovered their overwhelming political weight in the legislature and therefore felt little or no need for the USA as an ally. Moreover, the *Imbokodvo* wanted to be on the popular side of politics in which the Progressives had been basking, and gain legitimacy in the eyes of the Swazi people by appropriating the platform of the Progressives, which favoured the equality of Blacks and Whites, an end of racial discrimination and special political privileges for Whites, and immediate independence for Swaziland. The *Imbokodvo* abandoned its conservative political credentials and assumed the outlook of a pro-Swazi progressive nationalist party. Thus, in the aftermath of the June 1964 elections, the *Imbokodvo* became political turncoats *par excellence*, thereby distancing themselves from their original joint agenda with their White USA allies, which fundamentally upheld White privileges and rejected independence. That should not be taken to mean that the *Imbokodvo* and the USA were totally at loggerheads on every issue. There were issues on which the Committee was unanimous—and others over which they were bitterly divided.

The Committee was unanimous on issues related to the change of the status of Swaziland, the structure of the government, and whether Swazi culture and tradition should have a place in the new constitution. The politics of the protectorate status of Swaziland was related to the recognition of the *Ngwenyama* of Swaziland. The Committee had identified as its 'fundamental' problem: the restoration of what the Swazis regarded as the original treaty of the relationship that had been established between Swaziland and Britain in the late nineteenth century. This had recognized the kingship of the *Ngwenyama*, whereas the 1903 protectorate status did not explicitly do so. The original treaty was the Pretoria Convention of

---

[3] SNA: Swaziland Government. Report of Swaziland Constitutional Committee, 1966.

5   THE 1967 CONSTITUTION, INTERNAL SELF-GOVERNMENT ...   187

1881, which was a tripartite agreement signed by the British, Boers, and Swazis recognizing the independence of Swaziland under the Swazi king.[4] The Swazi monarchy often invoked this treaty to claim that Swaziland was already independent under a recognized sovereign with whom Britain should always deal, instead of the leaders of the political parties, the creation of which the British had encouraged, who were not entitled to governance of the kingdom of Swaziland under Swazi culture and tradition. Britain treated Swaziland as a British protectorate under the 1903 Act[5] in the context of the constitutional status and evolution of Swaziland, but the Swazi ruling class did not see it that way. The Swazi monarchists interpreted the constitutional development of their country as the process of 'regaining independence', translated as *inkhululeko* (freedom),[6] since Swaziland was said to have been independent under the 1881 and 1884 international conventions.[7] The monarchists emphasized Swaziland's independence, not its

[4]"Independence" should not be taken out of context and in the literally sense of the word. The British did not want the Boers to annex Swaziland for strategic reasons because they were seeking an outlet to the Indian Ocean through the territory. Paul Kruger, President of the South African Republic (or Transvaal) from 1883 to 1900, claimed that he was the rightful "King of the Swazis" and he was planning to construct a railway from Pretoria, the capital of South Africa to the Indian Ocean. The declaration of independence of Swaziland was simply a British obstructionist policy to contain Boer imperial ambitions. Independence should be seen in the light of European scramble for Africa (I. L. Griffiths, 'The Quest for Independent Access to the Sea in Southern Africa', *Geographical Journal* [1989], 378–391).

[5]On 25 July 1903 Britain issued the Swaziland Order-in-Council under the British Jurisdiction Act under which the administration of the territory was formally taken over as a Protectorate. The Order-In Council was a legal instrument which established the relationship between Swaziland and the UK in 1903, and provided the basic authority under which British administration was conducted during the colonial period. The Order placed Swaziland directly under British Colonial Administrators, who were vested with executive power and governed Swaziland on behalf of the British crown. The British colonial government was empowered to rule Swaziland by proclamations, which were issued periodically as need arose (J. S. M. Matsebula, *A History of Swaziland*, 3rd edition [Cape Town: Maskew Miller Longman, 1988], 179).

[6]SNA: Legislative Council Debates, 1966, 166–167.

[7]The 'independence' of Swaziland was guaranteed by the British and Transvaal governments in 1881 and 1884. In 1890, a provisional government was established, representing the Swazi, the British, and the Transvaal authorities to manage the excessive activities of European entrepreneurs. From 1894 to 1899, the Transvaal government undertook the protection and administration of Swaziland. The South African (Boer) War 1899–1902 saw the defeat of the Boers and the British imposition of their rule on Swaziland (P. Bonner, *Kings, Commoners and Concessionaires: The Evolution and Dissolution of the Nineteenth-Century Swazi State*, Vol. 31 [London: Cambridge University Press, 2002]).

'protectorate' status. The Secretary of State indicated the willingness of the British government to review the status of Swaziland from a protectorate to a protected state under a Treaty of Friendship with the British Crown, subject to the approval of Her Majesty and the *Ngwenyama*. The feeling was that Swaziland, as a protectorate, was little better than a colony, and the change was intended to enhance its status as something more than a colony.[8] This change made no fundamental difference, because Swaziland remained a colony in the technical and the practical sense of the word. But the politics of name change being pursued by the monarchists was to underscore the point that Europeans met Swaziland as a state under a monarch who should be treated as such, instead of advertising a political vacancy in the territory and inviting people to compete to fill it through elections. The monarch should therefore be incontestably factored into the constitution-making processes of Swaziland.

The Constitutional Review Committee made specific and detailed proposals that combined, in the Committee's view, the essentials of a modern democratic state with the traditional institutions of the Swazi people, with particular reference to Swazi kingship. It recommended that the *Ngwenyama* should be recognized as King of Swaziland and Head of State. Pending full independence, Her Majesty's Commissioner in Swaziland would retain responsibility for external affairs, defence, finance, and the internal security (including the use of the police force), and conditions of the public service. These reserved powers of Her Majesty's government were standard to all British dependent territories heading towards independence. In some territories, Her Majesty's Commissioner was usually in charge of finance, external affairs, defence, internal security, and other matters. The Committee recommended that the SNC would continue to advise the King 'on all matters regulated by Swazi law and custom', and should not be part of the constitution, while the three arms of modern government—the judiciary, legislature and executive—would be vested in the Constitution.

Furthermore, there should be a bicameral legislature consisting of a House of Assembly and Senate. The House of Assembly was to consist of a speaker, 24 elected members, and six members nominated by the

[8]SNA: Legislative Council Debates, 1966, 166–167.

5 THE 1967 CONSTITUTION, INTERNAL SELF-GOVERNMENT ... 189

Ngwenyama 'having regards to interests not already adequately represented', and the Attorney General, who would not have a right to vote.[9] The Senate would consist of a speaker and 12 members, six elected by members of the House of Assembly and six appointed by the King, also representing interests not otherwise adequately represented.

The Committee proposed eight electoral constituencies, comprising approximately 15,000 voters, with each returning three members to the House of Assembly. All bills were to be passed by a majority of both Houses and assented to by the King before they became law. In the event of disagreement, a joint sitting of both Houses would resolve the matter by a majority vote. Finance bills would be dealt with by elected members.

In addition, there should be a Cabinet, consisting of the Prime Minister, his Deputy and up to six other ministers. The Cabinet would advise the King. Allowance was made for the appointment of assistant ministers to assist the Cabinet members with their duties. Although the *Ngwenyama* would appoint a prime minister and cabinet, the British colonial separation of political office from civil service would be maintained and developed through the Public Service Commission and a Judicial Service Commission.[10] There was unanimity over these issues. Prince Makhosini Dlamini qualified this unanimity as a 'triumph for the *Imbokodvo* policy and as a wealthy gift to the people of Swaziland who returned [them] at the last elections'.[11] Because the *Imbokodvo* had shifted from their original conservative pro-White and anti-independence platform, serious cracks appeared between them and their USA allies. The *Imbokodvo* and the USA could hardly agree over the race question with reference to the electoral privileges accorded to Whites and the issue of the postponement of Swaziland's independence, which were part of the justification for the coalition between the two parties.

THE ACRIMONIOUS RACE QUESTION DURING THE APRIL 1966 LEGISLATIVE COUNCIL DEBATES

A typical characteristic of settler colonies in Southern Africa was the assertion of White superiority and the marginalization, and even exclusion, of

---

[9] Ibid.

[10] 'The Proposal for New Constitution', *Times of Swaziland*, March 25, 1966.

[11] Ibid., 162.

the Black majority from the governance. The feeling of the White minority was always that they were the torch bearers of civilization, and it was natural that they must lead the indigenous majority and enjoy special privileges. This thinking of the White Swazis, who overwhelmingly originated from apartheid South Africa, was expected. Against a background of the dominant position that the White minority enjoyed in Southern Africa, the predominantly White USA party defined the Swazi society as multi-racial and clamoured for White recognition as a distinct race from the indigenous Swazis. The Black majority, through the *Imbokodvo* party, advocated non-racial Swazi society in a constitutional order that treated everybody as equal and belonging to the same country irrespective of race, creed, religion, or ethnicity. However, the Whites did not see things in that same light. The USA party dissociated itself from the concept of a 'non-racial state' and demanded a separate European roll that would reserve half of the Legislative Council seats for the Whites in Swaziland. They argued that Whites not only warranted specific and separate representation, but also that their representation should be chosen by Europeans, even though Africans outnumbered Whites by some 30:1, given that there were over 270,000 Africans to 9000 Whites. They maintained that it was fair and reasonable that they should occupy half the seats in the House of Assembly because of their economic weight and the value of their technical know-how in the territory. The Swazi monarch had, hitherto, embraced this position of the White Swazis and this had resulted in the coalition between the *Imbokodvo* and the USA party before the 1964 legislative elections. This coalition, which had been meant to prevent the more radical Swazi political parties from gaining control of the legislature, had unravelled under new political circumstances in the aftermath of the 1964 elections.

The *Imbokodvo* discovered its own real power from its triumph in the June 1964 elections. The overwhelming victory had given the *Imbokodvo* leaders the confidence and a sense of security they had not previously enjoyed. Before the June 1964 elections, the Progressives had appeared truly threatening, as demonstrated by the mammoth crowd-pulling rallies they organized and the strikes they sponsored. The June 1964 elections dissipated the threat of the Progressives, as they did not win a single seat. This was possible because of the support the *Imbokodvo* received from the USA party. The Progressives were further weakened by post-election disillusionment and the carpet-crossings to *Imbokodvo*. The absorption of more Progressive elements into the *Imbokodvo* transformed it and built up

5 THE 1967 CONSTITUTION, INTERNAL SELF-GOVERNMENT ... 191

its sense of confidence, and it managed to undercut the appeal that these radical parties had enjoyed previously in the eyes of the masses.

The *Imbokodvo* came to realize that the Progressive stance that rejected reserved seats for the White minority and the establishment of a non-racial society was popular among Swazis and, therefore, had to be considered. The *Imbokodvo* was intent on cleaning up its image as a pro-White and a pro-apartheid party sponsored by South Africa. The pressure of the extraparliamentary political parties on the *Imbokodvo* was high, as Stephens observed during the April 1966 debates of the Legislative Council. During the April 1966 Legislative Council debates, Stephens of the USA White minority party observed:

> We know that Imbokodvo are under pressure from political parties and that the leaders of these parties have told us that their policy is to Africanise the service to the complete exclusion of the Whites... This is an anti-White move and a racial move... If the Imbokodvo gives an inch today, by eliminating the White roll, they are going to have a great difficulty in resisting further demands.[12]

The rapprochement between the *Imbokodvo* and the former Progressive leaders that had joined its ranks made the USA party suspicious and uncomfortable. As if this was not enough, the views of the *Imbokodvo* started changing and, in certain respects, approximated those of the Progressives, who had been advocating immediate independence, one-man-one-vote, a non-racial state, and White voting rights limited to those with British passports.[13]

The *Imbokodvo* was also increasingly becoming uncomfortable with the USA party because of its overt support of the project for the integration of Swaziland into apartheid South Africa, which was very unpopular among Swazis. Although Sobhuza had subscribed to the overtures of Prime Minister Verwoerd in the early 1960s, the scheme had been ridiculed and condemned by the Progressives before and during the 1964 election, and most Swazis were against it. By distancing itself from the USA party, the *Imbokodvo* was making a political statement to the effect that the monarch did not endorse the project of the integration of Swaziland into South Africa. The *Imbokodvo*'s changing position was captured in the April 1966

[12]SNA: Legislative Council Official Report, Hansard, 1965–1966, 175–177.

[13]See: SNA: Legislative Council Official Report, Hansard, 1965–1966.

session of the Legislative Council debates on the Committee's Report, which incensed their former allies of the USA party.

During the April 1966 Legislative Council debates, three members of the USA party—R. P. Stephens, W. Meyer, and E. G. Winn—distinguished themselves as a dissenting opinion and were referred to in the Legislative Council report as 'dissentients'.[14] They were the dissenting voices because they disagreed with their *Imbokodvo* allies and tabled a contrary motion amending the *Imbokodvo* constitutional proposals with regard to the equality between the White minority and Africans in the legislature, double electoral rolls for the two races, and the timing of independence. The USA party clamoured for a 50–50 representation of Blacks and Whites in parliament, separate electoral rolls for the two races, and the postponement of self-government and independence. Their justification was that Swazis were not yet sufficiently ripe politically to be able to govern themselves, and that the Swazi middle-class should first be created to make independence meaningful.[15] This was in stark opposition to the *Imbokodvo*'s new position which was demanding the establishment of a non-racial constitution, and a single electoral roll for all Swazi citizens, Black, Coloured, and White. Having a single electoral roll was, clearly, going to put an end to the reserved White minority seats that had been negotiated with the Swazi National Council in the early 1960s, and that was the basis of the alliance between the monarch and the Whites. In the event of a one-man-one-vote election, Whites no longer stood a good chance of being elected.

The divergent positions of the two former allies over the race question sparked fireworks in the House, as tempers flared in the heated debates. On 1 April 1966, Prince Makhosini Dlamini clearly stated the position of the *Imbokodvo* as one that was determined to ensure that the new constitution of Swaziland should provide for a non-racial state. This position was in line with the wishes of various interest groups, including political parties outside parliament, who wanted a non-racial state and one common roll for the whole territory. He emphasized that only a minority wanted a multiracial state, and that the majority would not bow to the wishes of the minority since they had been advised that, in politics, the majority must

---

[14]The use of the word 'dissentients' in the Legislative Council report and even the *Times of Swaziland*, refers to the minority with dissenting opinions. The Legislative Council document read: "I realize, Mr Speaker, that these dissentients are in the minority and have no following." See SNA: Legislative Council Debates, 1966, 163.

[15]SNA: Legislative Council Official Report, Hansard, 1965–1966.

5 THE 1967 CONSTITUTION, INTERNAL SELF-GOVERNMENT ... 193

always rule. He justified his position by arguing that the Constitutional Committee had agreed that all discriminatory laws should be repealed in the new constitution.

Prince Makhosini further reported that members of the USA party had dissociated themselves from the concept of a non-racial state, and that, without success, the *Imbokodvo* had struggled to persuade them to change their 'sectional and racial attitude for the common good of Swaziland and enable the constitutional Committee to present a unanimous Report'. He stated that he:

> knew that these [honourable] members felt that the Europeans warranted, not only specific and separate representation, but that their representatives should be chosen by Europeans; although Africans outnumber Europeans by some thirty to one. They considered it fair and reasonable that Europeans should occupy half the seats in the house of Assembly and hence the division ... We advocate equality for all men and we condemn discrimination based on colour ... If we accept the Europeans should have a separate voters' roll, how can we deny the same right of separate representation to the women, to the Roman Catholics, to the Portuguese, to the Jews, to the blind, to the Euro-Africans, to the teachers or indeed to anyone who feels he is in a special category? It is indeed a matter that we still have in our midst, when we have in the past, lived harmoniously.[16]

One of the White Swazis who proved to be a diehard supporter of the Swazi monarch was Todd, who endorsed the provisions of the Report and supported Prince Makhosini. He made it clear during the debate that he fully supported the new Constitution because it was acceptable to the large mass of the population of Swaziland, whether they were Swazi, White, or Eurafrican. He also supported it because it provided for a constitutional monarch, and he stated:

> I believe that I speak not only for the Europeans but for the Swazis when I say that this constitution, because it supports a monarchy for Swaziland, it is the real foundation to the stabilising influence in Swaziland. The Europeans are monarchists and the Swazis are monarchists. The Swazis have an old tradition of loyalty to their King and it would be unthinkable in Swaziland to devise a constitution that did not provide for a monarchy.[17]

---

[16]SNA: Legislative Council Debates, Official Report, Hansard, 1965–1966, 162–163.

[17]Ibid.

194   H. P. DLAMINI

As anticipated, three White members of the USA party—R. P. Stephens, W. Meyer, and E. G. Winn—dissented and tabled an alternative motion for amendment that demanded a separate European roll that would retain for the Europeans one half of the membership of the Legislative Council. The stakes for the White minority in Swaziland were high and these Whites put up a ferocious battle to save the last vestiges of White privilege through the legislature. The two White USA party members who spoke out in the House were R. P. Stephens and W. Meyer.

R. P. Stephens pointed out that the majority of the members of the USA party supported the constitutional proposals in every respect, except for the proposal on the voters roll and race. He agreed 'wholeheartedly with Prince Makhosini and Todd that the monarchy in Swaziland is the cornerstone to stability', but indicated that his party had reservations over the race issue and requested an amendment to allow Europeans to have a separate roll, because they were a significant and important minority on whose skills and investment the Swazi economy was built. The amendment was simply meant to reflect this reality. Stephens argued:

The object of our amendment is to try and accommodate in the constitution the realities with us at the moment. The reality is our people here are made up of two main races and our amendment will allow that part of the population, which is at the moment responsible for 99% of the farming, commercial, industrial, administrative and technical know-how, direct representation. This will give them and their children tangible proof that they are wanted as a permanent segment of the Swaziland community and that their standard and way of life will be permanently respected. The case of our recommendation is that we recognise the existence of two groups which, for want for a better term, I will refer to as races; and we maintain that, by ignoring this fact, we will do nothing to extinguish the patent differences between the two groups, mainly as entities in education, customs, tradition, capital, culture, technical skills, art and in many other ways.[18]

Stephens stated that the aim of the suggestion of the dissenting group was to 'obtain independence for Swaziland under a new constitution that [would] not shake the faith of [Europeans and Euro-Africans] in [Swaziland's] future'. The dissenting group maintained that 'a sudden 100% black

[18]SNA: Legislative Council Official Report, Hansard, 1965–1966, 171.

5 THE 1967 CONSTITUTION, INTERNAL SELF-GOVERNMENT ... 195

administered territory is unnecessarily revolutionary and may upset the progress of development'. The group felt that evolution was better than revolution. The anti-independence suggestion that the Swazi Whites were making in 1965 was totally unrealistic, because scores of African countries had already achieved independence and were operating in concert at the OAU headquarters in Addis Ababa.

Stephens argued that a constitution based on the concept of a non-racial society would not be suitable for Swaziland, since the country was multi-racial. He asked, 'why impose a non-racial constitution on a multi-racial state'. Stephens stated that there was a major difference between the approach of the USA party and the *Imbokodvo*. Whereas the *Imbokodvo* was advocating a non-racially based constitution in a society with more than one race, the USA was advocating a constitution for a multi-racial society and there was nothing wrong with that. It was a reality that the constitutional drafters had to take into consideration. If Swaziland was a non-racial state, the USA party would obviously ask for one electoral roll. To treat Swaziland as a non-racial state was untenable. In the words of Stephens:

> It certainly will not work 100%. Mr Speaker, if the *Imbokodvo* is completely honest when they want a non-racial state with the blacks and Whites completely integrated ... let us discuss the best way of achieving this ... they are not going to endear ourselves to the Whites by removing rights the Whites have had for over forty years. That is not the right way to win friends and keep them.[19]

W. Meyer was the second White politician to take to the floor of the House, and he also called for an amendment to the bill tabled by Prince Makhosini Dlamini that he alleged 'infringed' on White voting rights. He argued that the White minority constituted a special category and that the future of Swaziland hinged on their voting rights. Mistakes had been made in bequeathing to African countries the notion of one-man-one-vote, which had proved to be unworkable. Africans were not capable of handling European democracy. He then admonished:

> Let us hope that Her Majesty's government does realise by now that implementation of the political system of 'one man one vote majority rule' has

[19] SNA: Legislative Council Debates, Official Report, Hansard, 172–173.

always led to disaster and chaos. We do not blame the Swazi nation for grasping the opportunity of 'one man one vote majority rule' because they, like many other African states, are in an emotional dream; they are yet to awake and realise the responsibility of independence and what it all involves.[20]

Meyer indicated that there was no country in the world that could be called a 'non-racial' state and that many races were found in Swaziland. The Europeans had played an essential role in the development of Swaziland, and it was unjust to render them politically helpless in the one-man-one-vote system. Such a system would eliminate the European minority as an entity.[21]

In an arrogant and provocative manner, Meyer presented Whites as the indispensable movers of Swazi socio-economic life, and argued that Swazis had to rely on them or perish. He stated in clear terms that the economic prosperity of Swaziland was due to the presence of Whites, and that almost half of Swaziland belonged to Europeans who had developed it considerably. Meyer commented, sarcastically, that, without Europeans, Swaziland would have been a backward enclave and 'would have been where she was one hundred years ago'. Europeans brought light and development to Swaziland, and were the economic pillars of the territory. Because of their economic weight, he concluded, they should be entitled to special political rights on a separate roll.

In addition, Meyer ridiculed the idea of independence on the grounds that Swazis were not yet capable of governing themselves and needed more time. The issue of independence was to be approached piecemeal by introducing an interim period during which the Europeans would be given the 'opportunity and political power to enable him ... to lead Swaziland into a prosperous future.'[24] Africans, in his estimation, could not manage independence on their own; they still needed European expertise and tutelage. The quest for self-government and independence was not an urgent agenda to be pursued. Rather, the issue of European political rights should be addressed for the overall benefit of the territory. This would cause the Europeans to be committed and confident in their future in the territory.

[20] Ibid., 178.
[21] Ibid., 179.

5 THE 1967 CONSTITUTION, INTERNAL SELF-GOVERNMENT ... 197

Meyer stated:

> Mr Speaker, we respectfully ask Her Majesty's government to provide sufficient representation for the European by the European. This is the only way we will maintain the confidence of the European in Swaziland and a stable government. ... I am making an appeal to this House and to Her Majesty's government to make an exception in the case of Swaziland by taking account of the European's interest and the necessity to maintain his confidence in Swaziland, by giving the Europeans the opportunity to help the Swazi nation make Swaziland the only real independent country in Africa.[22]

The racist views of Stephens and Meyers on the indispensability of Whites in the survival of Swaziland's economy, and the incapability and unpreparedness of Blacks for self-government and independence, were pervasive in Southern Africa, particularly in Rhodesia and apartheid South Africa. It was difficult for White Swazis to disentangle themselves from this Southern African racial order. It was not, therefore, only in Swaziland that the White minority felt that Blacks were not ripe for independence and self-government, it was also the thought pattern of White settlers in Southern Africa.

Not surprisingly, Meyer's speech was not well-received in the predominantly Black House, given that he had literally denigrated Black Swazis and made allegations about their incompetency in managing the future of their country. Dr Msibi of the *Imbokodvo* flared as he took the first shot at Meyer. He could hardly hold himself together, and described Meyer as being 'racist' and 'short sighted' for highlighting the assumed shortcomings of Black Swazis, and the superiority and know-how of Whites:

> Mr Speaker, most of us have always believed that we are immune to shocks; but I can understand the silence of this House this evening. The last speaker's speech could not have shaken anybody more than it has shaken me today. His speech, Mr Speaker, is the last word in *intolerance, Nazism, Herevolkism and everything that we do not stand for. It is an epitome of man's inhumanity to man* ... We shall not be provoked by emotional speeches from the United Swaziland Association ... We know that Hitler discriminated on the basis of racism. We know that oppression has been carried on the basis of colour in Africa. We know that there are those today who are trying to increase their pocket today and satisfying their greed by discriminating on the basis

[22] Ibid., 180.

of colour in Southern Africa. There are those in our midst who, when we tell them that discrimination on the basis of colour is wrong, will say that we are anti-White ... [they will] shout 'agitator', 'agitator', when told that the colour of a man's skin is merely a biological phenomenon and has no reflection on his ability intellectually or otherwise, but the only agitators and the only anti-Whites I know...are those Whites who wittingly or unwittingly continue to advocate discrimination on the basis of the colour of the skin ... morphologically speaking, this country is multi-racial; ... [but] to base our laws on an a multi-racial status is folly .... We want therefore that before the law of this country, everyone should be equal ...[23] (Emphasis added)

He dismissed Meyer's claim that Whites ought to be given special privileges because of their role in the country's economy, and emphatically stated that Swazis were not in support of such an arrangement. He stated the Swazis wanted self-government and independence, and he did not think anybody could refuse them that.

Next, P. Dlamini rejected the amendment proposed by the USA party, pointing out those who had proposed the amendment under discussion 'were rude and arrogant' for telling Swazis that they were not ripe to be given 'responsibility for self-government, let alone independence', and that they owe their survival to Europeans who owned half of Swazi territory. Dlamini said from the utterances made it was clear that:

The United Swaziland Association would like to deny Swaziland self-government leading to independence. They say we are not ready and we are incapable of looking after ourselves. That may be so, but I cannot understand how they claim the patronage to look after us when they are in the same position as we are. Some sixty years ago or so ... the British government has been responsible for running this country over [both Swazis and Whites]. Now tell me, Messrs. United Swaziland Association, how do you come to have the qualifications and say you can rule better than the Swazi people? ... As far as I understand the position of a European in Swaziland *he is a guest* and this is the sort of gratitude we receive for our hospitality.[24] (Emphasis added)

In response, Fitzpatrick, of the USA party, tried to calm down tempers while distancing himself from the position of his party. He deplored the

[23] SNA: Legislative Council Official Report, Hansard, 1965–1966, 181–183.
[24] Ibid., 185.

5 THE 1967 CONSTITUTION, INTERNAL SELF-GOVERNMENT ... 199

fact that his party had proposed the amendment on the basis of cultural and traditional differences and on the *Herrenvolk* concept of the racial superiority of Whites. He stated that the 50–50 proposal was not realistic and had been rejected at the 1963 London Constitutional Conference. The British government was definitely going to reject such a proposal again. The Swazi people were generally hostile to the 50–50 principle and they would not entertain it under any circumstance. He acknowledged the fact that, if the 50–50 amendment were taken to London, it would simply delay self-government and independence.

S. Mbelu of the *Imbokodvo* majority party rose to call on members of the House to reject the amendment 'with a strong force because it deserved to be dealt with that way'. He noted that:

all [12] members of the [Constitutional Committee] were keen to produce a constitution which will bring about peaceful relations in Swaziland and they came to a point of differences whether the forecast should be on nationhood or should be on group exclusiveness. The African people all over Africa reject multi-racialism, Mr Speaker, because it is a negative approach to cooperation and the majority of the people regard it as pandering to European arrogance.[25]

He rejected all racialist concepts and stood for 'straight majority rule' and non-racialism, arguing:

When we say we stand for non-racialism we mean that we support the full development of the human personality. We support an active creation of conditions *which will blow to smithereens all group exclusiveness*. We believe that this will bring about a dynamic Swazi nation which will be committed to the tremendous task of building Swaziland ...[26] (Emphasis added)

When W. M. Magongo of the *Imbokodvo* party took the floor, he simply called on the House to reject the amendment being proposed by the three USA Party dissidents, because of its inclusion of the 50–50 representation in the legislature for Blacks and Whites, and because of the refusal of Swazi independence. He stated:

[25] Ibid., 191.
[26] Ibid.

200   H. P. DLAMINI

In a nutshell this amendment requires us to accept fifty-fifty. We have been told that Swazis are not yet able to govern themselves and that the Swazi middle class should first be created. Why should we waste our time on this and deny ourselves the opportunity of governing ourselves? We are asked here to reserve a separate roll for Europeans and Africans in the constitution. I say here and now that I reject that.[27]

D. J. Weir of the USA party took to the floor and also endeavoured to calm tempers. He remarked that the USA party had been thoroughly rebuked in the House, and that this might give the wrong impression that all USA members were 'traitors', which was not true. He explained how the USA party came by the 50–50 arrangement, and called for understanding and tolerance. He rejected the view expressed in the House that the European in Swaziland is a mere guest. He argued that the USA party did not stand for the suppression of any group in Swaziland.[28]

A. Gamedze of the *Imbokodvo* party called on the members of the USA party referred to in the Legislative Council report as 'dissentients'[29] to withdraw the amendment motion they had tabled because it was racist and unhelpful. He pointed to the fact that, in the Republic of South Africa, Whites only were allowed to legislate, while Blacks were ignored. In Swaziland, it was recommended that Whites should form part of the government, and they were asking for 50–50 representation and special consideration simply because they were White, despite their minority status. Gamedze stated that they had recommended equality before the law and rejected all forms of discrimination based on colour.[30]

Prince Masitsela Dlamini rejected the amendment proposed by the USA party like those before him, and advised them simply to withdraw it, because the majority in the House did not want it. The USA party, through Meyer, conceded to the position of the majority for the time being, but added that

[27] Ibid., 193.

[28] Ibid.

[29] The use of the word 'dissentients' in the Legislative Council report and even the *Times of Swaziland*, refers to the minority with dissenting opinions. The Legislative Council document read: "I realize, Mr Speaker, that these dissentients are in the minority and have no following." See SNA: Legislative Council Debates, 1966, 163.

[30] Ibid., 198.

5 THE 1967 CONSTITUTION, INTERNAL SELF-GOVERNMENT ... 201

they believed they were right in the position they took and would continue to fight for what they considered was best for Swaziland.[31]

After the debate in the Legislative Council, the draft constitution was sent to London for Her Majesty's government's consideration. The British government agreed with most of the proposals of the Constitutional Committee, but the thorny issue of the powers of the traditional monarch in a modern state was not addressed to its satisfaction. Was the *Ngwenyama* to have total control over rights to minerals, mineral oils, and land? Who should control these resources: the *Ngwenyama* as an individual, or the modern parliament that represented the people's voices? The *Imbokodvo* maintained that it should be the *Ngwenyama* in trust of the people, but the British did not agree with that type of management of national resources in a modern state. After much debate, the Secretary of State finally agreed that control over minerals be vested in the *Ngwenyama*, who would be advised by a committee. However, who was to constitute the committee? The Swazi argued that, according to Swazi traditional kingship, the committee should be appointed by the King in consultation with the SNC. In other words, the control over minerals would be an extra-parliamentary affair. The British pointed out that, since government would be in the hands of a Cabinet drawn from a parliament mainly elected by universal franchise, the committee should be appointed from Cabinet. The Secretary of State stated that it was:

> essential that the Central Government which was responsible for other aspects of the economic development of Swaziland should also control mineral development. To provide otherwise and to vest control in the traditional authority might well result in a clash with the central government which would have far reaching effects in Swaziland. Furthermore in view of its unique position, events in Swaziland would come in for close scrutiny and it was desirable to avoid creating procedures which would enable people to say that a traditional, rather than a democratic system, was being adopted. Clear ministerial responsibility would dispose of this criticism.[32]

According to the British, the ideal was that parliament in a modern state should emanate from competing political parties. The monarch, which was not an elective position, should be subordinate to an elected parliament.

---

[31] Ibid., 216.
[32] SNA: Swaziland Constitutional Proposals, October 1966.

202   H. P. DLAMINI

The *Imbokodvo* felt that the reluctance of the British to accept their viewpoint, that Sobhuza should be in charge of the control of minerals, was an indication of lack of recognition and trust in the *Ngwenyama*'s abilities, and was a deliberate act to deprive him and his people of the right to control revenue in accordance with their real national interests. The Swazis were clearly asking Britain to recognize the traditional model of kingship in Swaziland that had existed for more than one hundred years under totally different socio-economic conditions. Sobhuza's response was that Britain was applying its own traditional concept of constitutional monarch and not that of the Swazis. The argument of the monarchists was vacuous, in the sense that the British intended to bequeath to the Swazis a modern governance mechanism that would prioritize the people's voices and concerns through its elected representatives, and not those of an individual. The pro-monarchists were imagining a Swazi culture and tradition that never existed because pre-capitalist Swaziland had had a subsistence economy that had not developed into distinct primary, secondary, and tertiary economic sectors.

The British were inclined to ensure that the economic infrastructure of a modern Swaziland state should be managed by the modern political elite, who were equipped with the know-how to do so collectively, and not traditionalists or a single individual. The pro-monarchists did not contemplate the fate of Swazis if it transpired that a monarch was malevolent and unenlightened. What the British wanted the Swazis to inherit was a modern political system in which checks and balances existed, rather than a traditional one in which an individual arrogated power to himself at the expense of the elected institutions of the state. These disagreements between the British and the monarchists did not augur well for the accelerated pace of constitutional development in Swaziland.

Further pressures on the quickening of the pace of constitutional development in Swaziland came from the independence of the other High Commission territories. On 30 September 1966, Bechuanaland became the independent Republic of Botswana and, on 4 October 1966, Basutoland became the independent kingdom of Lesotho. J. Stonehouse, the British Parliamentary Under-Secretary for the Colonies, who was part of the independence ceremony of these countries, went to Swaziland with the intention of reconciling the differing viewpoints on the Swazi constitution between the British and the Swazi authorities. He met Sobhuza, local officials, political leaders, and a delegation from political parties to discuss the way forward for the making of a modern democratic Swaziland.

Dr Zwane of the NNCL, whose party was not represented on the Constitutional Review Committee because it had no seat in the Legislative Council, appealed to Stonehouse that a 'fully representative constitutional conference [should] be held in London by the end of October 1966 in which his party would want to be represented'.[33] Dr Zwane said Britain had found in 'White settler arrogance' and 'Swazi traditionalism' a reason to deny Swaziland a democratic constitution. He condemned the proposals in the Constitutional Committee report because it was biased against emergent political forces and denied them independent representation. He pointed out that the electoral system was biased in favour of the *Imbokodvo* while, structurally, the proposed three-member constituency without proportional representation made it difficult for small parties to gain representation. The large size of the constituencies accentuated the advantages of parties with greater resources, such as the *Imbokodvo*. Zwane further stated that the king would not be a true constitutional monarch because of his wide discretional powers. Moreover, Zwane's party argued that the SNC was an archaic body that was partisan, and was a 'mere breeding ground for Mbokodvoism and should be abolished and replaced by a college of chiefs with a fixed composition and with specified duties'.[34]

The British Under-Secretary of State indicated that 'no good purpose would be served by holding a constitutional conference in London', and that the British 'could well work out a constitution on the evidence already given'.[35] He stated clearly that, in a debate in the House of Commons in September 1966, the British government expressed its determination that the new constitution would provide for a constitutional monarch, and that political power would clearly be in the hands of the elected ministers.[36] He failed to persuade Sobhuza and the SNC to accept the British proposals for the control of mineral rights by the government that emanated from the parliament of the day.[37] When Stonehouse left, Sir Francis Lloyd made

---

[33] 'NNLC Wants London Talks on Proposed Constitution', *Times of Swaziland*, October 14, 1966.

[34] 'NNLC Wants London Talks on Proposed Constitution', *Times of Swaziland*, October 14, 1966.

[35] 'Constitution Ready? Stonehouse Meets Political Leaders', *Times of Swaziland*, October 14, 1966.

[36] 'Stonehouse on Powers of the King', *Times of Swaziland*, October 10, 1966.

[37] 'Constitution Ready? Stonehouse Meets Political Leaders', *Times of Swaziland*, October 14, 1966; Kuper, *Sobhuza II: Ngwenyama and King of Swaziland*, 271.

204 H. P. DLAMINI

another attempt in December 1966 to persuade the *Ngwenyama* of the wisdom of the British approach to constitutionalism whereby parliament should be supreme over all matters of governance. The *Ngwenyama* did not concede to Lloyd's advice because it touched on parliamentary control of his powers.

The response of the British government to the report of the Constitutional Review Committee was largely accommodating. On the basis of that report, the British government took the following decisions: Swaziland would be granted full internal self-government and they were ready to enter into an agreement with the Swazi king under which Swaziland would become a protected state; the *Ngwenyama* would be recognized as king; and Swaziland would achieve independence not later than the end of 1969. Britain proceeded with the enactment of the 1967 Constitution to enable the introduction of full internal self-government that would lead to independence.

THE MARCH 1967 CONSTITUTION

The penultimate constitution to independence in 1968 was the March 1967 Constitution. The Constitution was issued on 22 February and promulgated on 1 March 1967. It was essentially based on the proposals of the Constitutional Review Committee and reflected, to a large extent, the British Westminster constitutional tradition that was bequeathed to Britain's erstwhile colonies, with a bicameral legislature consisting of an Upper and Lower Legislative Assembly. It provided that Swaziland would gain independence under a monarch not later than 1969.

In contrast to the 1963 constitution, the new Constitution recognized the *Ngwenyama* as king and Head of State of Swaziland. The position of the *Ngwenyama* was, finally, firmly secured after a long struggle. The inclusion of the *Ngwenyama* as the king and Head of State of Swaziland was a victory for the *Imbokodvo* monarchists, who had been lobbying for the attribution of a more central and prominent role for the *Ngwenyama* against a background of British reluctance to do so in light of British constitutional tradition. Succession to the position of *Ngwenyama* would be governed by Swazi law and custom and, in the case of the absence or incapacity of the *Ngwenyama*, the *Ndlovukati* (Queen Mother) would act in his place in accordance with Swazi law and custom. The *Ngwenyama* was to enjoy immunities and privileges from criminal jurisdiction of the courts,

5 THE 1967 CONSTITUTION, INTERNAL SELF-GOVERNMENT … 205

and from being called as witness to any civil or criminal proceeding. Executive authority was vested in the *Ngwenyama*, who exercised it through the prime minister and his Cabinet. The *Ngwenyama* was to appoint the prime minister from the elected members of the House who appeared to him to likely to command the support of the majority of its members. With the advice of the prime minister, the *Ngwenyama* would appoint the rest of the members of the Cabinet from the House.

Under the 1967 Constitution, a new electoral system was introduced that was different from that under the 1963 constitution. A single voters' roll was introduced for all Swazis, and voting was based on universal adult suffrage. Swaziland was divided into eight constituencies, each returning three members to the House of Assembly. The *Ngwenyama* was to nominate six additional members of parliament to the 24 elected members, making a total of 30. The 30 parliamentarians then elected six senators, while the *Ngwenyama* nominated six others, making a total of 12. Thus, Swaziland's bicameral legislature of a House of Assembly of 30 members and a Senate of 12 members was established.[38]

Although the electoral system was an improvement in introducing a non-racial single voters' roll, it was harshly attacked by the President of the Swaziland's Student Union, N. J. Mhlongo, during the annual conference of the Union in Matsapha on 4 May 1967. The majority election system[39] introduced was criticized as a recipe for a one-party state, because the concept of a three-member constituency was 'a political manoeuvre to entrench the traditionalist-settler interests'.[40] The majority system made it impossible for other parties, particularly the small ones, to be represented in parliament.[41] Under the electoral system of winner-takes-all, the Progressives had no chance to be elected to parliament. They were strongest in the

---

[38] Ibid.

[39] There are basically two systems in parliamentary elections: the Majority Election System which allows the winner to take all the seats and the Proportional Election System which assigns seats to political parties according to the proportion of votes they obtain in an election. Both have advantages and disadvantages (For details on these systems see E. S. Herron, R. J. Pekkanen, and M. S. Shugart, 'Terminology and Basic Rules of Electoral Systems.' In E. S. Herron, R. J. Pekkanen, and M. S. Shugart [eds.], *The Oxford Handbook of Electoral Systems* [Oxford: Oxford University Press, 2018], 1; J. M. Colomer, 'Party System Effects on Electoral Systems.' In E. S. Herron, R. J. Pekkanen, and M. S. Shugart [eds.], *The Oxford Handbook of Electoral Systems* [Oxford: Oxford University Press, 2018], 69).

[40] 'Student Leader Attacks Constitution', *Times of Swaziland*, May 12, 1967.

[41] 'Student Leader Attacks Constitution', *Times of Swaziland*, May 12, 1967.

urban and industrial areas, and had a chance of winning some seats in areas where they were popular under the proportional representation system.[42] Under such a system, political parties are assigned parliamentary seats proportionally to the number of votes they get. Supporters of a small party are likely to be represented by at least one member of parliament rooted in their constituency. On the other hand, the *Imbokodvo* had a firm grip over the illiterate masses, who constituted more than 95% of the population. The idea of a majority system allowed the rural population to swallow up the urban and industrial areas. It was therefore difficult for the Progressives to make any inroads into the political system as designed by the colonial administration. The students sent their protest to the Secretary of State in London, but no action was taken.[43]

The new constitution allowed Her Majesty's government the reserved right to amend or replace any part of it. The British government was in charge of external affairs and defence, internal security, finance, and the public service. Where it was deemed necessary, the office of Her Majesty's Commissioner could initiate legislation through the Swazi House of Assembly. In essence, the Constitutional Review Committee made provisions for all the institutions necessary for the functioning of a parliamentary democracy for full internal self-government. All that was needed was to transfer the responsibilities and powers to the government of Swaziland. For this to happen, elections had to be held in April 1967.

The April 1967 General Elections and the Introduction of Internal Self-Government for Swaziland

General elections were held in Swaziland on 19–20 April 1967 under the revised constitution. The voting process was different from that of 1963 because, under the new constitution, voting was done on a single common roll, without reserved seats for Whites. The elections were contested by the *Imbokodvo*, the NNLC, the Swaziland United Front (SUF), and the SPP. It was meaningless for the White USA party to contest the elections, because the electoral code did not favour them since it was difficult to win a seat in a single roll election. The *Imbokodvo* followed the traditional

[42] Ibid.

[43] 'Student Leader Attacks Constitution', *Times of Swaziland*, May 12, 1967.

5 THE 1967 CONSTITUTION, INTERNAL SELF-GOVERNMENT …   207

channels of selecting candidates. Put differently, the candidates had to be the appointees of the *Ngwenyama*, and this ensured total compliance with his will. Such candidates were, therefore, mouthpieces of the *Ngwenyama*, to whom they were answerable, and not necessarily to their constituencies. They had to be the *Ngwenyama*'s perfect 'Yes men'. If they were to survive as politicians and enjoy political patronage, they had ceaselessly to sing the praises of the *Ngwenyama*.

Just as in the 1964 elections, the *Imbokodvo* derived most of its strength from cooperation with, and access to, the institutional resources of chieftaincy. The Swazi chiefs were at the beck and call of the *Ngwenyama*, and their role was to ensure that the rural population under their control voted for the *Imbokodvo* royal party. Only the *Imbokodvo* and NNLC were able to register the full 24 candidates throughout Swaziland, with three coming from each of the eight constituencies into which the territory was divided. The SPP mustered seven candidates and the SUF five.

Whites were not included in the *Imbokodvo* list in the 1967 elections, unlike as in the past. The initial reaction of most White Swazis was one of dismay and anxiety at the way their ally was treating them. Race had become an explosive issue about which the political parties had made a great deal of noise; Whites were associated with colonialism and apartheid, and it was not politically expedient to include them in any electoral list. The USA party had been overtly rejected by the *Imbokodvo* as a political ally, because other political parties were exploiting that relationship to their own ends by pointing to it as Sobhuza's open favouritism of a minority over indigenous Swazis.

The elections went on calmly and in an orderly manner. The result was a second successive victory for the royalist *Imbokodvo*, which won 79.4% of the vote and all 24 seats in the House of Assembly. The NNLC, which had no seats in parliament, had won 20.2% of the vote. O. Mabuza's SUF won 0.3% (681 votes), while J. J. Nquku's SPP won 0.2% (356 votes) of the votes cast (Table 5.2).[44]

The results of the elections reflected the nature of the electoral system, which allowed the party with the majority of the votes to have all the seats, whereas, under the proportional representation system of voting, the opposition would have been represented in parliament on the basis of their overall performance at the polls. Under the prevailing electoral

---

[44] 'Clean Sweep at Elections: Imbokodvo gets all Seats', *Times of Swaziland*, April 28, 1967.

208 H. P. DLAMINI

Table 5.2 Results of general elections held in Swaziland on 19–20 April 1967

Party	Votes	Percentage	Seats	±
Imbokodvo National Movement	191,160	79.4	24	+15
Ngwane National Liberatory Congress	48,744	20.2	0	0
Swaziland United Front	681	0.3	0	0
Swaziland Progressive Party	356	0.2	0	0
Total	240,941	100	24	
Valid votes	80,314	95.5		
Invalid/blank votes	3888	4.5		
Total	84,685	100		
Registered voters/turnout	106,121	79.8		

Source Nohlen et al., *Elections in Africa: A Data Handbook* (Oxford University Press, 1999), 868

system, no opposition party had a seat in parliament. Thus, after the April 1968 elections, Swaziland became a de facto one-party state. This was not promising for the future of democracy in the country.

The status of Swaziland changed from that of a protectorate' to that of a protected state after the April elections, as the British had promised, and this was celebrated by the *Ngwenyama*. The Protected State Agreement was signed on 24 April 1967 by Sobhuza as the King of Swaziland and Sir Francis Lloyd on behalf of Queen Elizabeth II of England. The *Ngwenyama* took the oath as King of Swaziland before a crowd of 20,000 people at Lobamba.[46] The politics of the new status of Swaziland as a protected state had to do with the recognition of the *Ngwenyama* by the British. The argument the Swazi monarchists had been consistently making throughout had been that Swaziland was a sovereign state according to the 1881 international convention, to which the Swazi monarch was a signatory. But the protectorate status that placed Swaziland under British rule created confusion, because Swaziland was being treated as a colony, whereas it was a sovereign state with a traditional Head of State. The monarchists felt this was not captured in British constitutional thinking. By insisting that Swaziland should sign an agreement with Britain as a protected state, the Swazi monarch was indirectly asking Britain to recognize the *Ngwenyama* as the real leader of Swaziland to whom power should be unconditionally transferred, rather than transferring power to the leader of a political party. This gymnastics of nomenclature did not imply any substantive constitutional change of the colonial status of Swaziland, because the territory was still treated as a colony and was still to be granted independence.

5 THE 1967 CONSTITUTION, INTERNAL SELF-GOVERNMENT ... 209

Following the 1967 Constitution, which provided for full internal self-government, Sobhuza announced the appointment of Prince Makhosini Dlamini as Prime Minister, who was duly sworn in by the Attorney General. Sobhuza appointed members of the National Assembly and Senate, taking into consideration interests that were not adequately represented. Since the *Imbokodvo* won every elected seat, the appointments posed no problem. The appointments were a unique opportunity for Sobhuza to compensate his White allies who could not be featured on the *Imbokodvo* electoral list because of political considerations, since Whites were associated by many with colonialism and oppression. The members of the House of Assembly appointed by Sobhuza to represent special interests and those elected are presented in Tables 5.3 and 5.4 gives the details of those elected to be senators.

The ministers and assistant ministers are given in Table 5.5.

Swaziland was granted full internal self-rule with a ministerial system of government as the last stage of the evolution of the territory to independence. The newly elected government's task was to engage in the constitutional processes leading to independence.

Towards the 1968 London Constitutional Conference

Prime Minister Prince Makhosini Dlamini's government assumed the key role of finalizing the Independence Constitution with the British government. In order to prepare the White Paper on the Constitution, the Swazi Cabinet asked members of parliament for written submissions for consideration in December 1967. Cabinet considered these submissions and incorporated some of them in the proposals for the Independence Constitution which it published as a White Paper in order to facilitate public debate on the document.[45] It is interesting to note that Dr Zwane's NNLC offered no comment on the White Paper when it was published. Zane was incensed at his exclusion from the Constitutional Review Committee and by the feeling that his criticism would have no effect on the *Imbokodvo*

---

[45] http://hansard.millbanksystems.com/commons/1968/jul/05/swaziland-independence-bill. HANSARD 1803–2005, 1960s–1968, 5 July 1968, Commons Sitting, Orders of the Day, Swaziland Independence Bill, HC Deb 5 July 1968, Vol. 767 cc1875-9031875 (accessed 29 June 2015).

210 H. P. DLAMINI

Table 5.3 Members of the Swazi National Assembly after the April 1967 general elections

	Member	Affiliation	Comment
1.	L. Lovell	Appointee of King Sobhuza	Former Legislative Council member
2.	R. P. Stephens	Appointee of King Sobhuza	Former Legislative Council member
3.	Rev. R. Forrester	Appointee of King Sobhuza	Former Legislative Council member
4.	J. S. Murphy	Appointee of King Sobhuza	Old Swazilander and Chairman of the Swaziland Tobacco Cooperative
5.	D. Hynd Stewart	Appointee of King Sobhuza	Euro-African. Served as observer during the 1963 London Conference
6.	D. Dlamini	Appointee of King Sobhuza	Successful businessman
7.	S. M. Dlamini	Elected member	Member of the Imbokodvo
8.	Dr M. Sukati	Elected member	Member of the Imbokodvo
9.	Prince Mfanasibili Dlamini	Elected member	Member of the Imbokodvo
10.	M. Ndlangamandla	Elected member	Member of the Imbokodvo
11.	M. N. Hlatshwako	Elected member	Member of the Imbokodvo
12.	A. K. Hlophe	Elected member	Member of the Imbokodvo
13.	R. V. Dlamini	Elected member	Member of the Imbokodvo
14.	A. Duba	Elected member	Member of the Imbokodvo
15.	J. B. M. Sukati	Elected member	Member of the Imbokodvo
16.	M. N. Gamedze	Elected member	Member of the Imbokodvo
17.	H. K. Dlamini	Elected member	Member of the Imbokodvo
18.	S. M. Shabalala	Elected member	Member of the Imbokodvo

(continued)

5 THE 1967 CONSTITUTION, INTERNAL SELF-GOVERNMENT ... 211

Table 5.3 (continued)

	Member	Affiliation	Comment
19.	M. S. Ndaba	Elected member	Member of the Imbokodvo
20.	Prince Makhosini Dlamini	Elected member	Leader on the Imbokodvo
21.	J. S. Mavimbela	Elected member	Member of the Imbokodvo
22.	Prince G. Dlamini	Elected member	Member of the Imbokodvo
23.	Z. A. Khumalo	Elected member	Member of the Imbokodvo
24.	A. D. Hlatshwako	Elected member	Member of the Imbokodvo
25.	B. A. Dlamini	Elected member	Member of the Imbokodvo
26.	E. S. Dhladhla	Elected member	Member of the Imbokodvo
27.	Dr A. M. Nxumalo	Elected member	Member of the Imbokodvo
28.	Prince Masitsela Dlamini	Elected member	Member of the Imbokodvo
29.	M. S. Matsebula	Elected member	Member of the Imbokodvo
30.	S. S. Nxumalo	Elected member	Member of the Imbokodvo

Source 'The King Names Six MPs', *Times of Swaziland*, May 5, 1967; 'Clean Sweep at Election Imbokodvo Gets All Seats', *The Times of Swaziland*, April 28, 1967

and the USA.[46] However, both the NNLC and the SUF had been consistently critical of the electoral code, which did not allow small parties the prospect of representation in parliament.[47] After public consultation, the Prime Minister submitted the White Paper to both the House of Assembly and the Senate for debate. A special meeting of the National Assembly was convened on 22 January 1968 to examine the White Paper.

The Prime Minister pointed out in the House of Assembly meeting that the government had to take a stand on what form the Independence Constitution should take in preparation for the forthcoming Constitutional

[46] Ibid.
[47] Ibid.

212 H. P. DLAMINI

Table 5.4 Senators elected by the House and appointed by King Sobhuza

	Senator	Affiliation	Remarks
1.	P. Dlamini	Imbokodvo	Elected by House
2.	J. M. Mamba	Imbokodvo	Elected by House
3.	B. Nhlabatsi	Imbokodvo	Elected by House
4.	B. Dlamini	Imbokodvo	Elected by House
5.	P. J. Braun		Elected by House
6.	M. W. Magongo	Imbokodvo	Elected by House
7.	M. Mdziniso (The only female)	Involved in welfare organisations; gender activist for enfranchisement of women	Appointee of the King
8.	G. Mabuza	Rural Development Officer and former member of Legislative Council	Appointee of the King
9.	D. Lukhele	Lawyer. He helped draft the 1963 petition against the Imposed Constitution	Appointee of the King
10.	Rev. A. B. Gamedze	Church Minister and Educator	Appointee of the King
11.	C. Todd	Former leader of EAC and close confident of King Sobhuza	Appointee of the King
12.	D. Fitzpatrick		Appointee of the King

Source Compiled from 'The King Names Six MPs, Five Senators Elected', *The Times of Swaziland*, May 5, 1967; 'Biographies, Nominated MPs and Elected Senators', *The Times of Swaziland*, May 5, 1967; and 'Six Nominated to Senate', *Times of Swaziland*, May 19, 1967

Conference in London on 19 February 1968. He urged that the Cabinet's proposals be accepted, and indicated that there were still some unresolved grievances relating particularly to the authority to control minerals and land. He spoke on the difficulties experienced by the Cabinet in reaching a compromise between the 'two irreconcilable views' of the Swazis and the British colonial authorities. He stated that the Swazis considered minerals to be the rightful property of the Swazi nation, and that these should logically be held in trust by the *Ngwenyama* for the Swazi people. He also argued that the profits derived from them would accrue to the Swazi nation and be used for its benefit, and pointed out that this proposition, contained in chapter V of the 1967 Constitution, had 'time and again been endorsed by the electorate.' However, the British did not agree with this viewpoint, which the Prime Minister described as 'the depth of the feeling

5 THE 1967 CONSTITUTION, INTERNAL SELF-GOVERNMENT ... 213

Table 5.5 1967 ministers and assistant ministers

		Ministry	Affiliation	Assistant ministers
1.	Prince Makhosini Dlamini	The Prime Minister's Office	Imbokodvo	Z. Khumalo
2.	M. Sukati	The Deputy Prime Minister	Imbokodvo	Prince Masitstela Dlamini
3.	L. Lovell	Minister of Finance, Commerce and Industry		S. S.Nxumalo
4.	Prince Mfanasibili Dlamini	Minister of Local Administration	Imbokodvo	B. Dlamini
5.	A. K. Hlophe	Minister of Agriculture	Imbokodvo	
6.	Rev. A. B. Gama	Minister of Education	Imbokodvo	
7.	P. Dlamini	Minister of Works, Power and Communications	Imbokodvo	

Source Compiled from 'King Names Seven Ministers', *The Times of Swaziland*, May 19, 1967; 'Swaziland's First Cabinet', *The Times of Swaziland*, May 19, 1967

and conviction of the Swazi Nation'. The British consistently argued that the control of these valuable assets should be vested in the Cabinet, and indicated that they were obliged to consider all interests other than those of the Swazi.[48]

In section 91 of the constitutional proposals that the British government was tabling, the disposition of mineral rights was placed under the ultimate control of the Cabinet. Section 91 also subjected the utilization of the proceeds from such mineral rights to the ultimate decision of the government of Swaziland. This was in contrast to the view of the Constitutional Committee, as reflected in the British White Paper of October 1966, which gave power to make dispositions of minerals and mineral oils to the *Ngwenyama*. The *Ngwenyama* would appoint a committee, after consultation with the SNC, to advise him to exercise his powers. The British and Swazi views were, therefore, irreconcilable. These views reflected the contradiction in the role of Sobhuza as *Ngwenyama* of the Swazi and Sobhuza as a king of a modern nation with a functioning parliament in the Westminster tradition. The proposal of Prime Minister Dlamini's government

[48]SNA: Swaziland House of Assembly. Official Report (Hansard), First Session. Sitting January 22, 1968.

214   H. P. DLAMINI

under chapter V of the White Paper was an attempt to reach a compromise solution between the views of the Constitutional Committee and those of the British government after lengthy consultations with the British government. In support of the government White Paper, the Prime Minister highlighted the importance of mineral resources and the responsibility of a modern government with regard to them:

> I wish to say that minerals are valuable assets and their development, lack of development, has a profound effect on the economy of the country as a whole. Mineral rights involve not only income to government through taxation but also various aspects of infrastructure to serve the country as a whole such as the construction of railways, roads, water and power. It is thought, therefore, that *it is only right and proper that the view of the government of the day should also be taken into account,* in addition to those owners of mineral rights, when any grants or dispositions are to take place. The views of this government can conveniently be taken into account by associating members of the Cabinet, in the committee advising the *Ngwenyama,* in the exercise of his rights over Minerals and Mineral Oils.[49] (Emphasis added)

The compromise put forward by the Cabinet was that the Minerals Committee should consist of the Commissioner of Mines (a government official), and four or six members, half of whom would be appointed by King Sobhuza II as *Ngwenyama* in consultation with the SNC, and half by him as king, acting on the advice of the Cabinet.

The next important point raised by the Prime Minister was the land issue. Prime Minister Dlamini felt that it was the responsibility of the British government to solve the British land alienation problem involving the ceding of large tracts of Swazi nation land to Europeans. He recalled that, after the British assumed protectorate status over Swaziland, it declared all Swaziland Crown land and appointed a Commission to partition this land between Europeans and the Swazis, who benefited from just one-third of the land. He pointed out that the land problem was causing social and economic problems that were threatening the political stability of the country and marring interracial relations. The Prime Minister wanted the land problem to be solved prior to independence. He therefore called on the House to support this motion in chapter V of the White Paper.

[49] Ibid., 3–4.

5 THE 1967 CONSTITUTION, INTERNAL SELF-GOVERNMENT ... 215

In parliament, King Sobhuza II's praise singers took to the floor to express their opinion about the White Paper. The first to speak from the floor was Elias S. Dhladhla. He went back to the old argument that the *Ngwenyama* should have absolute powers over land and mineral issues in Swaziland, because it was the wish of the Swazi people and, therefore, he called for the amendment of the government proposed motion accordingly. He stated:

> Mr Speaker, with regard to chapter 5, Land and Minerals... of the White Paper, I have to request leave of Mr Speaker to move an amendment of the White Paper proposals because I feel very strongly that there has been injustice done to the Swazis. This section... deals with a Mineral Committee which will consist of a Commissioner of mines and not less than four and not more than six other persons... What I fail to understand is the appointment of this Committee, half of whom shall be appointed by the *Ngwenyama*, acting on the advice of Cabinet. Mr Speaker, Sir, why on earth on the advice of Cabinet?... my argument... is that when we talk of the Cabinet we refer to the Ministers nominated by the leader of the political party that has won the general elections of the day...[50]

He pointed out that more than half of the land in Swaziland was held as farms or concession lands, which were fully protected under the Bill of Rights. Some members of the community had their properties fully protected by the law but:

> when it comes to legislation on the Swazi private property, which includes land, minerals and mineral oils... the White paper authors... should have the temerity and audacity to grant powers to Cabinet to exercise control over our Swazi private property which is under the trusteeship of the *Ngwenyama*? Surely this is not justice...[51]

He disagreed with the idea of Cabinet advising the *Ngwenyama* on matters relating to land and minerals, and proposed an amendment that read: 'The *Ngwenyama-in-Libandla* (SNC) shall appoint a Mineral's Committee which will advise him in the exercise of his rights of control of these assets on behalf of the Swazi nation.' He maintained that the wishes of the Swazi people that their King should control minerals and land should be

[50] Ibid., 12.
[51] Ibid.

216 H. P. DLAMINI

respected. He felt the Cabinet had gone too far in striking a 'compromise' and stated that the Cabinet:

> [had] no earthly right to tramp on what we regard as sacred ground. Mr Speaker, I nearly said they should rather resign than meddle with what is thought to be so dear to [the Swazi people].... Sir, the resolution [of Cabinet] could have been what they considered a reasonable compromise but we Swazis are not prepared and we do not believe that it is right for us to compromise, or to take chances with what we regard as our God-given possessions...[52]

He was seconded by S. M. Shabalala, who made a more restrained statement of Swazi wishes. He agreed that land and minerals were the God-given property of the Swazis that should be placed under the *Ngwenyama*, and cautioned Cabinet not to stray from the will of the Swazi people. The discussions that followed were acrimonious, as the parliamentarians aligned themselves in the pro- and anti-King Sobhuza II camp along racial lines.

Murphy noted that the proposer of the amendment, E. S. Dhladhla, and his seconder, Shabalala, were 'preaching to the converted', and expressed the fear that they were seeing 'a hornet's nest where one [did] not exist'. He congratulated the Prime Minister and his Cabinet for having produced 'a very accurate document'. He stated that, contrary to what some parliamentarians may be thinking, it was quite clear in the Government White Paper that mineral rights were vested in the *Ngwenyama* 'solely and entirely', and that he did not need anybody's advice. However, the Prime Minister and his Cabinet wisely went one step further by including a clause where certain people would be appointed on the advice of Cabinet to advise the *Ngwenyama*, but there was nothing to force the *Ngwenyama* to accept their advice. The White Paper 'wisely [mentioned] the Commissioner of Mines, which would comprise professionals and a technical team, to advise the *Ngwenyama* on the management of minerals because this was a technical exercise. Without such a committee, the Swazi people might be robbed of their mineral wealth by unscrupulous mining companies'. People with the technical knowledge were therefore needed because mining is a technological and not a traditional activity. He, therefore, congratulated the Cabinet and moved that the Government White Paper should be adopted.[53]

---

[52] Ibid., 13.

[53] Ibid., 16–17.

The Minister for Finance, Commerce and Industry, L. Lovell, pointed out that the problem for those asking for the Government White Paper to be amended arose from the clause that required that a committee should advise the *Ngwenyama* about the disposition of mineral rights. Such parliamentarians did not seem to grasp the dimension of the economics of mining, which is both domestic and international. Murphy pointed out that the Swazi parliamentarians were placing land and minerals on the same footing. The two belonged to the Swazi people, no doubt, but, 'when it comes to making grants of minerals, it is a far more complicated issue than to make grants or dispositions or sales of land'. The exploitation of minerals, which takes place deep underground, and the use of land for farming and grazing, and constructing buildings, are two different things. The *Ngwenyama* may not require any advice when it comes to a decision to dispose of land or to lease it but, when it comes to a decision as to whether you should grant a right of mineral prospection, expert advice would be required. The Minister then asked:

> Why should one take umbrage, why should one be upset because the Cabinet suggests that for this very difficult task the King should have at his disposal a Committee appointed by him to advise him? And advice regarding the disposal or grant to a particular mining company, or group of mining companies, not only requires the advice on the question of mining. It also requires advice on the whole question of economising of whether this mining proposition is favourable or unfavourable to the economy of the whole country.[54]

He pointed out that it was the government that provided the machinery for understanding the economy of the whole country. He stated that the Swazis had entrusted that task to their government, and they would expect that the *Ngwenyama* would welcome the advice of government on the general economic effects of the granting of a lease to a particular mining company. It was, therefore, in the best interest of Swaziland for the *Ngwenyama* to be well-advised by the government on the economy of the country. He felt there was no justification for not trusting Cabinet in the type of advice it would give to the King. Reacting to Dhladla's statement about the 'nerve, audacity and temerity' of Cabinet to suggest that the *Ngwenyama* should be advised on the disposal of minerals, Lovell retorted: 'I will accept...[that] it is audacious and an act of temerity to suggest that the Cabinet should

---

[54] Ibid., 24.

218   H. P. DLAMINI

place some advice at the disposal [of the *Ngwenyama*].' He questioned what was actually wrong with the King taking the advice from Cabinet. He wondered how advice to the King would endanger his 'sovereignty' or 'integrity', or the 'high repute' in which he was held.

Lovell asked the House what the British government would do with a proposal that the *Ngwenyama* should act without the advice of his Cabinet in a modern state. Lovell stated that the Swazi deputation to London would be able to have their constitutional document endorsed only if it included the clause that the *Ngwenyama* would seek the advice of the Cabinet and the SNC regarding the disposal of minerals. The minister warned that the British would reject any attempts to digress significantly from directives given about limitations on the powers of the monarch.

In concluding the heated debate, the Speaker of the House gave the floor to Dhladla, the mover of the amendment of the government White Paper, to sum up and make his position known after a lengthy explanation from Lovell. Dhladla did not address the crucial issues raised by Lovell on the importance of having Cabinet involved in mineral management in a modern economy due to its complexities. Rather, he expressed pity for Lovell, and asked him where international law was when Swazi land was being alienated by the British. In his words:

> I feel sorry for the Hon. Mr Lovell because he does not seem to realise the importance attached by the Swazis to this very important matter... I must say I was very disappointed after hearing the Minister... speaking about international Law and Justice because these are not new. Even when we were dispossessed of our land International Law and Justice were in existence. It is the nation which sent us here to bring back that which is their own, and it is our duty here to fulfil the wishes of the people. Mr. Speaker, I feel I will like to stay put on the amendment I have already moved and I will not be shaken.[55]

The amendment of the government White Paper to empower the *Ngwenyama* to have absolute authority over mineral and land resources was carried by 21 votes to 9, with voting reflecting a racial fault line with Swazis voting for and Europeans against the amendment.[56] The Swazis were essentially the King's men faithfully voting for the King, while the

[55] Ibid., 27.
[56] Ibid., 28.

5 THE 1967 CONSTITUTION, INTERNAL SELF-GOVERNMENT ...   219

Europeans were voting for the principles of Westminster parliamentary democracy and not necessarily against the King.

On 23 January 1968, the Prime Minister presented the White Paper to the Senate and urged the House to adopt its recommendations. There were two separate aspects to the proposals. The first related to the form of the constitution to be discussed between the representatives of Britain and Swaziland at a conference due to begin in London on 19 February 1968, and the second was about land alienation by the British at the expense of Swazis. The main issue of the first point was the irreconcilable positions of the British government and the Swazis over mineral rights. The Swazi Constitutional Committee's view, as reflected in the British Government White Paper of October 1966, was that the powers to dispose of minerals and mineral oils should be vested in the *Ngwenyama*, and that he should appoint a committee, after consultation with the SNC, to advise him to exercise these powers. The Swazi government proposal, as described in chapter V of the White Paper, was, in effect, an attempt to reach a compromise between the views of the Constitutional Committee and those of the British government. The Prime Minister emphasized in Senate, as he had earlier done in the Lower House, the importance of minerals to the economy of Swaziland, and the technicalities involved in handling them. He urged the Senators to approve the proposed compromise solution to the mineral issue in light of the explanation advanced. The second issue, about compensation for land alienation that had brought untold suffering to many Swazis, was raised, and the proposal was to request the British government to help the Swazi government to solve this crucial land problem prior to independence. Britain was held responsible for land alienation in Swaziland through its colonial legislation, and it was therefore incumbent on Britain to solve this problem. The second issue, dealing with land appropriation, did not elicit any serious debate and was forwarded to the British government to address. The main contentious issue was the amendment of the government bill that made the Cabinet an important body with regard to the control of minerals. The Swazis argued that the *Ngwenyama* should have absolute authority over mineral and land issues, while Whites subscribed to the supremacy of Cabinet in a typical Westminster parliamentary democracy.

The Swazi senator W. M. Magongo moved an amendment that read: 'The *Ngwenyama*-in-*Libandla* [Council] shall appoint a mineral committee to advise him in exercising his right of control of these assets on behalf of the Swazi Nation.'[57] The White Senator Braun immediately challenged Senator Magongo to explain exactly what that amendment meant. The Senator drew the attention of the House to the fact that what the government presented to Senate was the fruit of negotiations between the British and Swazi government, arguing that such negotiations always take place between governments. He stated that he had heard murmurings to the effect that the right of the Swazi nation had been taken away and given to government. He dissented from such views as being incorrect, and pointed to the fact that the government was elected by the Swazi people and therefore belonged to them. He explained that the government proposals that were the outcome of negotiations with the British, '[gave] the *Ngwenyama* absolute power in deciding how [mineral] rights [were] going to be disposed of'. Clause 80(2) read: 'The *Ngwenyama* may make grants, leases or other dispositions conferring rights or interests in respect of minerals and mineral oils but only exercises such powers after obtaining but not necessarily acting in accordance with the advice of the Minerals Committee'. The section of the Cabinet was merely to assist the Minerals Committee in giving it the benefit and experience of government members in its consideration of applications. Braun explained that the involvement of government did not constitute an encroachment on the rights of ownership of the *Ngwenyama*. After all, the government emanated from the Swazi nation and belonged to the Swazi nation, and modern governance was the responsibility of Cabinet acting on behalf of the *Ngwenyama* and the Swazi people.

This explanation appears not to have had any effect on the traditionalists, as they stood up to demonstrate their unalloyed loyalty to the *Ngwenyama* as the incarnation of the Swazi nation while refusing to acknowledge how Westminster parliamentary democracy works. Senator Magongo argued that the *Ngwenyama*-in-*libandla* should appoint members of the committee. Magongo made the argument that he regarded minerals as private property; in the same way that land was demarcated land and kept apart for its own use, others were leased land as their private property. Minerals were the property of the Swazi nation and government should stay off that domain in the same way that it stayed off private White farms. Cabinet should not advise the *Ngwenyama* on private property.

---

[57]SNA: Official Report of the Debates of the Senate Fifth Meeting of the First Session, January 23, 1968, 6.

Lady Senator Mdiniso supported Magongo, although in more moderate terms. She stated that the minerals under discussion now belonged to the Swazi nation under the control of the *Ngwenyama*, and agreed with the suggestion that the *Ngwenyama* should be empowered to appoint a committee of his choice to work with him.[58] She supported the idea that ministers should work with the *Ngwenyama* on condition that they were his choice. Senator Todd, a diehard supporter of the *Ngwenyama*, explained to the House that 'nobody [had] fought harder than [himself] for the principle that, as mineral rights were vested in the *Ngwenyama* for the benefit of the Swazi Nation, he should have a decisive say in the exploitation of the mineral rights'. He stated that the issue being raised 'on the amendment is more psychological than real', and revealed that he had 'consistently requested the British Government to allow the Swazi Nation to have a decisive voice in the exploitation of the minerals'. Todd explained that he knew the strong feelings of the British government about the mineral issue, and that the Constitutional Committee charged with responsibility of negotiating with the British government would have an uphill task in persuading the British government to allow the monarch to have total control over all matters affecting mineral rights at the expense of Cabinet. The Senator stated that it was impossible to exclude the government of Swaziland in the exploitation of these valuable assets, and advised senators not to tamper with the government proposal, which was a carefully balanced clause designed to meet both the government's and the *Ngwenyama*'s concerns. Todd, the *Ngwenyama*'s staunch supporter, had to speak the truth about the essence of parliamentary democracy and the operation of the cabinet system to the Swazis.

The clause in the draft stated that the *Ngwenyama* would make the decision on the advice of the Committee and, in Swazi tradition, the *Ngwenyama* was the head of the nation and made the decision for the Swazi nation. The government draft acknowledged the fact that there was a difference between the traditional and modern Swazi state, and the governance of the two were different. With respect to the modern Swazi nation, the *Ngwenyama* was expected to listen to two bodies: the Technical Committee, which was a government department, and the SNC, which was a traditional body, in order to make a decision on what was the best action to take regarding exploitation. It was not possible to assign such a technical

---

[58] SNA: Official Report of the Debates of the Senate Fifth Meeting of the First Session, January 23, 1968, 9–10.

222   H. P. DLAMINI

role exclusively to the king and the SNC, which was a traditional council. Todd took pains to explain that the Paper on mineral rights had no value if no minerals existed. He stated that, when he was in charge of the Mines Department, there were approximately 39 proved minerals in Swaziland, but there was no study that supported any expenditure on these minerals, because they were not of commercial value. The government of Swaziland spent money on mineral exploration annually and the budget for this was under the heading of the Ministry of Mines. This Ministry had to continue to function because of its specialization in handling such matters. The government could not be shut out of the domain of mineral management, which was a technical domain and was relevant to the national economy. Todd therefore invited the House to support the Government White Paper, which allowed the Technical Committee emanating from Cabinet and representatives of the SNC to oversee the management of minerals.

When Senator Braun took to the floor, he emphasized the point that there was need for free discussions and a democratic approach to matters of mineral management. He warned that the British government would not entertain a system of government that marginalized the Cabinet in favour of the king of Swaziland just because his supporters wanted it to be so. Referring to the Senators calling for the amendment of the government Bill, Senator Braun said:

> I do not think that we are entitled to expect of those who choose to act the role of opposition, that they will act as responsible opposition and that they will give a little careful thought to what they are doing before they move amendments of this nature. Now it is obvious that our government is going to have a difficult task ahead of it in persuading the Government of Great Britain to accept the proposals which the constitutional committee two years ago put forward in regard to minerals.... [According to the committee] minerals... would be in the control of the *Ngwenyama*. The Cabinet in their wisdom have devised this formula, namely, that there should be a committee which the *Ngwenyama* appoints and which will have on it as half of its Members people appointed by the *Ngwenyama* on the advice of the Cabinet. *And it is that half of a little Committee which is advisory only which seems to terrify the movers of this motion. Mr Speaker, this is like an elephant which is afraid of a mouse, and the mouse has not even growled.*[59] (Emphasis added)

---

[59] SNA: Official Report of the Debates of the Senate. Fifth Meeting of the First Session, January 23, 1968, 11.

5 THE 1967 CONSTITUTION, INTERNAL SELF-GOVERNMENT ... 223

Senator Braun maintained that the issue of mineral exploitation touched on several spheres of national life including communication, housing, education, and road infrastructure. This implied several government departments had to be involved in the matter. To exclude the Cabinet from having a say in this matter did not make any sense. He called on the movers of the amendment simply to withdraw it. Senator Fitzpatrick, another White senator, reminded the House of the technicalities involved in mineral management that required the attention of Cabinet. He warned that the British government would not accept the proposed amendment being tabled, because it kept out the Cabinet as the central body for decision-making. Despite all these explanations, the Swazis still refused to budge and kept on insisting on the supremacy of the *Ngwenyama* in all matters in the Swazi nation.

Senator Nhlabatsi took to the floor to insist on the amendment of the Government White Paper to allow the *Ngwenyama* exclusive rights over issues of mineral exploitation. His argument was that colonialism had not been fair to the Swazi people, and they trusted the *Ngwenyama* would act in the supreme interests of his people, who were generally poor. He opined that if the Cabinet and the Swazi nation had to appoint members of the committee to advise the *Ngwenyama*, there could be a conflict between the two.[60] The Senator appeared to be lost between the working of a modern and a traditional government, as he insisted that the *Ngwenyama* in Swazi tradition is the head of the Swazi nation. Another Swazi, Senator Mabuza, spoke about the colonial injustices suffered by the Swazis, and why the *Ngwenyama* should be trusted as the saviour of the Swazi people. Senator B. Dlamini felt that 'the aspirations of the Swazi people must be expressed' so that it could go on record. He explained that the elaborate explanations from all the parties were enlightening, but his thinking was that the Cabinet should not be above the *Ngwenyama*, and the people who elected them would not want to hear that they had negotiated a system of governance that places Cabinet above the *Ngwenyama*. He appreciated the difficulties of selling the Swazi viewpoint to the British government, but insisted that it was important for the British to know the feelings of the Swazi people. Finally, the proposed amendment was put to a vote and the Senate was again divided along racial lines. The numbers of votes are presented in Table 5.6.

[60] Ibid.

224 H. P. DLAMINI

Table 5.6 Senate vote on amendment of government White Paper to give the *Ngwenyama* absolute power over minerals and mineral oils

	Ayes	Noes
1.	Senator B. Dlamini	Senator P. T. Braun
2.	Senator D. Lukele	The Minister of Works, Power and Communication
3.	Senator G. M. E. Mabuza	Senator C. F. Todd
4.	Senator J. M. Mamba	Senator H. D. G Fitzpatrick
5.	Senator Mrs M. Mdziniso	
6.	Senator M. M. P. Nhlabatsi	
7.	Senator W. M. Magongo	
8.	The Minister for Education	

Source Compiled from SNA: Official Report of the Debates of the Senate. Fifth Meeting of the First Session, January 23, 1968, 20

The amendment in favour of the *Ngwenyama*'s overriding powers passed by eight votes to four, the strongest opposition being voiced this time by Senator Braun. Voting was on racial lines, with Whites voting against the amendment of the bill and Blacks in favour. The two Houses of Parliament finally resolved that mineral rights should be vested in the *Ngwenyama* as the head of the Swazi nation and, *ipso facto*, the trustee of its property. The proposed amendment took away the control of mineral rights from the modern government of Swaziland and gave it to the traditional authority. The two Houses, in essence, voted for an absolute monarch, rather than a constitutional one. This proposed constitution was a significant departure from the 1963 constitution, which marginalized the king and restricted him to the management of culture and tradition.

Prime Minister Prince Makhosini Dlamini's government made a request for independence on 6 September 1968. The same resolution requested Her Majesty's government to seek, at the appropriate time, the support of other member governments of the Commonwealth regarding Swaziland's desire to become a member of the Commonwealth. All the government proposals were sent to London.

The Secretary of State for Commonwealth Affairs convened a conference to discuss the final constitution of Swaziland on 19–23 February 1968 at Marlborough House in London. The Swazi delegates to the UK are given in Table 5.7.

Political parties not represented in parliament were excluded from the delegation. Dr Zwane of the extra-parliamentary opposition NNLC and his

Table 5.7 Members of the Swazi delegation to the UK to negotiate the Independence Constitution in February 1968

	Member	Affiliation	Comment
1.	Prince Makhosini Dlamini	Cabinet Minister	Imbokodvo
2.	A. K. Hlope	Cabinet Minister	Imbokodvo
3.	Polycarp Dlamini	Cabinet Minister	Imbokodvo
4.	Leo Lovell	Cabinet Minister	King Sobhuza's appointee
5.	Dr M. Nxumalo	Cabinet Minister	Imbokodvo
6.	Sir F. Lloyd	H. M. Commissioner in Swaziland	Government Official
7.	W. Ramsden	Attorney General	Government Official
8.	H. Roemmele	Secretary of the Cabinet	Government Official

Source Compiled from: 'London Talk', *The Times of Swaziland*, March 1, 1968

deputy, K. Samketi, did not take their exclusion kindly, and decided to go to London and stage a lie-down protest. Consequently, at the opening of the conference on Monday, 19 February 1968, Dr Zwane and K. Samketi staged a protest by lying down at the entrance of Marlborough House, thereby blocking delegates from entering the hall. Several delegates had to be given a hand as they stepped over the bodies of Dr Zwane and his deputy. The British police arrested them and took them away. A photograph of the two protesters, smiling and with their thumbs raised in African salute as they were being taken away by the police, appeared in several newspapers, including *The Times of Swaziland* (Fig. 5.1).[61]

According to George Thomson, Britain's Secretary of State for Commonwealth Affairs, all opinions, including those of the NNLC, were considered at the London talks. During his visit to Swaziland in October 1967, the NNLC and the SUF had submitted proposals that were critical of an electoral code that allowed the winner, by a simple majority, to carry all the seats. He therefore called for a single member constituency to replace the existing three-member constituency system. The Swazi government argued that the opposition had not presented their views when they had the opportunity to do so in Swaziland. The NNLC had proposed a 60-member constituency system, but the government had felt it would be inappropriate

[61] See. Dr. Zwane and Deputy Under Arrest in London for Protesting Their Exclusion from Constitutional Conference in Swaziland's Independence Constitution, *Times of Swaziland*, 1968.

Fig. 5.1 Leading opposition leader Dr A. Zwane and K. T. Samketi demonstrating at the entrance of Marlborough House, UK (*Source* Keystone Press/Alamy Stock photo)

for a small country such as Swaziland. The Swaziland delegation pointed out that, although the three-member system was entrenched in the Constitution and was therefore difficult to change, under the Constitution, the voting system would be determined by a simple parliamentary majority. The British advised that the provision forbidding a defeated member from

5 THE 1967 CONSTITUTION, INTERNAL SELF-GOVERNMENT ...   227

becoming a nominated member should be dropped from the constitutional proposals.[62]

On the issue of the *Ngwenyama*'s control over minerals and land, which the Swazi parliament wanted, the Colonial Office felt that there was no need for the Swazi delegation to insist on acceptance of this by the British government. It was clearly a matter that could be rectified after independence by a two-thirds parliamentary vote. The Attorney General, W. A. Ramsden, and the Queen's Commissioner, Sir Francis Lloyd, confirmed this position. The British, however, advised that it was not good for a newly independent country to start tampering with its constitution.[63]

The land issue was also raised in London in addition to the amendment. This was against the wishes of the White members of the delegation, who felt it was too delicate to handle. Prince Makhosini Dlamini made the argument that the national economy was growing, that the gap between the rich and the poor remained, and that this division was mainly between Whites and Blacks. He pointed out that 43% of the land was still in White hands, many of whom were absentee landowners who were resident in South Africa and who had vast acreages for grazing their sheep in winter. Others, as individuals or corporations, were engaged in cultivating or ranching on a large commercial scale. Yet, Swazis needed land for food and basic survival. Swazi areas were already congested, and farm tenants were insecure. The Swazi delegation placed the onus of finding the solution to the land problem on the British government. Citing the precedent of Kenya, where the British bought the so-called White Highlands for African resettlement, the Swazi delegation suggested that a similar path should be pursued by the British.

Prince Makhosini Dlamini warned that land shortage in Swaziland was a real problem, and would cause increasing economic pressure and racial tensions that would pose a serious challenge to the Swazi government after independence. He proposed compensation for the alienation of land under the Partition Proclamation of 1907 which favoured Whites and also for a further 500,000 acres of land, which the British had sold to Whites to finance its administration of the country. The British rejected this claim outright. Similarly, the British did not budge from their insistence on Swaziland

---

[62] 'London Talks. NNLC Views Were Put to the Conference', *Times of Swaziland*, March 1, 1968.

[63] Ibid.

228   H. P. DLAMINI

adopting a Westminster form of government, and the supremacy of parliament in modern governance. Before the close of the February 1968 London Conference, the British government informed the Swazi delegation that the Commonwealth Secretary General had confirmed that all members of the Commonwealth had agreed that Swaziland should become a member on attaining independence. Essentially, the Swazi delegation did not have its way in the UK, because the British government rejected the amendment of the government bill and the land issue was shelved.

On its return from the UK, the Swazi delegation was welcomed by a mammoth crowd at Oshoek. Prince Makhosini Dlamini said little, because 'Swazi tradition required him to report first to the *Ngwenyama* before discussing such matters with the people'.[64] According to Kuper, the delegation reported to King Sobhuza that they had been cordially received and agreements had been reached on most matters. The British had finally recognized the strength of Swazi claims to control minerals, and only the land issue had not been satisfactorily resolved.[63] This was not the exact picture of what transpired in London, because the British did not definitively give in to the idea of the *Ngwenyama* having monopoly over minerals and land. Over the issue of land alienation, not much was achieved, because it was more complicated than anticipated. Therefore, the land question had become linked with financial talks related to post-colonial British annual subventions to Swaziland. It was felt that financial talks would be held between the Swazi government and the British Minister of Overseas Development that could come later, after independence. This could take the form of a portion of the annual payment from Britain to Swaziland to keep the newly independent state solvent.[64] According to the Conference report, this last remaining dispute over land claims could be solved in the context of British financial assistance to the development plans of Swaziland following independence. Compensation for land alienation was considered a multimillion rand issue that had to be shelved until independence had been brought about.[65]

The British House of Commons debated the Swaziland Independence Bill in July 1968. The Bill provided for the independence of the kingdom of Swaziland within the Commonwealth. During the debate, some British

[64]'Independence Talks Continue in London', *Times of Swaziland*, February 23, 1968.

[65]http://hansard.millbanksystems.com/commons/1968/jul/05/swaziland-independence-bill. HANSARD 1803–2005, 1960s–1968, 5 July 1968, Commons Sitting, Orders of the Day, Swaziland Independence Bill, HC Deb 5 July 1968, Vol. 767 cc1875-9031875 (accessed 29 June 2015).

5 THE 1967 CONSTITUTION, INTERNAL SELF-GOVERNMENT ...   229

members of parliament questioned the wisdom of giving mineral control to the *Ngwenyama*, rather than to the Cabinet or the Legislature. The Under-Secretary of State for Commonwealth Affairs, W. Witlock, responded that 'whether wise or not, it [was] the feeling of the Swazis that the control and disposal of those rights should rest with the person who holds them and not with the government of Swaziland'. Also, the Swazi nation land was vested in the *Ngwenyama*, and not the Cabinet.

Responding to the members of parliament, Witlock said:

> Points have been made about mineral rights. What was agreed at the Independence Conference made no change whatsoever in the ownership of mineral rights. What is vested in the *Ngwenyama* in trust for the Swazi Nation under the present constitution will be unchanged. What the conference did was to deal with the disposal of what is held in trust for the Swazi nation, that is to say, the tribal Swazis and not the population as a whole, which includes Europeans and others.
>
> These rights are held by the Ngwenyama... and there can be no doubt that it is the desire of the large majority of the Swazis that this shall be so. Whether wise or not, it is the feeling of the Swazis that the control and disposal of such rights should rest with the person who holds them and not with the Government of Swaziland.
>
> The Swazis have their own way of making their own views known on how the *Ngwenyama* should conduct their affairs. The Independence Conference agreed that that there should be a minerals committee to advise the Ngwenyama-in-Libandla, which is the council of the whole nation; every adult male in Swaziland having the right to attend the Libandla. There is little need, therefore, to feel that as between the *Ngwenyama* and the Swazi nation there will be any dissatisfaction over this arrangement.[66]

The response of the Under-Secretary of State reflected a British accommodation to Swazi pressures to allow the *Ngwenyama* to have total control over mineral resources, but that was not the definitive answer of the British government. The response did not address the issue of the place of the Cabinet in regulating the modern economy of Swaziland, which was not in line with Westminster parliamentary democracy and not in the sphere of traditional governance.

[66] Ibid.

230 H. P. DLAMINI

The 1968 Independence Constitution, which the British ultimately approved,[67] was largely what the Swazi government had proposed, except for the checks and balances that were introduced on the powers of the *Ngwenyama* to render him accountable. The *Ngwenyama* was vested with the power to appoint the prime minister, to nominate six senators (half the Senate), and to nominate six members of parliament. He was made an executive authority and acted on behalf of Cabinet, which he appointed after consultation with the prime minister. The King participated in both the modern and traditional government. To ensure that these two were kept distinct, the monarchical institutions were not incorporated into the Independence Constitution. The constitution separated the SNC from modern government, whereas the SPP and the NNLC had proposed that it should be gradually and peacefully incorporated into the modern system of government.

The 1968 Constitution required the *Ngwenyama* to act on many issues in accordance with the advice of his Cabinet, rather than unilaterally. Article 12 of the Independence Constitution stated categorically that 'the constitution [was] the supreme law of Swaziland and if any law... [was] not consistent with this constitution, that law [would] to the extent of the inconsistency, be void'. It stated that any alteration of this specially entrenched provision would require a joint sitting of the House of Assembly and the Senate, with a majority of not less than three-quarters of all members, and that the decision should be submitted to the people's approval in a referendum that must be supported by not less than two-thirds of all valid votes cast. It was only after this process that the Bill would be submitted to the *Ngwenyama* for his assent. This was the essence of good governance that the British bequeathed to the Swazis. The checks and balances, and the subordination of the *Ngwenyama* to a modern cabinet did not please King Sobhuza, who wanted to reign supreme.

CONCLUSION

This chapter has demonstrated how the *Imbokodvo* and their USA allies constituted the Constitutional Committee that the British selected from the legislature that emanated from the 1964 elections. They were guided

---

[67] SNA: The constitution of Swaziland Statutory Instruments 1968, No. 1377, Africa, The Swaziland Independence Order, 1968, Made 25 August 1968, Laid Before Parliament 30 August 1968; Coming into Operation: Immediately Before 6 September 1968.

in their proceedings by tapping into the constitutions of other British territories, and the submissions of extra-parliamentary opposition parties and other interest groups. Following the establishment of the Constitutional Consultative Committee, the political collaboration between the two allies was no longer smooth sailing, because the *Imbokodvo* reneged on its original conservative and pro-White political platform, and adopted the radical stance of the Progressives, which had a wider appeal to Swazis. This schism had important implications on the constitutional debates in the Legislative Council in April 1966. The debates were characterized by fireworks between the *Imbokodvo* and USA over the issues of race, and the powers of the *Ngyemyama*. Whereas the *Imbokodvo* and the USA were unanimous on several components of the White Paper tabled in the House, including the inclusion of the *Ngwenyama* as the king and Head of State of Swaziland, the issue of voting rights for Whites and equal numerical representation between Blacks and Whites in the legislature divided the two bitterly. The separate voting roll for Whites was viewed as a form of apartheid politics and was exploited by the Progressive parties for electioneering purposes, and many Swazis supported them. The *Imbokodvo* wanted to eliminate this special electoral roll for Europeans on the grounds of the need to create a non-racial state in which everybody was equal before the law, because it was popular with the Swazi people and they were in a position of power to do so. The USA party dissented on the grounds that a single voters' roll would mean the political death of the White minority Swazis, despite their significant contribution to the Swazi economy. The exchanges between the two camps during the debates were heated and bitter and, eventually, the majority *Imbokodvo* party had its way with the establishment of a single electoral roll for all and the elimination of special political privileges for Whites. Whereas the *Imbokodvo* was unanimous that the *Ngwenyama* should operate as an absolute ruler with unfettered rights over the control of minerals and land issues, the USA argued for cabinet control of such spheres of the economy, in the spirit of Westminster parliamentary democracy.

Nonetheless the deliberations of the Constitutional Consultative Committee culminated in the 1967 Constitution, which was the penultimate Swazi constitution. It granted, for the first time, full internal self-government based on a bicameral legislature, and recognized Sobhuza as Head of State and king of Swaziland. When a delegation of the Swazi government went to London in August 1968 for the final constitutional talks before independence, the issue of land appropriation was shelved and the

232   H. P. DLAMINI

Swazi government failed to convince the British to amend the constitution so as to give Sobhuza absolute power without parliamentary control in a modern independent state.

REFERENCES

ARCHIVAL SOURCES

Swaziland National Archives
SNA: Legislative Council Official Report, Hansard, 1965–1966.
SNA: Swaziland Government. Report of Swaziland Constitutional Committee, 1966.
SNA: Legislative Council Debates, 1966.
SNA: Swaziland Constitutional Proposals, October 1966.
SNA, Swaziland House of Assembly. Official Report (Hansard), First Session. Sitting January 22, 1968.
SNA, Official Report of the Debates of the Senate Fifth Meeting of the First Session, 23 January 1968.
SNA: The Constitution of Swaziland Statutory Instruments 1968, No. 1377, Africa, The Swaziland Independence Order, 1968, Made 25 August 1968, Laid Before Parliament 30 August 1968; Coming into Operation: Immediately Before 6 September 1968.

NEWSPAPER ARTICLES

'The Proposal for New Constitution,' *Times of Swaziland*, March 25, 1966.
'Stonehouse on Powers of the King', *Times of Swaziland*, October 10, 1966.
'NNLC Wants London Talks on Proposed Constitution', *Times of Swaziland*, October 14, 1966.
'Constitution Ready? Stonehouse Meets Political Leaders', *Times of Swaziland*, October 14, 1966.
'Clean Sweep at Elections: Imbokodvo Gets All Seats', *Times of Swaziland*, April 28, 1967.
'Student Leader Attacks constitution', *Times of Swaziland*, May 12, 1967.
'Independence Talks Continue in London', *Times of Swaziland*, February 23, 1968.
'London Talks. NNLC Views Were Put to the Conference', *Times of Swaziland*, March 1, 1968.
'Dr. Zwane and Deputy Under Arrest in London for Protesting Their Exclusion from Constitutional Conference in Swaziland's Independence Constitution', *Times of Swaziland*, 1968.

BOOKS AND JOURNALS

Bonner, P. *Kings, Commoners and Concessionaires: The Evolution and Dissolution of the Nineteenth-Century Swazi State*, Vol. 31 (London: Cambridge University Press, 2002).

Colomer, J. M. 'Party System Effects on Electoral Systems', In E. S. Herron, R. J. Pekkanen, and M. S. Shugart (eds.), *The Oxford Handbook of Electoral Systems* (Oxford: Oxford University Press, 2018).

Griffiths, I. L. 'The Quest for Independent Access to the Sea in Southern Africa', *Geographical Journal* (1989), 378–391.

Herron, E. S., Pekkanen, R. J., and Shugart, M. S. 'Terminology and Basic Rules of Electoral Systems', In E. S. Herron, R. J. Pekkanen, and M. S. Shugart (eds.), *The Oxford Handbook of Electoral Systems* (Oxford: Oxford University Press, 2018).

Matsebula, J. S. M. *A History of Swaziland*, 3rd edition (Cape Town: Maskew Miller Longman, 1988).

INTERNET SOURCE

http://hansard.millbanksystems.com/commons/1968/jul/05/swaziland-independence-bill. HANSARD 1803–2005, 1960s–1968, 5 July 1968, Commons Sitting, Orders of the Day, Swaziland Independence Bill, HC Deb 5 July 1968, Vol. 767 cc1875-9031875. Accessed 29 June 2015.

PART III

Post-Colonial Phase

CHAPTER 6

The 1968 Westminster Constitution, the 1972 General Election, and Serious Challenges Confronting Constitutional Monarchism

INTRODUCTION

This chapter focuses on the era of the Westminster Constitution that provided for a Swazi-type constitutional monarchy. Constitutional monarchism had a rocky life span, because it was compromised by the African political environment, which favoured executive absolutism in the shape of a one-party dictatorship, and the hostility of the traditionalists to multipartyism. The crisis of constitutionalism in this chapter deals with government resistance to checks on its powers, and the promotion and protection of civil rights and liberties.[1] The crisis was triggered when the Opposition NNLC captured three seats in the May 1972 elections at the time King Sobhuza II

---

[1] Constitutionalism requires the division of power between the executive, legislature, and judiciary and between the central and local government. See, for instance, M. Brattan, 'Formal Versus Informal Institutions in Africa', In L. Diamond and M. F. Platter (eds.), *Democratisation in Africa: Progress and Retreat* (Baltimore: John Hopkins University Press, 2010); C. M. Fombad, 'The Swaziland Constitution of 2005: Can Absolutism Be Reconciled with Modern Constitutionalism?', *South African Journal on Human Rights*, 93, 1 (2007), 93–115; M. Sinjenga, 'Constitutionalism in Africa: Emerging Trends: The Evolving African Constitutionalism', *The Review-International Commission of Jurist*, 60 (1998), 23–28; and T. Lumumba-Kasongo, *Liberal Democracy and Its Critics in Africa: Political Dysfunction and the Struggle of Social Progress* (London: Radical International Publishing, Zed Books, 2005).

© The Author(s) 2019
H. P. Dlamini, *A Constitutional History of the Kingdom of Eswatini (Swaziland), 1960–1982*, African Histories and Modernities,
https://doi.org/10.1007/978-3-030-24777-5_6

237

238   H. P. DLAMINI

was contemplating emulating his counterparts elsewhere on the continent by doing away with the 1968 Westminster-inherited constitution and its corollary, multipartyism, in favour of royal absolutism. This chapter demonstrates how the government labelled Ngwenya, the Opposition candidate of the NNLC that won the 1972 elections, as a foreigner, but how the courts rejected the government stance. The tug of war between the judiciary and the government compromised the functioning of constitutional democracy in Swaziland.

THE SWAZI-TYPE CONSTITUTIONAL MONARCHY, 1968–1973

Between 1968 and 1973, Swaziland was a constitutional monarchy as prescribed by the constitutional drafters in Whitehall in the UK. Typically, a constitutional monarchy is understood as a state 'headed by a sovereign who rules according to the constitution'. Such a constitution may be 'written' and 'codified'—as, indeed, is the case with the vast majority of constitutional monarchies, although the British constitution is unwritten and uncodified.[2]

The era of constitutionalism in Swaziland deals with that short period during which there were checks and balances of the powers of government, and the protection and promotion of civil rights and liberties. Constitutionalism, in principle, required the division of power between the executive, legislature, and judiciary, and between the central and local government.[3] A constitutional monarchy differs from an absolute monarchy, in which the king serves as the sole source of power in the state and is not legally

---

[2]V. Bogdanor, *The Monarchy and the Constitution* (Oxford: Oxford University Press, 1997), 1; Wanda, 'The Shaping of the Modern Constitution of Swaziland: A Review of Some Social and Historical Factors', *Lesotho Law Journal: A Journal of Law and Developments*, 6, 1 (1990), 137–198; Examples of contemporary Constitutional monarchies include Cambodia, Denmark, Japan, Jordan, Kuwait, Lesotho, Luxembourg, Malaysia, Morocco, Netherlands, Norway, Spain, Sweden, Thailand, the United Kingdom of Great Britain and Northern Ireland.

[3]See, for instance, M. Brattan, 'Formal Versus Informal Institutions in Africa', In L. Diamond and M. F. Platter (eds.), *Democratisation in Africa: Progress and Retreat* (Baltimore: John Hopkins University Press, 2010); C. M. Fombad, 'The Swaziland Constitution of 2005: Can Absolutism Be Reconciled with Modern Constitutionalism?', *South African Journal on Human Rights*, 93, 1 (2007), 93–115; M. Sinjenga, 'Constitutionalism in Africa: Emerging Trends: The Evolving African Constitutionalism', *The Review-International Commission of Jurist*, 60 (1998), 23–28; and T. Lumumba-Kasongo, *Liberal Democracy and Its Critics in Africa: Political Dysfunction and the Struggle of Social Progress* (London: Radical International Publishing, Zed Books, 2005).

bound by any constitution. The constitution, in essence, vests all powers in the monarch and there is no clear separation of powers.[4] The monarchy is the incarnation of the state and this is best captured in the words of the French King Louis XIV (1638–1715), when he stated: 'l'état c'est moi' (I am the state).[5] What the British bequeathed to independence Swaziland was a constitutional monarchy in the liberal democratic tradition captured in the Westminster parliamentary system of government.

The 1968 Westminster constitution for Swaziland was a combination of modern and traditional governance features. The Western components of the constitution were reflected in the political institutions, and in Roman, Dutch, and common law legal institutions, while provisions were made for the traditional institutions of governance that were extra-parliamentary. The 1968 Westminster constitutional model bestowed on Swaziland encapsulated the main tenets of liberal democracy, including a written constitution, a multiparty system, a bill of rights, the separation of powers, and the independence of the judiciary. The Independence Constitution provided for a constitutional monarchy[6] tailored along Swazi custom and tradition, on the one hand, and the basic tenets of the Westminster constitutional model, on the other. Baloro noted that the balance of power between the various arms of government was defined in the constitution, although it very much tilted in favour of the monarchy and traditionalism.[7] This was reflected in the 'entrenchment of monarchal interests', which was noticeable in several aspects of the constitution. Chapter IV of the Constitution recognized the paramount nature of the Swazi monarchy, with the acknowledgement of King Sobhuza II as the king of Swaziland and Head of State. The paramount position of the queen mother (*Ndlovukati*) was equally recognized, as both she and the king were to enjoy immunity from taxation and legal proceedings.[8]

According to Swazi tradition, the king reigns along with his mother (or a ritual substitute). The king is viewed as the functional and administrative

---

[4] Bogdanor, *The Monarchy and the Constitution*, 1.

[5] Paul W. Fox, 'Louis XIV and the Theories of Absolutism and Divine Right', *Canadian Journal of Economics and Political Science/Revue canadienne de economiques et science politique*, 26, 1 (1960), 128–142.

[6] SNA, The 1968 Independence Constitution.

[7] Baloro, 'The Development of Swaziland's Constitution', 19–34.

[8] Ibid.

240   H. P. DLAMINI

Head of State, while the queen mother is the spiritual and national Head of State, with real power counterbalancing that of the king. In a bid to protect Swazi traditional political values, section 62(2) of the Constitution disallowed Parliament from legislating on any of the following: the office of the *Ngwenyama*; the office of the *Ndlovukati* (the queen mother); the authorization of a person to perform the functions of regent; the appointment, revocation of appointment, and suspension of chiefs; the composition of the SNC (defined as consisting of all adult male Swazis, exercising its function either in *libandla* or *liqoqo*); the annual *Ncwala* (kingship) ceremony; and the *libutfo* (regimental) system. These matters would continue to be regulated by Swazi law and custom, unless the SNC consented in writing to allow action by Parliament. These provisions were intended not only to preserve Swazi customary law and practices, but also to insulate the key issues of succession to the monarchy from interference by parliamentarians,[9] who were products of the elective principle. The positions of the king and the queen mother were, therefore, in the hands of traditional king-makers, who were allowed to exercise unfettered powers in determining royal succession without parliamentary control or interference.[10] These provisions represented 'significant departures from [the] Westminster model' because the 'supremacy of Parliament was limited by a stipulation that its legislative authority'could not extend to the traditional sphere of succession and governance.[11]

On the issue of control of the land and minerals, which was hotly debated before independence, Swazi culture and tradition were triumphant in entrusting those resources to the *Ngwenyama*, although he still had to rely on the advice of a technical committee. Under section 94 of the 1968 Constitution, all Swazi nation land was entrusted to the *Ngwenyama* on behalf of the Swazi nation. The *Ngwenyama*–in-*Libandla* had the power to exercise all rights of ownership regarding disposition, grants, or leases

---

[9] Succession to the British monarchy is regulated by Parliament. The next heir to the British throne is Prince Charles, Prince of Wales. It is therefore a public secret. This is not the case with the Swazi monarchical system, where the next heir is a guarded secret and is known only by a select few insiders.

[10] This is unlike the case in the United Kingdom where succession to the throne is regulated not only through descent, but also by Parliamentary statute (see A. Olechnowicz, 'The Monarchy', In D. Brown, G. Pentland, and R. Crowcroft [eds.], *The Oxford Handbook of Modern British Political History, 1800–2000* [Oxford: Oxford University Press, 2018], 205).

[11] J. H. Proctor, 'Traditionalism and Parliamentary Government in Swaziland', *African Affairs*, 72, 288 (1973), 274.

over all such lands. All rights to minerals and mineral oils were vested in the *Ngwenyama* in trust for the Swazi nation, subject to any subsisting interests or rights that were in force before 6 September 1968. The king was vested with the power to make grants, leases, and other dispositions with regard to minerals and mineral oils, provided that he consulted with the Mineral Committee before exercising any such rights.

The Mineral Committee was not an independent body but, rather, was appointed by the king-in-*Libandla*, which consisted of all adult Swazi citizens, under the terms of section 95(3) of the Constitution. The Chairman of the Mineral Committee was to be appointed at the discretion of the king, who was the only person in whom the power was vested to summon it. The British colonial government and Swazi Opposition parties had strenuously opposed such a constitutional provision, which invested such powers in the king at the expense of the Cabinet. The Swazi monarchists wanted the king's powers to be supreme, and not to be watered down by the dynamics of parliamentary democracy. The *Ngwenyama* was, no doubt, vested with substantial executive, legislative, and judicial powers, but the spirit of the 1968 Independence Constitution that was inherited from the British established a constitutional monarch who could act subject to Parliament and the advice of the Cabinet. That is why limitations on the King's powers were deliberatedly inserted in the Constitution.

The Constitution provided a bicameral legislature, comprising a National Assembly (Lower House) of 24 elected members and six nominated members and the Attorney General, and the Senate (Upper House) consisting of 12 members, six of whom were elected, while the remaining six were appointed by the king. In exercising the powers to appoint senators, the king was obliged to consult with the relevant bodies, and to ensure that special interest groups were also represented.

The Constitution vested all legislative authority in the king and Parliament, as constituted through elections and selection by the king. In order for any bill from Parliament to become law, the assent of the king was needed, even though, in terms of sections 72(2) and 76(1), he could not withhold his assent to an appropriation or money bill. In the case of other bills passed by both Houses of Parliament, if the king refused to assent, he could refer the whole bill or a section thereof for further consideration by Parliament. If, within 90 days of such referral, the bill was passed by a joint sitting of the Senate and the House of Assembly, it was then presented to the king for his assent. But what was to happen if the king refused the second opportunity to assent to the bill? The Constitution was silent on this.

In reality, this scenario of Parliament and the king being at loggerheads was not forseeable by virtue of the fact that Swaziland's Lower and Upper Houses were filled with deputies from the royal *Imbokodvo* party. But the fact that Parliament was given such powers in the Constitution to legislate and, possibly, to disagree with the king points to this important aspect of parliamentary control of the executive.

The Constitution vested executive authority in the king subject to certain limiting provisions. He was empowered to appoint the prime minister and his deputy, and to appoint up to eight ministers after consultation with the prime minister. In appointing the prime minister, the king was obliged to appoint a person who was an elected member of the House of Assembly, and who appeared to him to be the best candidate to command the support of the majority of the members of the House. Under this system, an Opposition prime minister could be appointed by the king if his party commanded the majority in the House of Assembly.

The prime minister was a political force in his own right, and could not be fired by the king unless the House of Assembly passed a vote of no confidence in the government of Swaziland. The other means by which to remove a prime minister from his post was following the holding of general elections in the country when the the resultant composition of the membership of the house no longer favoured the prime minister. In that case, the prime minister would not be able to command the majority of members in the House of Assembly and he would have to be removed. Furthermore, the office of the prime minister would be declared vacant in the following circumstances: where he ceased to be a member of Parliament, other than by reason of a dissolution of Parliament; where Parliament first met after dissolution and the prime minister was no longer a member thereof; or where he resigned from office. Similarly, a ministerial vacancy was said to occur: where the king, acting in accordance with the advice of the prime minister, so directed; where the prime minister resigned from office three days after the passage of a vote of no confidence in his government; or where another person had been appointed to the position of prime minister. The function of the Cabinet, comprising the prime minister and other ministers, was to advise the king in the governance of the country. The Cabinet was to be collectively responsible to Parliament for any advice given to the king and for any act performed by any minister in the execution of his duties. To underscore the collective nature of Cabinet responsibility further, the king could, by a written designation, assign responsibility to the prime minister

6 THE 1968 WESTMINSTER CONSTITUTION, THE 1972 GENERAL ...   243

or any minister, after consultation with the prime minister.[12] What clearly emerged from the provisions of the 1968 Independence Constitution, as Baloro points out, was the intention 'to establish a constitutional monarchy where the King would exercise executive powers which were, nevertheless, limited by...the Constitution, the...cabinet and also...Parliament'.[13] The constitutional limitation of the king's powers is precisely what did not go down well with the Swazi traditionalists, who interpreted it as undermining the *Ngwenyama*.

The 1968 Constitution as the basic and supreme law of the land was emphasized in section 2, where it was clearly stated that governance was subject to the Constitution. Section 28 of the Constitution stated that the king could 'do all things that belong to his office in accordance with the provisions of this constitution and of all other laws for the time being in force'. Thus, in the exercise of his executive functions, the king had to be mindful of the law, including Swazi law and custom, provided that such customary practices did not contravene the provisions of the Constitution, the supreme law of the land. The supremacy of the Constitution was underscored, implying that Swaziland was theoretically a state of law. In essence, the Independence Constitution established a democratic form of government, and provided for the rule of law, separation of powers, and an independent judiciary. In chapter II, the 1968 Constitution provided for a justiciable Bill of Rights that was enforceable by an independent judiciary.

No matter how much power the royal *Imbokodvo* would have wanted to retain for the monarch, the 1968 Westminster-tailored Constitution did clearly introduce checks and balances, and underscored the principle of constitutionality and not that of a hereditary monarch. The modern institutions of the Cabinet and Parliament were offshoots of the will of the people through elections, rather than through Swazi custom and tradition. It is for this reason that most of the provisions of the 1968 Constitution vested decision-making powers in the prime minister and his cabinet, instead of the hereditary *Ngwenyama*. This provision was constructed on the logic that:

> ...the Prime Minister, being an elected officer of government, was directly accountable, first to a largely elected House of Assembly which could vote

[12]SNA, The 1968 Independence Constitution.

[13]Baloro, 'The Development of Swaziland's Constitution', 23. For a similar viewpoint, see Wanda, 'The Shaping of the Modern Constitution of Swaziland', 178.

244   H. P. DLAMINI

him out of office by a resolution of no confidence and, secondly, that the Prime Minister was also ultimately responsible to the electorate who could likewise vote him out of Parliament.[14]

The in-built mechanisms in Swaziland's constitutional monarchy were never once put to the test, as the *Ngwenyama* appeared totally supreme, since the royal *Imbokodvo* party had total sway in both Houses of Assembly. This was facilitated by the fact that, in both the 1964 and 1967 elections held in colonial Swaziland, the *Imbokodvo* reigned supreme by winning either the overwhelming majority or all the seats. So, from the inception of multipartyism in Swaziland, it evolved as a de facto one-party state without experiencing the impact of an opposition party. The *Ngwenyama* did not need to worry, because there was no opposition in Parliament to challenge the government.

THE CONTRADICTIONS BETWEEN THE DEIFICATION OF THE *NGWENYAMA* AND CONSTITUTIONALISM

Contradictions were bound to arise between the Swazi traditional law and custom, which literally deified the *Ngwenyama*, and the unfolding of constitutionalism. Swazi traditional law and custom treated the *Ngwenyama* as an untouchable figure—a revered traditional warrior, and a political, military, and religious leader. The *Ngwenyama* was perceived as a near-deity in the eyes of Swazi people.

Under Swazi traditional customary practices, the name of the *Ngwenyama* was periodically drummed up during public occasions by royal praise singers as the descendant of great conquerors, a wise man, a loving and fatherly figure of the Swazi nation. These royal praise singers (*griots*) are not simply the repository of the past. They provide the masses with their moral roots, and are an aural library of Swaziland's contemporary events, and its immensely complex and rich cultural forms of expression. Royal praise singers are often present during public ceremonies and they remind the *Ngwenyama* not only of his ancestry, but also of his achievements.[15] Praise singers have a great impact on society, and are believed to

[14]Wanda, 'The Shaping of the Modern Constitution of Swaziland', 178.

[15]Praise singers/griots are not only found in Swaziland; they are representative of Africa. They make rich use of genealogy and history in performances on post-independence leaders including Senghor and Mandela (see P. Tang, *Masters of the Sabar: Wolof griot percussionists*

6 THE 1968 WESTMINSTER CONSTITUTION, THE 1972 GENERAL ...   245

have extraordinary abilities; their skills are passed down from one generation to another. One of the *Ngwenyama*'s popular praise songs was even taught in primary schools. The lyrics are presented below in *siSwati*, with an accompanying English translation.

TibongoTaSobhuza II	*Sobhuza II 's praises*
Dladla sembumbe, Simazima	Lion's claws that are very strong
Unyathele lwandle	You stepped on the sea
Lwandle lwakubalekela	The sea gave way
Lwandle lwakakhela izinkimbinkimbi	The sea rippled before you
Lwandle lwakakhela izikhawukhawu	The sea rippled before you
Sobhuza bebathe	Sobhuza they had said you
Kayikumchawula	Will never shake hands
USokhingi Jojie eNgilandi	With King George of England
Waze Wamchawula Ngembane wezulu	You eventually shook hands with him by lightning
Wazewavuma	He let you shake his hands
Lizulu lawufaka umbane	There were flashes of lightning
Wabambili	The lightning struck twice
Egodlweni KaNkhosazane eNgilandi	At the Palace in England
Bazebakudvumisa bathi	They applaud you and said
'Lobudvodza lobungaka'	You are a man/You are courageous!!
Wabutsatsaphi	Where did you get such courage?
Nkhweletjeni KaNgwane, KaMahlokohla?'	
Watsi: 'Wabutsatsa enkhabeni	You answered and said that
Lapha KuboNdvungunye	You got it from Ndvungunye
Lapha KuboSomhlolo	You got it from Somhlolo[a]

Source T. T. Ginindza, *Tibongo Temakhosi* (Cape Town: Longman Publishers, 1979)
[a]The poet alludes to King Sobhuza's genealogy (Ndvungunye and Somhlolo are the names of Sobhuza's forefathers)

Another engaging popular praise song of Sobhuza II, referred to as Sobhuza's *tibongo*, was sung by Mhlabeleli Dlamini, a member of the royal house, and taught in Swazi secondary schools. The song is pregnant with meaning and covers Sobhuza's dispatch of Swazi regiments to World War

of Senegal [Philadelphia: Temple University Press, 2007]; T. A. Hale, *Griots and Griottes: Masters of Words and Music [African Expressive Cultures]* [Bloomington: Indiana University Press, 2007]; and R. H. Kaschula and D. Samba, 'Political Processes and the Role of the Imbongi and Griot in Africa', *South African Journal of African languages*, 20, 1 [2000], 13–28).

246   H. P. DLAMINI

II to fight for the British, his entry into modern politics and, above all, the successive victories of the royal Imbokodvo in general elections.[16] These praise songs portrayed the *Ngwenyama* as a winner and conqueror, and were popular among the common folk[17]; they had the effect of making the *Ngwenyama* feel really good and great. These praise songs also caused him to disdain any type of challenge to his rule.

The Swazis were therefore used to the rituals of pouring encomiums on the king and deified him whenever the opportunity arose. The modern political platform did not provide exclusive space for praising the king round the clock, because opposition parties and the media had to play the critical role of watchdog of government action. The traditionalists were irked by this role and interpreted it as disrespect for royalty. During the May 1972 elections, the opposition literally vilified the monarch in its campaigns, to the utter embarassment of the commonality.[18] The ordinary Swazi people typically respected the king and the critique unleashed on the monarch during the 1972 election campaign was reminiscent of the behaviour between the *Imbokodvo* and the Progressive political parties during the 1964 election campaign—an embarrasing political culture that many Swazis had difficulty entertaining. The mindset of the traditionalists, that the monarch was to be worshipped and not criticized in a modern political system, did not augur well for the survival of constitutionalism in independent Swaziland.[19] Multipartyism was barely and painfully tolerated pending an opportune moment to do away with it.

---

[16] P. A. Dlamini, 'The Teaching of Oral Literature in Swazi Secondary Schools: A Critique' (MA diss., University of Cape Town, 2000, 58).

[17] Vail, Leroy and L. White, *Power and the Praise Poem: Southern African Voices in History* (London: James Currey Publishers, 1991).

[18] 'Dr Zwane Fined', *Times of Swaziland*, May 5, 1972; 'Dr Zwane in Court', *Times of Swaziland*, April 28, 1972.

[19] The traditionalism of the Swazi monarchy has made a number of writers to question whether it is feasible for a typical traditional monarchy to imbibe constitutionalism (see, for instance, Fombad, 'The Swaziland Constitution of 2005: Can Absolutism Be Reconciled with Modern Constitutionalism?'; C. M. Fombad, 'Challenges to Constitutionalism and Constitutional Rights in Africa and the Enabling Role of Political Parties: Lessons and Perspectives from Southern Africa', *The American Journal of Comparative Law* (2007), 1–45; and J. B. Mzizi 'The Dominance of the Swazi Monarchy and the Moral Dynamics of Democratisation of the Swazi state', *Journal of African Elections*, 3, 1 (2004), 94–119.

THE ROAD TO THE CRISIS OF CONSTITUTIONALISM IN SWAZILAND

The African Political Environment and Its Impact on Royal Political Thought

The road to the end of Swaziland's constitutional monarchy should not be seen as an exclusively internal development within Swaziland but, rather, as a common trend that was dictated and nurtured by events outside Swaziland. Developments in the African political environment—where, everywhere, multipartyism was being discredited in favour of a one-party state—were crucial, and served as an incentive to Swaziland to follow suit. The liberal democratic independence constitutions of independent Africa were mostly imitations of the constitutions of the former imperial masters . W. H. O. Okoh-Ogendo observes that the English-speaking African countries inherited the Westminster constitutional system with its liberal democratic flair, but this legacy did not have a 'happy history'. This was because 'almost without exception the independence documents…either ended up in military dustbins or [underwent] changes so profound and rapid as to alter their content and significance beyond recognition'.[20] The end product of these mutations was single-party or no-party authoritarian rule.

Kwame Nkrumah's Ghana set the tone for the death of the colonially inherited multiparty system; this pattern was followed by other African countries. Shortly after Ghana's independence, Nkrumah indicated that Africans should evolve forms of government that were different from the traditional Western pattern, but no less democratic in their protection of the individual and his inalienable rights. He posited that multipartyism was alien and divisive, and not conducive for the development of newly independent African states. In 1964, Ghana officially became a single-party state, and an act of Parliament ensured that there would only be one candidate for presidential elections.[21] Most African countries subscribed to

---

[20] H. W. O. Okoth-Ogendo, 'The Politics of Constitutional Change in Kenya Since Independence, 1963–69', *African Affairs*, 71, 282 (1972), 9–34.

[21] Commonwealth African states in the 1960s which established de jure one-party states include Ghana (1964–1966), Tanzania (1965), Malawi (1966). In the early 1970s, Lesotho, Zambia (1972), Sierra Leone (1978) followed suit. The first four states rejected the incorporation of a bill of rights as a substantive part of their single-party constitutions (see P. T. Omari and N. A. Ollennu, *Kwame Nkrumah: The Anatomy of an African Dictatorship*

248   H. P. DLAMINI

Nkrumah's logic following independence. This was so because the transplant of the Western multiparty democratic arrangement in Africa during the final stages of colonial rule had failed to take firm root in Africa.[22] In different ways, most African countries opted for the replacement of multipartyism with one-party states or military regimes. In the space of a few years after independence, authoritarian forms of government came to prevail on virtually the entire continent, perhaps with the exception of Botswana, the Gambia, and Mauritius.[23]

The African national leaders who subscribed to one-party rule premised their choice on the imperatives of national integration, because of the ethnic and social cleavages that characterized the political and social landscapes of their various societies. They argued that the constraints of social and economic development meant that their young and fragile states could ill afford the divisive trends inherent in opposition politics. Other proponents of the single-party state made a strong cultural argument that traditional African society was classless, and was always akin to consensus democracy and the one-party state, rather than multiparty culture.[24] Consequently, African statesmen came to the conclusion that the ideal political culture for Africa was a single-party or a no-party state. It was believed that it was only within this form of political organization that all the various preferences in their societies would be compelled to compete. This would guarantee national integration, avoid the fissiparous tendencies inherent in opposition politics, and harness the energies of their people towards nation-building.

[London: Africana Publishing Corporation, 1970]; M. L. Kilson, 'Authoritarian and Single-Party Tendencies in African Politics', *World Politics*, 15, 2 [1963], 262–294; R. H. Jackson and C. G. Rosberg, *Personal Rule in Black Africa: Prince, Autocrat, Prophet, Tyrant* [Berkeley: University of California Press, 1982]; and K. Nkrumah, R. Arrigoni, and G. Napolitano, *Africa Must Unite* [London: Heinemann, 1963]).

[22] G. M. Carbone, 'Political Parties and Party Systems in Africa: Themes and Research Perspectives', *World Political Science Review*, 13, 3 (2007), 1; S. Mozaffar and A. Schedler, 'A Comparative Study of Electoral Governance: Introduction', *Party Politics*, 11, 4 (2005), 395.

[23] H. W. O. Okoth-Ogendo, 'The Politics of Constitutional Change in Kenya Since Independence, 1963–69', *African Affairs*, 71, 282 (1972), 9–34; R. Schachter, 'Single-Party Systems in West Africa', *American Political Science Review*, 55, 2 (1961), 294–307; and N. Van de Walle, 'Presidentialism and Clientelism in Africa's Emerging Party Systems', *The Journal of Modern African Studies*, 41, 2 (2003), 297–321.

[24] A. Mohiddin, 'Ujamaa: A Commentary on President Nyerere's Vision of Tanzanian Society', *African Affairs*, 67, 267 (1968), 130–143.

6 THE 1968 WESTMINSTER CONSTITUTION, THE 1972 GENERAL ... 249

The trend of abandoning the inherited Westminster constitution and adopting the single party-state model resonated positively in the mind of the conservative Swazi monarch, who had never hidden his disdain for Western liberal democracy.[25]

Developments in the kingdom of Lesotho in Southern Africa[26] further reinforced the resolve of the Swazi monachy to discard its opposition, and review its multiparty culture. The ruling Basotho National Party (BNP) of Chief Leabua Jonathan that had won the 1965 general elections lost the first post-independence general election in 1970 to the Basotho Congress Party (BCP). Chief Jonathan refused to cede power, and declared himself *Tona Kholo* (*Sesotho* for prime minister). He suspended the British-tailored Westminster constitution and instituted a one-party state. Chief Jonathan justified this act on the grounds that the Western concept of democracy was not suitable for Africa.[27] The cultural argument on the lips of African statemen for discarding the Westminster constitution came to form part of King Sobhuza's arsenal for also disposing of the Westminster constitution. Swaziland also needed to revisit its colonially inherited constitution and its prevailing multiparty democracy, which had been described by the ruling African political class as foreign and ill-fitting in the African environment.

The 'fault' with Swaziland's Independence Constitution was not that it did not treat the *Ngwenyama* as an important political figure; he was treated as a constitutional monarch with the constraints of checks and balances. Following the general trend in post-colonial Africa of African heads of state finding fault with colonially inherited constitutions on the grounds

---

[25] King Sobhuza II had clearly distanced himself from liberal democratic practices in the 1960s but the British made it part of the Independence Constitution.

[26] The three British High Commission territories comprising Basutoland (Lesotho), Bechuanaland (Botswana) and Swaziland started a joint University in 1964 known as the University of Basutoland, Bechuanaland and Swaziland (UBBS) owing to South Africa's apartheid policy. Lesotho withdrew from UBLS in 1981 to form the National University of Lesotho (NUL). Swaziland and Botswana were on their own and decided to from form the University of Botswana and Swaziland (UBS). The UBLS later dissolved, leading to the birth of an autonomous University of Swaziland (UNISWA) in 1982. Developments in Lesotho were, therefore, closely followed in Swaziland owing to their common history and institutions of learning they shared.

[27] K. Matlosa, 'Democracy and Conflict in Post-apartheid Southern Africa: Dilemmas of Social Change in Small States', *International Affairs*, 74, 2 (1998), 330; V. Shale, 'Political Party Funding and Regulation in Lesotho and Mozambique', In J. Mendolow and E. Phelippeau (eds.), *Handbook of Political Party Funding* (Cheltenham: Edward Elgar Publishing, 2018).

250   H. P. DLAMINI

of being alien instruments that were not in line with African culture and tradition, Sobhuza wasted no time in attacking the 1968 Constitution as a prelude to its ultimate abrogation. He hated the liberal component of the Constitution that provided for multipartyism. He argued that multipartyism was not a reflection of democracy but, rather, a potential source of dissension and discontent described as *umbango* (fighting or conflict). During the speech marking Independence Day in 1968, King Sobhuza II suggested that multiparty democracy 'sets one group against the other only in the interest of gaining a brief day of power for themselves'.[28] King Sobhuza II interpreted the 1968 constitutional provisions that required him to act on the advice of the Cabinet as a restriction on his right to rule as *Ngwenyama*. In 1969, in an address to Swazi chiefs in Lobamba, the royal headquarters in Swaziland, he criticized the Constitution as being too rigid.[29] He did not like the liberal component of the Constitution that provided for multiparty elections. He pointed out that it was the Swazi nation that had the right to change the Constitution, not the government in Mbabane. When King Sobhuza dissolved Parliament on 15 March 1972, he invited parliamentarians to the Lobamba Royal *kraal* for a meeting on 26 March 1972, so that they could give an account of their stewardship for the last five years. The prime minister made a report on behalf of the members of Parliament in which he complained about the difficulties they faced in running the country because of the 1968 constitution. Sobhuza seized the opportunity to voice a public condemnation of the Constitution, which he felt had not succeeded in reconciling the Swazi and British ways of governance. Sobhuza stated that there was a need to review the Constitution so as to make it malleable and relevant to the needs of Swazis.[30]

In another address to the Swazi nation at Lobamba, on 19 March 1973, King Sobhuza put the following questions to Swazis: '(a) Are we really independent like the British, French, or Germans? (b) Do we have a Parliament that is supreme, like that of the British, French, and other independent nations? (c) Or are we nominally independent?'[31] The concern of the *Ngwenyama* was the fact that the Independence Constitution

---

[28] H. Kuper, *Sobhuza II, Ngwenyama and King of Swaziland: The Story of an Hereditary Ruler and His Country* (New York: Africana Publishing, 1978), 290.

[29] Kuper, *Sobhuza II: Ngwenyama and King of Swaziland*, 318–335.

[30] Ibid.

[31] Ibid.

6 THE 1968 WESTMINSTER CONSTITUTION, THE 1972 GENERAL ... 251

subordinated him to its provisions, and he did not like that. His counterparts elsewhere in Africa had changed their respective constitutions to enable them to concentrate powers in their hands and to function effectively without dissension.

To tamper with Swaziland's Independence Constitution would, thus, not be an unprecedented event in post-colonial Africa. Nonetheless, King Sobhuza needed a pretext to discard Swaziland's inherited Independence Constitution and its multiparty culture. There was nothing to worry the Swazi monarch, because all the members of both the House of Assembly and Senate elected on the eve of independence belonged to the royal *Imbokodvo* party and, de facto, this made Swaziland a one-party state with no opposition. King Sobhuza was, therefore, legally in a position to effect any constitutional changes he wanted, if he could only be patient with due process and follow the law to the letter. He planned to carry out constitutional changes after the May 1972 elelctions, which his party was sure to win overwhelmingly, as in the past.

The May 1972 General Elections and the Emergence of the Opposition NNLC

The May 1972 elections resuscitated an Opposition that had so far only had a legal existence but no parliamentary presence. The surfacing of an Opposition displeased the monarch: it posed a problem for him, since he could now be openly challenged. In a continent where one-party rule and authoritarian heads of state were in vogue, the Swazi Opposition party not only emerged in an unfavourable environment following the May 1972 elections, but was also unwelcome to the Swazi monarch.

The pre-independence elections that had taken place in Swaziland on a multiparty basis in May 1967 witnessed the royal *Imbokodvo* party sweeping all the seats. King Sobhuza expected a repeat of a similar feat. In anticipation of the general elections billed for 16–17 May 1972, King Sobhuza dissolved Parliament and the Senate on 15 March 1972.[32] The campaign manifestoes of the two main political parties promised political change in the event of victory. The *Imbokodvo* manifesto promised:

    i. A state with the *Ngwenyama* as its head;
    ii. Respect for Swazi institutions;

---

[32] 'May Elections', *Times of Swaziland*, March 17, 1972.

252   H. P. DLAMINI

iii. A free democracy based on the best Swazi tradition and modern constitutional law;

iv. A sound and stable government with an impartial and independent judiciary; and

v. The entrenchment of the freedom of the institutions of Kingship, and the Swaziland National Council and the Chiefs.[33]

But the government appeared to be paying mere lip service to its election slogans of 'free democracy' while emphasizing the respect and entrenchment of Swazi traditional institutions of governance. During the election campaigns, the Prime Minister, Prince Makhosini Dlamini, could not conceal his animosity towards the 1968 Constitution. Prince Makhosini Dlamini stated at Lobamba that the constitution inherited from the British was a problem for the Swazi government, and called for an amendment in favour of the transfer of more powers to the monarch. He made it clear that the Swazi nation did not like the constitution.[34] This proposed constitutional amendment towards concentration of more powers in the hands of the king in the campaign speech was contrary to the spirit of constitutionalism that underscores checks and balances between the various arms of government. This was also evidence of the fact that the Swazi government had made up its mind to change the constitution after the elections, because it was already complaining about it.

Dr Zwane's NNLC campaign slogan, in contrast, called for the following pro-liberal democratic principles:

i. The rule of law to be the watchdog of the Ngwane State [that is, the Kingdom of Swaziland] whose motto would be 'Freedom and justice';

ii. A Constitutional monarchy;

iii. An independent judiciary completely free from the country's Executive;

iv. Automatic citizenship for everyone born in the country;

v. Free labour unionism; and

vi. Freedom of speech, association, assembly and press.[35]

---

[33] 'Pledge', *Times of Swaziland*, April 14, 1972.

[34] Ibid.

[35] 'Dr A.P. Zwane's Historic Document', *Times of Swaziland*, May 12, 1972.

6 THE 1968 WESTMINSTER CONSTITUTION, THE 1972 GENERAL ...   253

By emphasizing the issue of equality before the law and the idea of a constitutional monarchy for Swaziland, the traditionalists were not happy with Zwane's NNLC, and were quick to represent the party as standing against Swazi culture and tradition, and the king, and working for his destitution. The traditionalists persistently spread the rumour that Zwane was out to destitute the king: this did not go down well with the Swazi people, and they turned their backs against the modernist politicians. In essence, the NNLC campaigned for a democratic Swaziland and a constitutional monarchy that operated within the parameters of the law. It advocated for the separation of powers in the true spirit of modern constitutionalism.

The monarchists campaigned strenuously against the modernist stance of the Opposition parties, and warned that voting for them was dangerous because of their alien ideas and their intention to compromise the Swazi traditional monarchy. King Sobhuza II joined the anti-Opposition party campaign by assuring Swazis that he would not be cowed into silence because of the fear of dethronement.[36] This type of statement from the monarch was clearly intended to demonize and alienate the Opposition from the common folk.

Apart from the negative misrepresentation campaign against the Opposition, the NNLC was rocked by internal conflict over plans to centralize leadership of the party and to make Dr Ambrose Zwane president for life shortly before the May 1972 elections, leading to a schism within the party. A splinter faction of the NNLC was led by Kingsley T. Samketti, who also decided to stand in the May elections, meaning that there were actually two NNLC candidates. The elections took place in Swaziland on 16–17 May 1972. The royal *Imbokodvo* party won its third successive victory with 78% of the votes, based on a voter turnout of 74.0% and claimed 21 of the 24 seats. Dr Zwane's NNLC managed to take the remaining three seats from the Mphumalanga constituency, which comprised a high number of farm workers, small farmers, and middle-class voters.[37] Table 6.1 captures the results of the May 1972 elections.

This was the first time in Swaziland's modern political history that the Opposition had qualified for the House of Assembly. But this occurred in an era in African history when multipartyism was being discredited almost everywhere on the continent as being 'alien' and 'unAfrican', and was being

---

[36]'Imbokodvo Candidate', *Times of Swaziland*, March 31, 1972.

[37]'Boycott at Parliament', *Times of Swaziland*, October 20, 1972.

254   H. P. DLAMINI

Table 6.1   The results of the May 1972 elections

Party	Votes	%	Seats +/	Seats /−
Imbokodvo National Movement	164,493	78.0	+21	−3
Ngwane National Liberatory Congress (Zwane)	38,554	18.2	3	+3
Ngwane National Liberatory Congress (Samketti)	6393	3.0	0	0
Swaziland United Front	797	0.4	0	0
Swaziland Progressive Party	582	0.3	0	0
TOTAL	210,819	100		
Valid votes	70,273	98.5		
Invalid/blank votes	1034	1.5		
Total	71,307	100		
Registered voters/turnout		74.0		

Source Nohlen et al., *Elections in Africa: A Data Handbook.* Oxford University Press, 1999, p. 868

assailed by a strong upsurge of authoritarianism. The reigning spirit in Swaziland was intolerance towards liberal democracy.

The capture of some parliamentary seats by the Swazi Opposition challenged the de facto one-party *Imbokodvo* regime that had reigned supreme after the 1964 and 1967 elections in Swaziland.[38] Neocosmos asserts that the NNCL was able to bring together the working class and a section of the well-to-do peasants, but this was not enough to pose any threat to the traditional aristocracy.[39] Motloso states that the Opposition leader, Dr Ambrose Zwane, won only one constituency, Mphumalanga, in the eastern part of the country, and his party's representation was not sufficiently significant to pose any threat to the royal *Imbokodvo* party. However, the important point is that the prospects of the Opposition's presence in the Assembly represented an alternative dissenting voice to that of the monarch.[40]

The election results confirmed the fears of the traditionalists, that the Independence Constitution was not a good document for Swaziland because it made allowance for the challenge to the royal prerogative.

[38] Ibid.

[39] M. Neocosmos, 'The Politics of National Elections in Botswana, Lesotho and Swaziland: Towards a Comparative Analysis', In M. Cowen and L. Laakso (eds.), *Multiparty Elections in Africa* (Oxford: James Currey, 2002).

[40] Motloso, 'Democracy and Conflict in Post-apartheid Southern Africa', *International Affairs*, 74, 2 (1998), 319–337; also see R. Levin, 'Swaziland's Tinkhundla and the Myth of Swazi Traditional', *Journal of Contemporary African Studies*, 10, 2 (1991), 1–23.

6 THE 1968 WESTMINSTER CONSTITUTION, THE 1972 GENERAL ... 255

Swazi constitutional experts state that the winning of three seats in Parliament by the Opposition amounted to what the Swazi royalists called a 'constitutional crisis' in Swaziland, and the unfolding of events from these May elections culminated in the royal repeal of the Independence Constitution.[41] The use of the word 'crisis' should not be taken to mean there was an internal or external threat to the institutions of the kingdom of Swaziland. The government manufactured the 'constitutional crisis' in order to do away with the Independence Constitution and its liberal democratic aspects that the government did not like. The Bhekindlela Thomas Ngwenya affair was a mere smokescreen for the government to discard the 1968 Independence Constitution and multipartyism.

THE BHEKINDLELA THOMAS NGWENYA AFFAIR, THE SWAZI PARLIAMENT, AND THE HIGH COURT

The Bhekindlela Thomas Ngwenya affair was a political controversy caused by the refusal of the *Imbokodvo* dominated House of Assembly to endorse the candidature of one Opposition candidate who won the May 1972 polls on the grounds that he was not a Swazi citizen. The Ngwenya affair pitted the government against the Opposition, and resulted in 'three of the most important judicial pronouncements in the short history of [Swaziland's 1968] constitution'.[42] It was a test case for Swaziland of the principle of the separation of powers in a nascent democracy, and of the role of the judiciary 'as the custodian of the constitution, fundamental rights and freedoms' in Swaziland.[43]

The Swazi monarchy wanted to use the Opposition candidate, Bhekindlela Thomas Ngwenya, as a scapegoat in order to execute its agenda of establishing political monolithism—which is essentially a negation of multiparty democracy—in Swaziland. The *Imbokodvo* dominated Parliament therefore initiated a crisis in order to get rid of the Opposition

---

[41] See H. S. Zwane, 'Constitutional Discontinuity and Legitimacy: A Comparative Study with Special Reference to the 1973 Constitutional Crisis in Swaziland' (A Dissertation for a Master Degree in Law, University of Edinburg, 1988); B. Khumalo, 'The Politics of Constitution-Making and Constitutional Pluralism in Swaziland Since 1973', *UNISWA Research Journal*, 10 (1996), 1–19; and T. Maseko, 'The Drafting of the Constitution of Swaziland', 1–22.

[42] Maseko, 'The Drafting of the Constitution of Swaziland', 31.

[43] Ibid.

256   H. P. DLAMINI

entirely.[44] Before the elected members of Parliament could be sworn in after the May 1972 elections, as was the tradition, the government alleged that one of the members of the Opposition NNLC, Ngwenya, was not a Swazi citizen. Although Ngwenya had been allowed by Swazi electoral law to stand as a *bona fide* Swazi citizen in the May 1972 elections, the Swazi government claimed after his election victory that they had discovered that he was not really a Swazi citizen. The Deputy Prime Minister, as the minister responsible for immigration, described Ngwenya as 'a South African citizen' in the Government Gazette Extraordinary, and declared him a prohibited immigrant that had to be deported to his country of origin.[45] On 25 May 1972, the Deputy Prime Minister served Ngwenya with a deportation order. He was arrested and held in jail in Matsapha for a few days, before being deported and handed over to the South African Police at the Oshoek border post. So, when Parliament opened, Ngwenya's seat was empty. After deportation, Ngwenya decided to return to Swaziland and was immediately arrested, charged with being in Swaziland illegally, and found guilty by a magistrate. He was sentenced to 12 days imprisonment. In the meantime, Ngwenya applied to the Swaziland High Court to have the Deputy Prime Minister's decision that he was a prohibited immigrant quashed. The case was clearly a political one that needed to be handled with expertise. Ngwenya's lawyer, Musa Shongwe, solicited the services of a renowned South African advocate, David Soggot,[46] to appear for his client. Ngwenya's legal representation applied to the High Court to have the order set aside. They prepared a dossier of affidavits in which they maintained that their client was born at Hluti, in Swaziland.[47] They stated that the fact that Ngwenya was born in Swaziland was enough evidence that he was a true Swazi citizen. Ngwenya's legal representation therefore filed an application to the High Court of Swaziland to have the order declaring him a prohibited immigrant and a citizen of the Republic of South Africa set aside. He also requested that the Court should explicitly rule that Ngwenya

[44] Interview with anonymous political activist and scholar in Swaziland.

[45] It was issued in terms of Section 9(1) (g) of the Immigration Act 32 of 1964, published under Government Gazette 45 of 1972.

[46] Soggott was not new to the politics of Swaziland and had represented Dr, Zwane and the other NNLC leaders during the trials connected with the 1963 workers' and Mbabane residents' strikes (Kuper, *Sobhuza II: Ngwenyama and King of Swaziland*, 334).

[47] 'Declared Prohibited Immigrant', *Times of Swaziland*, June 2, 1972.

was a citizen of Swaziland. The case was brought before Sir Philip Pike, the Chief Justice, and Acting Justice Johnson for a hearing.[48]

During the hearing, a pro-government official, M. Ntshangase, brought evidence in the High Court of Swaziland against Ngwenya that he was a South African citizen from Kanzkloof, and that his father was South African.[49] Ntshangase told the Court that Ngwenya was born at Ntonga in South Africa, near Kanzkloof. He revealed that he was an acting chief of that area when the Ngwenya clan came to him with an inheritance dispute concerning the estate of J. Ngwenya, the applicant's South African father.

Delivering judgement, the Chief Justice, Sir Philip Pike, observed that, in view of the importance of the matter, affecting as it did the fundamental rights of a person who claimed to be a citizen and who had been resident in Swaziland for some years before his deportation, the case had to be heard by a full bench of two judges. Meanwhile, the Court expressed its displeasure with the way the government had arrived at the conclusion that Ngwenya was not a citizen of Swaziland. Barrister Soggot argued fervently for his client, Ngwenya, pointing out that he was allowed to run in the elections because he qualified in the first place as a Swazi citizen. Since he won the election and belonged to the Opposition, they had to look for a pretext to disqualify him. After hearing oral evidence in court on 29 August 1972, the full bench, comprising the Chief Justice, Sir Philip Pike, and Acting Justice Johnson, ruled that Ngwenya was a Swazi citizen by birth and set aside the deportation order.[50] This meant that Ngwenya could take his seat in Parliament. The judicial arm of government had made its pronouncement, and it was now left for the government to comply accordingly. The government was furious and declared Barrister Soggot *persona non grata* in Swaziland. The government appealed against the High Court's ruling on 31 August 1972. Parliament was convened for October 1972 and the drama that unfolded showed that government was not willing to comply with the decision of the High Court.

The *Imbokodvo* dominated House was not prepared to respect the High Court ruling that confirmed the citizenship of the Opposition member of the NNCL, Ngwenya. The royal *Imbokodvo* parliamentarians did so by

---

[48] Bhekindlela Thomas Ngwenya v The Deputy Prime Minister 1970–76 Swaziland Law Report (HC) 88.

[49] 'Deportation Appeal', *Times of Swaziland*, July 28, 1972.

[50] 'A Boycott at Parliament', *Times of Swaziland*, October 20, 1972.

boycotting the swearing in ceremony of Ngwenya in Parliament billed for October 1972. The Opposition NNCL members went into the House of Assembly and took their seats, Ngwenya took his seat in the House next to the two other NNLC members, Dr A. Zwane and M. Masilela, while waiting for the other members of Parliament to come in for the swearing-in ceremony. At about 2.30 pm, when the sitting of Parliament was due to begin, the NNLC were the only members present in the House of Assembly. Other *Imbokodvo* members of Parliament were in the Assembly buildings but they kept away from Parliament in a bid to boycott the sitting, thereby making it impossible for a quorum to meet since the *Imbokodvo* had the overwhelming majority in the House. At 3.00 pm, the Speaker, accompanied by the clerk, the interpreter, and the Attorney General, David Cohen, formerly entered the House and observed that there was no quorum, and the sitting had to be postponed to another day.[51]

A joint sitting of both Houses—the National Assembly and Senate—was scheduled to take place on 17 October 1972. However, the Speaker received a letter from the Prime Minister, Prince Makhosini Dlamini, stating that the date was not suitable for the meeting owing to the problem of a quorum.[52] It was clear that the government party had decided to stay away from a sitting of its own Legislative Assembly because of Ngwenya's presence in the House. On receipt of the letter from the Prime Minister, the Speaker of the National Assembly sent it to all Senators and members of the House of Assembly. Parliament was unable to swear in the Opposition member.

Parliamentary Amendment of 1964 Immigration Act on Citizenship and Its Conflict with the Principle of Non-retroactivity of the Law

The Swazi Parliament, with its overwhelming majority of royalists, decided to make a new law and, in a twist of legal drama in a nascent independent state grappling with the law, implement it retroactively with regards to the Ngwenya case. This parliamentary act was clearly in violation of the principle of of non-retroactivity of the law.

---

[51]'A Boycott at Parliament', *Times of Swaziland*, October 20, 1972.

[52]'A Boycott at Parliament', *Times of Swaziland*, October 20, 1972.

6 THE 1968 WESTMINSTER CONSTITUTION, THE 1972 GENERAL ... 259

The principle of non-retroactivity of the law[53] is based on the fact that, as a general rule, laws shall have only a prospective effect and must not be applied retroactively in such a way as to apply to pending disputes and cases. This is expressed in the familiar legal maxim *lex prospicit, non respicit,* which means the law looks forward and not backward.[54] The jurisdiction of a court depends on the law existing at the time an action is filed. A statute continues to be in force with regard to all rights that had accrued prior to its amendment. The essence of this principle implies that a law's effect cannot be elastic so as to include past affairs and cannot pass judgement on events that occurred prior to its enactment. Rather, a law applies only to events that occur after its enactment. Thus, the date of application of a law is a decisive factor in determining a law's enforceability. All laws become applicable after their publication in the Official Gazette of the Swazi government. Jurists argue that the principle of non-retroactivity underscores the tendency of retroactive legislation to be unjust and oppressive, due to the likelihood of it being used to target and punish individuals for violations of laws not enacted at the time of the offence; to unsettle vested rights; or to disturb the legal effect of prior transactions, which is unconstitutional.[55]

Parliament was confident it would have its way with the Ngwenya case because of its overwhelming majority. While the government appeal against the Court verdict on Ngwenya's citizenship was still pending, it rushed a bill through to amend the 1964 Immigration Act that had qualified Ngwenya's participation in the elections. The intention of the amendment was to apply the new law retroactively to classify Ngwenya as a foreigner and to have the opportunity to deport him. Parliament then set out to enact a parliamentary law under a Certificate of Urgency clause that would allow it to act speedily to solve the 'citizenship' crisis.

Under the Certificate of Urgency clause, the government could enact a law to address a crisis if there were no constitutional provision for it,

---

[53] See R. H. Fallon Jr., and D. J. Meltzer, 'New Law, Non-retroactivity, and Constitutional Remedies', *Harvard Law Review* (1991), 1731–1833; and S. J. Hammer, 'Retroactivity and Restraint: An Anglo-American Comparison', *Harvard Journal of Law and Public Policy*, 41, 1 (2018), 409.

[54] http://saklawph.com/retroactivity/, Rule on Retroactivity of Laws—SAKLAW (Accessed September 8, 2018); R. H. Fallon, Jr. and D. J. Meltzer, 'New Law, Non-retroactivity, and Constitutional Remedies', *Harvard Law Review* (1991), 1731–1833; and Hammer. 'Retroactivity and Restraint: An Anglo-American Comparison', 409.

[55] Ibid.

260   H. P. DLAMINI

provided the enacted law did not contradict the spirit of the Constitution. Consequently, the government tabled an urgent bill amending the Immigration Act (No. 32) of 1964, which had qualified Ngwenya as a Swazi citizen by virtue of his birth and by virtue of the fact that he had lived in Swaziland continuously for more than five years. Parliament was convened to execute the amendment plan.[56] The Deputy Prime Minister, A. Z. Khumalo, tabled a motion in the House of Assembly: that the government should urgently endorse the amendment of the existing 1964 Immigration Act under which Ngwenya had qualified as a Swazi citizen. The government argued that, in reality, Ngwenya was not a Swazi citizen and that his father was from South Africa. Deputy Prime Minister Khumalo pointed out that there were a number of persons living in Swaziland who claimed that they belonged to Swaziland when they were not Swazis. He argued that the claims had brought confusion in the country, and there was need to set up a Special Tribunal to look into such cases. He stated:

> The Bill before you for your consideration proposes to amend the [1964] Immigration Act by the introduction of a *new section providing for the establishment of a Special Tribunal to deal with any issue as to whether or not a person belongs to Swaziland in terms of that act.* There will be a right to appeal to the Prime Minister against any decision of this Tribunal which will consist of five persons. These will be responsible men whose integrity I do not doubt at all.[57] (emphasis added)

The Deputy Prime Minister further proposed that a Special Tribunal of five people, under his chairmanship, be set up to look into the matter, and that the matter should no longer be heard in the courts of the land. He stated that the Special Tribunal would act according to the terms of the constitution, and pointed out that there would be a right for individuals to appeal to the Prime Minister. He asked the members of the House to give unanimous support to the Bill. He buttressed his position by stating that the courts in Swaziland were not in a position to deal with citizenship matters, because they were already congested with other issues and were not familiar with Swazi traditional customs and law. He argued that, if the court were to handle the matter of citizenship, it would be subjected to harsh criticism by Swazis, since the judges were not Swazis. Therefore, such

---

[56]'Immigration Bill Gazetted', *Times of Swaziland*, November 10, 1972.

[57]SNA, House of Assembly Hansard, November 1972, 270.

6 THE 1968 WESTMINSTER CONSTITUTION, THE 1972 GENERAL ... 261

interference should be avoided by letting the envisaged Special Tribunal handle the situation with due consideration to Swazi custom and tradition.

The first person to second the Deputy Prime Minister from the floor was the Minister of State for Foreign Affairs. He concurred with the Deputy Prime Minister that the citizenship issue had created problems in Swaziland. The Minister of State for Foreign Affairs stated that:

> It is a known fact that, when difficulties arise in some countries, points are presented which are not in accordance with their Constitution. One thing I am grateful for is that here in Swaziland we have always taken immediate steps to see that we frame clauses in our Constitution to tide us over difficulties. For instance, Mr Speaker, we have here the Deputy Prime Minister bringing up an amendment to this bill because of the controversy that has arisen here in Swaziland. The citizen question has created a lot of misunderstanding here in Swaziland. Not only does it put the country in the state of chaos, but it also affects the relationship between Swaziland and other countries ...[58]

The Minister of State for Foreign Affairs therefore endorsed the amendment of the 1964 Immigration Act. He pointed out that he hoped that the Deputy Prime Minister would ensure that the Special Tribunal was composed of people whose integrity was beyond doubt.

As expected, Dr Zwane, as the leader of the Opposition, strongly opposed the Bill. He argued that, in essence, the Bill had nothing to do with immigration, but was a political stunt to fight the NNLC. He pointed out that 'only a child...would be fooled and be deceived by the Imbokodvo'.[59] Dr Zwane saw the Bill as something that was presented in the House with the intention of destroying the NNLC as the only Opposition in the House. He stated:

> I am shocked that in terms of this immigration (Amendment) Bill of 1972...all powers of deciding as to who comes into this country and who goes out are now reserved for the Prime Minister....This House here has no power to make laws that are not subject to the jurisdiction of the courts. That is according to the constitution that I have in my hand.[60]

---

[58] SNA, House of Assembly Hansard, November 1972, 271.

[59] Ibid.

[60] Ibid.

262   H. P. DLAMINI

Dr Zwane emphasized that all laws that were passed by Parliament should be for the good of Swaziland, and should be in harmony with the Constitution. Parliament should not substitute the courts under any circumstance, and should not establish tribunals to handle immigration matters. He underscored his argument by stating that:

> The House has been given all the powers to effect some changes if it feels like it, as long as those changes are for the good of the country. The Constitution itself does point out that this House has powers to effect some alternations in the Constitution if they feel like it....There is a portion of the Constitution here which says: 'The Constitution is a supreme law of Swaziland; and if any other law is inconsistent with this Constitution, that other law, to the extent of the inconsistency, be void'. I therefore, Mr Speaker, wish to point out that this [Immigration Amendment Law] is void. ...it is un-constitutional. My party is going to fight this law inside this Chamber....And when I say outside this Chamber I mean the powers of the courts. This House here has no power to hijack the powers of the courts and vest them in the Prime Minister. I know this, of course, happens in fascist countries.[61]

In response to Dr Zwane, the Deputy Prime Minister argued that:

> [Dr Zwane] didn't feel satisfied that the Prime Minister should have the last say as far as this matter is concerned. I personally feel the Rt. Hon. Prime Minister should have the last say [in immigration matters] because he was elected by the nation. Mr Speaker, I would understand, perhaps if the matter would end up with me as the Head of the Tribunal not to go ahead, or to appeal to the Prime Minister. But if it is said that we appeal to the Prime Minister, I don't see what is wrong in that, because he is the one who is the Head of the present Government.[62]

Dr Zwane stood out as the lone voice that resisted parliamentary unconstitutionality and encroachment on the powers of the judiciary, but this had little or no impact in the House, which was overwhelmingly composed of *Imbokodvo* royalists. As was expected, the Assistant Deputy Prime Minister seconded the Deputy Prime Minister. He stated that he supported the amendment of the Bill wholeheartedly, and congratulated the Deputy Prime Minister for tabling it. He believed that the Bill would solve the

[61] SNA, House of Assembly Hansard, November 1772, 274.
[62] Ibid., 277.

6 THE 1968 WESTMINSTER CONSTITUTION, THE 1972 GENERAL ... 263

problem of people who claimed to be Swazis when they were not. The Minister for Agriculture also supported the Deputy Prime Minister, and condemned Dr Zwane for not supporting the Bill.

The Minister for Agriculture stated that:

> If the Member of the opposition party rejects this bill on grounds that it has been presented to the House merely to hit against his followers, does he imply that members of the opposition Party are elected by foreigners? If, for instance, you go to China, Japan, or anywhere else, I doubt whether permission can be granted to a person who is not a citizen. I must mention the fact that it wouldn't be right if a person just walked into your house and occupied your bed without seeking permission.[63]

As anticipated, the *Imbokodvo* dominated House of Assembly expectedly endorsed the Amendment Bill by an overwhelming majority.

The Attorney General described the work of the Tribunal as follows:

> the Special Tribunal, being an adjudicating authority, must in the case where any civil right or obligation is involved, give the case fair hearing within a reasonable time. It also provides in such a Tribunal that it would have to be independent and impartial. It also provides that the determination of that right shall be held in public ... Provisions of the section to which I have referred must be carried out by the special Tribunal. Section 6 of the Commission of Enquiry Act, which must be of the Tribunal must take an oath, and carry out their functions in the correct manner. Section 7 means that the secretary, who shall be appointed to this Commission and shall keep a record of the proceedings of the Tribunal. Section 9 means that in the case of equality of votes, the Chairman shall have a casting [vote]...The reference to section 10 means that the Tribunal may make rules not consistent with that act, for its own guidance as the time and place for their sittings, and generally as the conduct their proceedings.[64]

In essence, the 1972 Immigration Amendment Act provided for the establishment of a Special Tribunal to consider, where there may be doubt, whether a person was a citizen of Swaziland. The government further explained that the intention of the Immigration Amendment Act, which

---

[63] SNA, House of Assembly Hansard, November 1972, 276.

[64] Ibid., 278.

264   H. P. DLAMINI

set up a Special Tribunal, was to limit the number of non-Swazis and non-resident attorneys practising in Swaziland's courts.[65] In reality, the Special Tribunal was basically largely concerned with Ngwenya's birth place and his claim to citizenship.

The Deputy Prime Minister moved the same motion in Senate on the amendment of the 1964 Immigration Act and the establishment of a Special Tribunal to handle immigration matters. He made the same argument in Senate that had been made in the House of Assembly: that the courts were not capable of handling matters of citizenship that had a great deal to do with Swazi customs and tradition. He stated that cases such as 'our marriage ceremonies, *lobola*, and *khonta'ing* and such matters inevitably arise in consideration of whether or not a person belongs to the Swazi nation'.[66] Khumalo stated that letting the Special Tribunal to handle such cases was a way of protecting the courts against criticism by the public, who were aware of the fact that foreigners were ignorant of Swazi culture and tradition. Such criticism could lead to disrespect of the courts by the nation. He emphasized that such a situation should be avoided by allowing such cases to be handled by the Special Tribunal according to Swazi custom and tradition.

Senator Carl Todd supported the Deputy Prime Minister by pointing out that some countries set up a Special Tribunal when dealing with a case of whether a person was a citizen of that particular country. He stated that the House should not quarrel with such an amendment. The Senate supported the Bill.

Following the debates that took place in the Assembly and Senate, the Bill became law on 14 November 1972.[67] The amended Bill was to be applied retroactively on the Opposition candidate, with the intention of disqualifying him from the House. This retroactive piece of legislation by the pro-monarchical *Imbokodvo* Parliament was clearly politically motivated

---

[65] Ibid. The issue was not about limiting non-Swazis in the judiciary because a significant and high profile number of Commonwealth legal luminaries continued to serve in the Swazi judiciary in beyond the 2000s. Michael Mathealira Ramodibedi from Lesotho, for instance, was Chief Justice in Swaziland from 2010 until 2015 when he was fired by King Mswati III for alleged misconduct.

[66] SNA, House of Senate Hansard, November 1972, 148. *Lobola* is bride wealth tradition among Swazis while *khonta'ing* represents a token of a cow given to a Chief to obtain a piece of land for occupation and cultivation.

[67] 'Five Man Tribunal', *Times of Swaziland*, November 17, 1972.

6 THE 1968 WESTMINSTER CONSTITUTION, THE 1972 GENERAL ... 265

and was a travesty of justice because, in principle and practice, enacted laws are never retroactive in any modern state.

Could the Swazi Parliament, with an Attorney General considered as honourable and learned in the law, have acted in error? David Cohen, the Attorney General, could not have possibly erred in appreciating such an obvious legal principle. The point is that this was the common trend in Africa, where governmentst manipulated the law to achieve their objectives in flagrant violation of the legislation. It was therefore not a Swazi exceptionality. Clearly, Parliament had come under the sway of the monarchy to do all it could, including the exclusion of Nywenya, to neutralize the Opposition and pave the way for the destruction of the Independence Constitution, which did not uphold the absolute supremacy of the monarch as King Sobhuza II wanted. King Sobhuza was not concerned about legality: what was high on his agenda was the weakening and destruction of the Opposition, which was a widespread practice in vogue in post-colonial Africa.[68]

The parliamentarians ensured that Amended Bill could not be challenged in court and it empowered the Prime Minister to render any court ruling ineffective. Parliament intended to subordinate and eclipse the Judiciary in the Ngwenya affair by giving the Prime Minister the powers to counteract any decision of the Court that did not favour the government. Parliament ensured that, under the Amended Immigration Act, appeals against the decision of the Tribunal lay exclusively with the Prime Minister, a member of the *Imbokodvo*, whose decision was final. This Act made the government both the complainant and the judge in the Ngwenya case. The Act was, therefore, clearly designed to eliminate Ngwenya from Parliament and enfeeble the Opposition, which had a marginal presence in Parliament.

At the same time, the Amendment Bill usurped the powers of the court by establishing a Tribunal with power of sole adjudication on matters that would ordinarily be within the jurisdiction of the High Court. The civil rights referred to in the Bill are important rights, which at the time of the promulgation of the Constitution, could only be adjudicated on by the High Court. Rights of citizenship are civil rights, and there was nothing to suggest that such rights were to be excluded from the operation of

---

[68] Interview with anonymous Swazi legal experts November 10, 2015.

section 10(10)(b) of the 1968 Constitution. Barrister Maphalala[69] was, therefore, of the opinion that the establishment of the Tribunal was *ultra vires* the Constitution, and that Parliament was incompetent to adjudicate on the issue of the citizenship of Ngwenya.[70] Parliamentary intervention in the Ngwenya affair in opposition to the stance of the court was a glaring distortion of the principles of modern governance, although it represented a means to achieve the political goal of the Swazi monarchy, which was the termination of multipartyism in Swaziland.

The Special Parliamentary Tribunal established under the Amended Immigration Act (1972) to determine the Swazi status of Ngwenya included five members. The members of the Tribunal are documented in Table 6.2.

The government issued a summons against Ngwenya on 16 November 1972, claiming an order setting aside the High Court decision of 29 August 1972 that recognized and upheld his Swazi citizenship on the grounds it was obtained by perjured evidence. He was therefore subjected to the Special Tribunal set up by the government. The Special Tribunal was given a free hand to proceed with its case against Ngwenya. It held its first meeting on 8 December 1972 at Lobamba.[71] The purpose of the meeting was to set a date for the hearing of the claim by Ngwenya that he was a Swazi citizen. D. Luhkele represented the government, supported by two Johannesburg

Table 6.2 The members of the Special Tribunal to examine the Ngwenya citizenship affair

	Name	Comment
1.	J. F. G. Troughton	Chairman
2.	F. N. M. Dlamini	Member
3.	M. M. Mnisi	Member
4.	Chief M. Maziya	Member
5.	Prince Sifuba	Member

Source A Government Gazette Extraordinary: 'Five Man Tribunal', *The Times of Swaziland*, November 17, 1972

[69] He was the lawyer who stood for those who took the government of Swaziland to court over the illegality of the abrogation of the 1968 constitution.

[70] Bhekindlela Thomas Ngwenya v The Deputy Prime Minister 1970–76 Swaziland Law Report (HC) 88.

[71] 'Tribunal Meets', *Times of Swaziland*, December 8, 1972.

advocates, Goldstein and Mostert. Advocate Soggott from South Africa represented Ngwenya. The hearing was postponed until 9 January 1973. When the Parliamentary Tribunal finally met in January 1973, it invited Ngwenya to appear before it so it could determine his citizenship status—a matter that had already been settled by the High Court of Swaziland. But the Special Tribunal wanted to do things its own way according to the dictates of the monarchy. The Tribunal deliberated and came to the conclusion that Ngwenya was born in South Africa and was not a citizen of Swaziland. It stated that, although Ngwenya's parents may have been resident in Swaziland, he himself was born in South Africa and could not be considered a Swazi under the present amended law.[72] The amended law was therefore applied retroactively and Ngwenya was found to be a South African. He could not, therefore, sit in the Swazi Parliament because he was a foreigner.

Ngwenya did not take the politically motivated citizenship manoeuvring by the *Imbokodvo* Parliamentary Tribunal lying down. He challenged the competence and constitutionality of the Parliamentary Tribunal. He applied to the High Court of Swaziland praying that it declare the Immigration Amendment Act, 1972 *ultra vires* the Constitution and, to similar effect, the Special Immigration Tribunal established under it. The Swazi High Court, under Chief Justice C. J. Hill, did not favour Ngwenya, because it dismissed his application on grounds that the Parliamentary Act and the Special Parliamentary Tribunal were constitutionally valid.[73] But the High Court ignored the application of the principle of the non-retroactivity in the application of the Parliamentary Act. It should be noted that, prior to the establishment of the Parliamentary Tribunal, this same High Court presided over by Chief Justice Phillip Pike and C. J. Hill had adjudicated over this same case in favour of Ngwenya. The High Court had now changed its position, suggesting that some pressures had been put on it by the government. Chief Justice Phillip Pike had vacated his office before the court hearing[74] without any explanation, suggesting that he could have come under politial pressure to do so. Maseko notes that: 'the judgment [of the High Court] was clearly wrong, based on a deliberate

---

[72] Baloro, 'The Development of Swaziland's Constitution: Monarchical Reponses to Modern Challenges', 24–25.

[73] 'Tribunal Meets', *Times of Swaziland*, December 8, 1972.

[74] Maseko, 'The Drafting of the Constitution of Swaziland, 2005', 320.

268   H. P. DLAMINI

lack of appreciation of the relationship between the Act of Parliament, on the one hand, and the Constitution, on the other, as well as the role of the courts in protecting and promoting fundamental rights and freedoms'.[75] Furthermore, the legal principle of non-reactroactivity was grossly violated in legislating a law and applying it on the Opposition member of parliament retroactively. The legal untidiness of this case is therefore reflected by the fact that, under the 1964 Immigration Act, Ngwenya was a Swazi citizen and was allowed to run for a parliamentary seat. Under the 1972 Amended Immigration Act, which followed Ngwenya's victory at the polls, Ngwenya's citizenship was changed from that of a Swazi citizen to that of a South African citizen with the sole purpose of eliminating him from Parliament. This legal gymnastics was clearly politically motivated.

THE APPEAL COURT OF SWAZILAND RULING FOR THE OPPOSITION, AND THE STAND-OFF WITH GOVERNMENT

Ngwenya refused to accept the manipulation of his citizenship and decided to seek redress in the Appeal Court of Swaziland, which was the highest court in the land, and which had replaced the British Privy Council.[76] The Court of Appeal comprised three leading South African judges: J. P. Schreiner, J. A. Milne, and J. J. A. Smith.[77] The case was heard on 29 March 1973. The judges observed that section 134 of the Swaziland Independence Order dealt with the alteration of the Constitution, and this required a joint sitting of the Senate and the House of Assembly. The section further distinguished between 'entrenched' and 'specially entrenched' provisions, which were scheduled respectively in the two parts of schedule 4 of the Constitution. Entrenched and specially entrenched provisions both required that the amending enactment should be passed by no fewer than a three-quarters majority at the final reading of the joint

[75] Ibid., 321.

[76] Bhekindlela Thomas Ngwenya v The Deputy Prime Minister and the Chief Immigration Officer 1970–76, Swaziland Law Report (Court of Appeal), 123–126.

[77] It was a common practice in Swaziland to draw its Court of Appeal judges from South Africa to come occasionally to the country to conduct court sessions and return to South Africa. Swaziland did not have resident judges of the Court of Appeal and had to rely on South Africa. (Interview with anonymous legal authorities in Swaziland between November 1 and 16, 2015.)

6 THE 1968 WESTMINSTER CONSTITUTION, THE 1972 GENERAL ... 269

sitting. The entrenched provisions further required that, for alteration to be effected, a referendum had to be organized in which at least a two-thirds majority of the voters approved the amendment. What is important is the method of the alteration of the Constitution, which the *Imbokodvo* dominated Parliament failed to observe because they were impatient with due process.

The Court of Appeal observed that the Amendment Act was passed in the ordinary bicameral way, with each House sitting separately, and not together as required by the Constitution. The basis of Ngwenya's appeal was that the Act purported to bring an alteration in the Constitution without following the procedure of a joint sitting required by section 134 of the Constitution, implying that the alteration was invalid. Broadly speaking, the appellant's case was that the Constitution protected various rights belonging to Swazi citizens and, expressly or by implication, given the High Court jurisdiction to decide whether such rights had been infringed. In order to decide such issues, the Court had to decide whether the person affected was a Swazi citizen, as defined in chapter III of the Constitution. The Swazi Court of Appeal, therefore, declared the Immigration Act that had been enacted and applied retroactively was illegal. The Act was void, as it was beyond the powers of Parliament to enact, save in accordance with section 134 of the Constitution.[78] The Swaziland Court of Appeal had ruled accordingly, and the judicial arm of government had exercised its independence fully. It was now left for the Swazi government to uphold the independence of the judiciary and respect the principle of the separation of powers, which is the hallmark of constitutionality and its corollary, liberal democracy. This was an elegant landmark expression of the law and an unfolding of constitutionality in independence Swaziland that inevitably finds itself in the annals of Swazi political history.

The response of the royal *Imbokodvo* dominated Parliament to the decision of the Swazi Court of Appeal was, in the words of Baloro, 'swift and decisive',[79] and demonstrated the government's impatience with and lack of liberal democratic credentials, in which they had no interest and which they did not claim to possess. The government faulted the 1968 Independence Constitution for its legal woes, and declared that the Constitution

---

[78] Bhekindlela Thomas Ngwenya v The Deputy Prime Minister and the Chief Immigration Officer 1970–76, SLR (Court of Appeal), 123–126.

[79] Baloro, 'The Development of Swaziland's Constitution', 25.

270 H. P. DLAMINI

was 'unworkable' and that there was a 'constitutional crises' in Swaziland. By constitutional crisis, the government meant that the Court of Appeal ruling did not favour it and had, therefore, challenged the monarchy. The Swazi government tabled bills in both the House of Assembly and Senate simultaneously in which it elaborated on the theory of a 'constitutinal crisis' in Swaziland. From the constitutional crisis argument, the Swazi government contemplated revisiting the 1968 Independence Constitution. The two Houses of Parliament met simultaneously on 12 April 1973 to look into the 'constitutional crisis'. Given the importance of this historic event in Swaziland's post-colonial constitutional history, Appendix 10 presents a full list of the Cabinet and Members of the House of Assembly who engaged in the debate aimed at revisiting the Independence Constitution, which was described as 'unworkable'.

In the Swazi National Assembly, the Prime Minister moved a motion in Parliament on Thursday, 12 April 1973 that the Independence Constitution inherited from the British was 'unworkable'. He called on the King-in-Council 'to consider ways and means of resolving the constitutional crisis' and stated that 'the House of Assembly of the Kingdom of Swaziland and the individual members thereof [had placed] themselves entirely at the disposal of the King-in-Council'.[80] They had surrendered themselves to the King to do whatever he wanted to solve the crisis.

Speaking to the motion, the Prime Minister said:

> Since independence on the 6th of September, 1968, this House of Assembly and Senate have functioned in terms of, and by virtue of, the Constitution which was created and granted to Swaziland by way of a law passed by Parliament in the United Kingdom.

> The Constitution has proved to be the direct cause of difficult and sometimes insoluble problems in that:

> a. as a result of a number of provisions introduced into the Constitution as so-called safeguards, there is a significant derogation from the sovereign powers of legislation which should normally vest in His Majesty, the *Ngwenyama* of Swaziland;

---

[80] SNA, Official Report of the Debates of the House of Assembly, First Meeting (Vol. II) of the first Session of April 12, 1973.

6 THE 1968 WESTMINSTER CONSTITUTION, THE 1972 GENERAL ... 271

    b. Many unwarranted restrictions are placed on the executive powers of Ministers and of the King-in-Council resulting in the incapacity of the Executive to govern the country properly and without continuously encountering irksome and completely unjustifiable obstacles;

    c. It permits of particularly undesirable political activities, bordering on the subversive, and completely foreign to, and incompatible with, the normal way of life of the citizens of our country;

    d. The accumulated effect of the network of provisions derogating from sovereign powers of the legislature and the Executive renders the Constitution an ineffective instrument for the peace, order and good government of the country.[81]

The Prime Minister complained that the Constitution contained 'an intricate system for the entrenchment of the offending provisions which [was] wholly impracticable and effectively [prevented] Parliament from amending the Constitution'. He observed that this was 'an imposition on a free independent state of a set of restrictive conditions which [did] not apply even to the British Parliament itself'.[82]

The Prime Minister's motion captured the thinking of the traditionalist *Imbokodvo* about the 1968 Independence Constitution, which was intended to provide for a constitutional monarchy with checks and balances between the various arms of government, but which they were opposed to in favour of all powers being in the hands of the king. The entrenched clauses in the Constitution were intended to make it difficult for the manipulation of the Constitution according to the whims and caprices of the executive. What the British bequeathed to the Swazis was an instrument for the governance of a modern state in which sovereignty lay with the people, and the rule of the law was supreme. However, the thinking of the *Imbokodvo* traditionalists was that the *Ngwenyama* should reign supreme as a trusted benevolent despot without any restrictions on his powers. Constitutional checks and balances were interpreted as an infringment on the sovereignty of the Swazi people.

---

[81] SNA, Official Report of the Debates of the House of Assembly, First Meeting (Vol. II) of the first Session of April 12, 1973.

[82] SNA, Official Report of the Debates of the House of Assembly, First Meeting (Vol. II) of the first Session of April 12, 1973.

272   H. P. DLAMINI

After the Prime Minister's motion, speaker after speaker rose to support the motion. The Minister of Finance, R. P. Stephens, stated that he believed that 'the revision of the Constitution [was] in the best interest of the Kingdom of Swaziland and that a suitable revision [would] lead to a much better degree of...political stability'. He pointed out that there was nothing unusual in altering the Constitution, especially when it was felt that the Constitution was out of tune with the times and needs of Swazis. He cited the constitutions of great nations, such as that of the United States of America, which had been altered 25 times. In his turn, R. V. Dlamini argued that the Constitution was meant to serve the people, and not the other way around. The Minister of Agriculture also supported the motion and pointed out that the Independence Constitution was 'unworkable'. Like the Prime Minister, he said the Constitution was 'an imposition on a free independent state of a set of restrictive conditions which [did] not apply to the British Parliament itself'. He complained that 'in this constitution, as a result of a number of provisions introduced therein as so-called safeguards, there [was] a significant derogation from the sovereign powers of legislation which should normally vest in His Majesty and the Houses of Parliament'.[83] According to Maseko, the Opposition staged a walk-out of Parliament in protest against the manoeuvres of the *Imbokodvo* dominated House of Assembly before any voting.[84] The Prime Minister's motion to alter the Constitution was put to the House for a vote and was carried.[85]

Senate debated the issue on Thurday, 12 April 1973. Leading the discussion, the Minister of Justice pronounced the Constitution 'unworkable', and invited the King to intervene to solve the constitutional crisis that had arisen. He stated that the people of Swaziland whom they represented wanted this Constitution to be amended. All subsequent speakers supported this position. Senator Dr V. S. Leibbrandt endorsed the Minister's motion 'wholeheartedly' and argued that, while the 1968 Constitution may have suited Englishmen, it was doubtful whether it could suit Swazis 'who

[83]SNA, Official Report of the Debates of the House of Assembly, First Meeting (Vol. II) of the first Session of April 12, 1973.

[84]Maseko, 'The Drafting of the Constitution of Swaziland, 2005', 320. It is important to underscore this point because most pro-government interviewees give the impression that the opposition also voted in favour of the government motion and went as far as expressing their joy by dancing on the floor.

[85]SNA, Official Report of the Debates of the House of Assembly, First Meeting (Vol. II) of the first Session of April 12, 1973.

6 THE 1968 WESTMINSTER CONSTITUTION, THE 1972 GENERAL ... 273

[were] different in population, social and educational background' and the 'environmental differences and different levels of development', especially given the wish of Swazis to see the Constitution amended.[86] After the debate, Senate approved the motion.[87] Thus, the two Houses were unanimous that the 1968 Constitution was 'unworkable' and that there was a 'constitutional crisis' that required the Constitution to be 'amended'. The *Imbokodvo* members of Parliament placed themselves at the disposal of the King-in-Council. The parliamentarians then marched to the King's *kraal* at Lobamba, where the King, members of the traditional SNC, and a crowd of about 8000 people awaited them.[88] The stage had, therefore, long been prepared for political drama.

The constitutionality of members of Parliament placing themselves at the disposal of a traditional ruler and Head of State of Swaziland to solve a 'constitutional crisis' is definitely questionable within the provisions of the 1968 Constitution. There was no provision in the 1968 Constitution that disagreements between the various arms of government in a modern state should be solved by the surrender of the legislature to the executive in order to find a solution. This surrender was political drama *par excellence* that negated the essence of the functions of Parliament in sorting out constitutional issues and the idea of the separation of powers as sacrosanct. In modern governance, the sovereignty of the people is expressed through its elected parliamentarians. Parliamentary refusal to comply with the ruling of the Supreme Court, together with the negation of its responsibilities in the face of a crisis, was a scar on the constitutional history of Swaziland, and marked the personalization of power by the executive and the paving of a smooth path to the emergence of the typical African 'personal

---

[86]SNA, Official Report of the Debates of the Senate First Meeting (Vol. II) of the First Session, April 12, 1973.

[87]Ibid.

[88]See Appendix A: His Majesty's Speech during Repeal of the Westminster Constitution at Lobamba, April 12, 1973.

274   H. P. DLAMINI

rule', 'big man rule',[89] or 'presidentialist systems'[90] that were a common characteristic of post-independence political regimes in Africa.

Conclusion

The 1968 Swazi Independence Constitution did not find favour with the Swazi king because of its checks and balances on royal prerogatives, which the traditionalists interpreted as limiting the king's hands in governing his country the way he wanted. One-man rule also known as big-man rule, or autocratic one-party rule, was in vogue in Africa, and these prevailing circumstances were no incentive for the Swazi monarchy to persevere with constitutional democracy. The capture of three seats by the Opposition NNLC in May 1972 unsettled King Sobhuza at a time when he was contemplating doing away with multiparty democracy. This victory hurt the Swazi government, and it looked for a pretext to do away with the Opposition by accusing Ngwenya of being an undesirable alien in Swaziland and proceeding to deport him to South Africa. The Opposition resorted to the courts of the land and won their case against the government, as Ngwenya was declared a Swazi citizen and could, *ipso facto*, take his seat in Parliament. The government could not tolerate this trend of events and a stand-off set in. Swaziland bicameral legislature declared there was a constitutional crisis in the country and that the Westminster inherited constitution was unworkable. They surrendered their prerogatives to King Sobhuza II to solve the problem.

---

[89] R. H. Jackson, R. H. Jackson, and C. G. Rosberg, *Personal Rule in Black Africa: Prince, Autocrat, Prophet, Tyrant* (London: University of California Press, 1982); K. Kalu, 'Africa's "Big Men" and the African State', 36–50, In K. Kalu, O. Yacob-Haliso, and T. Falola (eds.), *Africa's Big Men* (New York: Routledge, 2018).

[90] N. Van de Walle, 'Presidentialism and Clientelism in Africa's Emerging Party Systems', *The Journal of Modern African Studies*, 41, 2 (2003), 297–321; O. Van Cranenburgh, "Big Men" Rule: Presidential Power, Regime Type and Democracy in 30 African Countries', *Democratization*, 15, 5 (2008), 952–973; and G. K. Kieh, Jr., 'The "Hegemonic Presidency" in African Politics', *African Social Science Review*, 9, 1 (2018), 5.

REFERENCES

ORAL INTERVIEWS

Interview with anonymous political activist and scholar in Swaziland.
Interview with anonymous Swazi legal experts November 10, 2015.
Interview with anonymous legal authorities in Swaziland between November 1 and 16, 2015.

ARCHIVAL SOURCES

Swaziland National Archives
SNA, The 1968 Independence Constitution.
SNA, The Immigration Act 32 of 1964, published under Government Gazette 45 of 1972.
SNA, Official Report of the Debates of the Senate First Meeting (Vol. II) of the First Session, April 12, 1973.
SNA, His Majesty's Speech during Repeal of the Westminster Constitution at Lobamba, April 12, 1973.
SNA, House of Assembly Hansard, November 1972.

Swaziland National High Court
Bhekindlela Thomas Ngwenya v The Deputy Prime Minister 1970–76 Swaziland Law Report (HC).

NEWSPAPERS

'Dr Zwane Fined', *Times of Swaziland*, May 5, 1972.
'Dr Zwane in Court', *Times of Swaziland*, April 28, 1972.
'May Elections', *Times of Swaziland*, March 17, 1972.
'Imbokodvo Candidate', *Times of Swaziland*, March 31, 1972.
'Pledge', *Times of Swaziland*, April 14, 1972.
'Dr A.P. Zwane's Historic Document', *Times of Swaziland*, May 12, 1972.
'Declared Prohibited Immigrant', *Times of Swaziland*, June 2, 1972.
'Deportation Appeal', *Times of Swaziland*, July 28, 1972.
'Boycott at Parliament', *Times of Swaziland*, October 20, 1972.
'Immigration Bill Gazetted', *Times of Swaziland*, November 10, 1972.
'Five Man Tribunal', *Times of Swaziland*, November 17, 1972.
'Tribunal Meets', *Times of Swaziland*, December 8, 1972.

BOOKS, JOURNAL ARTICLES AND THESES

Baloro, J. 'The Development of Swaziland's Constitution: Monarchical Responses to Modern Challenges', *Journal of African Law*, 38, 1 (1994), 19–34.

Bogdanor, V. *The Monarchy and the Constitution* (Oxford: Oxford University Press, 1997).

Brattan, M. 'Formal Versus Informal Institutions in Africa', In L. Diamond and M. F. Platter (eds.), *Democratisation in Africa: Progress and Retreat* (Baltimore: John Hopkins University Press, 2010).

Carbone, G. M. 'Political Parties and Party Systems in Africa: Themes and Research Perspectives', *World Political Science Review*, 13, 3 (2007).

Dlamini, P. A. 'The Teaching of Oral Literature in Swazi Secondary Schools: A Critique' (MA diss., University of Cape Town, 2000), 58.

Fallon, R. H., Jr., and Meltzer, D. J. 'New Law, Non-retroactivity, and Constitutional Remedies', *Harvard Law Review* (1991), 1731–1833.

Fombad, C. M. 'The Swaziland Constitution of 2005: Can Absolutism Be Reconciled with Modern Constitutionalism?', *South African Journal on Human Rights*, 93, 1 (2007), 93–115.

Fombad, C. M. 'Challenges to Constitutionalism and Constitutional Rights in Africa and the Enabling Role of Political Parties: Lessons and Perspectives from Southern Africa', *The American Journal of Comparative Law* (2007), 1–45.

Fox, P. W. 'Louis XIV and the Theories of Absolutism and Divine Right', *Canadian Journal of Economics and Political Science/Revue canadienne de economiques et science politique*, 26, 1 (1960), 128–142.

Hale, T. A. *Griots and Griottes: Masters of Words and Music (African Expressive Cultures)* (Bloomington: Indiana University Press, 2007).

Hammer, S. J. 'Retroactivity and Restraint: An Anglo-American Comparison', *Harvard Journal of Law and Public Policy*, 41, 1 (2018), 409.

Jackson, R. H., Jackson, R. H., and Rosberg, C. G. *Personal Rule in Black Africa: Prince, Autocrat, Prophet, Tyrant* (London: University of California Press, 1982).

Kalu, K. 'Africa's "Big Men" and the African State', 36–50, In K. Kalu, O. Yacob-Haliso, and T. Falola (eds.), *Africa's Big Men* (New York: Routledge, 2018).

Kaschula, R. H., and Samba, D. 'Political Processes and the Role of the Imbongi and Griot in Africa', *South African Journal of African languages*, 20, 1 (2000), 13–28.

Khumalo, B. 'The Politics of Constitution-Making and Constitutional Pluralism in Swaziland Since 1973', *UNISWA Research Journal*, 10 (1996), 1–19.

Kieh, G. K. 'The "Hegemonic Presidency" in African Politics', *African Social Science Review*, 9, 1 (2018), 5.

Kilson, M. L. 'Authoritarian and Single-Party Tendencies in African Politics', *World Politics*, 15, 2 (1963), 262–294.

Kuper, H. *Sobhuza II, Ngwenyama and King of Swaziland: The Story of an Hereditary Ruler and His Country* (New York: Africana Publishing, 1978).

Levin, R. 'Swaziland's Tinkhundla and the Myth of Swazi Traditional', *Journal of Contemporary African Studies*, 10, 2 (1991), 1–23.

Lumumba-Kasongo, T. *Liberal Democracy and Its Critics in Africa: Political Dysfunction and the Struggle of Social Progress* (London: Radical International Publishing, Zed Books, 2005).

Maseko, T. 'The Drafting of the Constitution of Swaziland, 2005', *African Human Rights Law Journal*, 8, 2 (2008), 312–336.

Matlosa, K. 'Democracy and Conflict in Post-apartheid Southern Africa: Dilemmas of Social Change in Small States', *International Affairs*, 74, 2 (1998), 330.

Mohiddin, A. 'Ujamaa: A Commentary on President Nyerere's Vision of Tanzanian Society', *African Affairs*, 67, 267 (1968), 130–143.

Mozaffar, S., and Schedler, A. 'A Comparative Study of Electoral Governance: Introduction', *Party Politics*, 11, 4 (2005), 395.

Mzizi J. B. 'The Dominance of the Swazi Monarchy and the Moral Dynamics of Democratisation of the Swazi State', *Journal of African Elections*, 3, 1 (2004), 94–119.

Neocosmos, M. 'The Politics of National Elections in Botswana, Lesotho and Swaziland: Towards a Comparative Analysis', In M. Cowen and L. Laakso (eds.), *Multiparty Elections in Africa* (Oxford: James Currey, 2002).

Nkrumah, K., Arrigoni, R., and Napolitano, G. *Africa Must Unite* (London: Heinemann, 1963).

Okoth-Ogendo, H. W. O. 'The Politics of Constitutional Change in Kenya Since Independence, 1963–69', *African Affairs*, 71, 282 (1972), 9–34.

Olechnowicz, A. 'The Monarchy', In D. Brown, G. Pentland, and R. Crowcroft (eds.), *The Oxford Handbook of Modern British Political History, 1800–2000* (Oxford: Oxford University Press, 2018).

Omari, P. T., and Ollennu, N. A. *Kwame Nkrumah: The Anatomy of an African Dictatorship* (London: Africana Publishing Corporation, 1970).

Proctor, J. H. 'Traditionalism and Parliamentary Government in Swaziland', *African Affairs*, 72, 288 (1973), 274.

Schachter, R. 'Single-Party Systems in West Africa', *American Political Science Review*, 55, 2 (1961), 294–307.

Shale, V. 'Political Party Funding and Regulation in Lesotho and Mozambique', In J. Mendolow and E. Phelippeau (eds.), *Handbook of Political Party Funding* (Cheltenham: Edward Elgar Publishing, 2018).

Sinjenga, M. 'Constitutionalism in Africa: Emerging trends: The Evolving African Constitutionalism', *The Review-International Commission of Jurist*, 60 (1998), 23–28.

Tang, P. *Masters of the Sabar: Wolof Griot Percussionists of Senegal* (Philadelphia: Temple University Press, 2007).

Vail, L., and White. L. *Power and the Praise Poem: Southern African Voices in History* (London: James Currey Publishers, 1991).

Van Cranenburgh, O. '"Big Men" Rule: Presidential Power, Regime Type and Democracy in 30 African Countries', *Democratization*, 15, 5 (2008), 952–973.

Van de Walle, N. 'Presidentialism and Clientelism in Africa's Emerging Party Systems', *The Journal of Modern African Studies*, 41, 2 (2003), 297–321.

Wanda, B. P. 'The Shaping of the Modern Constitution of Swaziland: A Review of Some Social and Historical Factors', *Lesotho Law Journal: A Journal of Law and Developments*, 6, 1 (1990), 137–198.

Zwane, H. S. 'Constitutional Discontinuity and Legitimacy: A Comparative Study with Special Reference to the 1973 Constitutional Crisis in Swaziland', A Dissertation for a Master Degree in Law, University of Edinburg, 1988.

INTERNET SOURCE

http://saklawph.com/retroactivity/, Rule on Retroactivity of Laws—SAKLAW (Accessed September 8, 2018).

CHAPTER 7

From King Sobhuza II's Auto-Coup D'état to the Era of Constitutional Void and Royal Benevolent Despotism

INTRODUCTION

This chapter examines how King Sobhuza II abrogated the Independence Constitution, which he deemed cumbersome, on 12 April 1973. The overthrow of the Constitution, which defines the parameters of the institutions of government, is what is technically labelled an auto-coup d'état,[1] similar to the those in the kingdom of Nepal and in Latin America. King Sobhuza II did not invent auto-coup d'états, and was not the first to stage one. In order to have a clear insight into the dynamics of an auto-coup d'état, an attempt has been made in this chapter to unpack a classic example from the kingdom of Nepal.

It is demonstrated in this chapter how the repeal of the Independence Constitution witnessed a protracted period of constitutional void marked by proclamations and decrees, and an extraordinary display of monarchical

---

[1]The concept of "auto-coup", which will be explained in detail in this chapter, deals with the overthrow of the constitution by a Head of State who came to power by constitutional means or a monarch who owes his position both to a dynastic line and the constitution.

© The Author(s) 2019
H. P. Dlamini, *A Constitutional History of the Kingdom of Eswatini (Swaziland), 1960–1982*, African Histories and Modernities,
https://doi.org/10.1007/978-3-030-24777-5_7

279

280 H. P. DLAMINI

absolutism, qualified as benevolent despotism[2] and guided democracy[3] in Swazi history. Using proclamations and decrees, the King governed with an iron fist, but also with the human face reflected in his humanism and parternalism. This was in contrast to the 'strong man' political model of Marcias Ngeuma and Idi Amin, which involved the mass detention and execution of hundreds of thousands of Africans. A succession of constitutional committees established to draft a new constitution consulted the Swazi people several times, but never succeeded in providing Swaziland with another constitution before King Sobhuza II's demise in 1982. Nonetheless, the King introduced guided democracy in the shape of a party-less *tinkhundla* system of elections under the control of the monarchy. These provided the Lower and Upper Chambers of the legislature, and a government under Prime Minister Maphevu Dlamini (b.1922–d.1979). Even with the inauguration of Parliament, the King continued to rule by proclamations and decrees.

THE CONCEPT OF A COUP D'ÉTAT AND AN AUTO-COUP D'ÉTAT

When the expression coup d'état is used, it frightens and unsettles many, because it is often used in the narrow sense of the word and is associated

---

[2]The expression "Benevolent Despotism" is coined from European history. Benevolent despotism refers to the conduct and policies of European absolute monarchs during the second half of eighteenth and early nineteenth centuries who were influenced by the ideas of the Enlightenment. They exercised absolute political power for the benefit of the people, rather than exclusively for themselves or the elites. Typical examples of benevolent despots included Frederick II of Prussia (1740–1786), Joseph II (1790) and Leopold II (1790–1792) of Austria, Catherine II (1762–1796) of Russia, See H. M. Scott (ed.), *Enlightened Absolutism: Reform and Reformers in Later Eighteenth Century Europe C. 1750–1790* (Basingstoke: Macmillan, 1990); Geoffrey Bruun, *The Enlightened Despots* (New York: Henry Holt, Rinehart and Winston, 1967); Adam Smith, X. V. Louis, X. V. I. Louis, Bourbon Spain, V. Philip, Hanoverian England, I. George, et al., 'Europe in the Age of Enlightenment, 1720–1789', *A Handbook of Civilization: Earliest Times to the Present* (1974): 308.

[3]Guided democracy, also called 'managed' or 'manipulated' democracy is a formally democratic government that functions as a *de facto* autocracy. The government controls elections so that the people can exercise all their rights without truly changing public policy. While they follow basic democratic principles, there can be major deviations towards authoritarianism. Under this qualified democracy, the state's continuous use of propaganda techniques prevents the electorate from having a significant impact on policy (Baladas Ghoshal, *Indonesian Politics, 1955–59: The Emergence of Guided Democracy* [K.P. Bagchi, 1982]).

with a military takeover of a government, this having been an endemic feature of politics in Africa until recently.[4] A coup d'état—also known simply as a coup, a putsch, or an overthrow—is an illegal and overt confiscation of a political power by the military or other elites within the state apparatus.[5] Although many studies tend to limit coup perpetrators to 'the armed forces', it is not exactly the case, because any elite who form part of the state apparatus, including civilian members of government, can also be perpetrators. Consequently, scholars have also increasingly focused on civilian coup d'états, and have adopted the concept of an 'auto-coup d'état' or 'self-coup' or 'auto-golpe'[6] as a form of coup d'état in which a nation's civilian leader repeals, suspends, dissolves or discard the constititution of the state. The civilian leader unlawfully assumes extraordinary powers not

---

[4]Since the end of the Cold War in 1989, coup d'états in Africa have declined and are no longer attractive. The African Development Bank study reveals that from 1970 to 1989 study there were 99 coup attempts in Sub-Saharan Africa. Thereafter, there was a decrease of about one third in two decades of which the most important reason is that the international community is hostile and intolerant to coups (see John Frank Clark, 'The Decline of the African Military Coup', *Journal of Democracy*, 18, 3 [2007], 141–155).

[5]Jonathan M. Powell and Clayton L. Thyne, 'Global Instances of Coups from 1950 to 2010: A New Dataset', *Journal of Peace Research*, 48, 2 (2011), 249–250.

[6]For the development of the concept of auto-coup d'état, self-coup or see Maxwell A. Cameron, 'Self-Coups: Peru, Guatemala, and Russia', *Journal of Democracy*, 9, 1 (1998), 125–139; Philip Mauceri, 'State Reform, Coalitions, and the Neoliberal Autogolpe in Peru', *Latin American Research Review* (1995), 7–37; J. Protzel, 'Changing Political Cultures and Media Under Globalism in Latin America', *Democratizing Global Media: One World, Many Struggles* (2005), 101–120; M. Hutt, 'King Gyanendra's Coup and Its Implications for Nepal's Future', *Brown Journal of World Affairs*, 12 (2005), 111; K. Hachhethu, 'Legitimacy crisis of Nepali monarchy', *Economic and Political Weekly* (2007), 1828–1833; K. M. Dixit, 'Absolute Monarchy to Absolute Democracy', *Economic and Political Weekly* (2005), 1506–1510; M. Hutt, 'Nepal and Bhutan in 2005: Monarchy and Democracy, Can They Co-exist?', *Asian Survey*, 46, 1 (2006), 120–124; Tevita Baleiwaqa, 'Reflections on the Civilian Coup in Fiji', *Coup: Reflections on the Political Crisis in Fiji* (2001), 24–30; Venkat Iyer. 'Courts and Constitutional Usurpers: Some Lessons from Fiji', *Dalhousie Law Journal*, 28 (2005), 27; Maxwell A. Cameron, 'Latin American Autogolpes: Dangerous Undertows in the Third Wave of Democratisation', *Third World Quarterly*, 19, 2 (1998), 219–239; Susan Berger, 'Guatemala: Coup and Countercoup', *NACLA Report on the Americas*, 27, 1 (1993), 4–7; Steven Levitsky, 'Fujimori and Post-party Politics in Peru', *Journal of Democracy*, 10, 3 (1999), 78–92; David Holiday, 'Guatemala's Long Road to Peace', *Current History*, 96, 607 (1997), 68; Eduardo Ferrero Costa, 'Peru's Presidential Coup', *Journal of Democracy*, 4, 1 (1993), 28–40. This concept is extremely helpful in this study in describing what King Sobhuza II actually did.

282   H. P. DLAMINI

granted under normal circumstances by the constitution. He engages in extra-constitutional governance after the overthrow of the constitution, which is the supreme law of the state. Exceptional measures are usually taken by the auto-coup leader, including the declaration of a state of emergency, reinforced by a curfew, and the suspension of civil courts and the institution of governance by proclamations and decrees.

Since an incumbent regime forms part of the constitutional order, the regime's overthrow of the constitutional order is considered illegal in strict constitutional terms, in the same way all military coups are treated.[7] With reference to the April 1973 repeal of the Constitution in Swaziland, one cannot escape from the fact that the issue in question was the excessive exercise of power by a traditional monarchy in modern politics. This fact takes us to the next question: whether, in the eyes of the Swazi people, King Sobhuza's actions were legitimate and acceptable. Hilder Kuper opines that the act of discarding the 1968 Independence Constitution by King Sobhuza II, followed by the imposition of one-man rule, was very popular among the Swazi people.[8] Following the trend of this logic, if it were the will of the Swazi people that the 1968 Constitution should be disposed of, then there was no room for any complaint. But the madding crowd cannot be used to legitimize what is illegitimate, because there was a clear constitutional route to be taken to revise or amend the constitution, and this was not followed. This is where the illegality of the abrogation of the Independence Constitution by a civilian leader lies.

Overview of Monarchical and Republican Auto-Coup D'états

King Sobhuza II was neither the first, nor alone, in jettisoning the Constitution in the spirit of an auto-coup d'état[9] when he found the Independence

---

[7] Tayyab Mahmud, 'Jurisprudence of Successful Treason: Coup D'etat & Common Law', *Cornell International Law Journal*, 27 (1994), 49.

[8] Kuper Hilda, *Sobhuza II, Ngwenyama and King of Swaziland: The Story of an Hereditary Ruler and His Country* (New York: Africana Publishing Company, 1978).

[9] Some randomly selected examples of civilian auto-coup d'états include King Letsie III of Lesotho August 17, 1994; President Boris Yeltsin of Russia 1993; President General Pervez Musharraf of Pakistan, November 3, 2007; President Mamadou Tandja Niger, June 29, 2009; President Viktor Yanukovich of Ukraine, September 30, 2010; President Nicolás

7 FROM KING SOBHUZA II'S AUTO-COUP … 283

Constitution irksome and became impatient with its functioning. There are several dozens of auto-coup d'états in recorded history that need not delay us here.[10] Nonetheless, Sobhuza's 1973 auto-coup d'état can be fully appreciated by comparing it with two appropriate historical parallels elsewhere. The first case, which is more appropriate for this study, since it deals with a monarchy, focuses on the perennial auto-coups that were often staged in the kingdom of Nepal which, as was Swaziland, was ruled by a king after periods of constitutional rule. The second case simply highlights the Peruvian auto-coup in the 1990s by a civilian president. Both coups were orchestrated by civilians.

Both the kingdom of Nepal[11] and Swaziland share common characteristics, because they were primarily traditional monarchies in outlook and upheld the divinity of the king, which was deeply entrenched in their cultures. Nepalese Hindu scriptures placed the king at the top of the state machinery. As a ruler, the king was an agent of the gods, and supposedly possessed divine powers. The notion of royal divinity, reinforced by the dynastic origin of kingship, gave the highest position in the state to the king, and it was his duty to maintain law and order, and to be obeyed faithfully by his subjects. The divinity in kingship meant that the king wase considered the supreme and sovereign power of the state, and it authorized him to reward or punish his subjects without being questioned. The concept of divinity tallied more with autocracy, rather than liberal democracy. It is in this spirit that such monarchs enjoying divine rights could take unilateral actions, such as staging a coup against their own institutions, because they believed they were acting not only in the best interests of their people, but also in line with their ordained culture and tradition.

The Nepalese king, Mahendra, staged a royal auto-coup d'état on 15 December 1960 against the inherited British Westminster constitution,

---

Maduro of Venezuela, March 29, 2017; Prime Minister Hun Sen of Cambodia November 16, 2017, https://en.wikipedia.org/wiki/Self-coup, retrieved October 19, 2018; Maxwell A. Cameron, 'Self-Coups: Peru, Guatemala, and Russia', *Journal of Democracy*, 9, 1 (1998), 125–139.

[10] See Footnote 9.

[11] The Kingdom of Nepal is located in South Asia between China in the north and India in the south, east and west. It was founded in 1768 by King Prithvi Narayan Shah, a Gorkhali monarch and it existed for 240 years until the abolition of the Nepalese monarchy in 2008 (see Quy-Toan Do and Lakshmi Iyer, 'Geography, Poverty and Conflict in Nepal', *Journal of Peace Research*, 47, 6 [2010], 735–748).

284   H. P. DLAMINI

owing to his frustration with the operation of parliamentary democracy.[12] He dismissed the elected government, banned political parties, and proceeded to imprison all prominent political party leaders. King Mahendra instituted a 'party-less' traditional *panchayat* (councils) system of government described as a meaningful democratic form of government that was closer to Nepalese traditions, and the system lasted for 30 years. The *panchayat* system constitutionalized the absolute power of the monarchy by making the king the Head of State and the sole authority over all government institutions, including the executive (cabinet) and legislature (parliament). In 1971, with the death of King Mahendra, his eldest son, Birendra, inherited the throne and the *panchayat* system. Finally, a People's Movement (*janandolan*), succeeded in obliging the king to lift the ban on political parties on 8 April 1990.

In 1990, the new Nepalese King, Gyanendra, staged another royal auto-coup d'état, because of conflicts with the goverrnment. He alleged that political parties had failed to contain violence, corruption, and the deteriorating economic situation in the country. The King suspended the constitution and imposed personal despotism on the country. He then formed a new government under his direct control. Media practitioners, intellectuals, and other members of civil society who were considered to be supporters of democracy were also arrested, or were subjected to restrictions on their movements.

The Nepalese monarchy later reinstated constitutional rule, but this did not survive for long. On 1 February 2005, the monarchy staged yet another royal auto-coup d'état after complaining of political corruption, chaos, and generalized mismanagement. King Gyanendra dismissed the Sheer Bahadur government, and declared a state of emergency in the country. Political leaders were either placed under house arrest or jailed. All kinds of communications—print media, radio, and television—were brought under control. King Gyanendra assumed all powers to rule the country directly as Chairman of the Council of Ministers for a specified period of three years. Bhuwan Upreti notes that King Gyanendra's action was uncalled for, as

---

[12] For more on the Nepalese royal auto-coup see Hutt, 'King Gyanendra's Coup and Its implications for Nepal's Future', 111; Hachhethu, 'Legitimacy Crisis of Nepali Monarchy', 1828–1833; Dixit, 'Absolute Monarchy to Absolute Democracy', *Economic and Political Weekly* (2005), 1506–1510; Hutt, 'Nepal and Bhutan in 2005: Monarchy and Democracy, Can They Co-exist?', 120–124; B. C. Upreti, *Maoists in Nepal: From Insurgency to Political Mainstream* (Delhi: Gyan Publishing House, 2008), 46.

there was no such urgency and no circumstances to justify declaring a state of emergency in the country. According to Bhuwan Upreti, the King's action was unconstitutional and the justification for assuming full powers for a three-year period was unclear. Auto-coup d'états were therefore endemic in the Nepalese kingdom.

The second example of an auto-coup d'état can be briefly explained and was staged by President Alberto Fujimori of Peru on 5 April 1992. This auto-coup, also known as the *Autogolpe* (in Spanish), involved the dissolution of the Peruvian congress and judiciary, and the presidential assumption of full legislative and judicial powers.[13] Fujimori embarked on curtailing the independence of the judiciary and constitutional rights, imposed a state of emergency and curfews, and enacted severe emergency laws to deal with any form of opposition. International reactions to the auto-coup involved condemnation from the international community, which was largely ignored.[14] Monarchies and republics have therefore reverted to auto-coup d'états as political instruments for the resolution of a crisis. King Sobhuza II's 1973 auto-coup d'état did not come out of the blue, because there were precedents.

THE OVERTHROW OF THE WESTMINSTER INHERITED CONSTITUTION IN 1973 AND THE MAKING OF A DESPOTIC MONARCH

King Sobhuza II found the 1968 inherited Westminster Constitution frustrating, as it unnecessarily constrained his kingly powers, and he decided to stage an auto-coup d'état on 12 April 1973. It has already been demonstrated that what triggered the royal hostility towards the 1968 Constitution of Swaziland, leading to its repeal, was the stalemate between the government and the courts over the citizenship of Thomas Ngwenya. The situation was triggered by the fact that the courts reinstated the Opposition parliamentarian's citizenship, to which the government was opposed. The Legislative and Executive arms of government then invited the King to

[13] Charles Dennison Kenney, *Fujimori's Coup and the Breakdown of Democracy in Latin America* (Notre Dame: University of Notre Dame Press, 2004); Maxwell A. Cameron, 'Self-Coups: Peru, Guatemala, and Russia', *Journal of Democracy*, 9, 1 (1998), 125–139.

[14] C. Sampford, 'Making Coups History', *World Politics Review*, 22 (2010), 1–10; J. Protzel, 'Changing Political Cultures and Media Under Globalism in Latin America', *Democratizing Global Media: One World, Many Struggles* (2005), 101–120.

286   H. P. DLAMINI

step in to resolve the crisis engulfing the nation 'the Swazi traditional way', rather than in the spirit of the 'imported' Westminster Independence Constitution. The parliamentarians informed the King they had placed themselves at his disposal.[15]

What the government called a 'constitutional crisis' was a topical issue in the nation, which was engaged in a tug of war with the courts over the Ngwenya affair. Public opinion was split between royalist supporters who were overwhelmingly rural, and the Progressives sympathizers of Zwane's NNLC opposition party, who were overwhelmingly the educated class, workers, and urbanites. It was generally expected that the King would speak to the crisis, since the Legislative and Executive arms of the government had invited him to do so. A popular *sibaya* (people's traditional parliament) meeting at the Lobamba Royal *kraal* was therefore scheduled for 12 April 1973.[16] There was great anxiety on that day, as many people were expecting changes to be made in the constitutional order, given the unfolding of the Ngwenya affair.

People had started arriving at the Lobamba royal *kraal* on the morning of 12 April 1973 to find a place and wait for the King, who usually arrived in the afternoon between 3.00 p.m. and 4.00 p.m. to address them. Leaving the Houses of Parliament, the peoples' representatives marched to the Lobamba Royal *kraal*, where a crowd of about 8000 people had already assembled.[17] The Cabinet fetched the monarch from his office and brought him to the *kraal*, where the people had assembled. The Prime Minister read the Resolution of Parliament surrendering itself to the King to solve the crisis. This was followed by the speech of Chief Sifuba, a leading member of the SNC, who addressed the monarch on behalf of the Swazi nation and told him that the Swazi people wanted 'complete sovereignty' and 'independence', and that the King should take steps to fulfil the 'wishes' of the Swazis by according to them a truly Swazi governance instrument.

---

[15]SNA, His Majesty's Speech to a large crowd at Lobamba on the Historic Occassion in the afternoon of the April 12, 1973 (SNA).

[16]In Swaziland the *Sibaya* is the traditional gathering of the Swazi people which usually holds at the Ludzidzini Royal Residence cattle byre, the country's traditional headquarters. The *Sibaya* is called People's Parliament which is open to Swazis of all social classes. The people take to the floor to express their opinion on a number of topics freely without censorship and without fear of persecution and a consensus is reached. The King usually uses the occasion to make important announcements and appointments.

[17]Kuper Hilda, *Sobhuza II, Ngwenyama and King of Swaziland: The Story of an Hereditary Ruler and His Country* (New York: Africana Publishing Company, 1978), 335.

After these preliminary niceties, it was now the long awaited moment for the King to intervene. The King's speech, which was recorded, then followed. His speech, titled 'To all my subjects: citizens of Swaziland'.[18] The speech was a carefully prepared proclamation in which, in essence, he repealed the 1968 Constitution; deployed the army and police in all strategic positions in Swaziland; dissolved Parliament; proscribed all political parties, including the royal ruling INM, and trade unions, and all political activities and meetings.[19]

The King blamed the shortcomings of the Constitution as being responsible for its unworkability in the Swazi context. He blamed the Constitution as 'the cause of growing unrest, insecurity, dissatisfaction with the state of affairs in [Swaziland] and an impediment to free and progressive development in all spheres of life'. The 'Constitution [had] permitted the importation into [Swaziland] of highly undesirable political practices alien to, and incompatible with the way of life in [Swazi] society, designed to disrupt and destroy' the 'peaceful and constructive' and 'essentially democratic methods of political activity'. 'Increasingly, this element [engendered] hostility, bitterness and unrest in our peaceful society.' In his monumental, historic speech, King Sobhuza II stated:

as a nation, we desire to march forward progressively under *our own Constitution* guaranteeing peace, order and good government and happiness and welfare of the people.

Now, therefore, I Sobhuza II, King of Swaziland, hereby declare that, in collaboration with my Cabinet Ministers and supported by the whole nation, *have assumed supreme power in the Kingdom of Swaziland and that all legislative, executive and judicial power is vested in myself and shall, for the timebeing, be exercised in collaboration with a Council constituted by my Cabinet Ministers.*

I further declare that to ensure the continuous maintenance of peace, order and good government, *my armed forces, in conjunction with the Swazi Royal Police, have been posted to all strategic places and have taken charge of all government places and all public services.*

I further declare that I, in collaboration with my Cabinet Ministers, hereby decree that:

---

[18]SNA, His Majesty's Speech to a large crowd at Lobamba on the Historic Occassion·in the afternoon of the April 12, 1973.

[19]Kuper, *Sobhuza II, Ngwenyama and King of Swaziland*, 332.

288   H. P. DLAMINI

(a) *the Constitution of the Kingdom of Swaziland which commenced on the 6th September, 1968 is hereby repealed.*

(b) All laws, with the exception of the Constitution hereby repealed, shall continue to operate with full force and effect and shall be construed with such modifications, adaptations, qualifications and exceptions as may be necessary to bring these into comformity with this and issuing decrees.

I will call upon the Attorney-General, Mr David Cohen, to read out further decrees designed to provide for the continuance of Administration, essential services and normal life in our country.[20]

King Sobhuza made it abundantly clear that he had repealed the Constitution and had 'assumed supreme power in the Kingdom of Swaziland and that all Legislative, Executive and Judicial power' were vested in him, and he was to exercise such powers 'in collaboration with a Council constituted of [his] Cabinet Ministers'. He repealed the Independence Constitution, subject to all other laws continuing to operate with full force and effect, but being construed in a manner that would bring them into conformity with the proclamation and ensuing decrees. According to the King, '[all] laws, with the exception of the Constitution that [was] repealed, [would] continue to operate with full force and effect and [would] be construed with such modifications, adaptations, qualifications and exceptions as [might] be necessary to bring these into comformity with this and other issuing decrees'. In the first instance, the Constitution, as the supreme law of the state, was repealed, and King Sobhuza automatically became the supreme authority of the state, or a type of a new human constitution. The Constitution was overthrown and King Sobhuza II made himself the Constitution from which all laws had to emanate. The Constitution was gone, but the laws of Swaziland to be implemented by the courts were to continue existing as in the past by the King's authorization and to conform with royal decrees.

One may ask whether repealing the Constitution and vesting all powers in himself is what the King meant by the desire of the Swazi people 'to march forward progressively under [their] own Constitution guaranteeing peace, order and good government and happiness and welfare of the

[20] Ibid.

7 FROM KING SOBHUZA II'S AUTO-COUP ... 289

people'. Scrapping the Constitution and substituting himself for the Constitution was an auto-coup d'état *par excellence*. A coup is a coup because it is an illegality that deals with the overthrow of the Constitution that is the supreme law that emanates from the popular will of the people and defines the institutions of the state. But coups fall into different categories, which is worth specifying.[21]

In the case of Swaziland, the coup fell in the category of a royal civilian auto-coups similar to those in Nepal. The several post-independence coups in Nigeria were generally military coups, which can provide useful insights that illuminate the Swazi case. Although the 1983 coup in Nigeria by General Babangida was a typical military coup, the nature and outcome were similar to those in King Sobhuza II's Swaziland. King Sobhuza II's royal auto-coup d'état, which necessitated governance by Orders-in-Council and decrees, was anti-constitutional and a negation of the basic notion of liberal democracy. The same is true of Babangida's 1983 coup d'état in Nigeria. The Swazi 1968 Constitution specified the method of effecting constitutional changes, which involved tabling the motion in a joint sitting of the House of Assembly and the Senate, and submitting the revised, amended, or new constitution to the Swazi people in a referendum for approval by a two-thirds majority of the electorate and then, finally, to the King for assent before any changes could be effected. The King was not prepared to follow this legal route; the way he abrogated the Constitution was definitely illegal. The Nigerian constitution did not provide for a change of a democratically elected government through a military coup d'état, because it was illegal.

Legal experts are unanimous about the illegality of Sobhuza's abrogation of the 1968 Independence Constitution[22] and, when the matter was ultimately taken to court in 2002 by civil society organizations, both the High Court and the Court of Appeal of Swaziland concurred that the 1968 Constitution was unlawfully repealed.[23] Scholars writing on the overthrow of the 1968 Independence Constitution did not conceive it as an auto-coup

---

[21] The types of coups include a military coup, a putch, a palace coup and an auto-coup.

[22] Ray Gwebu and Lucky Nhlanhla Bhembhe, Swaziland Court of Appeal Case Nos. 19/20, 2002 as yet (unreported), Zwane, Hlatshwayo and Khumalo.freedom house, etc.

[23] See Lucky Nhlanhla Bhembe v The King criminal Case 75/2002 (High Court), per Masuku; Nhlanhla Lucy Mbembe& Ray Gwebu and Another Criminal Case 75 & 11 of 2002 *per* Sapire CJ (Unreported).; Gwebu & Another.

290   H. P. DLAMINI

d'état,[24] probably because King Sobhuza was a civilian and the word was not yet in vogue. Scholarship and legal opinion pointed to the fact that Sobuza's repeal of the Constitution was unlawful or illegal, but they were short of calling the act an auto-coup d'état.[25]

The appropriate term for the illegality of overthrowing the 1968 Constitution is a royal auto-coup d'état, which has its precedence in the Nepal monarchy and elsewhere. King Sobhuza II unilaterally abrogated the Independence Constitution, arrogated all constitutional powers to himself, and started legislating by proclamations and decrees that became the supreme law of the land. King Sobhuza's proclamations and decrees replaced parliamentary legislation, since Swaziland operated without a parliament from 1973 to 1978. The act of repealing the Constitution and the institutionalization of governance by proclamations of Orders-in-Council and decrees is the hallmark of a typical coup d'état and dictatorship in Africa, and this is precisely what the Swazi monarch did.

King Sobhuza II's speech to the Swazi nation was the typical coup d'état speech frequently heard on African radios and televisions each time a coup d'état was staged. Sobhuza's speech echoed that by Brigadier Sani Abacha when President Shehu Shagari of Nigeria was overthrown on 1 December 1983 in favour of General Buhari, part of which went as follows:

Fellow countrymen and women, I, Brigadier Sani Abacha, of the Nigerian army address you this morning on behalf of the Nigerian armed forces. You are all living witnesses to the great economic predicament and uncertainty,

[24] See, for instance, Baloro John, 'The Development of Swaziland's Constitution: Monarchical Responses to Modern Challenges', *Journal of African Law*, 38, 1 (1994), 19–34; B. P. Wanda, 'The Shaping of the Modern Constitution of Swaziland: A Review of Some Social and Historical Factors', *Lesotho Law Journal: A Journal of Law and Development*, 6, 1 (1990), 137–178; Levin Richard, 'Swaziland's Tinkhundla and the Myth of Swazi Tradition', *Journal of Contemporary African Studies*, 10, 2 (1991), 1–23; Kuper, *Sobhuza II: The Ngwenyama and King of Swaziland*; S. H. Zwane, 'Constitutional Discontinuity and Legitimacy: A Comparative Study with Special Reference to the 1973 Constitutional Crisis in Swaziland' (Unpublished LLM Dissertation, University of Edinburgh, 1988); B. Khumalo, 'The Politics of Constitution-Making and Constitutional Pluralism in Swaziland Since 1973', *UNISWA Research Journal*, 10 (1996), 1–19.

[25] A Freedom House 2013 publication also considered the April 1973 Constitutional repeal a coup. In a *Freedom House* publication in 2013, the publishers stated that Freedom House is a U.S.-based government-funded non-governmental organization that conducts research and advocacy on democracy, political freedom, and human rights. Freedom House was founded in October 1941, and Wendell Willkie and Eleanor Roosevelt served as its first honorary chairpersons.

7 FROM KING SOBHUZA II'S AUTO-COUP ...   291

which an inept and corrupt leadership has imposed on our beloved nation for the past four years... *After due consultations over these deplorable conditions*, I and my colleagues in the armed forces have, in the discharge of our national role as promoters and protectors of our national interest, decided to effect a change in the leadership of the government of the Federal Republic of Nigeria and form a Federal Military Government. This task has just been completed. The Federal Military Government *hereby decrees the suspension of the provisions of the Constitution of the Federal Republic of Nigeria 1979 relating to all elective and appointive offices ... All the political parties are banned*; the bank account of FEDECO and all the political parties are frozen with immediate effect. *With effect from today, a dusk to dawn curfew will be imposed between 7 pm and 6am* each day until further notice. All airways flights have been suspended forthwith and all airports, seaports, and border posts closed. External communications have been cut ... Anyone caught disturbing public order will be summarily dealt with ...[26] (Emphasis added)

Sobhuza's discourse and that of Brigadier Abacha were very much similar, emphasizing the fact that the nation was confronted with a crisis that required urgent and decisive action to save the state craft from collapse. The Nigerian military decreed the suspension of the provisions of the Constitution of the Federal Republic of Nigeria, and banned all political parties. Sobhuza, like the Nigerian military, took draconian measures to ensure peace and compliance by suspending the Constitution, arrogating all powers to himself, ruling by proclamations and decrees, and also banning all political parties. The Swazi military and police forces were positioned in all strategic parts of Swaziland as a deterrent to any eventuality.

The Nigerian military imposed a dusk to dawn curfew between 7 p.m. and 6 a.m. each day until further notice. King Sobhuza also imposed a similar curfew, and deployed the armed forces to strategic areas. The Nigerian military warned that anyone caught disturbing public order would be summarily dealt with. King Sobhuza's proclamation also prohibited all meetings and processions of a political nature except with the prior consent of the Commissioner of Police. To good effect, it was decreed a criminal offence, punishable by a six-month term of imprisonment, for any person to form or attempt to form a political party, or to organize or attend any meeting, procession, or demonstration of a political nature in contravention of the

---

[26]S. W. Obotetukudo (ed.), *The Inaugural Addresses and Ascension Speeches of Nigerian Elected and Non-elected Presidents and Prime Minister, 1960–2010* (Lanham, MD: University Press of America, 2010), 178–179.

292   H. P. DLAMINI

proclamation. Furthermore, the Swazi Prime Minister was empowered to detain any person for a renewable period of 60 days. Any person released after such detention could be detained again as often as may be deemed necessary in the public interest, and no court was allowed to enquire into or make any order in connection with such detention. This draconian proclamation provided the government of Swaziland with enough weapons in its arsenal to crush any form of political activity by Opposition groupings.[27]

The Swazi 1968 Independence Constitution defined the scope of executive, legislative, and judicial action. Consequent on the abrogation of the Independence Constitution, the Legislative, Executive and Judicial branches of government were equally repealed, and King Sobhuza II automatically assumed all constitutional powers, as all legislative, executive and judicial powers were vested in him. The King was now the constitution and all the provisions of the constitution were construed to be emanating from the King. Everything belonged to the King and emanated from the King. King Sobhuza used personalized expressions such as 'my subjects', 'my people', 'my cabinet ministers', and 'my armed forces' in the wording of the 1973 proclamation and decrees to demonstrate a sense of ownership. Everything belonged to him and everything was his.

As King Sobhuza II repealed the Constitution, he simultaneously reappointed the Prime Minister and Cabinet of Ministers with whom he exercised powers in council, and decreed other essential services to continue functioning. The King's proclamation stated that all laws, with the exception of the Constitution, which had been repealed, were to continue to operate with full force and effect, and were to be 'construed with such modifications, adaptations, qualifications and exceptions as may be necessary to bring them into conformity' with the decrees that would be issued. The Proclamation was therefore immediately followed by a decree of the King-in-Council which retained certain key provisions in the repealed Constitution, including those relating to judges, government officials, public servants, members of the Police, and the Prison Services. The proclamation read:

> All Judges and other Judicial Officers, Government Officials, Public Servants, Members of the Police Force, the Prison Service and Armed Forces shall continue in office and shall be deemed to have been validly appointed.

---

[27]SNA, Swaziland Government Gazette Extraordinary, Vol. XII, Mbabane, Tuesday April 7, 1973, No. 578. Proclamation by His Majesty King Sobhuza II.

They shall carry out their duties and shall be entitled on the existing basis to their remuneration.[28]

The King decreed in Council that:

4. All persons who at the date hereof held office as Prime Minister, Deputy Prime Minister, Minister, Minister of State, Assistant Minister, Secretary to the Cabinet and Attorney-General in terms of Chapter VII of the repealed constitution shall continue in office *at the discretion of the King*. They shall continue to carry out their duties and functions (subject to such modifications as may be necessary as a result of this decree) and shall be responsible to the King; ...

(a) All land and rights in and to land previously vested in the Government shall now *vest in the King* and the reference in Chapter VIII to the Government shall, where the context permits, be taken as a reference to the King;

...

8. Chapter XI of the repealed Constitution shall again come into force and shall be construed with such modifications, adaptations, qualifications and exceptions as may be necessary to bring it into conformity with this and ensuring decrees. *In particular any reference to the House of Assembly or both chambers or the procedures for enacting financial legislation shall be interpreted as references to the King-in-Council and/or decrees issued by the King as the context requires.*

Until further notice, *all persons who have lost office as a result of the repeal* of the Constitution, *including all members of the Senate and the House of Assembly, shall be entitled to receive the emoluments which they would have received but for the repeal of the Constitution.*[29]

Swazis did not actually suffer significant losses, and continued to serve the government at the discretion of the King, who was technically the Constitution. King Sobhuza II had discarded the Constitution as the supreme law of the state and had assumed supreme authority by vesting in himself all the powers of the state. The King could now freely arrogate to himself all effective executive powers, rather than the Prime Minister, as was provided under the Independence Constitution. Under the Westminster Constitution, the Prime Minister and his Cabinet were answerable to the legislature,

---

[28] SNA, Proclamation by His Majesty King Sobhuza II April 12, 1973, The Government Printer, Mbabane (Issue 4).

[29] SNA, Proclamation by His Majesty King Sobhuza II April 12, 1973, The Government Printer, Mbabane (Issue 4).

294   H. P. DLAMINI

which represented the voice of the Swazi people. Under the King's 1973 proclamation, the Prime Minister and his Cabinet were no longer to be responsible to the legislature, which had been discarded, but directly to the King, who no longer needed to act in accordance with the advice of the Prime Minister. This means Swaziland was no longer a constitutional monarchy after the April 1973 auto-coup d'état. It became an absolute monarchy, since King Sobhuza II was not answerable to any constitution but, rather, to himself. King Sobhuza II's auto-coup d'état did not render the state services dysfunctional. It simply transferred the constitutional foundations of the nation to King Sobhuza, and he became the constitutional referral point in Swaziland because he was now the new constitution. All services continued, but at the discretion of the King.

The April 1973 auto-coup d'état signified, in essence, a transition from a constitutional monarchy with relatively broad powers that were shared with the Cabinet, in line with the tradition of parliamentary democracy, to an an absolute monarchy that was unchecked by the limitations of any constitutional provisions, since the constitution had been abrogated. Like France's Louis XIV (1638–1718), the King was the personalization of the state and could rightly claim: *l'état cést moi* (I am the state) and the state is me.[30] This concept depicts royal absolutism in political terms with King Sobhuza as a classic case; it is a concept of proprietary kingship—the King as the owner of everything, and the sole fountain of rights and privileges in the kingdom of Swaziland. The April 1973 new order thus established the King as the sovereign and proprietor of the Swazi nation. The King was the supreme law and sovereignty emanated from him. He was no longer the recipient of delegated functions and authority from a constitutional document. The inherent right and authority in his person belonged to him and were not delegated; they did not come from another source but from himself. This was largely the totalitarian position of the King and he governed-in-council without a legislature until 1978, when he decided once more to establish a bicameral parliament elected through a system of Swazi traditional electoral methods known as *tinkhundla*. But the reinstatement of Parliament did not stop King Sobhuza II from governing by proclamations and decrees, because he was still the constitution. By opting

---

[30] *l'état cést moi* is a common expression in constitutional history which captures the notion of royal absolutism. (See T. Shields, 'L'état C'est Moi?', *Africa Report*, 33, 6 [1988], 49; H. H. Rowen, '"L'Etat c'est a moi": Louis XIV and the State', *French Historical Studies*, 2, 1 [1961], 83–98).

to govern without a constitution, King Sobhuza had chosen to sail in a constitutional void in which his modus operandi was the use of proclamations and decrees.

One must not lose sight of the fact that King Sobhuza II had his eyes on the constitutional developments of other independent African nation-states, and he was behaving no differently than other African heads of state, who tended to assume supreme authority by vesting executive, legislative, and judicial powers of the state in themselves as absolute leaders, otherwise referred to as 'big men rulership'. The difference lies in the fact that King Sobhuza II completely jettisoned his country's constitution while equally exercising a 'big man rule' by concentrating all powers in his hands. But his civilian African counterparts did not dispose of their respective constitutions. They simply panel-beat their constitutions to their taste and conserved them, while exhibiting all the characteristics of 'big men rule' by concentrating all powers in their hands and acting extra-constitutionally. King Sobhuza II was no more absolute than the majority of his African counterparts after independence.[31] The problem with King Sobhuza II was that he opted to govern without a constitution, and this got him into problems with Swazi civil society. The real problem confronting the Swazi monarch was not royal absolutism, but the flagrant absence of a constitution and the governance by proclamation and decrees.

The Attitude of the Swazi Legal Fraternity Towards the April 1973 Repeal of the Constitution

There was no immediate challenge to the abrogation of the Independence Constitution and the institution of governance by proclamation and decrees, given that King Sobhuza II was the law and the law was King Sobhuza. Wanda notes that the King clearly acted outside the law and that there was no judicial challenge to his actions from Swazis. The issue was

---

[31] For the concentration of powers in hands of chief executive in Africa, see Ted Robert Gurr, Keith Jaggers, and Will H. Moore. *Polity II: Political Structures and Regime Change, 1800–1986* (Ann Arbor, MI: Inter-University Consortium for Political and Social Research, 1990); O. Van Cranenburgh, '"Big Men" Rule: Presidential Power, Regime Type and Democracy in 30 African Countries', *Democratization*, 15, 5 (2008), 952–973.

296   H. P. DLAMINI

never brought to the courts for a more reflective and objective legal opinion.[32] There was clearly no room for that, given that anybody who dared could be detained without charge. The 1973 decree also had a provision for detention without charge in the public interest of any person for a renewable period of 60 days. It was the King-in-Council who determined the detention, which could not be challenged in any court of law. Any legal challenge to the 1973 constitutional appeal could go nowhere.

That the 1973 proclamation and decrees were not challenged did not mean that Swazi legal practitioners would maintain their silence forever. The opportunity to speak out on the issue of the repeal of the Independence Constitution was provided by the democratic whirlwind that started blowing through the African continent from the late 1980s,[33] uprooting one-party states, and leaving multipartyism and the expansion of the democratic space in their wake. Although the overwhelming majority of legal practitioners of liberal democratic inclination were very critical of the repeal of the Constitution, the pro-monarchists used cultural arguments to support it.

Taking advantage of this new liberal political environment, different advocates—conveniently labelled the Legal School of Liberal Advocates[34]—stood up to challenge the 1973 repeal of the Independence Constitution and to call for the return to the constitutional order *ante*. In this light, they called for the simple nullification of the King's proclamation of 12 April 1973, and all subsequent decrees made thereunder, on the grounds that they were invalid and unconstitutional. These critics were unanimous that King Sobhuza acted in illegality by abrogating the Constitution and

[32] Wanda, 'The Shaping of the Modern Constitution of Swaziland: A Review of Some Social and Historical Factors', 137–178.

[33] Samuel P. Huntington, 'Democracy's Third Wave', *Journal of Democracy*, 2, 2 (1991), 12–34; C. Manning, 'Assessing African Party Systems After the Third Wave', *Party Politics*, 11, 6 (2005), 707–727.

[34] These advocates, who became active mostly after King Sobhuza II's demise, were treated as a school of thought because of their common hostility towards the jettisoning of the 1968 independence constitution and the concentration of all powers in the hands of the monarchy. They found it irksome that the King assumed supreme authority at the expense of the constitution, by vesting executive, legislative and judicial powers of the State to himself. They felt that the idea of supremacy of the King was inherently inconsistent with constitutionalism, democracy and good governance and was not conducive to the protection, promotion and enjoyment of fundamental human rights, basic freedoms and civil liberties.

that this illegality persisted as long as the monarchy relied on proclamations and decrees as instruments of governance. As was expected, P. M. Dlamini, the Attorney-General, who served as the principal legal advisor to government, argued forcefully *per contra*. The tug of war between the Legal School of Liberal Advocates and the Attorney-General set in, and was useful in x-raying question of the constitutionality of governance without a formal written constitutional document in Swazi history.

The chief proponents of the hypothesis regarding the illegality of the repeal of the Constitution included Advocate L. M. Maziya (instructed by Ben J. Simelane & Associates) and J. Simelane.[35] The hypothesis was constructed on the premise that it was illegal to have scrapped the 1968 Independence Constitution in the first place, because it was the supreme law of Swaziland and there was no constitutional provision for repeal. The 1968 Constitution only provided for alterations to be made to the Constitution. It did not state anywhere that the Constitution should be discarded under any circumstance. Section 2 of the Constitution provided as follows: 'This Constitution is the supreme law of Swaziland and if any other law is inconsistent with this Constitution, that other shall, to the extent of the inconsistency, be void.' Section 134 of the Constitution made provision for the alteration of the Constitution and provided that, for such alteration, a joint sitting of the Senate and House of Assembly would be summoned for the purpose in accordance with the provisions of Schedule 1. Schedule 1 provided for the summoning and procedure of the joint sittings of both Chambers of Parliament. The proposed alteration would then be submitted to the people in a referendum for approval, following which it would be assented by the King to become effective as law.

Advocate L. M. Maziya remarked that King Sobhuza II was not interested in any amendment following due process but, rather, an outright repeal.[36] King Sobhuza II's justification for repealing the Constitution was that there was 'no constitutional way of effecting the necessary amendments to the constitution because the method prescribed by the constitution itself was wholly impracticable and would bring about the disorder which any

---

[35] CRIM.CASE NO. 20/02, In the matter between: LUCKY NHLANHLA BHEMBE Applicant VS THE KING, Respondent CORAM: SAPIRE. C. J. MASUKUJ. For Applicant: Adv. L. M. Maziya (instructed by Ben J. Simelane & Associates) For Respondent: Mr P. M. Dlamini (Attorney-General) JUDGEMENT 17/09/02.

[36] It should be re-emphasised that these critiques were not made at the time King Sobhuza II repealed the constitution but in 2002.

constitution was meant to inhibit'. The intention of the King was not to amend or revise the Constitution, but to repeal it altogether because of its perceived negative effects. The question of repealing the Constitution posed a legal problem, because there was no provision in the Constitution for such a procedure to be followed. The procedure King Sobhuza II followed was therefore illegal. The Legal School of Liberal Advocates noted that it was not clear where the King derived 'the power and authority to repeal the Constitution', and that 'the repeal of the Constitution was [therefore] unlawful'. It was asserted that anything that followed the repeal was therefore unlawful. Advocate L. M. Maziya opined, 'there [appeared] to be no source of the King's power to issue the 1973 Decree and the ensuing ones. This was not provided for in the Constitution or in any other law. The irresistible conclusion, in view of the foregoing is that the King did not have such power.' He emphasized that, 'It [was] therefore clear that the extraordinary procedure of repealing the Constitution was not specially identified and defined in the 1968 Constitution. The power exercised was not derived from the Constitution. The source from which it was derived is unknown.'[37]

Consequently, 'the purported repeal of the Constitution' by King Sobhuza II was 'null and void' and had 'of no force or effect for the reason that the procedure for amending the Constitution set out therein was not followed' in effecting any change in the Constitution. The King therefore had no power in law to legislate by decree, inasmuch as there was no enactment purporting to give him such power. The 1973 proclamation and every decree and its offspring were therefore tainted with illegality. The proclamation, which was the source from which the 1973 decree drew its power and validity 'was poisoned because it was illegal', and this 'poison...[ran] in the veins of all other Decrees as they draw their power and existence from the 1973 Proclamation and Decree'.[38]

---

[37] CRIM.CASE NO. 20/02, In the matter between: LUCKY NHLANHLA BHEMBE Applicant VS THE KING, Respondent CORAM: SAPIRE. C. J. MASUKUJ. For Applicant: Adv. L. M. Maziya (instructed by Ben J. Simelane & Associates) For Respondent: Mr P. M. Dlamini (Attorney-General) JUDGEMENT 17/09/02.

[38] Ibid.

Reverting to Kelsen's Grundnorm (basic norm) legal theory,[39] the School of Advocates made a submission that the April 1973 Royal proclamation and decree never assumed the status of Kelsen's Grundnorm. P. M. Dlamini (Attorney-General) argued that the 1973 Royal proclamation and decree did effectively assume the status of Kelsen's Grundnorm. In order to appreciate the arguments of the protagonists on this vexing question of Grundnorm theory for the governance of Swaziland, it is necessary to highlight what Kelsen's Grundnorm theory is all about.

According to the Grundnorm theory, the legal order of any country that has not undergone any territorial change remains the same, and is considered valid so long as it is established and upheld by any given government. The size of Swaziland did not change after the 1973 events marked by the repeal of the Independence Constitution. Swaziland remained Swaziland. It does not matter whether the constitutional change was legal or constitutional. Whatever legal order such a government establishes remains valid and enforceable as long as the territory remains the same. According to Kelsen's Grundnorm theory:

> The legal order remains the same as long as its territorial sphere of validity remains essentially the same, even if the order should be changed in another way than that prescribed by the Constitution, in the way of a revolution or a *coup d'état*. A victorious revolution or a successful *coup d'état* does not destroy the identity of the legal order which it changes.[40]

Following this logic, Sobhuza II's auto-coup of April 1973 instituted a proclamation and decree as a new legal order of legislating over Swaziland, which remained the same country with no change in the size of its territory. King Sobhuza II's proclamation and decrees were therefore a new legal order over the same territory. King Sobhuza II's proclamation and decrees did not destroy the identity of the existing legal order at all. Although Sobhuza II repealed the Independence Constitution, he proclaimed, inter alia:

---

[39] M. Swarup, 'Kelsen's Theory of Grundnorm', manupatra.com/roundup/330/Articles/Article%201.pdf (accessed September 3, 2018).

[40] M. Swarup, 'Kelsen's Theory of Grundnorm', manupatra.com/roundup/330/Articles/Article%201.pdf (accessed September 3, 2018).

300 H. P. DLAMINI

- That all laws, except the Constitution thereby repealed would continue to operate with full force and effect and would be construed in a manner that would bring them into conformity with that and ensuing decrees;
- That all Judges and other Judicial Officers, Government Officials, Public Servants, Police, Prison and Armed Forces would continue in office and would be deemed to have been validly appointed;
- That certain portions of the repealed Constitution ... which ... were identified were reinstated.[41]

The legal anatomy of Swaziland remained almost literally the same. In other words, the events of April 1973 only resulted in the repeal of the Constitution, but this was not followed by an overhaul of the existing laws in Swaziland. Significant portions of the Independence Constitution were retained in their entirety. Sobhuza killed the Independence Constitution but he resurrected the Constitution in himself and became the supreme law of Swaziland. So, in the legal history of Swaziland, King Sobhuza II became the supreme law of Swaziland following the April 1973 auto-coup. Kelsen's Grundnorm theory stated that:

a revolution or coup d'état ... if ... victorious in the sense that the persons assuming powers under the change can successfully require the inhabitants of the country to conform to the new regime, then the revolution [or coup d'état] itself becomes a law-creating fact because thereafter its own legality is judged not by reference to the annulled Constitution but by reference to its own success.[42]

What this theory infers, in essence, is that law is meant for man and not the other way round. The maker of a new political order also makes the laws that govern that order, and the precedent laws should no longer be a reference point. By successfully repealing the Independence Constitution, King Sobhuza II created a new legal order to which the people of Swaziland subscribed. The Attorney-General implicitly recognized the fact that the events of April 1973 amounted to a coup. The 1968 Constitution,

---

[41] SNA, Proclamation by His Majesty King SOBHUZA II April 12, 1973, The Government Printer, Mbabane (Issue 4) (Emphasis mine).

[42] M. Swarup, 'Kelsen's Theory of Grundnorm', manupatra.com/roundup/330/Articles/Article%201.pdf (accessed September 3, 2018).

which was repealed, was replaced with King Sobhuza II's proclamations and decrees, which saved portions of the old Constitution. The Attorney-General opined that the repeal was successful, and that King Sobhuza II imposed himself as the legal order emanating from his proclamations and decrees, which were efficacious and which the Swazi people accepted. In rebuttal to the lawyers prayer that the 1968 Constitution should be re-instituted, the Attorney-General argued that it was not possible, because constitutional legality in Swaziland was henceforth judged not by reference to the annulled Independence Constitution, but by reference to the King's legal order in the shape of proclamations and decrees. References were no longer supposed to be made to the 1968 Independence Constitution but, instead, to the 1973 proclamation and decrees which had been accepted by Swazis and had become efficacious.

Whether King Sobhuza mobilized security forces and draconian legislation to render the new legal order efficacious is not the point. In the view of the Attorney-General, the proclamation and decrees did become efficacious and gained continuity in the kingdom of Swaziland. King Sobhuza II's coup succeeded and, in line with the Grundnorm theory, the King's proclamations and decrees became the new legal order.

The Attorney-General opined that the post-April 1973 proclamation and decree created a new legal order that was efficacious, and regulated the behaviour and actions of the people of Swaziland. He posited that the validity of a new legal order did not depend on whether the old Independence Constitution was changed by a lawful method. He stated that King Sobhuza's repeal of the Constitution was not challenged and compromised, and his proclamation and decrees survived his era and became a settled efficacious Grundnorm. The issue of the legality of Sobhuza's proclamation and decree was therefore laid to rest.

The pro-monarchical legal experts[43] did not find anything wrong with King Sobhuza II's repeal of the Independence Constitution and the concentration of all powers in his hands as an absolute monarch. They found solace in the cultural argument to support King Sobhuza II's assumption of supreme authority of the state after repealing the Independence Constitution. They felt that the idea of the supremacy of the king is inherently

---

[43] These legal experts who did not conceal their unalloyed support for the Swazi monarchy preferred to be anonymous when I granted them interviews on several occasions in 2015 and I was ethical in respecting their wishes.

302   H. P. DLAMINI

consistent with traditional governance in Swaziland.[44] They argued that, under traditional Swazi law and custom, effective political, military, and religious powers were vested in the monarch who exercised it in conjunction with its various advisory councils—such as the *Libandla*. Consequently, the repeal of the Independence Constitution in 1973 should not be seen in negative light, because the King was an absolute ruler in Swazi culture and tradition so far as the Swazi nation was concerned. Thus, in terms of Swazi law and custom, the King did nothing wrong in 1973, because he traditionally held supreme power in the kingdom of Swaziland, since all executive, legislative, and judicial powers were vested in him. The powers of the King were therefore immutable and he enjoyed customary protection under the traditional idiom *umlomo longacali manga* (the mouth that never lies) which, in essence invoked royal infallibility in the exercise of his functions.[45] The royalists also made the argument in *siSwati: makoti nakafika ekhaya, umgcokisa ngendlela yalopho ekhaya*, which can loosely be translated to mean that after the bride is taken in marriage, the bridegroom is at liberty to dress her the way he wants. In other words, after Swaziland assumed independence, it was at liberty to undertake political reforms according to its needs and the way it wanted.[46]

Following the postulation regarding Swazi culture and tradition, the April 1973 auto-coup d'état can be interpreted as the popular will of the Swazi people to establish a governance order to which the people were used. Such an argument is unquestionably logical and plausible, particularly among the rural population, who were still basking in the memories of a traditional Swazi state. But, in an independent modern Swazi state, this was definitely anachronistic, and weakened by the fact that a modern state has a more sophisticated organization and composition than a traditional state, and is not structured like a pre-colonial state with a simplistic subsistence economy and simple social organization.[47]

---

[44] They opted for anonymity.

[45] For more on the concept of Swazi royal infallibility, see Angelo Dube and Sibusiso Nhlabatsi, 'The King Can Do No Wrong: The Impact of the Law Society of Swaziland v Simelane No & Others on Constitutionalism', *African Human Rights Law Journal*, 16, 1 (2016), 265–282.

[46] Interview with anonymous legal luminary.

[47] For more on simple social stratification of traditional African societies, see A. Tuden and L. Plotnicov (ed.), *Social Stratification in Africa* (New York: Free Press, 1970); R. H. Bates,

The Attitude of the International Community to the April 1973 Repeal of the Independence Constitution

The reaction of the international community to the April 1973 overthrow of the Constitution was largely shaped by the principle of non-interference contained in the OAU and UN Charters, and by the fact that African political regimes had all evolved towards totalitarianism. Both the OAU and the UN provided in their Charters the principle of non-interference in the internal affairs of a sovereign state. In Article 3(2) of the OAU Charter, for instance, member states declared and adhered to the principle of non-interference in the internal affairs of other states.[48] The two important partners of Swaziland—Britain and South Africa—were supportive of the Swazi monarchy in the Cold War context because of its known conservative and anti-communist stance since Swazi independence in 1968.[49] King Sobhuza II had expressed his disdain for the Soviet blend of 'socialism', and even banned the circulation of communist literature in Swaziland following independence.[50] He never expressed any intention of pursuing any brand of socialism, unlike other African countries had done at one point or another, and he never threatened to nationalize foreign-owned industries in Swaziland.[51] Sobhuza's monopolization and consolidation of power after the April 1973 Constitutional repeal also 'meant to convey the picture of stability through a policy of traditionalism and continuity of the economic

Modernization, Ethnic Competition, and the Rationality of Politics in Contemporary Africa. *State Versus Ethnic Claims: African Policy Dilemmas*, 152 (1983), 171.

[48] U. O. Umozurike, 'The Domestic Jurisdiction Clause in the OAU Charter', *African Affairs*, 78, 311 (1979), 197; P. D. Williams, 'From Non-intervention to Non-indifference: The Origins and Development of the African Union's Security Culture', *African Affairs*, 106, 423 (2007), 253–279.

[49] For King Sobhuza II anti-communist stance, see P. H. Bischoff, 'Swaziland: A Small State in International Relations', *Africa Spectrum* (1986), 175–188; T. Simpson, '"The Bay and the Ocean": A History of the ANC in Swaziland, 1960–1979', *African Historical Review*, 41, 1 (2009), 90–117.

[50] R. P. Stevens, 'Swaziland Political Development', *The Journal of Modern African Studies*, 1, 3 (1963), 327–350; C. P. Potholm, *Swaziland: The Dynamics of Political Modernization*, vol. 8. (Berkeley: University of California Press, 1972); Isobel Winter, 'The Post-colonial State and the Forces and Relations of Production: Swaziland', *Review of African Political Economy*, 4, 9 (1977), 27–43.

[51] P. H. Bischoff, Paul-Henri, 'Swaziland: A Small State in International Relations', 175–188.

304   H. P. DLAMINI

status quo'.[52] So, when Sobbhuza abrogated the 1968 Constitution, the British High Commissioner in Swaziland wrote a few days after the incident that he had obtained instructions 'to tell the Swazi Government that Her Majesty's Government proposed business as usual'.[53] South Africa, an important economic partner of Swaziland, found nothing wrong with the abrogation of the Swazi Independence Constitution, and was, instead, full of praise for the Swazi monarch.

The South Africa, radio and press took particular interest in this development, and the South African Broadcasting Service's 'Current Affairs' programme, which was generally considered to echo the sentiments of the apartheid regime, considered the 1973 Swazi constitutional repeal in a favourable light. The South African media noted that King Sobhuza II did not act from fear that the government party would be voted out of office; nor were there any tribal tensions. The King acted in the best interests of his people. The media expressed the view that Swaziland was one of the most prosperous Black states; was endowed with rich agricultural and mineral resources, and plentiful water; and had a per capita income that was more than twice that of Lesotho and Botswana. The South African government was of the opinion that King Sobhuza II was compelled to act in the best political interest of Swazis in a bid to enhance peace and national concord. The South African Broadcasting Service was full of praise for Sobhuza and the Swazi traditional system of government by concensus. It stated:

> Quite simply, King Sobhuza believed that the Swazi [traditional] system of government was better for the Swazi people. Certainly, it is thoroughly democratic. The Libandla, the King's Council, is open to all Swazi males or their representative and the King gives effect to the consensus the Libandla establishes. The system has indeed been described as a classic example of rule by consultations and consent.[54]

The South African endorsement of the April 1973 Swazi royal auto-coup and conservative traditional political system is understandable. Apart from the pro-Western stance of the Swazi government, British and South African capital dominated certain sectors of the Swazi economy up to 1968. After

---

[52] Ibid., p. 176.

[53] P. Q. Magagula, 'Swaziland's Relations with Britain and South Africa Since 1968' (PhD dissertation, Durham University, Durham, UK, 1988), 100–103.

[54] Ibid.

independence, however, South Africa became the main economic partner of Swaziland, supplying the country with more than 95 per cent of its imports by way of a freight haulage system operated by South African Railways. The growth in the manufacturing and mercantile sectors was driven mainly by South African capital.[55] South Africa had not only invested heavily in Swaziland's economy, Swaziland was a member of the Pretoria-dominated Southern African Customs Union (SACU). During the 1980s, Swaziland made financial gains from certain South African businesses that used Swazi territory as a transshipment point in order to circumvent international sanctions on South Africa.[56] Whereas, the Swazi monarch did not pose any threat to apartheid South Africa, Swaziland's Opposition manifested open sympathy with South African radical Black nationalist movements. The Opposition NNCL did not conceal its intentions to open its doors to the ANC in the event of victory.[57] South Africa was, therefore, comfortable with the conservative, despotic political order in Swaziland.[58]

UNDERSTANDING THE POLITICS AND REALITY OF SOBHUZA'S ROYAL BENEVOLENT DESPOTISM AND PATERNALISM

It is clear that the abortion of the Independence Constitution in April 1973 led to the rise and consolidation of an absolute despotic monarchy in Swaziland under King Sobhuza II. Although the coup gave King Sobhuza II absolute powers, he hardly abused them; he functioned more as a

[55] J. Daniel, 'The Political Economy of Colonial and Post-colonial Swaziland', *South African Labour Bulletin*, 7, 6 (1982), 90–113; J. S. Crush, 'The Parameters of Dependence in Southern Africa: A Case Study of Swaziland', *Journal of Southern African Affairs*, 4, 1 (1979), 55–66.

[56] Daniel, 'The Political Economy of Colonial and Post-colonial Swaziland', 90–113.

[57] SITE, EISA. 'Swaziland: Demise of Democracy and the Consolidation of Autocracy (1968–1986)', *Update* (2008), https://www.eisa.org.za/wep/swaoverview3.htm (accessed October 15, 2015); Freedom House. 'Swaziland: A Failed Feudal State', *Freedom House* (2013), https://freedomhouse.org/.../Swaziland-%20A%20Failed%20Feudal% 20State%2015% (accessed October 15, 2015).

[58] Although ANC bases were found in Swaziland, it should be noted that Swaziland was never a member of the frontline states. The Swazi monarchy did not have the military resources to contain ANC activities on its territory. It had to rely on South African intelligence operatives to go after the ANC in Swaziland, especially after signing the 1982 secret pact with South Africa to uproot the ANC from Swazi territory.

benevolent despot than a tyrant and blood thirsty monster, unlike some of his African contemporaries. It is pertinent at this juncture to interrogate the concept of royal Swazi benevolent despotism in order to establish a relationship between despotism and benevolence.

How can a monarch who concentrates all powers in his hands in the spirit of absolutism still qualify as benevolent? It is a mistake to assume that an absolute or despotic ruler is necessarily negative and backward because he does not display democratic credentials. Historically, it is tenable to argue that a despotic leader can equally be benevolent, benign, and dedicated to his people. King Sobhuza II's despotism in Swazi history needs to be qualified. He was a monarch who exercised absolute political power, but a monarch with a 'human face' and 'heart', displaying none of the characteristic cruelty of post-colonial African leaders that were notorious for wanton political persecution and extermination of their political opponents.

While radiating an aura of fatherliness, the monarch consciously endeavoured to empathize and identify with his people in their culture, tradition, and dress code (Fig. 7.1).[59]

Fig. 7.1 King Sobhuza II, dressed in traditional attire and barefoot to empathize with Swazi masses, September 6, 1968 (*Source* Eswatini National Archives)

The cornerstone of King Sobhuza II's despotism were his proclamations and decrees aimed at curtailing civil liberties and holding political opposition at bay. His 1973 proclamation and decrees banned political parties, and prohibited all meetings and processions of a political nature except with the prior consent of the Commissioner of Police, which it is likely would never be given. Consequently, the proclamation made it a criminal offence, punishable by a six-month term of imprisonment, for any person to form or attempt to form a political party, or organize or attend any meeting, procession, or demonstration in contravention of the law.

The decrees designed to outlaw political parties were Decrees 11, 12, and 13, which read as follows:

11. All political parties and similar bodies that cultivate and bring about disturbances and ill-feelings within the Nation are hereby dissolved and prohibited.

12. No meeting of a political nature and no procession or demonstration shall be held or take place in any public place unless with the prior written consent of the Commissioner of Police; and consent shall not be given if the Commissioner of Police has reason to believe that such meeting, procession or demonstration, is directly or indirectly related to political movements or the riotous assemblies which may disturb the peace or otherwise disturb the maintenance of law and order.

13. Any person who forms or attempts or conspires to form a political party or who organizes or participates in any way in any meeting, procession or demonstration in contravention of this decree shall be guilty of an offence and liable, on conviction, to imprisonment not exceeding six months.[60]

These decrees were reinforced with the Prime Minister's powers, together with the power to detain any person for a period of 60 days, renewable without trial or charge. The activities of labour unions were largely curtailed, and they were allowed a very tiny margin of operation.

---

[59] Reminiscences of King Sobhuza in the course of collecting oral data from both his supporters and detractors between 2014 and 2016 were general positive in terms of how he handled those opposed to him and his overall fatherly figure.

[60] See SNA, Proclamation by His Majesty King Sobhuza II April 12, 1973, The Government Printer, Mbabane (Issue 4).

308   H. P. DLAMINI

This type of draconian decree imposed a seemingly permanent state of emergency in Swaziland throughout Sobhuza's reign, and gave the government enough weapons in its armoury to crush any form of political activity by the Opposition. This was a typical African 'big man rule' phenomenon,[61] which was upheld by this apparent permanent state of emergency emanating from the 1973 proclamation.

King Sobhza II undeniably radiated the hallmark of a typical despotic monarch. But Sobhuza's despotism must be nuanced and qualified, because he was never like his contemporaries in Africa, who were blood-thirsty tyrannical despots. The reign of African leaders in King Sobhuza II's time, and even thereafter, was generally catastrophic in human rights terms, characterized by mass detentions, and the torture and deaths of African citizens. Suffice it to give a picture of the human rights situation in Africa during King Sobhuza II's time with just two notorious examples from Equatorial Guinea and Uganda. Equatorial Guinea gained its independence in 1968, like Swaziland, under President Francisco Macías Nguema, who transformed himself into a despotic leader, a tyrant, and a mass murderer. Out of a total population of 300,000, an estimated 80,000 were killed.[62] In 1974, the World Council of Churches reported that large numbers of people had been murdered and one-quarter of the population of Equatorial Guinea had fled abroad, while the prisons were overflowing with political prisoners. On 25 December 1975, Macías Nguema ordered 150 alleged coup plotters executed.[63] He was therefore engaged in genocide of unprecedented scale in that country's history until his removal from power in 1979 by Teodoro Obiang.[64] President Idi Amin of Uganda was another very bad case. Idi Amin's eight-year reign of terror in Uganda (1971–1979) was characterized by widespread killing and torture. Over 300,000 Ugandans lost their lives.[65] He murdered peoples from all walks of life suspected of plotting against him. Hundreds of prominent men and women among

[61] See R. H. Jackson, R. H. Jackson, and C. G. Rosberg, *Personal Rule in Black Africa: Prince, Autocrat, Prophet, Tyrant* (London: University of California Press, 1982).

[62] S. Baynham, 'Equatorial Guinea: The Terror and the Coup', *The World Today*, 36, 2 (1980): 65–71; W. G. Clarence, 'Equatorial Guinea: An African Tragedy' (1990), 603–604.

[63] Ibid.

[64] Ibid.

[65] R. J. Rummel, 'Power, Genocide and Mass Murder', *Journal of Peace Research*, 31, 1 (1994), 1–10; R. J. Rummel, 'Democide in Totalitarian States: Mortacracies and Megamurderers', In *The Widening Circle of Genocide* (Routledge, 2018), 3–40.

the dead included cabinet ministers, Supreme Court judges, diplomats, university rectors, educators, Catholic and Anglican churchmen, hospital directors, surgeons, bankers, tribal leaders, and business executives.[66] President Amin used members of death squads, including the chillingly named Public Safety Unit and the State Research Bureau, to terrorize his own people. The Swazi monarchy was in no way close or comparable to the hideous behaviour with regard to human life practised in both Equatorial Guinea and Uganda, and elsewhere in Africa.

King Sobhuza II's draconian decrees allowed the government a free hand to randomly arrest political agitators and opponents. But these decrees were sparingly used and actually lay fallow most of the time, giving the impression that they were fierce paper tigers. It is for this reason that John Daniel[67] observed that, when the human rights situation of Swaziland is 'measured against most Third World dictatorships, Swaziland [would qualify as] a human rights paradise'. Let us now turn to examine how King Sobhuza II used his draconian decrees against the political opposition to his rule posed by political leaders in 1973 and 1978, and trade unionists in the second half of the 1970s.

The 1973 Arrest and Detention of the Leadership of the Opposition NNLC for 60 Days

Shortly after the passage of the proclamation and decree of 12 April 1973, the Swazi government proceeded with the first detention of Swazis for political reasons. The Opposition NNLC, which had won three seats in Parliament in the 1972 elections, was not expected to back down without a fight following the banning of Opposition parties. The urban centres, workers, students, and the educated elite who gave the NNLC Opposition three seats in Parliament were all waiting for Zwane's response to the King's bombshell decree banning political parties, which had been entrenched in Swaziland since 1960, because he represented the hope of the Progressives and had to reassure them. Zwane was clearly under pressure from his followers to riposte. In his capacity as the voice of the Opposition, Zwane

---

[66] Ibid.

[67] J. Daniel, 'The Political Economy of Colonial and Post-colonial Swaziland', *South African Labour Bulletin*, 7, 6 (1982), 106.

310 H. P. DLAMINI

expressed the view that the kingdom of Swaziland was heading into unacceptable dangerous despotism as all the civil rights were swept away by the king. He made scathing criticisms of the Prime Minister for championing the destruction of democracy in Swaziland, and this statement was treated by the Swazi authorities as defamation.[68] Using the legal provision that allowed for the detention without trial, for a (renewable) period of 60 days, of individuals suspected of causing public disorder, seven key leaders of the Opposition NNLC—Dr Zwane, S. Myeni, M. M. Motha, T. B. Ngwenya, J. Groening, M. M. Mathonsi, and B. Mbuli—were arrested to pre-empt any protests and held in detention.[69] The detention was a clear signal to the Swazi public that the Swazi monarchy meant business about clamping down on any Opposition voices, and had made real its threat by arresting and detaining the chief Opposition figures. King Sobhuza II did not stretch his nets to catch political agitators beyond the principal political leaders. There was therefore no massive arrest of the Swazi Opposition.

King Sobhuza II was in a position of absolute power with his proclamations and decrees to do whatever he wanted. But he combined the massive powers that the draconian decrees gave him to contain opposition to his rule with some conciliatory overtures by humbling himself to negotiate a *modus vivendi* with the political Opposition. This attitude is explained by the fact that, in King Sobhuza II's mind, he was the 'father' and 'protector' of all Swazis. He privileged the making of peace with every Swazi as the 'king of all Swazis'. King Sobhuza II therefore magnanimously sent several emissaries to the Opposition leaders in detention to encourage them to reconcile with him as a precondition for their rehabilitation and freedom. He requested T.B. Ngwenya—the controversial Opposition figure whose case in court witnessed the defeat of the government, setting in motion a crisis—to remain in Swaziland and enjoy royal pardon and favours on the condition that he renounced his Opposition stance and declared loyalty to him.[70] Such an offer placed Ngwenya in a difficult position, because he had

[68] Department of State, Diplomatic Cables, Full text of "State Dept cable 1973-125658"—archive.org; https://archive.org/stream/State-Dept-cable-1973-125658/StateDept. Publication date 1973 (accessed May 19, 2015).

[69] A. R. Booth *Swaziland: Tradition and Change in a Southern African Kingdom* (Boulder, CO: Westview Press, 1983), 75.

[70] Declassified/Released US Department of State EO Systematic Review June 30, 2005, https://www.wikileaks.org/plusd/cables/1973MBABAN01945_b.html (accessed April 2, 2015).

been in the political spotlight in Swaziland and the courts had upheld the issue of his citizenship, which the pro-monarchists interpreted as a challenge to the King and the Progressives celebrated as victory for the separation of powers and modernity. Ngwenya was in the awkward position of pleasing his constituents by remaining adamant, or conceding to the overtures of the monarch and having his freedom and royal favours. Ngwenya chose to reject the king's offer to pursue the matter of his citizenship in court. Against a background of his obstinacy, King Sobhuza had no choice but to deport him to South Africa on 28 June 1973 on the grounds that he was not a citizen of Swaziland.[71]

King Sobhuza II also extended a hand of fraternity to Dr Ambrose Zwane, leader of the outlawed NNLC Opposition party, offering him an amnesty if he declared loyalty to him and refrained from Opposition politics. The King promised to release him after 60 days' detention and definitively close the chapter of any differences with him, unless he committed another offence in violation of the Kings Order-in-Council by engaging in political activities again.[72] Like Ngwenya, Dr Zwane found himself in the difficult position of compromising his principles regarding the liberal democratic Swaziland for which his supporters were yearning. Dr Zwane turned down the King's offer and opted to be incarcerated for another 60 days but, according to the Police Commissioner, Timothy Velabo Mthethwa,[73] Zwane later indicated he had no intention of seeking further incarceration and he was released.[74] The other detainees, who were considered 'small fish', were released unconditionally after 60 days. After Zwane accepted being released, he lived in Swaziland freely and ran his clinic as a medical doctor in Manzini until 1978 when, once again, he got into trouble with the authorities.

Developments in 1978 forced the Opposition out of their reserve. King Sobhuza II's 1978 proclamation envisaging the re-establishment of

---

[71] Ibid.

[72] Ibid.

[73] Timothy Velabo Mtetwa was Swaziland's first Royal Swaziland Police Service (RSP) Commissioner from 1972–1981. He was responsible for policing in the tumultuous years following the 1973 Royal Proclamation (See Sandile Nkambule, 'First Police Commissioner TV Wants to Service History Book', *Observer*, Saturday October 15, 2016).

[74] Declassified/Released US Department of State EO Systematic Review June 30, 2005, https://www.wikileaks.org/plusd/cables/1973MBABAN01945_b.html (accessed April 2, 2015).

312   H. P. DLAMINI

a bicameral parliament through the *tinkhundla* no-party system meant the era of multipartyism was definitely over in Swaziland. Reinstating the legislature without concurrently unbanning the Opposition to participate in the elections was worrisome, because it effectively sealed the hopes of political parties from ever competing in any elections in Swaziland again. Discussions about the unbanning of political parties and agitations for it naturally gripped public attention. Critical voices among the educated elite and the working classes were raised in favour of the reintroduction of competitive party politics, and these forced the security apparatus to be on the alert. The Police proceeded to arrest some 15 suspected individuals, including Dr, Ambrose Zwane and Prince Dumisa Dlamini, using the decree on detention for 60 days without trial of individuals suspected of causing public disorder.

The cases of Dr Zwane and Prince Dumisa Dlamini are worth examining so as to reveal King Sobhuza II's benign rehabilitation policy towards political opposition to his rule. The Police sought out Dr Zwane who was picked up on 10 February 1978 at his clinic in Manzini city and taken to a high-security prison where he was incarcerated without charge.[75] Zwane and certain incarcerated Opposition figures eventually escaped from Swaziland and sought exile in Tanzania.[76] The fact that detainees of such a calibre were able to escape shows, to a certain extent, the laxity of the detention. Prince Dumisa Dlamini did not escape and, while he was still held in detention, King Sobhuza II offered him an olive branch of peace and reconciliation, if he could agree to abdicate from politics, pay an oath of fealty to him, and be rehabilitated as a free citizen. Prince Dumisa Dlamini reconciled with the king on his terms and was appointed to head a government parastatal. At the point of King Sobhuza II's demise, Prince Dumisa Dlamini had become a prominent figure in Swaziland owing to royal patronage.

King Sobhuza II may have been a despot, but he was a benign and paternal one. His treatment of political opponents was one of bite, blow, heal, and reconcile, rather than one of political assassinations and disappearances

---

[75]'Swazi Opposition Leader, a Doctor Arrested Once Again at His Clinic', *The New York Times Archives*, February 11, 1978.

[76]Life in exile is definitely not easy and Zwane negotiated his way back to Swaziland through the good offices of President Julius Nyerere of Tanzania who got into a deal with the Swazi government which resulted in a royal pardon for Zwane and his return to Swaziland on condition that he agreed 'to abide by the laws of the country and never made any political party agitation'. He died in Swaziland in 1998.

that characterized some post-independence African political regimes. John Daniel states that, by 1980, King Sobhuza II's Swaziland had no political detainees because they had all been released, making Swaziland a real paradise of human rights[77] in a continent that was tainted with jails full of political prisoners.

Trade Union and Student Challenge to Sobhuza's Rule and the Response of the Government

King Sobhuza II largely contained and eliminated political opposition to his rule, but Swazis still looked for alternative outlets to challenge him—through trade unions with the support of students. Trade unions, like political parties, came under scrutiny. But there was a major difference between the two because of their respective objectives. Trade unions were not purposely established to capture political power, although they were used as instruments to fight for workers' rights and also express political dissent. Trade unions were legal and were tolerated, but official policy was hostile to their existence on the grounds that they, like political parties, were 'un-Swazi', constituted divisive forces in society, and their activities had the capacity to impact adversely on the investment climate. Unlike political parties, which were banned outright, trade unions were generally not banned. Nonetheless, the provisions of the state of emergency were equally applied to undermine their operation. Under these regulations, any gathering of a political nature of 10 or more individuals required police authorization, which was hardly ever given. It did not even matter if the agenda of the unions was clearly to elect their office bearers. The emergency regulations forced trade unions into inactivity, but they still managed to occupy public space when their grievances built up. A few examples can be offered here.

A march by striking railway workers in 1975 was broken up with tear gas by the Swazi police. The Swaziland National Union of Teachers staged a strike under the leadership of Albert Heshane Shabangu over salaries in October 1977. This was overwhelmingly supported by a wave of student demonstrations that were suppressed by riot police, and mass arrests were made to contain the situation. Because of the strike, the Teachers Union

---

[77] J. Daniel, 'The Political Economy of Colonial and Post-colonial Swaziland', *South African Labour Bulletin*, 7, 6 (1982), 106.

314   H. P. DLAMINI

was banned. There was also a violent strike by sugar workers in 1978.[78] These strikes had a deleterious effect on trade unionism, because almost all trade unions were outlawed. A total of nine registered trade unions existed in Swaziland in January 1970. Before King Sobhuza II's demise, except for a microscopic trade union of bank workers formed in the early 1970s, none was functioning. Due to its small size and its recognition by the employers, the bank workers union was allowed to exist. Moreover, the size of the union precluded it from being a threat to the larger Swazi political establishment.[79] Trade unions were generally banned because of strikes, but this was not followed by prolonged detentions or any form of witch-hunting of Swazis. Every Swazi was considered a human being under Sobhuza's despotic rule.

FROM ATTEMPTS AT FILLING THE CONSTITUTIONAL VOID TO THE RE-ESTABLISHING OF A PARLIAMENT UNDER THE *TINKHUNDLA* SYSTEM

The idea of repealing the Independence Constitution in April 1973 and governing Swaziland thereafter without a constitution but with proclamations and decrees was taken hastily. It was a bad move that embarrassed the government, owing to the popular uproar against the move as unnecessary and untenable in the governance of a modern state. It was gathered that this awkward situation was caused by some pro-royalist hardliners who constantly put pressure on King Sobhuza to do away with the Constitution, which they saw as document that gave the courts the authority to challenge the government. Furthermore, they feared that the Opposition was gradually growing in strength due to people's discontentment, and that this would lead to the weakening and eclipsing of the monarchy. To avert this situation, they put pressure on the King to do away with the Constitution and, above all, multipartyism without having contemplated the implications of such measures on governance. For one thing, civilians do not govern with proclamations and decrees in Anglophone Africa; as a colonial legacy and tradition, it was out of place to do so. Proclamations and

---

[78] J. Daniel, 'The Political Economy of Colonial and post-colonial Swaziland', *South African Labour Bulletin*, 7, 6–7 (1981), 90–113.
[79] Ibid.

decrees are totalitarian governance instruments reserved for military dictatorships in Africa and civilian governments were not expected to rely on military instruments of governance.[80] Sobhuza's reliance on proclamations and decrees as a civilian was a real embarrassment into which the conservative pro-royalists had led him. It was a novel type of high-handed governance system that raised eyebrows: there was intensive debate in public about the feasibility of governing a modern state without a constitution,[81] and the monarch had a lot of explanations to give a bewildered nation. According to US declassified diplomatic cables, the government of Swaziland consulted Western embassies on how to handle the mess of repealing the Constitution: the advice was that King Sobhuza II had to return to constitutional order as soon as possible. This explains why, within just a week of repealing the Constitution, the Swazi government made an announcement assuring the public and the international community that the royal proclamation was only an interim measure, and that a Constitutional Commission would be appointed that would work towards establishing a new constitution that was pertinent to Swazi traditions and international trends as soon as possible.[82] But the government did not commit itself to any fixed deadline regarding when a new Constitution would be ready. The King later promised that, within a six-months deadline, he would appoint a Constitutional Committee that would work on a new form of hybrid democracy based on a combination of Swazi and Western values, and report to him.[83]

Members of government on their part attempted to allay the fears of Swazis about the constitutional void by making various promises to the people. The Minister of Justice, Senator P. Dlamini, announced on 4 May

---

[80] For more information on governance by decree and order-in-council during state of emergencies, see W. E. Scheuerman, 'Survey Article: Emergency Powers and the Rule of Law After 9/11', *Journal of Political Philosophy*, 14, 1 (2006), 61–84; A. F. Uduigwomen, *Schools of Law and Military Decrees* (Calabar: Ebenezer Printing Press & Computer Services, 2000); V. T. Le Vine, 'The Fall and Rise of Constitutionalism in West Africa', *The Journal of Modern African Studies*, 35, 2 (1997), 181–206; J. H. Pain, 'The Reception of English and Roman-Dutch Law in Africa with Reference to Botswana, Lesotho and Swaziland', *The Comparative and International Law Journal of Southern Africa* (1978), 137–67.

[81] Such concerns about the governing of Swaziland were expressed in the media (see 'New Constitution Coming: Official', *Times of Swaziland*, May 4, 1973).

[82] Kalley, J. 'Swaziland Election Dossier 2003' (2003), 3–4. https://www.eisa.org.za/pdf/ED_Swaziland2003.pdf (accessed 23 October 2014)

[83] 'Constitutional Commission to Be Set Up: Decree Is Temporary', *Times of Swaziland*, April 20, 1973.

316   H. P. DLAMINI

1973 that a new constitution was being drafted that would take into account the nation's hopes, aspirations, and historic and cultural background. King Sobuza also despatched a delegation to New York to explain why he had repealed the Independence Constitution. The delegation comprised government ministers and certain prominent diehard monarchists such as Prince Ncabaniso Qhawe Dlamini, the grandfather of this author, and Brigadier Fonono Dvuba.[84] The message of the delegation to the US government was that Swaziland was in search of a new constitution that would respond to its historical realities and to the specificities of Swaziland, and that there were royal commissions on the ground consulting with the people on the appropriate constitution to be drafted for Swazis. In a press briefing in New York, the Minister of Industry, Mines and Tourism indicated that a new constitution for Swaziland was in preparation and he estimated that it would be ready within six months time.[85] However, this did not happen, as further consultations with the people continued.

On Independence Day, 6 September 1973, the King announced the establishment of a Royal Constitutional Review Committee. The members of the committee included Polycarp Dlamini as Chairman, David Cohen, the Attorney-General, Arthur Khoza as Secretary, and Prince Sifuba as a member. [86]The Royal Constitutional Review Committee was tasked with travelling throughout Swaziland to obtain the views of Swazis on the type of constitution they wanted. They were to enquire into the fundamental principles on which the kingdom of Swaziland's constitution should be based, having regard to the history, culture, and way of life of the people of Swaziland, and the need to harmonize these facts with the modern principles of constitutional and international law.[87] After the fact-finding exercise, the Royal Constitutional Review Committee recommended a mixed constitutional system that contained both Swazi traditional values and Western political traditions.

In 1974, a more robust Committee was established to continue consulting the people on the issue of a new constitution for Swaziland, with

---

[84] Interview with Prince Majawonke Dlamini. The people of the chiefdom of Mbelebeleni still remember the praises King Sobhuza II had for the US delegation in a speech the king made during his birthday at Mankayane in 1973.

[85] 'New Constitution Coming: Official', *Times of Swaziland*, May 4, 1973.

[86] J. S. M. Matsebula, *A History of Swaziland*, 261.

[87] 'Constitution Committee Appointed', *Times of Swaziland*, September 21, 1973.

Table 7.1 Swaziland Royal Constitutional Committee

Kuseni Hlophe	Chairman
Velaphi Dlamini	Secretary
Mkhulumandvulo Mamba	Member
Buya Mdiniso	Member
Magangeni Magongo	Member
Prince Mabandla Dlamini	Member
Prince Mahhomo Dlamini	Member
Prince Gabheni Dlamini	Member

Source Public Library of the US Diplomacy, Constitutional Commission Makes its Report, 13 June 1975. Matsebula, 265

similar terms of reference as the initial Committee.[88] The representatives comprising the Royal Constitutional Committee are given in Table 7.1.

On 12 June 1975, the Chairman of the Royal Constitutional Committee announced that they had presented their final report to King Sobhuza on the key elements to be included in the new constitution. Although the Swazis were not sensitized to the main issues concerned in the making of a modern constitution, the Royal Constitutional Review Committee reported that Swazis wanted a 'no-party state', with the traditional SNC being the only decision-making body, and that there should be a two-chamber House of Parliament composed of an Assembly and a Senate.[89] The recommendations from the Constitutional Committee appeared to be confusing, as they proposed that decision-making in a modern state should be reserved for the traditionalists of the SNC while, at the same time, recommending the creation of a bicameral House of Assembly without specifying what its functions would be.

The King reviewed the Royal Constitutional Committee's report in collaboration with the SNC and proceeded to appoint another committee that would draft the new constitution.[90] On the basis of the 1975 report submitted by the Royal Constitutional Committee and the advice of the SNC, King Sobhuza decided to institute a traditional system of governance for Swaziland known as the *tinkhundla* system. It would be put in place by

[88] 'Constitution Committee', *Times of Swaziland*, September 13, 1974.

[89] Public Library of the US Diplomacy, Constitutional Commission Makes Its Report, June 13, 1975, http://www.wikileaks.org/plusd/cables/1975MBABAN00987_b.html (accessed June 28, 2015).

[90] Ibid.; Matsebula, *A History of Swaziland*, 265.

318   H. P. DLAMINI

means of an Order-in-Council. It was, however, only in March 1977 that the King announced in specific terms that he was contemplating replacing the parliamentary system of government based on multiparty democracy, as contained in the repealed 1968 Constitution that Swazis were used to, with a new system of government based on Swazi traditional elements that had no room for multipartism. In October 1978, the *tinkhundla* based system of election was formally passed under the Establishment of Parliament Order, 1978, and the Regional Councils Order, 1978.[91] The Order establishing the *tinkhundla* system revolved around the king, and Swazi culture and tradition. All candidates had to be independent of any political party and stand as individuals with the approval of the chiefs who were answerable to the monarch.

Towards Understanding the Origin and Changing Role of the *Tinkhundla* in Swazi Political History

The *tinkhundla* was originally a grouping of chiefdoms in the kingdom of Swaziland designed by King Mswati II (ruled c. 1840–c. 1865) for purposes of administrative and military mobilization. King Sobhuza II revived the *tinkhundla* traditional administrative units in the 1930s, as part of his policy of revitalizing the traditional regimental system that was in terminal decline. He also used the *tinkhundla* during World War II as recruitment units for labour and soldiers for the war effort.[92] The *tinkhundla* was not, therefore, initially intended for electoral purposes, and did not form part of the electoral system when multiparty politics was introduced in colonial Swaziland.

The British colonial administration established and delimited Electoral Constituencies or Districts for election purposes with the introduction of competitive politics. The 1967 election that proceeded independence was conducted according to a block vote system[93] in an arrangement that

---

[91] Ibid.

[92] Levin, 'Swaziland's Tinkhundla and the Myth of Swazi Tradition', 1–23.

[93] In the Block-voting system voting takes place within carved electoral constituencies in which multiple political parties present candidates. It is a winner takes it all system because political party whose candidates obtain an absolute majority wins all the seats. It is sometimes criticised for advantaging parties that have only a slight electoral advantage and heavily penalising those groups that have substantial minority support (see D. M. Farrell, *Electoral Systems: A Comparative Introduction* (Houndmills: Palgrave Macmillan, 2011).

was enshrined in the Swaziland 1968 Independence Order. The House of Assembly election of 1972 in independent Swaziland was organized along the block vote system under which Swaziland was divided into eight large constituencies, delimited by independent Delimitations Commission. Each constituency returned three members to the House of Assembly. Each voter had three ballots and the three candidates with the highest number of votes in each constituency were elected by plurality in the multiparty context.

In October 1978 the establishment of the Parliament of Swaziland Order was finally published with the intention of re-establishing Parliament after the King had repeatedly promised Swazis after he abrogated Parliament in 1973. The 1978 Parliament of Swaziland Order introduced the new *tinkhundla* electoral system which did not revive competitive party politics but established a party-less elections. Swaziland was divided into 40 *tinkhundla* or electoral districts each of which elected two representatives to form an electoral college, which then elected the Members of the House of Assembly. Parliamentarians were therefore to be indirectly elected. The King appointed an Electoral Committee to supervise elections. The architects of the *tinkhundla* system of government projected it as a home-grown system. It incorporated elements of the African one party system, Swazi traditional governance with the Swazi King and chiefs at the centre, and elements of Western governance.[94]

[94]The philosophy of the *Tinkhundla* system is developed in the Imbokodvo Policy document titled: *A handbook to the Kingdom of Swaziland, Swaziland Government Information Services, The Philosophy, Policies and Objectives of the Imbokodvo National Movement*; also see Report of the Tinkhundla Review Commission; Government Gazette Extraordinary, No. 855 of 1992. For a more comprehensive study on the Tinkhundla system of government, see, T. Mkhaliphi, 'The Extent to which the Tinkhundla-Based System of Government Articulates the Decentralization Principles: A Practitioner's Analysis', Paper presented at a Research Seminar, University of Swaziland, February 11, 2015; M. A. Mamba, 'Tinkhundla: A Study of A System' (MA thesis, University of Swaziland, 2006); A. M. Mkhatshwa, 'An Assessment of the Tinkhundla System of Government, 1973–2003' (BA Project, University of Swaziland, 2004); P. H. Bischoff, 'Why Swaziland Is Different: An Explanation of the Kingdom's Political Position in Southern Africa', *Journal of Modern African Studies*, 26, 3 (1988), 457–471; Baloro, 'The development of Swaziland's Constitution: Monarchical Response to Modern Challenges', 19–34; Wanda, 'The Shaping of Modern Constitution in Swaziland: A Review of Some Social and Historical Factors', 137–178.

African Party-Less Guided Consensus Democracy

The *tinkhundla* system of government espoused a 'party-less' system of government reminiscent of traditional African politics, which was based on consensus and not competing political party formations.[95] The no-party system was Swaziland's response to the emergence of single parties on the continent brought about by an autocratic president who was usually its automatic chairman. Instead of establishing a single political party to which everybody belonged, the *tinkhundla* elevated King Sobhuza as the fountain of politics in Swaziland, with the responsibility of directing political activities in the kingdom in collaboration with the SNC and his chiefs in a conflict-free harmonious atmostphere without wrangling among Swazis. Thus, the *tinkhundla* system vested sovereignty in the King[96] and not the people of Swaziland, and positioned him as a parental benevolent despot.

Since the idea of political parties, whether single or multiple, smacked of Westernization, Sobhuza endeavoured to distance himself from political parties and invented something typically Swazi. He did this by stating clearly in the Order-in-Council of 1978 that all political parties remained banned, and that it was unlawful for anyone to organize and canvass for political support under the banner of a political party. Although the Order-in-Council made Swaziland a party-less state, the Swazi King incarnated and radiated the spirit of a typical one-party-state in Africa, since he and his acolytes were the sole authority to select candidates for political office in the same way as the ruling single-party machinery in one-party African countries monopolized the animation of political life in the country.

The similarities between the African one-party state model and the *tinkhundla* no-party state model were, therefore, glaring to such an extent

---

[95] President Julius Nyerere of Tanzania had convincingly argued that traditional Africa was a classless society and this structure did not necessitate Western multiparty democracy. Rather, the one-party consensual system was more appropriate and closer to African culture and tradition (see A. Mohiddin, 'Ujamaa: A Commentary on President Nyerere's Vision of Tanzanian Society', *African Affairs* [1968], 130–143; K. W. Grundy, 'The "Class Struggle" in Africa: An Examination of Conflicting Theories', *The Journal of Modern African Studies*, 2, 3 [1964], 379–393.

[96] The *Tinkhundla* system entrenched the absolutism of the Swazi monarchy comparable to absolutism of pre-eighteenth century revolutionary France.

that it was almost impossible to distinguish between the two models.[97] The governments of the one-party states in Africa, just like the government of Swaziland, were made up of individuals drawn mainly from the ruling party or the defunct royal *Imbokodvo* that had wrestled power at independence. In both the one-party and the *tinkhundla* models, there was a clearly identifiable culture of the systematic neutralization of the Opposition through a series of strategies, including coercion, co-optation, accommodation, and exclusion. The President of the one-party-state was usually the chairman of the national party and he maintained tight control over its operations. The Swazi King was the source of all authority, like the chairman of the single party, and was responsible, in collaboration with Swazi chiefs, who were answerable to him, for the choice of officials to all elective offices. Using his over-bearing influence in the *tinkhundla* system, the Swazi King prevented the Western-educated radicals and reformers from gaining any foothold in the political arena during the first *tinkhundla* parliamentary elections in 1978.

WHAT WAS TRADITIONAL ABOUT THE FIRST *TINKHUNDLA* PARTY-LESS PARLIAMENTARY ELECTIONS OF 1978?

The *tinkhundla* electoral system was run by Swazi traditionalists. The 1978 Order created the following bodies:

i. the National Electoral Committee to supervise the elections; and
ii. the Electoral College to elect members of parliament.[98]

The mandate and machinery of conducting elections to the Electoral College, and, ultimately, to Parliament, was vested in an Electoral Committee comprising seven persons to oversee elections of members to the Electoral College and Parliament in line with Swazi traditional practices (Table 7.2).

After King Sobhuza had repeatedly promised his people he would restore Parliament, a general election was held on 27 October 1978 under the

---

[97] H. P. Dlamini, 'The Tinkhundla Monarchical Democracy: An African System of Good Governance?' In Olga Bialostocka (ed.), *New African Thinkers Agenda 2063: Culture at the Heart of Sustainable Development* (Cape Town: HSRC PRESS, 2018).

[98] SNA, Establishment of Swaziland Parliament Order, King's Order-in-Council No. 23 of 1978.

322   H. P. DLAMINI

Table 7.2 Members of the Electoral Committee

Name of Member	Comment
1. Gwece Dlamini	Chief Electoral Officer
2. Shadrack J. S. Sibanyoni	Executive Officer
3. Mndeni S. Shabalala	Member
4. Mabalizandla Nhlabatsi	Member
5. Major Magomeni Ndzimandze	Member
6. Richard Velaphi Dlamini	Member
7. Ndleleni Gwebu	Member
8. Chief Mfanawenkosi Maseko	Member

Source 'Election details announced', The Times of Swaziland, 17 October 1978

control of the traditionalists. The new *tinkhundla* system strengthened the position of the country's traditionalists since going to Parliament depended on them, as those who had the last word, and not the people. Due to significant demographic shifts of the population of Swaziland—numbered at 547,452 in 1978, having been about 300,000 in 1960— the number of seats in the 1978 elections was increased to 50, from the 24 seats at the 1972 election. The elections were not preceded by voter registration, and it was the responsibility of chiefs to ensure that only Swazi citizens voted in the elections.[99]

The character, breadth, and real mandate of the Electoral Committee were detailed in section 4 of the Establishment of Parliament in Swaziland Order, 1978 as follows:

Without derogating from the generality of section 3 thereof, the Electoral Committee shall:
(a) lay down guidelines and directives for the conduct of elections of the Inkhundla level and at the Electoral College;
(b) be represented by at least two persons, not necessarily members of the Committee at each meeting of any Inkhundla convened as hereinafter provided for the purpose of electing two delegates to the Electoral College;

[99]Tom Lodge, Denis Kadima and David Pottie (eds.), "Swaziland" in: Compendium of Elections in Southern Africa (2002), EISA, 328–330

(c) be present at the election by the Electoral College of members of Parliament or in the majority of its members; and
(d) be responsible for the proper conduct of the elections at Tinkhundla or the Electoral College, as the case may be, having regard to the traditional practices at meetings and elections of the Swazi nation, save in so far as such practices may be inconsistent with the directives and guidelines laid down by the Electoral Committee.[100]

The Electoral Committee acted under the tight control and supervision of the *indvuna yetinkhundla* (chief) who was defined as the person appointed by the King as the *indvuna* over the *tinkhundla*. This *indvuna* and his cabinet were directly answerable to the King.

On 12 October 1978, the King summoned the SNC to the *sibaya* (people's open parliament) and announced that he was sending his men to the *tinkhundla* to explain to Swazis how the *tinkhundla* electoral system worked. The King's emissaries consisted of Mndeni Shabalala, Prince Gabheni, Velaphi Dlamini, Chief Mfanawenkosi Maseko, Mabalizandla Nhlabatsi, Ndleleni Gwebu, and Capt. Montgomery Ndzimandze and Prince Dabede who represented the *Ngwenyama*. Even though the King had sent emissaries throughout the country to explain the nature and purpose of the *tinkhundla* elections, confusion still arose over many aspects of the elections, particularly the issues of holding elections without the registration of voters, the nomination of candidates standing for the elections, and even the procedure for elections. Matters were compounded by the fact that the election had been planned in a legal vacuum because the new constitution, under which it was to be conducted, had not yet been promulgated. The election decree had simply stated that the constitution would be promulgated after the people and the King had accepted it.[101]

It was expected that, before an election took place in a modern state, the National Electoral Committee would have provided general information on the election concerning polling stations; the qualification of voters in terms of age, citizenship, and residency; the registration of voters; and essential statistics that were accessible to the electorate. Voters should have attained voting age, should be in possession of a voter's card and identity card , and

[100]SNA, Establishment of Swaziland Parliament Order, King's Order-in-Council No. 23 of 1978.

[101]T. Lodge, D. Kadima, and D. Pottie (eds.), "Swaziland" in: Compendium of Elections in Southern Africa (2002), EISA, 328–330

324   H. P. DLAMINI

be aware of their polling stations. The candidates running for the various offices should have been made known to the electorate in advance of voting day so as to allow them to make informed choices. These preliminaries were never organized, because the traditionalists had their own way of doing things that negated the essentials of any electoral process.

No voter registration took place before the 1978 *tinkhundla* elections. There was the feeling that there was no need for one, since every electorate was supposed to be known by the chief and his inner council. The electorate consisted of every adult male or female aged from 18 years, and they were expected to go to the nearest *inkhundla* for the voting exercise. Although no documentary proof of age or citizenship was demanded, it was the duty of each chief, through his councillors, to see that all the people voting and contesting for positions were genuine and qualified Swazi citizens.[102]

The *tinkhundla* voting system was steeped in a traditionalism of which the pillar of the system was King Sobhuza II and Swazi traditional authorities, who were his faithful acolytes. Forty *tinkhundla* electoral constituencies were established in the kingdom of Swaziland. Villages and their chiefs were grouped into electoral constituency areas known as council areas, each council area (*inkhundla*) being under the control of an area chairman, the *ndvuna*. In the second half of the 1970s, Sobhuza II appointed one Supreme Chairman as the Officer in charge of a *tinkhundla* (an *indvuna yenkhundla*). Local chiefs controlled their local councils, but the chairman of the *tinkhundla* was appointed by the *ndvuna ye tinkhundla*. Matters from chiefs' local councils could be referred to the local *nkhundla* before being taken to the SNC. Each *nkhundla* had its own inner executive committee (*bucopho*). Elections took place within the 40 *tinkhundla* constituencies under the control of traditional authorities.

For electoral purposes, the 40 *tinkhundla*s (electoral constituencies) that represented administrative or council units would elect two out of four candidates to form an Electoral College to go to Lobamba for an electoral meeting to elect 40 members (not from themselves) for the House of Assembly by secret ballot. An order of the King was to determine the date, time, and place of the election of parliamentarians.

Voters did not elect their representatives directly, because their primary responsibility was to elect members of the Electoral College. It was the responsibility of the Electoral College to select candidates for Parliament,

---

[102] J. S. M. Matsebula, *A History of Swaziland* (Longman, 1988), 267.

implying that parliamentary elections were indirect. In the 1978 poll, in which an estimated 55 per cent of the potential voters participated in electing members of the Electoral College, 80 out of 160 candidates were chosen. The Electoral College was slated to elect 40 parliamentarians and the King was to nominate 10 others, bringing the total number of parliamentarians to 50. These 50 people would be sworn in as members of Parliament. The parliamentarians would, in turn, elect 10 people and the King would nominate a further 10 to the Senate or Upper House. These 20 people would then be sworn in as Senators.

The First and Last *Tinhkhundla* General Elections of 27 October 1978 Under King Sobhuza II

King Sobhuza II's repeated promises to Swazis to restore Parliament were fulfilled by the holding of a general election under the *tinkhundla* system on 27 October 1978. This October 1978 *tinkhundla* election was the only one that the monarch organized before his demise, and was unprecedented in the electoral history of Swaziland—from the selection procedure of the nominees to the election proper that involved the Swazi population. The *tinkhundla* elections started with the formation of the Electoral College of 80 members, which Swazis were invited to elect.[103] Voters were registered, although everybody was expected to attend the polls where they were resident. Every adult male or female from 18 years of age was invited to go to the nearest *inkhundla* (chief's *kraal*) for the voting booth and some had to trek distances of about 30 kilometres, or even more. The issue of identification and citizenship was left in the hands of the chiefs and their traditional councils. The polling booth was a temporary enclosure erected for the purpose that had four passages leading out from it. A chief's *inkhundla* inner committee (*bucopho*, or traditional councillors) nominated four candidates of either sex in each of the 40 *tinkundla* constituencies from which the public was to elect two. The public was excluded from the nomination process of the candidates, and their role was restricted to electing two from the four. The traditional authorities were unquestionably the preponderant determinants of who should be elected, while the general public was reduced the role of mere electors.

---

[103] A graphic illustrated account of this first Tinkhundla election is provided by Matsebula, *A History of Swaziland*, 266–270. Except otherwise indicated any allusion to this election it taken from Matsebula.

At midday on 27 October 1978 (voting day), the public was invited to close their eyes for a prayer. After the prayer, the local area chairman (*indvuna yenkhundla*) announced the names of the four nominees who were expected to make brief acceptance speeches, and each was shown a stool provided at the entrance of the passage leading out of the enclosure. It was the *indvuna yenhkundla* who gave a brief biography of each nominee to help the electorate make informed decisions. The nominees were not supposed to speak beyond their acceptance speeches.

The voting process was very dramatic and required that each person walked through the passage where the person of their choice sat. The two nominated candidates who obtained the highest number of votes were declared winners. The counting of the votes was done by two officials on either side of the passage who took stock of the voters as they filed out of the passages. The totals were handed to other senior officials who channelled them to the electoral officer to take to the local *indvuna yenkhundla*, who was mandated to announce the two winners who were then transported to Lobamba to wait for further instructions.

On 5 November 1978, the elected members of the Electoral College of the kingdom of Swaziland all assembled at the Lozitha Royal Palace, where the king instructed them on how to elect 40 members of Parliament. The King advised them to be judicious and to elect people of integrity who would serve the nation. He urged them not to be guided by race, gender, place of birth, age, or level of education. He appointed an electoral officer to take charge of the elections.

The Electoral College initially nominated 60 candidates to stand for parliamentary elections on 13 November 1978, following a thorough check on their integrity and citizenship that included their home address, chiefs, and local *indvuna*. One candidate was disqualified on the grounds that he was a civil servant. Of 59 candidates, the Electoral College elected 40 on 16 November 1978, and the King added 10 nominees, bringing the total to 50.

These *tinkhundla* maiden parliamentarians were sworn in on 16 January 1978. Soon after the parliamentarians had elected 10 Senators and the King had nominated 10 more, the 20 Senators were sworn in on 17 January 1978. Out of a House of 70 legislators, there were six Whites, three Eurafricans, and four Swazi women. The indirect elections at the secondary level under the *tinkhundla* system produced the members of Parliament (see Appendix B). The King also appointed members of the Cabinet (see Table 7.3).

7 FROM KING SOBHUZA II'S AUTO-COUP ... 327

Table 7.3 Members of Cabinet emanating from the tinkhundla system

1.	Prime Minister	Major General Maphevu Dlamini
2.	Deputy Prime Minister	Mshamndane Sibandze
3.	Minister of Commerce, Industry and Mines	Prince Ncaba
4	Minister of Agriculture	Abednego Kuseni Hlophe
5.	Minister of Education	Archdeacon Sphetse Dlamini
6.	Minister of Finance	J. F. L. Simelane
7.	Minister of Health	Dr Samuel Hynd
8.	Minister of Home Affairs	Prince Gabheni
9.	Minister of Works, Power and Communications	Dr V. S. G. Leibbrandt
10.	Minister of Justice	Polycarp Dlamini
11.	Minister without portfolio	R. V. Dlamini

Source Official Report of the First Meeting of the First Session of the Third Parliament of Kingdom of Swaziland, 16th and 19th January 1979

The names of the assistant ministers are presented in Table 7.4. Bicameralism was inherited from the 1968 Constitution with Lower and Upper Houses.[104] On 18 January 1979, the King called the nation to the *sibaya* (traditional parliament) where he introduced the new parliamentarians and ordered the Governor of Lobamba to announce the reappointment of Major-General

Table 7.4 Deputy ministers and assistant ministers

	Ministry	*Name of deputy minister*
1.	Deputy Minister for Agriculture	Prince Mahhomu
2.	Deputy Minister for Education	W. M. Magongo
3.	Minister of State for Establishments and Training	Enock B. Simelane
4.	Deputy Minister of Labour	Chief Bhekimpi Dlamini
5.	Deputy Minister of Finance	J. R. Masson
6.	Deputy Minister of Works, Power and Communications	Dabulumjiva Nhlabatsi
7.	Deputy Minister of State for Foreign Affairs	Lawrence Mncina

Source Official Report of the First Meeting of the First Session of the Third Parliament of Kingdom of Swaziland, 16th and 19th January 1979

[104] See SNA 1968 Constitution.

328   H. P. DLAMINI

Maphevu as the Prime Minister. On 19 January 1978, the King officially opened the new Parliament.

The Cabinet and Royal Absolutism

The 1978 Order-in-Council establishing the *tinkhundla* system of government served further to consolidate and entrench the powers of the Swazi monarchy. It vested the executive authority of the country in the King. He was empowered to appoint the Cabinet, including the Prime Minister, Deputy Prime Minister, and all ministers, at his discretion. Unlike under the 1968 Constitution, the King was no longer required to have regard to the political make-up of the House of Assembly since multipartyism had been banned, and every member of the House was a royal appointee and faithful. The King was no longer obliged to consult the Prime Minister in appointing ministers to the Cabinet. In theory, the doctrine of collective responsibility to Parliament had been explicitly preserved in Swaziland. In practice, it would seem that the Prime Minister and his Cabinet ministers ranked at par both before Parliament and the King, because 'the Prime Minister [could] not legally dismiss or even discipline … a member of his Cabinet whom he found wanting in the execution of his duties'. The tenous position of the Prime Minister was further underscored by the provisions of section 71(2) of the establishment of the Parliament of Swaziland Order 1978, which empowered the King to dismiss the Prime Minister or any other minister from office at any time. He could remove the Prime Minister if there were a resolution of no confidence in him, or if the government of Swaziland was passed by the House of Assembly, or if he were unable to perform the duties of his office, or was guilty of misbehaviour. There was, however, some limitation to the King's power to dismiss the Prime Minister contained in the following proviso to section 71(2):

> Provided that before removing the Prime Minister or other Minister from office on the ground of any such inability or misbehaviour, the King shall appoint a tribunal consisting of a Chairman and two other persons to enquire into the matter and report to the King on the facts thereof and render such advice to the King as it may deem fit.[105]

---

[105] Establishment of the Parliament of Swaziland Order, King's Order-in-Council No. 23 of 1978.

Section 71(4) seemed to take away what was provided in section 71(2) by stating that the enquiry by the tribunal was subject to the following conditions: it was to be held in camera; its members were appointed by the King only; its appointments were not to be published in the Government Gazette; it prepared a confidential report for the King only; and the proceedings and regularity of the inquiry and its conclusions were not challengeable in any court of law. In practice, King Sobhuza was answerable to nobody. The King never instituted any inquiry before the dismissal of prime ministers.

Essentially, the *tinkhundla* system of a party-less democracy[106] that King Sobhuza established by the 1978 Order effectively set up and legalized a monolithic political order in which the Swazi monarch reigned supreme. The Legislature and Cabinet were composed of his appointees, and he was at liberty to hire and fire any official.

THE PARADOX OF THE COEXISTENCE OF ELECTED LEGISLATIVE AND EXECUTIVE ORGANS OF GOVERNMENT, AND THE CONTINUITY OF DECREES AND ORDERS-IN-COUNCIL

Perhaps the singular most important event of constitutional importance during Sobhuza's years of constitutional void was the establishment of the *tinkhundla* system that allowed for elections into the House of Assembly

---

[106]Democracy under one-party or 'party-less' rule is a distinct political model that stands out in its own category. In Swaziland, as in other African countries which used to have legally established one-party states, it is not appropriate to think in conventional terms of a government and an opposition to describe the regime as democratic. "Single party" or "party-less" states also claim to be democratic in the sense that they allow free discussions, within fairly broad limits but they proscribe free association outside the single party system. Those who disagree fundamentally with the ruling party or regime are not allowed to form rival political party to promote their own agenda. They must either keep quiet and conform, or seek to advance their cause by resorting to unconstitutional means. A different yardstick is therefore needed to evaluate "democracy" in a one part or "party-less" state from a multiparty regime. (For more on democracy under one party rule see W. Tordoff, 'Tanzania: Democracy and the One-Party State', *Government and Opposition*, 2, 4 (1967), 599–614; G. Schubert, 'Democracy Under One-Party Rule? A Fresh Look at Direct Village and Township Elections in the PRC', *China Perspectives*, 46 (2003); K. J. O'Brien and L. Li, 'Accommodating "Democracy" in a One-Party State: Introducing Village Elections in China', *The China Quarterly*, 162 (2000): 465–489; B. Magaloni and R. Kricheli, 'Political Order and One-Party Rule', *Annual Review of Political Science*, 13 (2010), 123–143.

330   H. P. DLAMINI

and Senate, and which made it possible for King Sobhuza to form a government with a degree of legitimacy. Parliament, which had been forcefully dissolved in 1973, was able to resurface in 1978, holding its first meeting on 16 January 1979. The 1978 Establishment of the Parliament of Swaziland Order nominally returned legislative powers to the people. One would have expected that the re-establishment of the Legislature would mean the return to constitutional order.[107] This did not happen, because King Sobhuza was still taking his time to provide Swaziland with a constitution.[108] Sobhuza believed the *tinkhundla* system of government was appropriate for Swazis, because it accommodated consensus and societal harmony, as opposed to the Western model of competitive canvassing of votes in a multiparty context.[109] The Swazi monarch continued to rule by decrees and Orders-in-Council despite the fact that Parliament had been instituted, because Swaziland had no constitution.

Conclusion

This chapter examined King Sobhuza II's auto-coup d'état against the Independence Constitution that resulted in a constitutional void. Proclamations and decrees became unprecedented instruments of governance to the uneasiness of all, and successive royal commissions to draft and adopt a replacement constitution for Swaziland never came to fruition. Although King Sobhuza was a typical despot *par excellence*, he was a despot with a difference. Unlike his African counterparts—such as Macias Ngeuma and Idi Amin, who slaughtered hundreds of thousands of their citizens suspected of opposing their rule, King Sobhuza II never engaged in such excesses. Rather, he excelled as a benevolent and paternal despot, for which he should be remembered in history. His political opponents were generally detained for short periods of time, and he characteristically showed compassion and

---

[107] The 1978 Establishment of the Parliament of Swaziland Order nominally returned legislative powers to the people, declaring that the monarchy could issue no further royal decrees until a new constitution entered into force.

[108] King Sobhuza and his successor continued to issue a number of Decrees, which purported to amend the 1973 Proclamation and Decree. These included the King's Proclamation No. 1 of 1981, King's Decree No. 1 of 1982; The Tribunal Decree of 1987; Decree No. 1 of 1999; Decrees Nos. 1, 2 and 3 of 2001, which all seek to amend certain portions of the Proclamation.

[109] Interview with Prince Majawonke Dlamini at Manzini Extension 6, June 22, 2015.

7 FROM KING SOBHUZA II'S AUTO-COUP ... 331

fatherliness towards them, and kept the door for reconciliation and rehabilitation permanently open. Before the demise of Sobhuza II, Swaziland did not count a single political prisoner in its jails, thereby making Swaziland a haven for human rights in Africa.

It was also revealed in this chapter that King Sobhuza II, like any despot in his era, did away with multipartyism and introduced the *tinkhundla* non-party political system as Swaziland's version of a 'party-less' or single-party state. King Sobhuza II established the *tinkhundla* traditional system of government in Swaziland by the Proclamation instrument of the 1978 Order-in-Council. The *tinkhundla* were actually electoral constituencies whose responsibility was to initiate the process of voting royal nominees to Parliament. Under the *tinkhundla* system, the Legislature and Cabinet of pro-King Sobhuza II supporters were established. The *tinkhundla* was a monolithic system under the firm control of the Swazi monarch, and made it possible for King Sobhuza to reign supreme with the total compliance of his people.

References

Oral Interviews

Interview with Anonymous Legal Luminary.
Interview with Prince Majawonke Dlamini.

Archival Sources

Swaziland National Archives
SNA, 1968 Swaziland Constitution.
SNA, His Majesty's Speech to a large crowd at Lobamba on the Historic Occassion in the afternoon of the April 12, 1973 (SNA).
SNA, Swaziland Government Gazette Extraordinary, Vol. XII, Mbabane, Tuesday April 7,1973, No. 578. Proclamation by His Majesty King Sobhuza II.
SNA, Proclamation by His Majesty King Sobhuza II April 12, 1973, The Government Printer, Mbabane (Issue 4).
SNA, *A Handbook to the Kingdom of Swaziland, Swaziland Government Information Services, the Philosophy, Policies and Objectives of the Imbokodvo National Movement.*
SNA, Report of the Tinkhundla Review Commission; Government Gazette Extraordinary, No. 855 of 1992.
SNA, Establishment of Swaziland Parliament Order, King's Order-in-Council No. 23 of 1978.

332 H. P. DLAMINI

NEWSPAPER ARTICLES

'First Police Commissioner TV Wants to Write History Book', *Swazi Observer*, October 15, 2016.

'Constitutional Commission to Be Set Up: Decree Is Temporary', *Times of Swaziland*, April 20, 1973.

'New Constitution Coming: Official', *Times of Swaziland*, May 4, 1973.

'Constitution Committee', *Times of Swaziland*, September 13, 1974.

'Constitution Committee Appointed', *Times of Swaziland*, September 21, 1973.

HIGH COURT OF SWAZILAND REPORTS

Lucky Nhlanhla Bhembe v The King Criminal Case 75/2002 (High Court), per Masuku; Nhlanhla Lucy Mbembe & Ray Gwebu and Another Criminal Case 75 & 11 of 2002 *per* Sapire CJ (Unreported).; Gwebu & Another.

Ray Gwebu and Lucky Nhlanhla Bhembhe, Swaziland Court of Appeal Case Nos. 19/20, 2002 as yet (unreported), Zwane, Hlatshwayo and Khumalo.freedom house.

PROCLAMATIONS AND DECREES

King's Proclamation No. 1 of 1981, King's Decree No. 1 of 1982.

The Tribunal Decree of 1987; Decree No. 1 of 1999.

Decrees Nos. 1, 2 and 3 of 2001.

BOOK, JOURNAL ARTICLES AND THESIS

Baleiwaqa, T. 'Reflections on the Civilian Coup in Fiji', *Coup: Reflections on the Political Crisis in Fiji* (2001), 24–30.

Baloro, J. 'The Development of Swaziland's Constitution: Monarchical Responses to Modern Challenges', *Journal of African Law*, 38, 1 (1994), 19–34.

Bates, R. H. 'Modernization, Ethnic Competition, and the Rationality of Politics in Contemporary Africa', *State Versus Ethnic Claims: African Policy Dilemmas*, 152 (1983), 171.

Baynham, S. 'Equatorial Guinea: The Terror and the Coup', *The World Today*, 36, 2 (1980), 65–71.

Berger, S. 'Guatemala: Coup and Countercoup', *NACLA Report on the Americas*, 27, 1 (1993), 4–7.

Bischoff, P. H. 'Swaziland: A Small State in International Relations', *Africa Spectrum* (1986), 175–188.

Bischoff, P. H. 'Why Swaziland Is Different: An Explanation of the Kingdom's Political Position in Southern Africa', *Journal of Modern African Studies*, 26, 3 (1988), 457–471.

Booth A. R. *Swaziland: Tradition and Change in a Southern African Kingdom* (Boulder, CO: Westview Press, 1983).

Bruun, G. *The Enlightened Despots* (New York: Henry Holt, Rinehart and Winston, 1967).

Cameron, M. A. 'Latin American Autogolpes: Dangerous Undertows in the Third Wave of Democratisation', *Third World Quarterly*, 19, 2 (1998), 219–239.

Cameron, M. A. 'Self-Coups: Peru, Guatemala, and Russia', *Journal of Democracy*, 9, 1 (1998), 125–139.

Clarence-Smith, W. G. 'Equatorial Guinea: An African Tragedy' (1990), 603–604.

Clark, J. F. 'The Decline of the African Military Coup', *Journal of Democracy*, 18, 3 (2007), 141–155.

Costa, E. F. 'Peru's Presidential Coup', *Journal of Democracy*, 4, 1 (1993), 28–40.

Crush J. S. 'The Parameters of Dependence in Southern Africa: A Case Study of Swaziland', *Journal of Southern African Affairs*, 4, 1 (1979), 55–66.

Daniel, J. 'The Political Economy of Colonial and Post-colonial Swaziland', *South African Labour Bulletin*, 7, 6 (1982), 90–113.

Dlamini, H. P. "The Tinkhundla Monarchical Democracy: An African System of Good Governance?' In Olga Bialostocka (ed.), *New African Thinkers Agenda 2063: Culture at the Heart of Sustainable Development* (Cape Town: HSRC Press, 2018).

Dixit, K. M. 'Absolute Monarchy to Absolute Democracy', *Economic and Political Weekly* (2005), 1506–1510.

Do, Q. T., and Iyer, L. 'Geography, Poverty and Conflict in Nepal', *Journal of Peace Research*, 47, 6 (2010), 735–7480.

Dube, A., and Nhlabatsi, S. 'The King Can Do No Wrong: The Impact of the Law Society of Swaziland v Simelane No & Others on constitutionalism', *African Human Rights Law Journal*, 16, 1 (2016), 265–282.

Farrell, D. M. *Electoral Systems: A Comparative Introduction* (Houndmills: Palgrave Macmillan, 2011).

Ghoshal, B. *Indonesian Politics, 1955–59: The Emergence of Guided Democracy* (K.P. Bagchi, 1982).

Grundy, K. W. 'The "Class Struggle" in Africa: An Examination of Conflicting Theories', *The Journal of Modern African Studies*, 2, 3 (1964), 379–393.

Gurr, T. R., Jaggers, K., and Moore, W. H. *Polity II: Political Structures and Regime Change, 1800–1986* (Ann Arbor, MI: Inter-University Consortium for Political and Social Research, 1990).

Hachhethu, K. 'Legitimacy Crisis of Nepali Monarchy', *Economic and Political Weekly* (2007), 1828–1833.

334   H. P. DLAMINI

Holiday, D. 'Guatemala's Long Road to Peace', *Current History*, 96, 607 (1997), 68.

Huntington, S. P. 'Democracy's Third Wave', *Journal of Democracy*, 2, 2 (1991), 12–34.

Hutt, M. 'King Gyanendra's Coup and Its Implications for Nepal's Future', *Brown Journal World Affairs*, 12 (2005), 111.

Hutt, M. 'Nepal and Bhutan in 2005: Monarchy and Democracy, Can They Co-exist?', *Asian Survey*, 46, 1 (2006), 120–124.

Iyer, V. 'Courts and Constitutional Usurpers: Some Lessons from Fiji', *Dalhousie Law Journal*, 28 (2005), 27.

Jackson, R. H., Jackson R. H., and Rosberg, C. G. *Personal Rule in Black Africa: Prince, Autocrat, Prophet, Tyrant* (London: University of California Press, 1982).

Kenney, C. D. *Fujimori's Coup and the Breakdown of Democracy in Latin America* (Notre Dame: University of Notre Dame Press, 2004).

Khumalo. B. 'The Politics of Constitution-Making and Constitutional Pluralism in Swaziland Since 1973', *UNISWA Research Journal*, 10 (1996), 1–19.

Kuper, H. *Sobhuza II, Ngwenyama and King of Swaziland: The Story of an Hereditary Ruler and His Country* (New York: Africana Publishing Company, 1978).

Levin, R. 'Swaziland's Tinkhundla and the Myth of Swazi Tradition', *Journal of Contemporary African Studies*, 10, 2 (1991), 1–23.

Le Vine, V. T. 'The Fall and Rise of Constitutionalism in West Africa', *The Journal of Modern African Studies*, 35, 2 (1997), 181–206.

Levitsky, S. 'Fujimori and Post-party Politics in Peru', *Journal of Democracy*, 10, 3 (1999), 78–79.

Lodge, T., Kadima, D., and Pottie, D. (eds.). "Swaziland" in: Compendium of Elections in Southern Africa (2002), EISA, 328–330.

Magagula, P. Q. 'Swaziland's Relations with Britain and South Africa Since 1968', PhD dissertation, Durham University, Durham, UK, 1988, 100–103.

Magaloni, B., and Kricheli, R. 'Political Order and One-Party Rule', *Annual Review of Political Science*, 13 (2010),123–143.

Mahmud, T. 'Jurisprudence of Successful Treason: Coup D'etat & Common Law', *Cornell International Law Journal*, 27 (1994), 49.

Mamba, M. A. 'Tinkhundla: A Study of A System', MA thesis, University of Swaziland, 2006.

Manning, C. 'Assessing African Party Systems After the Third Wave', *Party Politics*, 11, 6 (2005), 707–727.

Matsebula, J. S. M. *A History of Swaziland* (Johannesburg: Longman, 1988).

Mauceri, P. 'State Reform, Coalitions, and the Neoliberal Autogolpe in Peru', *Latin American Research Review* (1995), 7–37.

Mkhatshwa, A. M. 'An Assessment of the Tinkhundla System of Government, 1973–2003', BA Project, University of Swaziland, 2004.

Mohiddin, A. 'Ujamaa: A Commentary on President Nyerere's Vision of Tanzanian Society', *African Affairs* (1968), 130–143.

Obotetukudo, S. W. (ed.). *The Inaugural Addresses and Ascension Speeches of Nigerian Elected and Non-elected Presidents and Prime Minister, 1960–2010* (Lanham, MD: University Press of America, 2010).

O'Brien K. J., and Li, L. 'Accommodating "Democracy" in a One-Party State: Introducing Village Elections in China', *The China Quarterly*, 162 (2000): 465–489.

Pain, J. H. 'The Reception of English and Roman-Dutch Law in Africa with Reference to Botswana, Lesotho and Swaziland', *The Comparative and International Law Journal of Southern Africa* (1978), 137–167.

Potholm, C. P. *Swaziland: The Dynamics of Political Modernization*, vol. 8 (Berkeley: University of California Press, 1972).

Powell, J. M., and Thyne, C. L. 'Global Instances of Coups from 1950 to 2010: A New Dataset', *Journal of Peace Research*, 48, 2 (2011), 249–250.

Protzel, J. 'Changing Political Cultures and Media Under Globalism in Latin America', *Democratizing Global Media: One World, Many Struggles* (2005), 101–120.

Rowen, H. H. '"L'Etat c'est a moi": Louis XIV and the State', *French Historical Studies*, 2, 1 (1961), 83–98).

Rummel, R. J. 'Power, Genocide and Mass Murder', *Journal of Peace Research*, 31, 1 (1994), 1–10.

Rummel, R. J. 'Democide in Totalitarian States: Mortacracies and Megamurderers', In *The Widening Circle of Genocide* (Routledge, 2018), 3–40.

Sampford, C. 'Making Coups History', *World Politics* Review, 22 (2010),1–10.

Scheuerman, W. E. 'Survey Article: Emergency Powers and the Rule of Law After 9/11', *Journal of Political Philosophy*, 14, 1 (2006), 61–84.

Schubert, G. 'Democracy Under One-Party Rule? A Fresh Look at Direct Village and Township Elections in the PRC', *China Perspectives* 46 (2003).

Scott, H. M. (ed.), *Enlightened Absolutism: Reform and Reformers in Later Eighteenth Century Europe C. 1750–1790* (Basingstoke: Macmillan, 1990).

Shields, T. 'L'état C'est Moi?', *Africa Report*, 33, 6 (1988), 49.

Simpson, T. '"The Bay and the Ocean": A History of the ANC in Swaziland, 1960–1979', *African Historical Review*, 41, 1 (2009), 90–117.

Smith, A., Louis, X. V. Louis, X. V. I., Spain, B. Philip, V., England, H. George I. Theresa, F. W. I. M. 'Europe in the Age of Enlightenment, 1720–1789', *A Handbook of Civilization: Earliest Times to the Present* (1974), 308.

Stevens, R. P. 'Swaziland Political Development', *The Journal of Modern African Studies*, 1, 3 (1963), 327–350.

Tordoff, W. 'Tanzania: Democracy and the One-Party State', *Government and Opposition*, 2, 4 (1967), 599–614.

Tuden, A., and Plotnicov L. (Ed.). *Social Stratification in Africa* (New York: Free Press, 1970).

336 H. P. DLAMINI

Uduigwomen, A. F. *Schools of Law and Military Decrees* (Calabar: Ebenezer Printing Press & Computer Services, 2000).

Umozurike, U. O. 'The Domestic Jurisdiction Clause in the OAU Charter', *African Affairs*, 78, 311 (1979), 197.

Upreti, B. C. *Maoists in Nepal: From Insurgency to Political Mainstream* (Delhi: Gyan Publishing House, 2008), 46.

Van Cranenburgh, O. '"Big Men" Rule: Presidential Power, Regime Type and Democracy in 30 African Countries', *Democratization*, 15, 5 (2008), 952–973.

Wanda, B. P. 'The Shaping of the Modern Constitution of Swaziland: A Review of Some Social and Historical Factors', *Lesotho Law Journal: A Journal of Law and Development*, 6, 1 (1990), 137–178.

Williams, P. D. 'From Non-intervention to Non-indifference: the Origins and Development of the African Union's Security Culture', *African Affairs*, 106, 423 (2007), 253–279.

Winter, I. 'The Post-colonial State and the Forces and Relations of Production: Swaziland', *Review of African Political Economy*, 4, 9 (1977), 27–43.

Zwane, S. H. 'Constitutional Discontinuity and Legitimacy: A Comparative Study with Special Reference to the 1973 Constitutional Crisis in Swaziland', Unpublished LLM Dissertation, University of Edinburgh (1988).

SEMINAR PAPER

Mkhaliphi, T. 'The Extent to which the Tinkhundla-Based System of Government Articulates the Decentralization Principles: A Practitioner's Analysis', Paper presented at a Research Seminar, University of Swaziland, February 11, 2015.

INTERNET SOURCES

CRIM.CASE NO. 20/02, In the matter between: LUCKY NHLANHLA BHEMBE Applicant VS THE KING, Respondent CORAM: SAPIRE. C. J. MASUKUJ. For Applicant: Adv. L. M. Maziya (instructed by Ben J. Simelane & Associates) For Respondent: Mr P. M. Dlamini (Attorney-General). JUDGEMENT 17/09/02. https://swazilii.org/sz/judgment/high-court/03/3. Accessed August 27, 2018.

Declassified/Released US Department of State EO Systematic Review June 30, 2005. https://www.wikileaks.org/plusd/cables/1973MBABAN01945_b.html. Accessed April 2, 2015.

Department of State, Diplomatic Cables, Full text of "State Dept cable 1973–125658"—archive.org; https://archive.org/stream/State-Dept-cable-1973-125658/StateDept. Publication date 1973. Accessed May 19, 2015.

Examples of civilian auto-coup d'états include King Letsie III of Lesotho 17 August 1994; President Boris Yeltsin of Russia 1993; President General Pervez Musharraf of Pakistan, November 3, 2007; President Mamadou Tandja Niger, June 29, 2009; President Viktor Yanukovich of Ukraine, September 30, 2010; President Nicolás Maduro of Venezuela March 29, 2017; Prime Minister Hun Sen of Cambodia November 16, 2017. https://en.wikipedia.org/wiki/Self-coup. Accessed June 20, 2018.

Kalley, J. 'Swaziland Election Dossier 2003' (2003), 3–4. https://www.eisa.org.za/pdf/ED_Swaziland2003.pdf. Accessed October 23, 2014.

Public Library of the US Diplomacy, Constitutional Commission Makes Its Report, 13 June 1975. http://www.wikileaks.org/plusd/cables/1975MBABAN00987_b.html. Accessed June 28, 2015.

SITE, EISA. 'Swaziland: Demise of Democracy and the Consolidation of Autocracy (1968–1986)', *Update* (2008) https://www.eisa.org.za/wep/swaoverview3.htm. Accessed October 15, 2015; Freedom House. 'Swaziland: A Failed Feudal State', *Freedom House* (2013). https://freedomhouse.org/.../Swaziland-%20A%20Failed%20Feudal%20State%2015%. Accessed October 15, 2015.

Swarup, M. 'Kelsen's Theory of Grundnorm'. manupatra.com/roundup/330/Articles/Article%201.pdf. Accessed September 3, 2018.

'Swazi Opposition Leader, a Doctor Arrested Once Again at His Clinic', *The New York Times Archives*, February 11, 1978. https://www.nytimes.com/1978/02/12/archives/swazi-opposition-leader-a-doctor-arrested-once-again-at-his-clinic.html. Accessed August 21, 2018.

CHAPTER 8

Conclusion

What sparked constitutional developments in colonial Swaziland in 1960, and what direction did these developments take by the time of King Sobhuza's demise in 1982? This book about the constitutional history of Eswatini (formerly known as Swaziland) has shown that what triggered the constitution-making processes in colonial Swaziland was the rise of nationalist movements in Africa after World War II. The actions of these movements culminated in the independence of Ghana in 1957, followed by the momentous independence year of 1960, when 13 new African nations became independent and took their seats in the UN Assembly as sovereign states, bringing the number to 22. These developments accelerated the whirlwind of decolonization across the African continent. The British colonial authorities responded to these developments and the simmering nationalist agitations of Swazis by unleashing the process of constitution-making. This took place with the full engagement of the Swazi political elite, who were the certain inheritors of the departing colonial authorities.

The Swazi political elite comprised the Swazi monarchy, the White Swazis, and the Western-educated modern political leaders. These stakeholders constituted a configuration that was rarely found in non-settler African colonies. In the constitutional development of Nigeria, Ghana, and Malawi, for instance, the leaders of modern political parties took the lead in the constitutional processes, not traditional rulers. White settlers were

© The Author(s) 2019

H. P. Dlamini, *A Constitutional History of the Kingdom of Eswatini (Swaziland), 1960–1982*, African Histories and Modernities, https://doi.org/10.1007/978-3-030-24777-5_8

339

absent, and neighbouring states did not attempt to intervene in the constitutional developments of these territories. This was not the case with Swaziland, where the influence of the traditional monarchy and the White settlers was all-pervasive and preponderant. Neighbouring South Africa interfered, and even competed, with the British colonial authorities in shaping the constitutional developments in Swaziland. This concatenation of actors makes the constitutional developments of Swaziland somewhat unique.

The Swazi stakeholders were able to navigate and negotiate within the Westminster constitutional framework provided by Britain. Starting from the early 1960s, the Western-educated elite engaged in forming political parties, in order to capture power from the departing British colonial authorities in the same way as Ghana's Kwame Nkrumah and other members of the Western-educated elite in British Africa. These parties included the Swaziland Progressive Party, led by John June Nquku; the Ngwane National Liberatory Congress, under the leadership of Dr Ambrose Zwane; the Swazi Democratic Party, under Sishayi Nxumalo; and the Mbandzeni National Convention, under Clifford Nkosi and Dr George Msibi's Convention Movement. They endorsed the replica of Westminster parliamentary democracy in Swaziland anchored on popular sovereignty, one-man-one-vote, and a ceremonial monarchy. The Western-educated elite in politics enjoyed the support of the intelligentsia and workers who were anxious for societal transformation along modernist lines.

The British and the Western-educated elite set out to establish a Swazi kingdom which, constitutionally, would be a parliamentary democracy with a ceremonial king: it was the standard British practice in her African dependencies to rely on modern politicians heading political parties. While recognizing the importance of the monarchy in Swazi society, the British felt the Swazi king, as a traditional ruler, was ill-fitted for the business of modern governance, and should restrict himself to traditional matters. An additional quality of the Western-educated class of politicians was that they were adept followers of Kwame Nkrumah's brand of nationalism, which called for the immediate independence of Swaziland and 'Africa for Africans'—meaning the nationalization of all sectors and services of the economy. This was the agenda of the modern political leaders who had constituted political parties and the substance of their constitutional debates.

The endeavour by both the British colonial administration and the modern political leaders to relegate the Swazi king to a mere ceremonial head in the transition politics to independence hurt the Swazi monarchists, who felt the king was the only legitimate leader of the Swazi people and that the issue about to whom the British should transfer political power was already settled and was not open for debate. King Sobhuza II and the SNC were opposed to the formation of political parties in colonial Swaziland and to the liberal democratic agenda that allowed one-man-one-vote; this was regarded as 'alien' and 'unAfrican'. The Dlamini dynasty had historically ruled the largely homogenous Swazi society, and the King saw himself as the logical heir of the new political order the British were instituting. The Swazi monarchists expected that the British would deal directly with King Sobhuza in all talks related to decolonization, rather than the leaders of political parties who were not traditionally entitled to govern. King Sobhuza's legitimacy was not to be put to the test through ballot box democracy, since it was ancestrally derived, and upheld by culture and tradition. The monarchists felt that Sobhuza's education and exposure to Western ways were additional qualifications for him to be the successor of the departing British administration. Swazi chiefs and their rural population, who constituted the bulk of the Swazi population, were faithful supporters of the monarchy.

For King Sobhuza II to counter the British anti-monarchical attitude in Swaziland there was no choice but to court and placate the White Swazis and apartheid South Africa, both of whom were ready to support the King to further their own interests. The White Swazis, operating under the EAC led by Carl Todd, were a ready ally of the Swazi monarchy, because they felt threatened by the nationalization and independence discourse of the modern political leaders. The Whites therefore supported the conservative monarchy at the expense of the modern political leaders, whose agenda for nationalization and immediate independence threatened their investments in Swaziland. The Swazi monarch and the White minority therefore constituted an alliance to stem the rising tide of the Western-educated politicians in Swaziland. The White community in Swaziland was economically influential, and backed the Swazi monarch in opposing the modernization schemes pursued by the modern political leaders out of self-interest.

Apartheid South Africa's rapprochement with King Sobhuza II was essential, because the King represented the type of conservative political ideology that kicked against liberal democracy and one-man-one-vote, because such a stance was not good for the apartheid minority White regime. South Africa could not be neutral in Swazi politics due to the location of the territory as a landlocked state. South Africa, therefore, intervened in Swazi affairs through its proxies: the Swazi monarch and the White Swazis. Meanwhile, some White liberals and the Swazi Student Union supported the platform of modern political party leaders.

The constitutional debates in the early 1960s were essentially between two main camps: the progressive modern political leaders, and the conservative monarchists with their White backers. A clear ideological battle line between the two was drawn. For the Swazi Progressive leaders of the Western school of modernization, the political playing field had to be level for everybody, and the Swazi people should speak through the polls on the basis of one-man-one-vote. They insisted that, regardless of their race, the Swazi people should exercise their full sovereignty through the ballot box in the same way other African territories had done. The Swazi King and the traditional SNC were against political modernization through popular sovereignty and ballot box democracy, because these methods constituted a challenge to the traditional Swazi political *status quo* and were considered 'foreign' and 'unSwazi'. The monarchy should be allowed to manage the selection process through acclamation in the traditional way, and the land tenure system should not be changed through nationalization. The White community supported the conservative Swazi monarchy, because they trusted the traditionalists as being the best partners who would protect their economic interests rather than the modern politicians.

As a security strategy, South Africa attempted to replicate itself in Swaziland through its proxies by supporting separate electoral colleges and methods of voting for Blacks and Whites. While standing against full-scale liberal democracy in the shape of universal adult suffrage for Black Swazis on grounds that it was 'unSwazi', King Sobhuza II supported it for 'Whites only' on the grounds that it was European political culture. He stood for separate political treatment for Blacks and Whites from the perspective of separate development along racial lines. Swazis were to be selected for the legislature by the King through the traditional process of acclamation, while Europeans could vote on the basis of universal adult suffrage.

In a bid to placate the Whites for reasons of political expediency, Sobhuza also advocated equal numerical representation for Blacks and Whites in the Legislature, despite the fact that Whites numbered just 9000 while Swazis numbered 270,000. This offer may have sounded crazy, and the modern political leaders used this to mobilize Swazis against their king. But King Sobhuza II knew what he was doing was incredibly unpopular, which was not necessarily what he believed in as later events revealed. The British, like the modern political leaders, were heatedly opposed to this equal representation of Blacks and Whites in the Legislature as being unreasonable and

8 CONCLUSION 343

untenable. The two camps—the Progressives and Conservatives—stuck to their positions, making progress in constitutional talks difficult throughout the early 1960s.

By the time the British government invited the various protagonists from Swaziland to the London Conference in January 1963 to prepare a constitution, no agreement had been reached. The London Conference, as expected, came to nothing despite the efforts of the colonial administration to strike a compromise. The monarchists and the modern political leaders were reluctant to concede to any arrangement under which they would fade out of the political scene. The two camps were therefore engaged in a battle for political ascendency in the new political order Britain was creating. The British were so frustrated with the Swazi political elite that they decided to impose a constitution on Swaziland in December 1963.

The 1963 Constitution largely reflected British constitutional views, but was also envisioned to be a compromise document intended to address the peculiar situation in Swaziland, and to satisfy all the various political inter- est groups in the territory and have them represented in the Legislature. This compromise constitutional document did not produce the desired effect, because it did not satisfy any of the stakeholders. The conservative monarchists cried foul due to the total marginalization of King Sobhuza, who was given a token ceremonial role in the Constitution, since Britain did not expect a traditional ruler to be engaged in modern politics. The White community under Todd rejected the Constitution because equal European and African representation was not included in it and the tradi- tional monarchy, which they preferred to the modern political leaders, was marginalized. The modern political leaders rejected the Constitution on the grounds that it did not provide for one-man-one-vote under universal adult suffrage, and it favoured the White minority who were disproportion- ately overrepresented in the Legislature. Britain ignored these protests and announced general elections in June 1964 that would provide a political road map for Swaziland.

The 1964 elections were a watershed in the constitutional history of Swaziland, because they produced the first legislature, which had the peo- ple's mandate to design the Constitution and determine the fate of the Swazi political elite in modern politics. The elections were opened exclu- sively to political parties in the territory. King Sobhuza II was caught off- guard in his conservative game, because he was opposed to political parties as 'alien' and had previously not considered it logical to form one. The implications of King Sobhuza II not participating in the 1964 elections

344   H. P. DLAMINI

were clear, and South Africa and the Swazi Whites persuaded King Sobhuza II to form a political party urgently even though it was against the colonial policy of the British, which disallowed traditional rulers from indulging in party politics. The traditional SNC engineered the formation of the royal *Imbokodvo* National Movement in response, while the White settlers also formed the United Swaziland Association, and the two parties immediately formed an alliance to fight for the 24 envisaged electoral seats in the June 1964 elections.

Of prime importance was the fact that the royal *Imbokodvo* and White United Swaziland Association won all the seats, while the modern political parties of the Western-educated class won none. The overwhelming number of seats in the Legislature went to the royal *Imbokodvo*: King Sobhuza II was able to position himself at the centre of modern Swazi politics and champion the revision of the 1963 imposed constitution, under British supervision. This was a rare case in the constitutional history of British dependencies: the constitution-making exercise excluded the Western-educated nationalist politicians and privileged a traditional ruler and his White supporters. It was also a deviation from the post-1945 British politics of power devolution, of which the beneficiaries were the Western-educated elite and not the conservative African traditional rulers.

The Constitutional Committee appointed from the Legislature deliberated on the new constitution that was intended to introduce self-government leading to independence without the input of the leaders of the Progressive political parties. But the deliberations of the Constitutional Committee generated unexpected fireworks between the two allies, whose rapport had quickly fallen asunder. The royal *Imbokodvo* and their United Swaziland Association allies could no longer trust each other in the aftermath of the June 1964 elections, due to breaches of their initial agreements and the increasing rapprochement between the *Imbokodvo* and renegade elements of the Progressive party leaders outside Parliament. King Sobhuza II turned out to be a skilful politician, as he quickly incorporated the ideas of the Progressives after winning the 1964 elections and, by so doing, hurt his White allies very badly. King Sobhuza II's party abandoned the idea of numerical equality for Blacks and Whites in the Constitution and, instead, opted for the equality of all races before the law without providing special political privileges for Whites. Further, King Sobhuza II called for the independence of Swaziland as soon as possible, demonstrating that he had virtually become as progressive as the Progressives. The White United Swaziland Association party members on the Constitutional Committee

8 CONCLUSION 345

felt betrayed and fought back, but without success due to the numerical strength of the *Imbokodvo* members. The Whites fought in the House of Assembly and Senate against the overwhelming powers of the monarchy contained in the constitutional draft to be sent to the British government, but still to no avail.

The divisions among the Swazi political class led to the tardy introduction of full internal self-government in colonial Swaziland in 1967. Whereas most African countries were already independent by the mid-1960s, Swaziland was not endowed with full internal self-government for the first time until 1967. The 1967 Constitution was the penultimate constitution that enacted internal self-government in Swaziland before independence. Britain insisted that King Sobhuza II should be subordinate to Parliament in the spirit of the parliamentary system of government. But the monarchists felt this constitutional document was out of tune with Swazi culture and tradition, in which the Swazi King was supreme. When a delegation of the Swazi government went to London in August 1968 for the final constitutional talks before independence, the royalists failed to convince the British to amend the Constitution to give King Sobhuza II absolute power without parliamentary control in a modern independent state. The monarchist quest for royal absolutism was therefore defeated before independence. This book shows the reluctance of the Swazi monarchists to accept that the powers of the king should be held in check by constitutional instruments. The monarchists continued to view modern governance through the lens of the autocratic royal culture and tradition of the Swazi people.

Like other African countries, Swaziland became independent in September 1968 under the British-tailored Westminster Constitution, but the Constitution had a short life span after having functioned smoothly for barely five years. This is explained by the fact that Swaziland was not spared from constitutional developments in other parts of the continent, where a common tendency among Anglophone independent African states, and also certain other non-English speaking states, had been to amend, revise, or alter the British-tailored Westminster Constitution.[1] These constitutional changes also went hand-in-hand with the collapse of multipartyism and its replacement with autocratic single-party regimes, often justified on grounds of adjusting to the realities of African culture and tradition.

[1] Other non-English speaking African states also amended their constitutions.

346   H. P. DLAMINI

These developments appealed to the conservative instincts of the Swazi monarch, who was no lover of the Westminster liberal democratic Constitution of checks and balances.

Unlike elsewhere in erstwhile British Africa, the Swazi monarch actually repealed the Independence Constitution in 1973 and began ruling by Orders-in-Council and decrees. This book has demonstrated that King Sobhuza II actually staged a royal auto-coup d'état by overthrowing the Constitution, which led to the incarnation of the institutions of government that were legally put in place. Although scholars have elaborated on the illegality of the royal abrogation of the 1968 Westminster Constitution, they were short of describing it as a coup d'état. This book has therefore conceptualized King Sobhuza II's 1973 abrogation of the Independence Constitution in appropriate terms as an auto-coup d'état, which supports adding him to the list of historic coup leaders in contemporary African history.

King Sobhuza's auto-coup d'état inaugurated an era of constitutional void in Swazi history that remained in place before his demise in 1982, despite the establishment of a series of Constitutional Committees to provide Swaziland with a new constitutional document. Civilian regimes in post-colonial Africa were generally autocratic in outlook, with constitutional documents that were manipulated at random according to their whims and caprices. They at least governed with a constitution. The Swazi monarch provided a rare case of civilian modern governance taking place in a constitutional void for a protracted period of time.

Ruling by Orders-in-Council and decrees without legislative instruments is what made King Sobhuza II a total autocrat. Royal absolutism was upheld by a series of draconian decrees that held any opposition to King Sobhuza's rule at bay. King Sobhuza II's royal absolutism was combined with paternalism through which he treated Swazis of all schools of thought as his subjects. The absolutism of the Swazi monarch was beyond doubt, but more needs to be done to qualify it within its real political and historical context. King Sobhuza II set himself in place as the constitution of Swaziland. He was a despot, but differentiated himself from the likes of Idi Amin and Macias Nguema because he towered as a benevolent despot—an important fact that has eluded scholarship on African politics. King Sobhuza II combined benevolence and absolutism in the sense that he strived to bring his political opponents into the fold and rehabilitate them. Most of King Sobhuza II's opponents agree that he was a simple, fatherly figure who endeared himself to many by his openness to all Swazis. He went barefoot with them, danced with them, and dined with them. At the time of his demise in 1982, Swaziland had no political prisoners and King Sobhuza II's Swaziland went down on the records as an oasis of human rights in a continent where Africa's rulers massacred and imprisoned their citizens for political reasons.

The *tinkhundla* system that King Sobhuza II established was used to provide Swaziland with a Legislature in 1978. The *tinkhundla* system enabled him to have total control over the political processes in Swaziland, and had come about because of his overwhelming obsession with the idea of creating peace and stability in his country. While he rejected and resisted constitutionalism and liberal democracy, the Swazi monarch still subscribed to bicameralism and a cabinet system headed by a prime minister. However, such an arrangement insisted on the close supervision of elections and the whole process of governance. Other African heads of state also tended increasingly to concentrate powers in their own hands, and eternalized themselves in power like a typical African monarchy. The high propensity manifested by the Swazi monarch to monopolize power and to reject liberal democracy is no different from its counterparts elsewhere in Africa. King Sobhuza II's Swaziland was an absolute monarchy that he created from the prevailing historical circumstances: his political order was essentially a hybridity that created space for the traditional and the modern. It was an order with a real human face.

Appendix A: King Sobhuza II's Speech of April 1960

Your Honour and Gentlemen

We are met here to consider and talk about what is happening in the world today. We have seen from reading newspapers and hearing radio reports that there is quite an unrest and a number of things happening around us. I am sorry that the day has proved unsuitable in that we find that the weather is inclement and that therefore the roads are not very nice to drive on; but I hope that is an omen of something good that may come from what we are trying to do here today. [Rain is an auspicious omen.]

The unrest and many disturbances that I have mentioned just now alarm us and cause us to wonder where the world is leading to, and in particular Africa. The Prime Minister of the United Kingdom in his speech at Cape Town mentioned something to the effect that Africa is on the crossroads—they did not know which side they might have to choose of the two worlds, East or West; he was convinced that the only way to solve the problem would be by treating the African people in a humane way, and in a way that would so satisfy them that they would not join in the struggle that is at present taking place between the East and the West. But as we see the day to day events taking place we feel unhappy about what is happening in Africa, so much so that we cannot pride ourselves in Swaziland that we are not included in the struggles that are taking place elsewhere; nor can we

© The Editor(s) (if applicable) and The Author(s),
under exclusive license to Springer Nature Switzerland AG,
part of Springer Nature 2019
H. P. Dlamini, *A Constitutional History of the Kingdom of Eswatini (Swaziland), 1960–1982*, African Histories and Modernities,
https://doi.org/10.1007/978-3-030-24777-5

350 APPENDIX A: KING SOBHUZA II'S SPEECH OF APRIL 1960

say that we are better off in any way. I personally think that we are utterly in the midst of the trouble. There is no room for complacency.

The most disturbing factor which I think is the source of all trouble in Africa is fear. If only we could get rid of that fear complex we would have solved all our problems. Let us consider what the source of fear is. Now let me explain it in this way—a human being is an animal like other animals; then in this analogy, consider what animals do when they are in fear, and I come to certain conclusions. I have observed that an animal such as a lion will kill a male cub when it is still young, kill it, because once it grows to maturity, it may be a danger to it. So is the case with a human being; it has also got that instinct, with this exception only—that a human being has got the power of thinking ahead on any proposition before him. One finds two types of human beings. There is one type that will bring up his children in such a way that they will become very cruel and unhuman because they have been brought up in a rough way at home, and another type of person will bring up his children in the spirit that they are his children, his responsibility and the future prop of his declining years. Even if he beats the child, he only does so in order to teach him or give him a training of some kind, and when he is grown, the child will say, 'Oh how my father did beat me'; but the father will be in the position to say that 'I wanted you to be a man and by my discipline, I have brought you to what you are now.' And in his own private talks, the child will be able to tell his comrades and friends: 'You know, I was brought up by my father, under hard discipline, but that was good for me and has made me what I am today.' The other child who has been brought up in a brutal manner in a cruel way, when grown will try to do what was done to him by his father. We have come to the conclusion therefore that the difference between human beings and animals is that in the case of human beings where the child has been brought up in a reasonable, humane way, the child will develop to be a good citizen but when the child has been brought up in a brutal and unreasonable way, he may develop to be something unruly, difficult and a bad man generally.

Next we come to consider what happens in the case of the treatment of races be they White or Black. Let us take for instance the case of Europeans and place them in the position of parents who have to bring up their child and we watch how they bring up the child. We find that what actually happens today is that the Europeans will so handle the African that they would not like to see him grow and try to be something to contend with. The treatment the African receives is such that it aims at keeping him just at

APPENDIX A: KING SOBHUZA II'S SPEECH OF APRIL 1960 351

that level so that he does not achieve complete independence. In a way you could say that the European is defending himself, is protecting his interests. Can anyone tell me if it is a good state of affairs that the European must seek to protect his interest in this way? What will be the position if the White man acts thus? The African too will seek to do that at some stage. There are many ways of stifling the development of a person so that he does not grow or does not thrive.

One way would be the elder man will not give full rights to the younger one. Another way is so to apply economic pressure that the African has no incentive to develop. In certain cases you will find that there are many obstructions that are in the way of the development of the younger man. Yet another way is to deny him a full and fundamental education that will enable him to stand on his own, as a man. All those are ways and means of trying to debar the progress of the junior man to develop to the stage where he compares with his senior.

I read the other day something that was said by the leader of the Opposition in the Union, Sir de Villiers Graaff, where he said that he did 'not think that the people overseas who thought that there should be equality even in the economic world were genuine in what they said'. He thought that that would never obtain. He thought they merely meant that there should be equality in a shallow way because no African can hope to be on the same level with the European at the present moment. When I read the article, I wondered what Sir de Villiers really meant, what sort of equality was he referring to, that of stature, or what? I could hardly appreciate his idea, because as an African together with many others we are looking for fair play and justice only. All that the African people seek to achieve is to be able to face their own problems themselves rather than have things done for them by some other person. The type of equality and fair play that we are referring to is not such as to demand that even though someone has his own property here we will try to oust him from that property of his or show off in any way. All we need is fair play in every sphere of life, that's all that we are asking for. Having read that article I felt I wasn't at all convinced that Sir de Villiers had grasped what type of equality we are striving for. I thought of what's happening up in North Africa.

In casting my thoughts over this and wondering what actually it was that was worrying the whole of Africa, and looking around in my predicament, I read one article from a man in East Africa, in Kenya, who says: 'No, we are not actually trying to deprive some other person of his own right, we want rights of our own.' And another one came out from Nyasaland

352   APPENDIX A: KING SOBHUZA II'S SPEECH OF APRIL 1960

who says: 'We are not out to fight against Europeans – we realize that we must live together with the Europeans.' I said: 'This is exactly what we have been thinking ourselves, because, when someone says "We don't want Europeans here, we don't want Europeans with us" I just wonder really if those people are saying so genuinely from the bottom of their hearts. Truly speaking, one wonders if there is anything at all in that type of talk.'

Personally I feel that no man with all his senses and a good citizen could ever think of depriving one of his own property and still remain complacent with somebody else's property. People who try to do such things are those who have had ill-treatment like a child that has been ill-treated from its earlier stages, which usually thinks: 'If one day I grow, I will pay back to this person.' That type of person I am referring to now, is such as we have read about in papers who say: 'Let the Europeans go back overseas' and speak in an unreasonable way like that. But I would like to give an assurance to this House here and now that personally I feel that no true African would think in terms of trying to oust a person from his house or think that he can just chase his neighbours out.

I have often wondered what it is really that these people are struggling for or are striving for when they say that they are trying to establish White protectorates and things of that nature which don't seem to make any sense to me. And I think that's where the danger of the whole thing is. It is a danger that I think is threatening us even in this country Swaziland. I have read that we are trying to get more and more immigrants into Swaziland and I have read also that even though the Union did not want to have immigrants from elsewhere they are now trying to open their doors to get as many people from outside as possible. I think that they will go wrong. That's where the conflagration is going to start which will lay waste the whole countryside.

Let me take for example what is happening in the Union. I am sure that they haven't got a proper solution of the problem how to settle the Africans in that country. Now they are seeking to bring in more and more Europeans. What will the Indians do? The Indians will wonder why they should be debarred from entering the Union, they are human beings like anybody else, and so will the Chinese and other Asians, they also have a right to live. Everybody else will demand: 'Why am I precluded from entering the Union if these other countries have a right to send their people as immigrants into South Africa?' And then there is also the position in which one finds there are Africans who are not allowed to go out into other countries—they are in South Africa all the time and are refused permits or

APPENDIX A: KING SOBHUZA II'S SPEECH OF APRIL 1960   353

passports for going out. They will join the other people that are struggling against what is happening in South Africa and they will join hands with those to whom Mr. Macmillan was referring when he pointed out, 'Let us beware of trying to work the situation in such a way that will estrange ourselves from the Africans and make them join the East instead of going with us.'

To drive my point home, let me make an illustration of what happens among the Swazi. When a man has to reprimand his wife, often there will be found an ill-intentioned man who will come to the wife and say: 'How sorry I feel for you because your husband always scolds you and treats you badly and I would do something better for you.' Such a man is a bad man. And we feel that such a man in the political world is Russia and others like her. Now if you try to stop the Africans from doing what they would like to achieve by way of entering Territories outside the Union or the Asians and others from entering into South Africa, you are really setting against each other the East and West. Personally, I think that among the Africans, there is no need whatsoever, nothing required by way of immigration laws and things of that nature to regulate the migration of the people.

All that type of legislation emanates from the fear complex that is there all the time and each man wants to protect himself. Each side fears that if there are more and more people of the other section coming in they must protect their rights so that these people that come in will not eventually swallow them up. Actually what I mean is that by bringing in more and more Europeans, the country's government is trying to equalize the position so that some day when it is needed to vote the Europeans should not be found to be in the minority or have lesser numbers. There I feel personally that there is nothing to fear, 'they fear leopards in the dark where they do not exist'.

In the protection that they are seeking in this manner, they are getting themselves into worse positions than they would otherwise have been in. Let us take for instance, the example in the Union or Rhodesia; if, say, people were to be told that they are now placed on equal footing or equal rights in all respects, how many educated persons would be found with adequate education to supply all commodities that are necessary in modern life, how many years would it take them to get to that stage? Or let us take a hypothetical case where by some miracle we would suddenly find that Europeans had all disappeared and left the country and we are left in Africa without any Europeans at all. What could we do? Where would we get

354 APPENDIX A: KING SOBHUZA II'S SPEECH OF APRIL 1960

trains? Where would we have the electricity, power, or the commodities that we have learnt to use with comfort nowadays?

Now seeing that each of us is seeking to find a proper protection as to his rights in future, in what way shall we have this assurance that the European is not going to be ousted from any country and the African is assured of a proper place for his posterity. It is for that reason then, gentlemen, that I have asked for this meeting to take place here today so that we can consider, confer together and find out a way which will make us have a common understanding and how we can remain in peace knowing that we are here settled and going to live together. Now even if one may deceive oneself by saying that it is only the Europeans that are seeking security for their future, the truth is that also the Africans would like to get assurance of what is going to happen with them in future. I say so because it is common practice among the Europeans that when he lends out money, he must have security, a surety for what will happen in the event of the client failing to pay the money. In Africa we have also got to look into the practices of the Africans as to whether the practice used to obtain whereby when one borrowed money it was necessary to have some sort of surety. This one thing I know among the Africans, that if you marry a woman and you pay cattle as *lobola*, those cattle are there as security—you are buying the right to have the children and your wife is also bound at her husband's *kraal* because she feels that she cannot leave the children there. She knows that if she were to leave her husband's people, she would have forsaken her children, have abandoned any right to her children because the children were actually bought by her husband's people by the *lobola* that they paid. And if she were to decide to desert her husband's *kraal*, she would have to leave the children behind. So far I have been trying to deal with the situation of the whole world but now I'd like to come nearer home and refer to Swaziland in particular.

We find that what is the source of trouble elsewhere obtains even in Swaziland. Indeed I have read from the newspapers that this country, too, seeks to bring in a lot of people from outside, and somebody else mentioned on a certain occasion that we need to have people from outside, for the development of the country. And that has caused me much concern—I feel this is the source of all problems that are going to come.

Our practice, and indeed what we uphold in Swaziland, is a position where people will come into the Territory of their own free will, when they feel that there is something for which they want to come into the Territory, not because they have been invited or told to come in numbers into the

APPENDIX A: KING SOBHUZA II'S SPEECH OF APRIL 1960   355

country. I wonder how this House feels about that, whether they think that is the way in which we are going to solve our problems.

I draw attention to the policy of the government overseas; a glimpse into their policy will show what their aim is about the whole of Africa. You will find that the policy now is to let go. They feel that to be sitting on a people, in that old Imperialist and Colonialist fashion when they are unhappy and all that, is not a healthy state of affairs. Give them independence and let them carry on their own—just in the way that Mr Harold Macmillan mentioned in Parliament in Cape Town. And you will realize that the West as a whole—England, America and others that are grouped together as the West—their ideas, their policy now is that people should look after their own affairs. The White people should have nothing to complain about. The Black people should not find cause to complain either. If that would come to pass, that state of affairs where there will be peace, between the White and the Black—these Western countries would be very happy—they will sing 'Halleluja'.

And it is for that reason that even in Swaziland one has heard a number of people here and there coming out with views and ideas that we should come together and work together for the wellbeing of our country. We have this one great fortune in Swaziland that we live together as one—there is no underdog—we just live as a community. And this lack of equality elsewhere does not exist in Swaziland—we are all equal.

We should now look for a way which will make us feel at home, feel that we are quite secure in this country, but how shall we go about getting this security that we seek? Even if there are difficulties I don't think that they are insurmountable. Many a difficulty has had to be surmounted. We can have difficulties of whatsoever a nature, but we should find ways and means of trying to fight against those difficulties and live together in peace. I have already mentioned that the metropolitan government has already expressed a desire that we should manage our own affairs. A number of men have been to consult me about whether it wouldn't be a good idea to meet together and join in the Advisory Council as one Council.

I have decided to place my dreams before you here present. At first I thought I would hold back my views and leave the matter in the hands of my Council and those men who were desirous to discuss it, and await their views. I thought that my Council would confer together and discuss these matters with the European Council or government and with ordinary members of the public to find out ways and means of how to come together and develop something that would be of help to the country. But because of the turn of events that have been taking place in North Africa, in East

356 APPENDIX A: KING SOBHUZA II'S SPEECH OF APRIL 1960

Africa, in Central Africa and elsewhere, I began to realize that probably I was making a mistake by sitting quiet—now I am convinced I must say my mind, however wrong it may be—a number of people may not agree with me but I think I'd better express my mind now. And even though perhaps what I am going to say now may probably prejudice the position in that some people may try to follow what I have already said without reasoning it out, I am now going to say out what my feelings are on the subject.

I think it would not be a good idea to join with the Advisory Council, for these two reasons: firstly, we are a protectorate and the set-up of a protectorate is such that the people are an entity on their own, a people that have their own institutions, have got to carry on in the way that they have been wont to do, but they go to someone to protect them who has got to bring them up, teach them certain things in which they feel they are deficient until such time as they feel they are fully developed. And then he hands over.

And you find that the protecting power, as we have heard is the practice among the Germans, when they are protecting a certain state, instead of developing that state to a state of being able to stand on its own feet, they begin to absorb that particular state. And that causes ill feeling from the state which was expecting to be brought up and which was being nursed until it was able to stand on its own feet. They feel that they have now been deprived of their rights.

Now I will ask His Honour the Resident Commissioner and the Secretary from Swazi Affairs now to listen intently. What I am going to say will probably be somewhat sore to them but I would ask them to bear with me and just listen to what I am saying. It may help them because sometimes to speak the truth, even though it may be painful, does help. The members of the Council may probably think that I am spoiling their chances by saying much and more than I should have said but, well, let them bear with me. A man always has bad ideas sometimes has also got to be listened to, so please listen to this.

I believe at the present moment, there is quite a lot of talk in Council sessions with government on matters concerning immigration laws and deportation laws, so much so that decision on one law has been withheld for an inordinately long time and the government feels that the Council is so delaying matters that now the High Commissioner's Office is becoming very impatient on these things, and the Council feels 'What is government trying to do with us? They are probably leading us into something that

APPENDIX A: KING SOBHUZA II'S SPEECH OF APRIL 1960 357

we've never heard of or are going to ruin our country' and things of that nature.

I did not like to participate in these discussions because, even though I am a man, a member of the Council, they have the chance to discuss matters among themselves and convince one another on these matters before I come in. But now I begin to feel that I should really come out with the truth and ask the Council 'Why don't you say so and so', which will make the position quite clear to the government, and why doesn't government do so and so and so and so, so that this matter may be cleared up.

I am of opinion that the mind of the Council is working on these lines: 'That instead of government protecting us they are now taking away some of our powers – they are now suppressing us.' Take for instance the deportation draft Proclamation. The Swazis wonder why it should be the government that has got to deport people rather than people should be deported by the Swazis if they have to be. It is felt that government should be in a position to deport Europeans but the African people who have come into the Territory should only be deported by the National Administration—the Swazi Authority.

A number of these members of the Council here present have got relations of some kind in the Union somewhere. Chief Confirm here with us, has his senior brother in the Lydenburg district. Councillor Nhlabatsi has always told us that when the boundaries were first set up his home was on the Swaziland side of the line but the boundary has shifted time and again and now they don't know how they got to be in the Union. Mnt. Madevu's physical father used to live in the Carolina district. The Secretary to the Nation has got some of his people living in the Transvaal and others living in Swaziland. A number of Royal *kraals*, some of them in the Barberton district, others in the Carolina district, are under my direct control in the same way as other Royal *kraals* of past reigns are under my care today.

Now if these people were to come back to Swaziland and we accept them to come back to Swaziland and should there be something wrong because they were born outside the country, they become deported by government. What does that bring up in the minds of the Swazis? That is what is really causing a lot of difficulty among the members of the Council on this draft Proclamation that we are doing something that is not known among the Swazi. They fear that when the whole *Libandla* is called upon, they will censure them rather severely, they will tell them that they have exceeded their powers in accepting this thing because it has got great repercussions,

358 APPENDIX A: KING SOBHUZA II'S SPEECH OF APRIL 1960

great difficulties behind it, if it is going to bring about dismissal or deportation of Africans in Swaziland without the authority of the Swazi—it is something unheard of.

I don't know if this has been explained to government by the Council but this that I am explaining is the reason why they have been so very adamant about it, and that they also feel that our rights are being whittled off. Instead of being brought up properly we are now being swallowed up. In all this I have been trying to explain how a protecting government can help to protect and develop and bring up a nation that is not yet developed, to a stage where it can stand on its own feet. I will not now deal with the Convention of 1894 but I will refer to the Order-in-Council which enjoins government that when they make laws in the country they will respect Swazi law and custom.

Thirdly, as I mentioned, I don't think that the Advisory Council can join together with us. The set-up, the way of life of the European is such that it is individualistic and he has his own practices which are peculiarly his own. That is their tradition, but we have our own traditions too. No man can say that that one is not as good as the other one but I will say that mine is the better tradition.

By way of illustrating what I am saying I would like to point out that in the European culture, you find that if I married a wife, my wife is my own and she is not a woman of the household of my family. A wife does not belong to the family but she is my own. I am her husband and nobody else has got anything to do or to say to her. According to Swazi custom, she is your wife, she is your family's wife, belonging to the family as a whole. Among the Europeans if there is a misunderstanding in the house, the husband will run to the magistrate and report, 'Oh my wife does not want to share a bed with me.' If the wife has got some difficulty in the house, she goes to report to the Court—and then the newspaper reporters are there and they are ready to report. And then the Court Order is given—you should make it up and if you are not able to make it up within so many days, come back to me. Among us Africans we feel that that is not good behaviour. With us, if the man had such a situation in the house, he, if it is the woman that is becoming difficult, reports the matter to his parents. If his parents no longer lived, he reports to friends or relatives and they come and discuss the matter and get it over—it is not broadcast to the whole world so that everybody should know what's happening—that these are no longer sharing their bed, etc. A family matter of that nature is referred to the King, to the Court only as a last resort, and we feel that that is a better procedure than to report everything to the Court rather than have it settled amicably at home.

In so saying, I am trying to point out that the Europeans and Africans are not yet at the stage where they would be able to meet and discuss things profitably in such gatherings as the Advisory Council. But I do not mean that they should not meet, I think that we should by all means find a way of making these two meet.

But we regard the Advisory Council as having a lower status than our Council. We cannot meet the Advisory Council in its present stage as an Advisory Council and in order that we should join it, let its status be raised to that of a Legislative Council. Only then can we come together. At that stage, we will come together on equal basis, discuss matters of the Territory of Swaziland as a whole. It would not lower our prestige, our dignity as a protected people who have their own institutions and rights, but it will raise us both to a stage where we could together confer on matters of state and legislate for the country. We would not be taking a retrogressive step there. Now there again, as I have mentioned, these people have been brought up on different ideas. How will they come together, join up only at the top levels? I think a solution to that would be that the Advisory Council, the European public, should elect their own men under their system of election, and we would get our men, chosen by us to meet and legislate for the country. They would all then join together. It would be better to call the method that of federation, where we would not count how many represent so and so and how many represent that unit, but they will merely meet as a federation together.

If we met on these lines and the Africans came with their own system, I think it would solve the situation. I do not see how we can try to adopt European ways of doing things which we don't know. Yes it is quite true that we should copy those good practices that the Europeans have, but when we come to consider what is this democracy of which they speak you ultimately get lost in the idea—I do not even understand what is meant by democracy—because each man will display his wealth and say that he wants to do so and so and bring out certain monies with the idea to do so and so but one without capital will not be able to do any of these things or display. When people speak of democracy, one wonders what democracy it is they want to maintain because we, the Africans as a matter of fact, have bigger numbers than the other people but one cannot understand what is meant by democracy when one thinks on those lines.

360 APPENDIX A: KING SOBHUZA II'S SPEECH OF APRIL 1960

Let us regard this as a practice, as a European practice, because to speak of democracy, I don't think would be the correct word, because democracy is not there. A man promises his constituency that 'I will do so and so for you, I will certainly achieve so and so for you' and then he is not able to do it. I think it would be better democracy if people went into it in the same way as de Gaulle took up his position in France. He was called by the people to come to their rescue as they were in difficulty in this way. He came with that mandate. There's nothing that he has promised the people that he would achieve for them. Actually, I appreciate it was the people that suggested that he should be appointed. I thought that was a good form.

If only we could be able to extricate Africa from this idea of one man, one vote, I am sure we would have achieved our objective. Even this federation that I referred to, that we have heard of in Central Africa, if it aims at one man, one vote, I am sure it will not be a success. Whether it is a federation for the White or the Black, it would not be successful. Because if the parties fear that the one party, the Black or White, supersedes the other, then there will be fear that they will swallow all the others' own opinion, whether it is right or wrong, it is my opinion. I would like to hear from you, what you suggest could be done to save this country.

Source: H. Kuper, *Sobhuza II Ngwenyama and King of Swaziland: The Story of an Hereditary Ruler and His Country* (London: Gerald Duckworth, 1978), 210–217. This speech, reproduced by Kuper, is a taped translation from *siSwati* to English. Excerpts of it are also found in *The Times of Swaziland*. (See 'The Ngwenyama, Sobhuza II C.B.E. Gives Expression to His Views on the Constitutional Future of Swaziland'. *The Times of Swaziland*, 1 July 1960, vol. 58, no. 27.)

Appendix B: Members of Parliament Under the *Tinkhundla* System

1.	Princess Phetfwayini
2.	Mphithi Luka Dlamini
3.	Mambonjwana S. Nkambule
4.	Peter Shovela Munro
5.	Robert Makhanyambeni Dlamini
6.	Walter William Mordaunt
7.	Malaveni Mgwagwanana Ginindza
8.	Samson Msunduzeni Dlamini
9.	Dr Sishayi S. Nxumalo
10.	Joseph Nduna Mamba
11.	Ben Gregory Bennett
12.	Bhizeni Wilson Dlamini
13.	Paulos Mfanawendlela Ginindza
14.	Chief Mlimi Nicholas Maziya
15.	Chief Mandzanga Ndabenkulu Ndwandwe
16.	Ephraim Nyambezi Dlamini
17.	Chief Malamlela Magagula
18.	Mshefane Daniel Shongwe
19.	Mhlanganyelwa Mbonani Michael Shongwe
20.	Ernest Phenyane Mamba

(continued)

© The Editor(s) (if applicable) and The Author(s),
under exclusive license to Springer Nature Switzerland AG,
part of Springer Nature 2019
H. P. Dlamini, *A Constitutional History of the Kingdom of Eswatini (Swaziland), 1960–1982*, African Histories and Modernities,
https://doi.org/10.1007/978-3-030-24777-5

362 APPENDIX B: MEMBERS OF PARLIAMENT UNDER…

(continued)

21.	Chief Sibengwane Magomba Ndzimandze
22.	Magwece Jeremiah Mkhatshwa
23.	Chief Mnikwa William Dlamini
24.	Austin Sangoma Vanda Dlamini
25.	Gawulela Jeremiah Zwane
26.	Naphtali Mlungeli Mahlalela
27.	Makhalane Paul Dlamini
28.	Prince Maquba
29.	Prince Mekiseni Enock
30.	Mengameli Amon Matsebula
31.	MafaPheleon Sibandze
32.	Sylvester Saustin Sankwenteya Mokgokong
33.	Mandinda Bhembe
34.	Ndawombili Fred Dlamini
35.	Precious Shungube

Source Official Report of the First Meeting of the First Session of the Third Parliament of Kingdom of Swaziland, 16–19 January 1979

INDEX

A

Abacha, Sani, 290, 291
Amin, Idi, 6, 280, 308, 309, 330, 346
Apartheid South Africa, 9, 22, 34, 55,
    57, 58, 73, 91, 130, 147, 149,
    151, 156–159, 164, 178, 179,
    190, 191, 197, 305, 341
Arden-Clarke, Charles, 87
Attorney-General, 135, 189, 209, 227,
    241, 258, 263, 265, 288, 293,
    297, 300, 301, 316
Auto-coup, 24, 25, 279–283, 285,
    289, 290, 294, 299, 300, 302,
    330, 346

103, 107, 108, 110, 111, 113,
    116, 121, 122, 130, 151, 171,
    176, 193, 199, 201, 203, 213,
    214, 219, 221, 222, 230, 280,
    315, 317, 344, 346
Constitutional Committee Delegation,
    100
Constitutional Review Committee, 24,
    171, 175–177, 179, 183–186,
    188, 203, 204, 206, 209, 316,
    317
Constitutional talks, 13, 20, 22, 52,
    54, 57, 66, 83, 91, 93, 94, 113,
    115, 116, 129, 133, 173, 231,
    343, 345

C

Cohen, David, 154, 258, 265, 288,
    316
Colonial affairs, 141
Commissioner of Police, 291, 307
Constitutional Committee, 23, 37, 38,
    83–85, 87, 91, 94–96, 98–101,

D

Dabede, 323
Despotic monarch, 285, 308
De Symons Montagu George Honey,
    41
Dlamini, Dumisa, 53, 153, 312
Dlamini, P.M., 297, 298

© The Editor(s) (if applicable) and The Author(s),
under exclusive license to Springer Nature Switzerland AG,
part of Springer Nature 2019
H. P. Dlamini, *A Constitutional History of the Kingdom of Eswatini
(Swaziland), 1960–1982,* African Histories and Modernities,
https://doi.org/10.1007/978-3-030-24777-5

364 INDEX

Douglas-Home, Alexander, 83

E
Electoral College, 319, 321–326, 342
Eurafrican community, 117
Euro-African Welfare Association, 99, 118
European Advisory Council (EAC), 19, 20, 22, 41, 42, 54, 55, 58, 72, 74, 75, 78, 79, 84, 87–89, 91–95, 97, 100–122, 130–134, 139, 142, 144, 147–149, 151, 172, 177, 341

G
Gabheni, 323
Gwebu, Ndleleni, 323

H
High Commission Territories, 36, 37, 43, 72, 134, 147–149, 175, 202
Hlophe, A.K., 77, 100, 105, 140, 171, 173
Hynd, D., 77, 107, 117–119

I
Imbokodvo, 23, 24, 130, 157–160, 162–171, 173–176, 178, 179, 183, 184, 186, 189–193, 195, 197, 199–204, 206, 207, 209, 230, 231, 242–244, 246, 251, 253–255, 257, 258, 261–265, 267, 269, 271–273, 321, 344, 345
Independence Constitution, 14, 16–20, 22–24, 33–35, 38, 49, 57, 184, 209, 211, 225, 230, 239, 241, 243, 247, 249, 251, 254, 255, 265, 269–272, 274, 279,

282, 283, 286, 288–290, 292, 293, 295–297, 299–305, 314, 316, 330, 346

K
Kelsen's Grundnorm legal theory, 299–301
Khoza, Arthur, 170, 316
King-in-Council, 270, 271, 273, 292, 293, 296

L
Legal practitioners, 296
Legal School of Liberal Advocates, 296–298
Legislative Council, 14, 19, 20, 24, 38, 41, 42, 65, 71, 72, 74, 75, 78–82, 88, 89, 94, 96, 97, 101, 104, 106–108, 111–114, 120–122, 129, 133–136, 140, 141, 146, 147, 151, 160, 167, 171–175, 179, 183–186, 189–192, 194, 200, 201, 203, 231, 359
Lloyd, Francis, 169, 171, 173, 176, 177, 185, 203, 204, 208, 225, 227
London Conference, 113, 115–117, 120, 122, 130, 131, 134, 151, 177, 228, 343
Lord Landsdowne, 141

M
Mabuza, O.B., 169
Mabuza, O.M., 51, 86, 95, 147, 176
Macmillan, Harold, 70, 71, 74, 77, 156, 159, 353, 355
Makhosini, 140, 158, 160, 170, 174, 175, 177, 184, 185, 189, 192–195, 209, 211, 213, 224, 225, 227, 228, 252, 258

Marwick, Brian, 83, 85, 100–102, 118, 147, 154, 159, 160, 162, 169
Mbandzeni National Convention (MNC), 53, 117, 340
Mthethwa, Timothy Velabo, 311

N

Ndwandwe, Sishayi Simon, 12, 361
Nguema, Macías, 6, 308, 346
Ngwenya, Thomas, 255, 285
Nhlabatsi, Mabalizandla, 77, 223, 322, 323
Nquku, J.J., 22, 51–53, 73, 82, 84, 86, 92, 95, 98, 118, 147, 169, 176, 207, 340
Nxumalo, A., 86, 169

P

Political parties, 9, 11, 12, 14, 22, 23, 34, 38, 44, 49, 50, 53, 58, 75, 76, 78, 81, 89, 92, 93, 101, 106, 112, 118, 119, 121, 122, 139, 142, 143, 151–153, 155, 156, 158–160, 162–164, 166–170, 173, 176, 178, 187, 190–192, 201, 202, 206, 207, 224, 246, 251, 284, 287, 291, 307, 309, 312, 313, 320, 339–341, 343, 344
Polycarp, Dlamini, 140, 173, 174, 225, 316, 327
Proclamation and decrees, 279, 280, 282, 290–292, 294–299, 301, 307, 310, 314, 315, 330
Progressives, 4, 5, 11, 18, 21, 23, 34, 38, 43, 44, 49–51, 53–55, 57, 58, 66, 72–74, 76, 81, 82, 86, 87, 90–100, 103–106, 109–112, 114–117, 120–122, 129–134, 139, 146, 147, 152–154, 158, 159, 163–165, 168–170, 174, 177, 179, 183, 186, 190, 191, 205, 206, 231, 286, 309, 311, 343, 344

R

Referendum, 75, 109, 110, 114, 115, 131, 132, 142–144, 160, 166, 173, 178, 230, 269, 289, 297
Resident Commissioner, 37, 41, 42, 48, 52, 74, 77, 83, 84, 87, 88, 95, 96, 102, 119, 131, 132, 135, 147, 356
Royal auto-coup, 16, 17, 283, 284, 289, 290, 304, 346

S

Samketi, H.Y., 116
Sandys, Duncan, 117, 119, 120, 130, 141, 169
Secretary of State for the Colonies, 83, 103, 114, 117, 132, 171, 186
Shabalala, S.M., 210, 216, 322, 323
Shabangu, Albert Heshane, 313
Sifuba, 266, 286, 316
Swazi monarchy, 5, 15, 16, 23, 56, 73, 75–77, 94, 129, 158, 187, 239, 255, 266, 274, 303, 309, 310, 328, 339, 341, 342
Swazi National Council, 17, 19, 20, 22, 38, 44, 51, 87, 90, 111, 137, 140, 143, 145, 155, 158, 161, 173, 192
Swaziland Order-in-Council of 1903, 135

T

Teeling, W., 141
Tinkhundla, 25, 167, 168, 280, 294, 312, 314, 317–331, 347, 361

366 INDEX

Todd, C.F., 20, 22, 42, 54, 57, 58, 84, 85, 87, 91–95, 100, 108–111, 113–115, 121, 122, 130, 131, 133, 142–145, 149, 150, 166–168, 171–174, 176, 178, 185, 193, 194, 221, 222, 224, 264, 341, 343

U

United Nations General Assembly, 69, 98

V

Verwoerd, 52, 56, 147–150, 191

W

White community, 19, 20, 22, 23, 34, 38–40, 54, 58, 74, 78, 81, 113, 121, 122, 133, 137, 146, 151, 153, 154, 159, 178, 341–343

Z

Zwane, A.P., 22, 51–54, 73, 86, 95, 98, 116, 146, 150, 153, 155, 162, 169, 173, 176, 203, 209, 224–226, 252–254, 258, 261–263, 286, 309–312, 340